LEGAL
STUDIES
AS
CULTURAL
STUDIES

for the fire next time

LEGAL STUDIES AS CULTURAL STUDIES

a reader in (post)modern critical theory

marie ashe
david s. caudill
drucilla cornell
costas douzinas
teresa l. ebert
nancy fraser
eugene d. genovese
peter goodrich
gayatri chakravorty spivak
ronnie warrington

edited by jerry leonard

STATE UNIVERSITY OF NEW YORK PRESS

Published by
State University of New York Press, Albany

For information, address the State University of New York Press,
State University Plaza, Albany, NY 12246

Production by Christine Lynch
Marketing by Theresa Abad Swierzowski

Library of Congress Cataloging-in-Publication Data

Legal Studies as cultural studies : a reader in (post) modern critical
  theory / edited by Jerry Leonard; Marie Ashe ...[et al.].
     p.   cm.
  Includes bibliographical references and index.
  ISBN 0-7914-2295-X (acid-free). — ISBN 0-7914-2296-8 (acid-free)
  1. Culture and law. 2. Critical legal studies. I. Leonard,
Jerry, 1963–   . II. Ashe, Marie.
K487.C8L44 1995
340'.115—dc20   94-9240
                                                      CIP

10 9 8 7 6 5 4 3 2

CONTENTS
LEGAL STUDIES AS CULTURAL STUDIES: A READER IN (POST)MODERN CRITICAL THEORY

ACKNOWLEDGMENTS

The following articles were originally published as indicated below. I would like to thank both the authors and the publishers for their permission to reprint these texts.

"Freud and Critical Legal Studies: Contours of a Radical Socio-Legal Psychoanalysis," by David S. Caudill, originally appeared in the *Indiana Law Journal*, volume 66, number 3 (Summer 1991), pp. 651–697, and is reprinted with permission.

"Mind's Opportunity: Birthing a Poststructuralist Feminist Jurisprudence," by Marie Ashe, originally appeared in the *Syracuse Law Review*, volume 38 (1987), pp. 1129–1173, and is reprinted with permission.

"Foucault and (the Ideology of) Genealogical Legal Theory," by Jerry Leonard, is a slightly revised version of a text which originally appeared in *Legal Studies Forum*, volume XIV, number 1 (1990), pp. 3–25, and is reprinted with permission.

"Constitutions and Culture Studies," by Gayatri Chakravorty Spivak, originally appeared in the *Yale Journal of Law & the Humanities*, volume 2 (1990), pp. 133–147, and is reprinted with permission.

"Sex, Lies, and the Public Sphere: Some Reflections on the Confirmation of Clarence Thomas," by Nancy Fraser, originally appeared in *Critical Inquiry*, volume 19 (Spring 1992), pp. 595–612, and is reprinted with permission.

"'A Well-Founded Fear of Justice': Law and Ethics in Postmodernity," by Costas Douzinas and Ronnie Warrington, originally appeared in *Law and Critique*, volume II, number 2 (1991), pp. 115–147, and is reprinted with permission.

"Time, Deconstruction, and the Challenge to Legal Positivism: The Call for Judicial Responsibility," by Drucilla Cornell, originally appeared in the *Yale Journal of Law & the Humanities*, volume 2 (1990), pp. 267–297, and is reprinted with permission.

"Critical Legal Studies as Radical Politics and World View," by Eugene D. Genovese, originally appeared in the *Yale Journal of Law & the Humanities*, volume 3 (1991), pp. 131–156, and is reprinted with permission.

"Sleeping with the Enemy: An Essay on the Politics of Critical Legal Studies in America," by Peter Goodrich, is published in the *New York University Law Review*, volume 68, number 2 (1993), pp. 389–425, and is printed here with permission.

"Writing in the Political: Resistance (Post)Modernism," by Teresa L. Ebert, originally appeared in a special issue of *Legal Studies Forum*, volume XV, number 4 (1991), pp. 291–303, devoted to Transformative Discourses in Postmodern Social, Cultural and Legal Theory, guest edited by Jerry Leonard, and is reprinted with permission.

INTRODUCTION: (POST)MODERN LEGAL STUDIES AS (CRITICAL) CULTURAL STUDIES

JERRY LEONARD _____

> ...because the political agenda of theory is not to legitimize one
> meaning over all others but to interrogate the very institutional
> bases of the production of meaning, whether multiple or
> singular. To ask, in other words, not which meaning is most
> legitimate, but what makes possible this legitimation; to ask
> how the currently privileged anchor of all meaning—the literary
> or legal text—came to be legitimated in the first place; to ask
> not that more texts should be thus legitimated (a reformist
> project) but that this apparatus of legitimation itself be
> dismantled.
>
> —Madhava Prasad[1]

This is not a book. After Blanchot, if the "book" is understood "as
repository and receptacle of knowledge,"[2] then *Legal Studies as
Cultural Studies* marks *the absence of the book* and the activation
of reading *otherwise*. The project of legal studies as cultural
studies sets forth a series of intersecting and often conflicting
interrogative possibilities more so than firmly settled answers or
solutions. And moreover, the issues raised through these pages
are *political* through and through, and indeed involve, perhaps
most importantly, the theorization of "the political" itself in the
(post)modern moment. In a very general sense, as Teresa L. Ebert
has recently put it, such writings at once question *why* the
existing social order is (un)just "the way it is" and also *why not*
order things otherwise. Developing out of the philosophically and
politically overlapping arenas of the Conference on Critical Legal
Studies (emerging in the United States around 1977) and
Contemporary Cultural Studies (emerging in Britain with the
Birmingham School around the mid-to-late 60s), what is
ultimately at stake is the untiring insistence on the possibility of
global social justice, and, more specifically, the question of the

role of historical "subjectivity" in the dominant legal and cultural orders.

This is not a book, but rather, following Foucault, three *dossiers* investigating at different levels of analysis the problematics of social justice underlying contemporary critical theory. Whereas the repositive book would have already hailed the reader toward/into the passivizing post of the consumer, the tourist of "knowledge," *Legal Studies as Cultural Studies* offers and foregrounds instead an active, restless and urgent post-(modern) space for the reader as critical *interventionist* and *collaborationist* in the productive historical development of radical intellectual struggles for change. Further on in this introduction I shall return to mark the "ludic" (neo-liberal pluralist) posts of Blanchot and Foucault, with which I opened this text, in partisan (committed and collectivist) rather than merely eclectical terms.

What is called "cultural studies" today is first of all not a "given" or stable domain of activities and inquiries but rather a highly contested field of questioning and theorizing through which a broad range of conflicting visions of social justice get elaborated.[3] From this general conceptualization of contemporary cultural studies as a social arena in which, to paraphrase Marx, individuals become conscious of a range of collective conflicts over the *just* and "fight it out" at the level of meanings, I take the position that a critical, rigorously interrogative approach to law and legal institutions must play a key role. Thus *Legal Studies as Cultural Studies* is put forward here as an advocacy of the integrative, globally inclusive commitments of Critical Legal Studies[4] and Contemporary Cultural Studies[5] toward the development in theory and/*as* practice of an economically and politically fair, just and publicly accountable organization of social space, relations and resources. The most general goal of this project, then, is to contribute to the construction and legitimacy of a public forum in which cultural studies may be elaborated as a broad-ranging contestation of (in)justice under the historical limits and contradictions of transnational capitalist patriarchy and (post)modern culture.

While the general agenda here is to in a certain sense produce an open(ing) space for the contestation of cultural studies as an intervention in the discourses of world justice, this formulation itself soon becomes intellectually unproductive insofar as it tends to suggest a vacuous "anything goes" pluralism *under the very banner of the idea of "contestation."*[6] In other words, while it does help I think to frame cultural studies as an inquiry into the conflictedness of "justice" in the contemporary world, it is necessary to go further in registering somewhat more precisely the lines of theoretical battle traversing cultural studies. I would now like to move in this direction by offering very schematic outlines of three broad approaches to contemporary cultural studies. I shall designate them, first, "Experiential" Cultural Studies; second, "Textual" Cultural Studies; and third, "Critical" Cultural Studies. As just one further preface to the outlines, I should point out that "culture" here designates exclusively neither the "high Culture" of bourgeois "Fine Arts" nor the "popular culture" of, for instance, MTV, Madonna, reruns of *The Love Boat* or *Gilligan's Island* and so forth. "Culture" in cultural studies, rather, conceptually encompasses both of (and more than) these sorts of "high"/"low" categories by staking out the collective ensemble of artifacts, practices, and spaces enmeshed in the production and dissemination of *meanings* and *knowledges*. Culture, in short, is anywhere "the real" is constructed and made sense of, and the different approaches to cultural studies aim in differing ways to account for that "sense" of what is, or what can count as, "real." (Post)modern cultural studies intervenes in the historical and social intelligibilities of *reality* in a world in which "reality" appears ("makes sense") quite differently depending upon the subject's position along the material social matrices of race, gender, sexuality, and class.

"Experiential" Cultural Studies and its approach to cultural meaningfulness may generally be formulated as follows: Experiential Cultural Studies "affirms" the many, highly variegated ways in which meanings emerge for individuals through their direct, "sensuous" interactions ("experiences") with the world of things and others: This is a study, a writing, a reading, or an affirmative "recounting" which fundamentally addresses the question of what is "real"—and this frame of address is most often put forward by or on behalf of those who have historically suffered various kinds of oppression and exploitation and who have, as well, been denied the possibility of having their oppressions articulated in public—i.e., having them "known." Experiential Cultural Studies gives "voice" to such experiences or otherwise provides something of a "window" on that reality as a step toward changing it.

Following such relatively recent events as the videotaped police beating of Rodney King in Los Angeles, California, or the sheer refusal of police in Milwaukee, Wisconsin to take seriously the bizarre goings-on around the residence of Jeffrey Dahmer—until it was far too late—the *politics* of the "public" ostensibly "served and protected" by the police has become an urgent site of contestation and resistance: an *Other* public's collective realization of injustice which was an essential factor in the south-central L.A. uprisings emerging in response to the King "incident." By late September of 1993, however, Ted Koppel could confidently open his *Nightline* broadcast to millions of Americans by saying that the health and welfare of (white) policemen recently sentenced to prison had become a real question of "the principles of justice" because of the daily violences they were subject to amidst the "general" prison population. Again here the political anxiety and the politics of knowledge fueling Koppel's "report" is that the health and welfare of prisoners only *really* becomes a "principle of justice" when the general conditions of prison life "really" touch corrupt white policemen, while the daily historical "experiences" of dehumanization for the "general population" of black inmates can be regularly and routinely ignored. The wider political and social meaning of "minority" here is cynically reversed in order to "serve and protect" even the embarrassingly crude "fall guys" of the dominant social interests.

In the very opening moves of Steven Connor's book *Postmodernist Culture: An Introduction to Theories of the Contemporary* (1989), Connor offers an eloquent articulation of the Experientialist stance, but also going further to critically suggest its limits in the complex division and privileging of "experience" over and against "knowledge":

> The difficulties of knowing the contemporary are well known. Knowledge, it is often claimed, can only be gained and enjoyed about what is in some sense over and done with. The claim to know the contemporary is therefore often seen as a kind of conceptual violence, a fixing of the fluid and formless energies of the urgently (but tenuously) present *now* into a knowable and speakable form, by fundamental and irrevocable acts of critical choosing. This formulation rests upon a sense of the inherent division between experience and knowledge, a belief that, when we experience life, we can only partially understand it, and when we try to understand life, we are no longer really experiencing it. According to this model, knowledge is always doomed to arrive too late on the scene of experience.

Much of the critical and theoretical work in philosophy and the social sciences over the last twenty or so years gives us reason to suspect this division, reason to wonder whether knowledge and experience may not be joined in a much more complex continuum. It may be that experience is always, if not actually determined, then at least interpreted in advance by the various structures of understanding and interpretation which hold at particular moments in particular societies, and different regions of those societies. Indeed, the very relationship in which experience and knowledge are taken to stand may also be a reflex of such structures of knowledge and understanding. From this it would follow that our present way of conceiving the opposition between experience and knowledge as (for example) one between transience and fixity, itself has its origin and history in particular knowledge structures.[7]

In a way which is quite pertinent to the present volume, the "liberatory" impulse of the Experientialist position lies behind the G.I.P. (*Groupe d'information de prisons*) project initiated by Foucault. In the "conversation" between Foucault and Deleuze, "Intellectuals and Power," Deleuze underscores their Central objective "to create conditions that permit the prisoners themselves to speak."[8] In the present collection, variously articulated elements of Experiential Cultural Studies may be traced through the texts of Marie Ashe, David S. Caudill, Eugene D. Genovese, and Nancy Fraser. Jerry Leonard's text also examines in detail Foucault's genealogical project.

I indicated above that the different modes of cultural studies all in one way or another produce (and, on a certain level, assume) differing "accounts" of the existence and circulation of meanings in culture. Whereas Experiential Cultural Studies takes account of "what" kinds of truths-as-"experiences" have been denied and silenced throughout history, "Textual" Cultural Studies transforms the question of "what" (is left out) into, as Jane Gallop puts it, a highly "complexifying"[9] account of *how* various "other" truths are systematically relegated to the spaces of cultural (non)sense which Derrida has powerfully articulated with the notion of "margins"—and, conversely, how one may read otherwise *from* the margins. Textual Cultural Studies, through "readings" and re-writings of texts of culture, microscopically examines (or more precisely, *analyzes*) "how" various potentials of meaningfulness or signification are repressed and kept tenuously in abeyance within the dominant patterns of the "taken for granted," the meanings which are made to seem "obvious" and unquestionable (and thus unalterable) precisely by the drive of "commonsensual" desire (common sense/consent) to "forget" whatever it is not, what it lacks, and yet exactly what it needs in order to secure and maintain the kind of imaginary "sense" which Lacan terms "*méconnaissance*": the plenitude of ("self")centeredness operative in various notions of "individualism" all the way up from Descartes and through Sartrean existentialism.

Whether the decentering of the metaphysical self, particularly in the historical moment of a globally "dispersing" capitalism, constitutes an "oppositional" modality, however, is still a very serious site of disagreement. The question becomes the historical one of what kind of "self" is subject to decentering, and hence the role of decentering as a contestation of social inequalities. Long before Derrida signaled the era of deconstruction, Marx clearly understood that the working class as a whole and every individual of that class has already been materially "decentered"—"alienated"—from effective collective control of labor and the products of labor. Thus Marx and Engels in *The Communist Manifesto*, while in a certain sense calling for the internationally transformative "deconstruction" of capitalism ("from below"), do *not* at the same time call for the "decentering" of the revolutionary proletariat: on the contrary, they emphatically conclude the *Manifesto* with the call for worldwide solidarity among the diversely constituted working class. "WORKERS OF THE WORLD, *UNITE!*"

Textual Cultural Studies, in any event, reads/writes against the grains of the dominant in order to activate the Nietzschean *ressentiment*, the resistance offered by the sense of "counter-memory" in Foucault, and the "other" histories of domination articulated through the Subaltern Studies project.[10] In her translator's introduction to Derrida's *Dissemination* (1981), Barbara Johnson offers the following elaboration of the Textual project:

> Deconstruction is not a form of textual vandalism designed to prove that meaning is impossible. In fact, the word "deconstruction" is closely related not to the word "destruction" but to the word "analysis," which etymologically means "to undo"— a virtual synonym for "to de-construct." The deconstruction of a text does not proceed by random doubt or generalized skepticism, but by the careful teasing out of warring forces of signification *within the text itself.* If anything is destroyed in a deconstructive reading, it is not meaning but the claim to

unequivocal domination of one mode of signifying over another. This, of course, implies that a text signifies in more than one way, and to varying degrees of explicitness. Sometimes the discrepancy is produced...by a double-edged word, which serves as a hinge that both articulates and breaks open the explicit statement being made. Sometimes it is engendered when the figurative level of a statement is at odds with the literal level. And sometimes it occurs when the so-called starting point of an argument is based on presuppositions that render its conclusions problematic or circular.

Derrida [in *Of Grammatology*] defines his reading strategy as follows:

> The reading must always aim at a certain relationship, unperceived by the writer, between what he commands and what he does not command of the language that he uses. This relationship is not a certain quantitative distribution of shadow and light, of weakness or of force, but a signifying structure that the critical reading should *produce*.

> In other words [Johnson continues], the deconstructive reading does not point out the flaws or weaknesses or stupidities of an author, but the *necessity* with which what he *does* see is systematically related to what he does *not* see.[11]

In the present volume, Textual Cultural Studies is most emblematically put forth in the writings of Gayatri Chakravorty Spivak and Drucilla Cornell, and also through the texts of Costas Douzinas and Ronnie Warrington, and Peter Goodrich (as well as, again, Ashe's feminist poststructuralism). The most directly sustained contestation of "textualism" is set out in this volume by Teresa Ebert (and to a lesser extent by Leonard in the critique of Foucauldian genealogy).

As Johnson's commentary on deconstruction makes clear, Textual Cultural Studies mobilizes a form of "critique" which is not to be confused with the moralistics of "criticism" ("flaws" and "stupidities" of individual authors). As critique, Textual "close readings" inquire into the possible presuppositions—the "unsaid" —at the foundations of thought systems: an investigation of presuppositions, in other words, aims at bringing such a disturbing degree of interrogative pressure to bear on the assumed "hinges" of established meanings and values as to inaugurate scenes of "crisis" at which, to use a self-consciously figurative language, the "bottom drops out" and what were once the apparently stable "grounds" of coherence begin to rumble and shift and become "in-determinate" according to "how" the discourses of such grounds are *read* by differing readers and in different institutional contexts.

It is in the reading of such social and institutional "contexts" —within which "texts" are themselves read—that the very meaning of "critique" itself becomes unstable and contestatory. In his *Deconstruction: Theory and Practice* (1982), Christopher Norris establishes most incisively the theoretical terrain for the battle over "critique." "Only in following through the logic of deconstruction," Norris writes, "rather than meeting its challenge halfway, can thought escape this imprisonment by the metaphors of its own frozen discourse. Nietzsche remains at the last a disturbing threat to the 'taken-for-granted' rhetoric of Marxist theory."[12] The call to radicality in Norris' advocation of a mode of Textual Cultural Studies which undermines "frozen" or entrenched discursive formations is one shared by "Critical" Cultural Studies. For Critical Cultural Studies, however, the "critique" of the *conditions of possibility* of the "frozen-ness" of commonsensical or automatistic thought structures is pursued most vigorously not only at the level of "discourses," "meta-phors," or "rhetorical" features in and of themselves—at the level of their immanent "within-nesses"; rather, the "critique" produced by the reading/writing practices of Critical Cultural Studies becomes in a certain sense trans-textual (as well as trans-experiential) by aiming to situate and theorize "texts" within precise historical and social formations.

Just as Textual Cultural Studies shifts from the Experiential question of "what" constitutes "the real" into the analysis of "how" the real is discursively fabricated and susceptible of de-construction (a teasingly incessant "raveling" and "unraveling") through the rhetorical playfulness and figurality of counter metaphors, Critical Cultural Studies pressures the very "taken-for-grantedness" of "metaphoricity" itself (the historicizing Marx contra Norris's rhetoricizing Nietzsche) by examining the question of why, under a given set of historical conditions of existence, certain meanings are put into radical question—why, in short, "frozen" or reified signs of "knowledge" may operate in (un)questionably "obvious" ways for political and economic reasons which can be demystified and grasped historically rather than "naturally."[13] The "critique" mobilized by Critical Cultural Studies is lucidly set out in Marx's 1859 preface to *A Contri-bution to the Critique of Political Economy*. Here Marx writes:

The guiding principle of my studies can be summarized as follows. In the social production of their existence, men inevitably enter into definite relations, which are independent of their will, namely relations of production appropriate to a given stage in the development of their material forces of production. The totality of these relations of production constitutes the economic structure of society, the real foundation, on which arises a legal and political superstructure and to which correspond definite forms of social consciousness. The mode of production of material life conditions the general process of social, political and intellectual life. It *is not the consciousness of men that determines their existence, but their social existence that determines their consciousness.* At a certain stage of development, the material productive forces of society come into conflict with the existing relations of production or—this merely expresses the same thing in legal terms—with the property relations within the framework of which they have operated hitherto. From forms of development of the productive forces these relations turn into their fetters. Then begins an era of social revolution. *The changes in the economic foundation lead sooner or later to the transformation of the whole immense superstructure. In studying such transformations it is always necessary to distinguish between the material transformation of the economic conditions of production, which can be determined with the precision of natural science, and the legal, political, religious, artistic or philosophic—in short, ideological forms in which men become conscious of this conflict and fight it out.* Just as one does not judge an individual by what he thinks about himself, so one cannot judge such a period of transformation by its consciousness, but, on the contrary, this consciousness must be explained from the contradictions of material life, from the conflict existing between the social forces of production and the relations of production. No social order is ever destroyed before all the productive forces for which it is sufficient have been developed, and new superior relations of production never replace older ones before the material conditions for their existence have matured within the framework of the old society. Mankind thus inevitably sets itself only such tasks as it is able to solve, since closer examination will always show that the problem itself arises only when the material conditions for its solution are already present or at least in the course of formation....The bourgeois mode of production is the last antagonistic form of the social process of production— antagonistic not in the sense of individual antagonisms but of an antagonism that emanates from the individuals' social conditions of existence—but the productive forces developing

> within bourgeois society create also the material conditions for
> a solution of this antagonism. The prehistory of human society
> accordingly closes with this social formation.[15]

Still even in this formulation, the recurrent articulation of the
"ideological forms in which *men* become conscious" of the social
conflict over justice itself requires "fighting it out": fighting it out
over the reach and scope of "ideology" and hence ideology
critique, and even over the very conceptual terrain of "the social"
at stake in such struggles. This "becoming conscious," in other
words, calls to the front precisely the question of "the subject"
and its political "significance" in critical theory. As Maria Mies
indicates in *Patriarchy and Accumulation on a World Scale* (1986),
significantly quoting from Roswitha Leukert's unpublished text,
"Weibliche Sinnlichkeit": "'The beginning of human history is
primarily not a problem of fixing a certain date, but rather that of
finding a materialist concept of man [the human being, the
subject] and history.'"[15]

In the (post)modern cultural moment of late capitalism, the
work of the critic becomes trans-disciplinary and global. Ernest
Mandel writes in *Late Capitalism*: "*The real idol of late capitalism
is...the 'specialist' who is blind to any overall context.*"[16] Clearly it
is the "political" (genealogical) Foucault, the champion of the
"specific" intellectual, who becomes a main oppositional representative in relation to the very idea of a globally systemic
materialist critique of existing modes of oppression. Derrida's
classic formulation, "There is nothing outside the text," as well
articulates a mode of self-enclosed textual "specialism" which,
ideologically, blocks an explanatory and transformative examination of the material "overall context." Under the pressure of
the deconstructive "war on totality"[17] throughout the 70s and
80s, the framing question from the "New Left" *Social Text*
Collective—*Universal Abandon?*[18]—is deeply symptomatic of the
immense impact of deconstructive discourses in the contemporary West, as well as, again, the "subtle" philosophical way in
which the discourses of deconstruction guard against a global-
systemic materialist critique of (post)modern capitalist patriarchy. As already suggested, in the present collection Teresa
Ebert's text directly engages these issues, punctuating the
volume's conclusion by writing a transformative politics back
into the "post" of (post)modern intelligibilities of resistance.

Although, as I established in the opening, this project draws
upon Blanchot's notion of "absenting the book" and Foucault's

notion of the "dossier," it is important in my view to not merely "use" such work as if such use were not, at this historical moment, a situated/situating use—a productive use, in other words, which differs from and contests such concepts of (re)ordering which have themselves emerged with the "New World Order." For Blanchot "the absence of the book" in fact constitutes nothing less than the arche-deconstructive maneuver in which the "book" (the Holy Bible as the exemplary Book of the Law of the Father) signifies the very possibility/impossibility of "concept" and "order" in conventional sense. By writing an "absence" into the book, Blanchot deconstructively marks the apocalypse of any such apparently stable, monological, unitary or undivided "concept." Traditional Law and Order, in other words, is internally subverted by the incessantly "slipping" law of the signifier: in Derrida's formulation, the law of *différance* according to which the order of signification is never the "same" as itself but constantly differing in space and deferring in time. The essential point, however, is that the deconstruction of the Law of the Father (the orthodox book) produces not so much the end of "order" altogether, but rather the inauguration of a new, plural, "dissenting" order traversed by the randomatics of aleatory "chances" and "risks" at the level of meaningfulness.

Along the same lines, Foucault's "dossier" is at bottom marked by the Nietzschean genealogical sense of "a play of hostile forces" without any necessarily determining point of departure or end: while apparently non-closural, this is in any event a suspiciously naturalizing, panhistorical "will" to power/knowledge. The notion of the dossier is introduced in Foucault's foreword to *I, Pierre Rivière,* one of the first published works growing out of the G.I.P.:

> ...it was a "dossier," that is to say, a case, an affair, an event that provided the intersection of discourses that differed in origin, form, organization, and function—the discourses of the cantonal judge, the prosecutor, the presiding judge of the assize court, and the Minister of Justice....All of them speak, or appear to be speaking, of one and the same thing;...But in their totality and their variety they form neither a composite work nor an exemplary text, but rather a strange contest, a confrontation, a power relation, a battle among discourses and through discourses. And yet, it cannot simply be described as a single battle; for several separate combats were being fought out at the same time and intersected each other...[19]

The essential moment lies here in the subtle "qualificational" tone of: "in their totality and their variety...*several separate* combats were being fought out at the same time..." Foucault displays in this way the infinite "capaciousness" of the genealogist as grand (neo-pluralist) host. As Foucault repeats to his interlocutors from the French journal *Esprit* in 1968, "Now, I am a pluralist...I am a pluralist: the problem which I have set myself is that of the *individualization* of discourses."[20] Not only is Foucault anxious in general about "theorizing" a battle over the general intelligibility of "events"; beyond this, he most certainly as well wishes to avoid the accusation of even "describing" a "single" battle "simply," and thus opts precisely for the neo-liberalist heterogenealogical stance of "acknowledging" both the "severalness" as well as the "separateness" of microcombatics.

In the wake of such super-subtlety in Blanchot/Derrida/Foucault/...,today, while displacing "orthodoxy," this stance of the critic has become the new heterodoxy which in the last analysis simply makes it possible for one to say everything, "allow" everything (i.e., be ethically "tolerant"), and thus essentially say nothing at all that anyone "reasonable" could possibly take issue with: the critic as indeterminist, tiptoeing in, around and between every "severally separate" local combat. While the move to point up the dividedness or multiple con-flictedness of the signs of culture is a necessary one, clearly my point here is to contest the limits of such a move in its currently institutionalized renarration of liberal pluralism as well as its massively widespread appeal as a basic threshold concession for "inclusion" within neoconservative, ad hoc "coalition building." George Bush perfectly articulated this idea in the slogan, "We want radical reform!", which finds only trivial disagreement from the "new" U.S. President, Bill Clinton. The horror behind "radical reform" is that Bush was not only speaking to America, but the entire world of the "New World Order." The question becomes "radical reform" in whose interests, whose new order?

The "differences" activated through the absenting of the book and the emergence of the dossier, I believe, must urgently be theorized with a sense of their global organization and possible coordinative relations under contemporary racist patriarchal capitalism. This is the sense in which my earlier mapping of differing approaches to cultural studies is not merely "descrip-tive" or infinitely "capacious." Rather, while producing a map of differences, I do not simply abandon the "concept" of cultural studies but in fact argue for the global horizon offered by Critical Cultural Studies as a principled materialist inclusion and supersession—not an eclectics—of the discourses of experientiality and textuality.

The three dossiers of this project, then, are all—within as well as between their differing and uneven articulations—scenes of intersection and difference. Beyond Foucault's intimations, however, I maintain that they are not "several separate combats" but rather a series of interrelated—or better, structurally interconnected—discourses which investigate these three main axes: (1) the historical and material positions of the subject; (2) the differentially conflictual operations of the sign; and (3) the political dimensions of contemporary theory in the struggles against injustice. The dossiers constitute the overlapping and often conflictual opening arguments for the "case" of legal studies as cultural studies.

In this introduction I have self-consciously drawn upon materials which are themselves by and large "introductory" or in some sense "exemplary" in nature, thus providing critical pedagogues and readers at least one possible set of texts in relation to which this volume itself may be read. At the end I have also provided an inclusive bibliography of works cited. I have refused "summarizing" the texts, however (or rather I have not "summarized" in the conventional sense), because actively and relentlessly producing the critique-al knowledges of a project such as this is the principal challenge of the partisan readers to whom the (post)modern reader addresses itself.

"Summarizing," of course, goes on all the time in cultural/ legal practices—in the classroom, at the seminar table, at conferences, in the courtroom, and so forth. My point, however, is that summary is always already a differentially positioned summary, and it is this (subject) positioning which needs clarification. Thus in this introduction I have sought to foreground the broad discursive movements within which the specific texts of this volume may (arguably, I believe) be located. If this seems a rather rude form of "pigeonholing," it is indeed because I believe "critical" theory—understood even in the most general sense imaginable—demands the taking of a stand, a self-reflexively argued-for intellectual and political positioning; and such a praxis is blatantly defeated through the widespread eclecticism of most "critical scholarship" in contemporary cultural/ legal studies.

There is finally a most important sense in which the present collection is not a "book" but rather, through the mediations of signifying practices, a politically and historically symptomatic "ensemble of social relations."[21]   Intervening in the discursive order of the anthology, *Legal Studies as Cultural Studies* symbolically articulates a particular historical configuration of knowledges.   It is "plural" but not evenly so; it is a "collection" but not haphazardly so; it is constituted by "differences" but they are not formal but political, not panhistorical but acutely symptomatic of the political economy of knowledge under the pressures and limits of (post)modern capitalist patriarchy.

As the opening epigraph from Madhava Prasad argues, the radical critical (post)modern text (whether an anthology or not) aims at clarifying its decisive and unrelenting opposition to the totality of the status quo by aggressively promoting a radical social critique—a radical social theory—of its enabling conditions, rather than a superficial "celebration" of itself, its "differences," its "utopian impulse" and so forth.   In this way the (post)modern reader refuses the dead weight of "books" and instead involves itself actively, consciously and committedly in that which it had always already been involved, if only at a less reflexive level of intelligibility: the politicization of knowledge, and not merely so as to "reform" but to exert as much pressure as possible on the dominant understandings of all social texts.

It is in this sense as well that the cultural function of the anthology itself is put in question.   The main issue is not merely that anthologies "say something about" the politics of inclusion/ exclusion, about the center and the margin, but moreover that such local (still "bookish") configurations of the politics of representation are themselves symptomatic of and intrinsically connected to far wider configurations of social unrest, conflict, contradictions, and resistance.   Because today it is so overwhelmingly clear that Experiential and Textual modes of cultural/legal studies represent the dominant discourses of (post)modernism—at once within and outside of this volume— the decisive question is not simply that of a "better representation" of Critical Cultural Studies (e.g., to make its agendas more "appealing"); on the contrary, it is a question of further and more rigorously clarifying the starkly material reality that Critical Cultural Studies (and its deployment as critical legal studies) "represents" not just another politics of inclusion (a "difference within") but rather a socialist politics of revolution.

Refusing the complacency of the book, then, *Legal Studies as Cultural Studies* in the final instance is a registration of the class struggle in theory. In this way the reader becomes a consciously produced and displayed ensemble of social relations and struggles. The reader signifies not a "utopian impulse" but rather a concrete moment of resistance. *The reader becomes a social critique and a collective indictment.* The determinant question necessarily becomes a "crude" one: the call of neo-bourgeois liberal justice as a multilayered and "immanent" politics of inclusion within the "newly" emerging forms of capitalist patriarchy on a world scale? or rather, revolutionary justice as a multivalent and "transformative" politics of the destruction of global capitalist patriarchy and its replacement by an entirely different historical construction and organization of socialist praxis?

I argue for this kind of reconceptualization of "critical theory" in general, as always already having been involved in such questions and theoretical problematics requiring more and more rigorous clarification in all modes of social praxis: that is, in writing, in pedagogy, in the formation of reading collectives, in local community, national and international forms of organization and service, in short, in "everyday life." This means, as I also argue through the title of this volume, that the radical theorization of the "post" of the subject in her/his historical relationship to "modern" society ("civil-ized" society) and all of the differentially articulated juridical positions of this existing society requires the most demanding, innovative, daring, and relentless investigation and elaboration. This is the kind of theory of (post)modern legal studies as (critical) cultural studies which I advocate and defend.

Contemporary cultural studies is reconceptualized through this collection as a profoundly contested "court," an historical political "trial" of critical knowledges. What is ultimately on trial at the shifting center of these contestations is the subject of justice, the historic means of bringing social justice into the contemporary world through the unity of radical theory and practice. As each dossier demonstrates, such a project involves the sustained interrogation of the conditions of possibility of injustice as it exists in different forms around the world. Taking a difference here with the volume edited by Stephen Greenblatt and Giles Dunn, *Redrawing the Boundaries: The Transformation of English and American Literary Studies* (1992),[22] *Legal Studies as Cultural Studies* is not content with "revisionism" and does not seek merely to "redraw" old boundaries in new ways. Instead the project proposes an examination of why and how "boundaries" exist to begin with. Hence the "as" in legal studies *as* cultural studies is neither interdisciplinary, antidisciplinary, nor postdisciplinary, but trans-disciplinary and bent toward transformations.

I would like to thank a few people whose sustained support for this project helped make it possible: Clay Morgan at SUNY Press, Jack Balkin, Bernard S. Jackson of Deborah Charles Publications in England, Leonard G. Buckle of the American Legal Studies Association and the Program in Law, Policy and Society at Northeastern University, and David Ray Papke, editor of *Legal Studies Forum.* Especially I wish to thank Mas'ud Zavarzadeh and Donald Morton for their critical intellectual support and sustained encouragement for this project and its fundamental development at Syracuse University in the late 80s/early 90s and afterwards.

NOTES

1. Madhava Prasad, "The New (International) Party of Order? Coalition Politics in the (Literary) Academy," *diacritics,* 22.1 (1992): 38.

2. Maurice Blanchot, "The Absence of the Book," in *Deconstruction in Context: Literature and Philosophy,* ed. Mark C. Taylor, Chicago: University of Chicago Press (1986): 382.

3. I do *not* mean to suggest here that there are no "dominant" modes of contemporary cultural studies. There are also quite clearly dominant modes of "critical" legal studies. Broadly speaking, for both cultural studies and critical legal studies, the dominant discursive mode is an eclectical celebration of poststructuralism. Further on in this introduction I directly address this issue.

4. On Critical Legal Studies generally, see the collection edited by Allan C. Hutchinson, *Critical Legal Studies* (Totowa, New Jersey: Rowman & Littlefield Publishers, 1989).

5. On Contemporary Cultural Studies generally, see the volume edited by David Punter, *Introduction to Contemporary Cultural Studies* (London: Longman, 1986). Also see Patrick Brantlinger, *Crusoe's Footprints: Cultural Studies in Britain and America* (New York and London: Routledge, 1990).

6. American neo-liberal academics of "multiculturalism," such as Gerald Graff with the notion of "Teach the Conflicts," have in this way

precisely attempted to recuperate and contain radical theories and pedagogies of critique. See Graff, "Teach the Conflicts," in *The Politics of Liberal Education*, eds. Darryl J. Gless and Barbara Herrnstein Smith (Durham and London: Duke University Press, 1992) 57–74.

7. Steven Connor, *Postmodernist Culture: An Introduction to Theories of the Contemporary* (Oxford and Cambridge: Easil Blackwell, 1989) 3.

8. Michel Foucault, "Intellectuals and power," in *Language, Counter-Memory, Practice: Selected Essays and Interviews*, trans. Donald Bouchard and Sherry Simon, ed. D. Bouchard (Ithaca, New York: Cornell University Press, 1977) 206.

9. See generally Jane Gallop, *Around 1981: American Feminist Literary Criticism* (New York and London: Routledge, 1992).

10. See Ranajit Guha, ed., *Subaltern Studies I: Writings on South Asian History and Society* (Delhi: Oxford University Press, 1982). See also Gayatri Chakravorty Spivak, "Subaltern Studies: Deconstructing Historiography," *In Other Worlds: Essays in Cultural Politics* (New York and London: Routledge, 1988) 197–221.

11. Barbara Johnson, "Translator's Introduction," in Jacques Derrida, *Dissemination*, trans. B. Johnson (London: University of Chicago Press, 1981) xiv–xv, emphasis in original. Johnson is quoting Jacques Derrida, *Of Grammatology*, trans. Gayatri Chakravorty Spivak (Baltimore: Johns Hopkins University Press, 1976) 159, emphasis in original.

12. Christopher Norris, *Deconstruction: Theory and Practice* (London and New York: Methuen, 1982) 89.

13. For a sustained articulation of radical critique-al (post)modern theory, see Mas'ud Zavarzadeh and Donald Morton, *Theory, (Post)Modernity. Opposition: An "Other" Introduction to Literary and Cultural Theory* (Washington, D.C.: Maisonneuve Press, 1991).

14. Karl Marx, *A Contribution to the Critique of Political Economy*, trans. S.W. Ryazanskaya, ed. Maurice Dobb (Moscow: Progress Publishers, 1970) 20–22, emphasis added.

15. As I indicate, this is Maria Mies's quotation as well as translation of Roswitha Leukert's text. See Mies, *Patriarchy and Accumulation of the World Scale: Women in the International Division of Labour* (Atlantic Highlands, New Jersey: Zed Books, 1986) 48. Mies (re)reads "man" as "the human being," and I am (re)reading this further as "the subject" of critical theory in (post)modern cultural studies.

16. Ernest Mandel, *Late Capitalism*, trans. Joris De Bres (London and New York: Verso, 1978) 509, emphasis in original.

17. Jean-Francois Lyotard, *The Postmodern Condition: A Report on Knowledge*, trans. Geoff Bennington and Brian Massumi (Minneapolis: University of Minnesota Press, 1984) 82.

18. Andrew Ross, ed., *Universal Abandon? The Politics of Postmodernism* (Minneapolis: University of Minnesota Press, 1988).

19. Michel Foucault, ed., *I, Pierre Rivière, Having Slaughtered My Mother, My Sister, and My Brother...: A Case of Parricide in the 19th Century*, trans. Frank Jellinek (Lincoln and London: University of Nebraska Press, 1975) x.

20. Michel Foucault, "History, Discourse and Discontinuity," trans. Anthony M. Nazzaro, *Salmagundi* 20 (Summer-Fall 1972): 226, emphasis in original.

21. K. Marx, "Theses on Feuerbach," in *The Marx-Engels Reader* (1978) 145.

22. Stephen Greenblatt and Giles Dunn, eds., *Redrawing the Boundaries: The Transformation of English and American Literary Studies* (New York: Modern Language Association Publications, 1992).

Dossier I

THE SUBJECT

1

DAVID S. CAUDILL _____

Freud and Critical Legal Studies: Contours of a Radical Socio-Legal Psychoanalysis

"The success of critical legal studies will be in part determined by the extent to which they succeed in bringing together the diverse theoretical, traditions on which they seek to draw."[1]

INTRODUCTION

In the growing literature associated with Critical Legal Studies ("CLS"),[2] one occasionally reads that the movement, in part, employs Freudian ideas.[3] The same is said of the Frankfurt School,[4] but one can easily point to the writings of Herbert Marcuse[5] and Erich Fromm[6] for unambiguous developments and revisions of Freud's work. While numerous references to Freudian psychoanalysis or social theory appear in CLS scholarship,[7] the connection between Freud and CLS is not clear. Indeed, Robin West's recent exposition of Freudian jurisprudence counts critical legal theorists among Freud's opponents.[8]

This Article explores the use of Freudian concepts in CLS. However, because of the scattered and often incongruous references to Freud in CLS writings, and the attendant necessity of relying upon literature outside the CLS canon (including Freud's own work and the work of some of his disciples, revisionists and critics), the present effort includes an inquiry as to what Freud might mean to CLS. More generally, this Article should offer some insights as to how CLS—an amalgam of many intellectual movements and methodological techniques—borrows from (and assumes familiarity with) various theoretical traditions.

In Part I, I consider the problems inherited by CLS as a critique of legal ideology, namely the difficulties in defining ideology and describing its operation, and the need for self-criticism on the part of the ideology critic. In Part II, I briefly re-introduce several of Freud's famous notions about the individual and society. Part III consists of a series of qualifications and distinctions concerning the somewhat narrow scope of this analysis, all necessitated by the understated fact that Sigmund Freud, like Karl Marx, is a major figure in Western thought and society. Much of Freud's writing and influence will thus be ignored in the pages that follow.

Parts IV and V discuss, respectively, the so-called Freudian Left[9] (especially Marcuse) and the influence of Freud on Struc-turalists (especially Jacques Lacan). Neo-Marxian Critical Theory and Structuralism generally are acknowledged to be founda-tional to much that we call CLS scholarship.[10] In Part VI, I explore several actual and possible connections between CLS and the Freudian tradition, and conclude by suggesting some avenues for clarifying and developing that relationship. Finally, Part VII focuses on the use of Freudian concepts in the explication and critique of legal ideology, with particular reliance upon Lacan (and Althusser's commentary on Lacan), Peter Gabel and the early Habermas.

The primary aim of this study is not to explain Freud's views, as legions have done already, but rather to contribute to the understanding of CLS and its potential in American legal scholarship.

I. CLS AS A CRITIQUE OF LEGAL IDEOLOGY

While there is no central or core theory shared by all scholars associated with CLS, conceiving the eclectic movement as a form of ideology-critique helps to explain the methodology and terminology of many CLS adherents. Ideologies, in the sense of worldviews or cultural belief systems, generate and inform communal life and thought. When an ideology is hidden (or *unconscious*), its power to obscure alternatives and to create false necessities is greatest. The critique of ideology seeks to disclose belief systems not only to enhance understanding and mean-ingful communication within a community, but to challenge and change social processes. Two problems, however, confront the ideology critic. First, is there evidence of ideologies, and how they operate, for example, within legal processes and institutions? Second, how does the critic overcome his or her own belief system, or, more generally, on what basis does the critic recommend change?

"Ideology" has various meanings. In some Marxian formulations, the term has pejorative connotations—ideology as false consciousness—and refers to that which masks social contradictions and thereby legitimizes oppressive institutions.[11] "Ideology" is also used to describe the coherent set of collective beliefs of any social group[12] In CLS literature, the term "ideology" often connotes "the beliefs that individuals hold about law or the set of beliefs, ideas, and values embodied in the legal institutions and legal materials...of a particular society."[13] However, ideologies also operate, according to some CLS scholars to marginalize alternatives and, distort social knowledge—a pejorative sense of the term.[14]

Some political theorists and sociologists have questioned the assumption that members of a society share a common set of beliefs that constitutes common sense or that legitimizes asymmetrical relations of power. David McLellan theorizes that a dominant ideology will generally be accepted by the ruling class, but that lower classes may be ignorant of, or indifferent to, the dominant ideology.[15] John Thompson argues that societies are more likely "stabilized by virtue of the diversity of values and beliefs and the proliferation of divisions between individuals and groups."[16] Ideology, for Thompson, is not grounded in consensus, but in everyday language where "meaning is mobilized in defense of [relations of] domination."[17] The study of ideology is therefore construed as an investigation into "the ways in which meaning (signification)" legitimates, hides and neutralizes power in society.[18]

Even if a workable definition of ideology is established as a common set of beliefs or as a set of limitations on thought and power embedded in everyday language, questions remain as to how legal ideology works—how is "the population in general or some particular section...influenced by the ideological products of the legal process?"[19] Compounding the problem, a program of ideology-critique proceeds in the shadow of its own ideology, and critics must account, in a process of self-reflection, for their own ideological presuppositions or, in another formulation, their given, linguistic framework. Critical legal theorists can escape neither belief nor language in their analyses of legal culture.

These problems, coupled with the recurring accusations that CLS literature is vague, incomprehensible, impractical and nothing but Legal Realism revisited, plague critical legal research. My thesis is that psychoanalytic theory offers insights with which to confront some of the problematic aspects of CLS— insights that are already contained within the radical traditions on which CLS draws.

II. FREUDIAN PSYCHOLOGY

A. Influence and Ideas

Within the history of psychology, Sigmund Freud's psycho-analytic theories represent (in Kuhnian terms) a revolutionary breakthrough between paradigms. As with Einstein in physics, we identify pre-Freudian and post-Freudian perspectives on the problems of the discipline.[20] Freudian psychoanalysis has also influenced sociology[21] and political theory,[22] as well as literature, art, education, religion and other disciplines.[23] Perhaps most important, however, is the popularly acknowledged impact of Freud on our lives in general.[24] "Much that was new in psychoanalysis has become accepted wisdom in our culture and has been absorbed even by people who have not read Freud[]...."[25]

At the same time, many of Freud's formulations have been ignored or have met with hostility in academia.[26] Freudian theory is often the source of controversy, especially among psychiatrists, and it continues to challenge traditional ways of thinking about human nature.[27]

While the theories and influence of psychoanalysis are the subjects of thousands of books and articles, one may identify several key ideas associated with Freud. First, the recognition of sexuality as a fundamental and complex motivational force, and the theory of repression in which painful desires and ideas are driven into the unconscious, have been considered two of Freud's major discoveries.[28] Second, Freud is primarily responsible for the therapeutic approach that promises access to the dynamics of mental life.[29] Third, and most important for the present study, Freud's later writings suggest that the concepts of sexuality, repression and the unconscious, as well as the psychoanalytic therapeutical method, are not only significant for understanding and helping the individual, but are useful in social analysis.[30]

B. Dynamics of the Mind

As is well-known, Freud's later theory of personality introduced three mental systems: the id, the ego and the super-ego. The id is the primary, subjective reality, existing prior to the individual's experience of the world. Driven by instinct, it functions, in the service of the primordial *pleasure principle*, to avoid pain and find pleasure.[31] The id may be bound or controlled, however by the ego, a secondary mental process, which is in, turn governed by the *reality principle*.[32] The reality of the external world requires thinking or problem-solving, a plan of action and control of instinctual desires. The ego also, in its adjustment function, governs the super-ego, which consists of moral ideals and the conscience, including traditional values and other social ideals learned in childhood.[33] Roughly, then, the id corresponds with biological processes, the ego with the higher mental processes (and interaction with reality) and the super-ego with socialization and cultural tradition.[34]

Faced with the frustrations, conflicts and anxieties of life, the ego may seek realistic solutions or deny, falsify or distort reality through various defense mechanisms.[35] Repression, for example "forces a dangerous memory, idea, or perception out of con-sciousness," and thereby blinds a person to the internal or external threat.[36] Projection, another defense mechanism, is the process of objectifying neurotic or moral anxiety, wherein the individual unconsciously rationalizes away personal respon-sibility by blaming another.[37] As with repression, projection is an escape from conscious self-examination and results in a distor-tion of reality. Reaction formations likewise hide awareness of an instinct by concentrating on its opposite.[38] As an example, extreme notions of chastity may be a denial of one's sexual desires; more generally, rigid conformity with any social rules may be a denial of one's rebellious desires. Fixation and regression, also defense mechanisms, are related to stopping or reversing psychological growth to avoid anxiety.[39] In all of these cases, the ego deals with anxieties by distorting or denying reality.[40]

Freud's early work on hypnotism with Josef Breuer con-vinced him that some psychological afflictions are caused by repressed episodes, and that if a patient can bring to conscious-ness and verbally express his or her feelings, the affliction may be cured.[41] The psychoanalytic method as developed by Freud involved overcoming the patient's predictable resistance and then

analyzing and interpreting the previously unconscious material.[42]
For example, anxiety hysteria, a form of transference neurosis,
symbolizes or dramatizes for the analyst a conflict between the id
and the ego, the primitive and the ethical self; similarly,
psychosis results from a conflict between the ego and the
external world, and narcissistic neurosis from a conflict between
the ego and the super-ego.[43] Significantly, these disturbances
are, for Freud, present in varying degrees in all people.[44] Thus,
everyday jokes, slips of the tongue, fantasies and dreams reveal
the workings of the unconscious and the universality of the
illusions and tensions within each person's mind.

Although psychoanalysis grew into an international movement in the decades following Freud's death (infiltrating much of
Western social and literary study) and then fell into disrepute
among mainstream psychologists, a renewed interest in Freud
and the psychoanalytic tradition is apparent outside the
discipline of psychology and even within some of the discipline's
movements (such as object-relations theory).[45] That tradition,
neophytes quickly realize, is a picture of disagreement and
uncertainty. Beyond mere revisionism, some schools of thought
inspired by Freud have developed theories that are fundamentally different from Freud's.[46] Nevertheless, nearly all
psychoanalytic approaches seem to share the concept of a
dynamic and ordinarily inaccessible unconscious in which the
residues of childhood and various instinctual (especially sexual)
impulses motivate everyday thought and action.[47]

C. Freud and Society

While psychoanalysis can be viewed solely as an explanatory
model for individual human behavior "it also contains the
possibilities for an approach that analyzes the mechanisms by
which the social world enters into the experience of each individual, constructing the human 'subject' and reproducing itself
through the perpetuation of particular patterns of ideology."[48]
Just as the individual represses threatening ideas, society
represses the individual.[49] Just as the individual seeks to control
powerful instincts, "civilization is built upon a renunciation of
instinct.."[50] Freud believed that the primordial and dangerous
passions of the individual must be controlled by inherently
oppressive social structures.[51] While these discoveries may be
helpful in social analysis one immediately notices that they invite
pessimism and provide the basis for an implied conservatism
rather than for a radical ar or utopian critique of the status quo.

However, Freud's views on sexuality, a seemingly individual and private matter, are particularly instructive for radical social analysis. First, if one accepts Freud's thesis that infants have a rich sexual life—a polymorphous perversity that seeks pleasure without inhibitions—then social repression of such infantile sexuality is, at some point on the road to adulthood, justified. The implication is that "normal" sexuality is not biological and that, in anthropological terms, different societies will have different views of normality, and in critical terms, alternatives to socially acceptable sexuality are imaginable.[52] Second, and more important to the present study, is "the recognition that what Freud describes is the way society enters into the essence of the human individual, organizing the instincts where usually we consider that we are most privately ourselves."[53]

In the radical Freudian scheme, it is *not* that an already established individual consciousness is conditioned or shaped by social interaction, but rather that society has an unconscious and formative effect on individual experience and perception of oneself and others.[54] That is, our social relations are "themselves only available because of the particular ideological structures that dominate within a society."[55] In this view the impulses and feelings that appear to be so much a part of our "selves" are actually products of our socialization.[56]

From the point of view of the critic of ideology, a profound ambivalence persists in Freud's social writings. On the one hand, Freud was not hopeful about radical social change and even criticized such hopes as a mere search for consolation.[57] On the other hand, the radical tradition inherited from Freud the promise of the power to analyze, "to display the unconscious roots of personal and social action, to make this material open to awareness and hence to make ideology open to inspection and change imaginable."[58] Freud's preoccupation with illusions, despite his descriptive and positivistic—"scientific"—goals, could not help but suggest the possibilities for emancipation and demystification.[59]

To begin my inquiry, I will revisit two traditions—Critical Theory and Structuralism—that build in part upon Freudian ideas. Significantly these, two traditions are most often identified as the forerunners of critical legal scholarship, and both signal a latent role for psychoanalytic theory in critical legal studies. First, however, the breadth of Freudian scholarship and the narrow scope of the present study must be briefly acknowledged.

III. QUALIFICATIONS AND DISTINCTIONS

In the foregoing summary of Freudian theory, and in the remainder of this study, much of Freud's own work and the work of many of his followers and critics has and will be ignored. While my focus is solely on Freud's relevance for the critical legal enterprise, a series of qualifications will serve to acknowledge other uses of Freud and psychoanalytic theory in law.

First, I am almost exclusively concerned with the social aspect of psychoanalysis, although assessing the implications of Freud's theories for society requires attention to his early work on the individual psyche as well as his later writings about culture. Nor will I discuss the international psychoanalytic movement, which builds upon Freud's clinical work and writings, involves an entire field of research and writing on individual, and especially abnormal, psychology, and is of course part—but not an uncontroversial part—of the practical tradition of psychotherapy and psychiatry.[60]

Second, I will limit my commentary to Freud's impact upon the Left and its concerns with ideology, power structures, freedom and criticism of the status quo. I will not attempt to describe either the numerous other movements of Neo-Freudianism or Freudian revisionism,[61] or the general effect of Freudian ideas upon Western culture.[62]

Third, I am not here concerned with the relationship between Freud and law generally, including the relationship between mainstream law practice and psychiatry or psychology,[63] the more traditional views concerning the utility of psychoanalysis for legal scholarship (including Frank's analysis of the myth of coherency,[64] Bienefeld's reconsideration of the Oedipus complex,[65] Goldstein's warnings concerning the limits of psychoanalysis,[66] Ehrenzweig's "psychosophy, "[67] and Schoenfeld's contemporary synthesis[68]), and Freud's own views on law and legal institutions (although I will address the latter in one limited context[69]). Thus, I will not be concerned with the legal problems of criminal behavior, the insanity defense or the testimony of psychiatric experts, although each are relevant to the general study of psychology and law.[70]

Finally, I will emphasize neither feminism[71] nor the current trends in literary theory[72] in my exposition, even though both fields are pertinent to the topic of Freud and the legal Left. Freud's ideas about gender and language continue to inspire scholars and to produce controversies that are important but beyond the scope of this Article. The analysis that follows is based upon my conception of Critical Legal Studies as an ideology critique, and the actual and possible uses of Freudian theory within that framework.

IV. FREUD AND CRITICAL THEORY

"[T]he laws are made by and for the ruling members...."[73]

While the contemporary Left is accustomed to, if not always comfortable with, the potential alliance between Marx and Freud, the Frankfurt School's early introduction of psychoanalysis into Neo-Marxian Critical Theory was bold and unconventional.[74] Max Horkheimer and Theodor Adorno clearly were interested in integrating the two traditions,[75] notwithstanding the tension between Freud's pessimism (regarding social change) and Marxian revolutionary hopes.

Erich Fromm, for a time, helped to reconcile Marx and Freud, although he later disassociated himself from the Frankfurt School and orthodox Freudianism. Fromm's identification of "psychoanalytic mechanisms as the mediating concepts between individual and society" established for the Neo-Marxists a Freudian component in social criticism.[76] Freud's theory of psychic repression of essential needs, for example, is strikingly analogous to Critical Theory's idea of social oppression, and in both cases people are considered to be generally unconscious of the process.[77]

Horkheimer welcomed the growing psychological supplement to Marxian theory, as did Adorno, yet both grew dissatisfied with Fromm's revision of Freud's work.[78] It was not Fromm, but Herbert Marcuse, who finally rescued for Critical Theory the revolutionary Freud.

Marcuse's *Eros and Civilization* plays several roles for those inspired by Critical Theory and enamored of Freud. First, the book is a criticism of Freudian revisionism. Marcuse retains, at least for their symbolic value, some of the most controversial concepts in Freud's theory: the death instinct, the primal horde and the killing of the primal father. While this "archaic heritage" rejected by the revisionists "defies common sense, it claims, in its defiance, a truth which common sense has been trained to forget."[79] Second, Marcuse did not accept Freud's pessimism (concerning society) and implied conservatism, finding instead a critical and liberating tendency, or "hidden trend," in psycho-analysis.[80] Third, Marcuse argued that "Freud's individual psychology is in its very essence social psychology."[81]

In the preface to the first edition of *Eros and Civilization*, Marcuse immediately identifies the psychological with the political:

> [F]ormerly autonomous and identifiable psychical processes are being absorbed by the function of the individual in the state— by his public existence....[P]rivate disorder reflects more directly the disorder of the whole, and the cure of personal disorder depends more directly than before on the cure of the general disorder.[82]

External repression, Marcuse continues, is internalized as self-repression; in Freudian categories, the repressions of the ego ("in the service and at the behest of the super-ego")[83] became "unconscious, automatic as it were...."[84] Rather than simply accommodating reality, the super-ego enforces *past* reality, the status quo.

Marcuse takes seriously Freud's instinct theory, especially the dualism of the Life (or *Eros*) and Death (or *Thanatos*) instincts, in order to advocate liberation from repression of such primary drives. He distinguished basic repression (necessary for civilization) from *surplus* (or unnecessary) repression, and suggests that the latter is a standard for measuring the repressiveness of each stage in the history of our culture.[85] Marcuse also emphasizes Freud's distinction between the pleasure principle and the reality principle, but the latter becomes in today's capitalist society the "performance" principle, an instrument of domination. "We designate it as *performance principle* in order to emphasize that under its rule society is stratified according to the competitive economic performances of its member."[86] Domination becomes rationalized administration, and the life-enhancing energy of Eros slowly withers in today's society.

Assessments of Marcuse's synthesis of psychoanalysis and critical social theory vary. Paul Robinson's sympathetic commentary on *Eros and Civilization* suggests not only that Marcuse was *the* Freudian Left, or at least its major figure, but also that Marcuse succeeded in bringing Freudian theory into line with the categories of Marxism.[87] Stephen Frosh is less impressed, finding that, in Marcuse's individualistic and libertarian analysis, "social relations are reduced to pure, unproblematic and unmediated encounters between totally unalienated individuals." A genuinely radical psychoanalysis, Frosh argues, needs to concern itself with social structures as well as specific others, "themselves the carriers of social and ideological messages."[88]

Before considering the lesson for legal theorists in Marcuse's Freudianism and Frosh's warning, another tradition influenced by Freud and influential in CLS should be considered.

V. FREUD AND STRUCTURALISM

"I suddenly realized...that an intellectual movement could be fashionable without being understood."[89]

Because Structuralism (and, as I will use the term, various post-structuralisms that are not radically anti-scientific) implies a search for universal mental structures manifested in human behavior, literature, and social relationships and institutions, it is not surprising to find Freudian concepts employed and refined by thinkers in the Structuralist tradition. Lévi-Strauss, a founder of the movement, claimed psychoanalysis, alongside geology and Marxism, as one of his "three mistresses."[90] His discovery in myths of universal and unifying structures was a type of cultural psychoanalysis, analogous to bringing the unconscious into consciousness.[91] Freudian conceptions of the unconscious continued to be influential in Structuralist thought, especially in the writings of Althusser,[92] Ricoeur,[93] Foucault,[94] and, less directly, Derrida.[95] The most obvious integration of psychoanalysis and Structuralism, however, is found in the work of Jacques Lacan.

Even a brief description of Lacan is problematical, for he "makes much of the fact that he cannot be systematized, that he cannot be 'understood,' that to understand him is to reify and misconstrue him...."[96] Given such warnings, the aim of these remarks is less to capture the essence of Lacanian theory than to establish the relationships between psychoanalysis and Structuralism and, more broadly, between psychoanalysis and radical social theory.

Ego formation occurs, for Lacan, "through distortions analogous to the reflections of mirrors within mirrors...."[97] He identifies as fundamental the "mirror-stage" in the child's development, the child's initial awareness of itself before the experience can be verbalized or understood.[98] This first impression or image becomes the basis for construction of a "self" and for all relationships to come. Thereafter, the child becomes aware of the mother (the "other body"), of the father (the "Law") and sexual differences, and of gender roles; concurrently the child discovers language itself.[99] The imaginary order is thus replaced by the symbolic order, Lacan's terms for "the pre-given structure of social and sexual roles and relations which make up the family and society."[100] With the passage into the symbolic, however, the child loses direct access to the imaginary possession of reality, and emerges into the restless world of language and repressed desire.[101]

The unconscious, for Lacan, is structured like a language—"a constant fading and evaporation of meaning, a bizarre 'modernist' text which is almost unreadable and which will certainly never yield up its final secrets to interpretation."[102] The ego, or consciousness, represses the turbulence by "provisionally nailing down words on to meanings," but articulation is always an approximation of truth. The "imaginary" reappears in the conscious and necessary attempt to view oneself as reasonably unified and coherent.[103] As analyst, Lacan adopts the Freudian emphasis upon dreams as a means of approaching the unconscious, but Lacan also examines, in Structuralist fashion, the analysand's speech and associations in general, as well as the breaks and irregularities in speech patterns.[104] Defense mechanisms parallel literary devices in the analysis of the language of the unconscious (or of the id, of desire), which interacts with the language of culture (ordinary speech).[105] Moreover, as a constructive theorist, Lacan proposes a radical new language of enjoyment and fantasy liberated from unhealthy repressions.[106]

Several implications of Lacanian theory are apparent for radical social theory. First, Structuralism as a literary theory helps explain how a legal text, for example, might "intimidate us because we do not see how the language got there in the first place."[107] The power of such a text, with its hidden assumptions, lies in a suppression of its mode of production not unlike the ego's repression of its own self-constructive processes.[108] Second, Althusser's theory of ideology implicitly relies on Lacan in explaining how we come to submit to dominant ideologies.[109] "We tend to see ourselves...as free, unified, autonomous, self-generating individuals; and unless we did so we would be incapable of playing our parts in social life."[110] Nevertheless, we are in fact bound to the social structure that gives us purpose and identity through its signs and social practices.[111] Like Lacan's child with its mirror-image, the individual subject is supplied with an idealized image, a misrecognition, of autonomy and freedom.

VI. CRITICAL LEGAL STUDIES AND THE PSYCHOANALYTIC TRADITION

A. Traces of Freud in CLS

"I think how people get over neuroses is just incredibly mysterious. You're talking about it just like Freud, in which, you know, you just spin the wheel, and whatever slot the little ball drops into becomes the truth. Now we've got collective getting over neuroses."[112]

Explicit references to Freud appear now and then in CLS literature, but Freudian or near-Freudian terminology abounds. Peter Gabel, who employs a concept of false consciousness in his works, speaks of the "collective projection and internalization of an imaginary political authority" as the "mass-psychological foundation of democratic consent."[113] Gabel has also, however, questioned the adequacy of Freud's theory of "an alienated ego resulting from the necessary renunciation of instinctual desires" and attempted to improve, by phenomenological description, both the Freudian and Marxian stories of alienation.[114]

David Trubek has characterized legal thought as "a form of denial, a way to deal with perceived contradictions that are too painful for us to hold in consciousness."[115] Moreover, for Trubek, critical legal scholars are like Freudian analysts in bringing "to '*consciousness*' what is hidden by hegemonic world views."[116] Mark Kelman, likewise, identifies Freudian themes in the CLS emphases upon unconscious self-construction of reality and distortion of reality by avoidance or denial.[117] James Boyle's article on the "politics of reason," in which he attempts to develop a sort of tool kit for the CLS project, remarks that Habermas' compelling "idea of belief structures that were once necessary to group survival but are now merely empty and repressive traditions has definite Freudian overtones."[118] Finally, Thomas Heller, in his helpful study of Structuralism in critical legal thought, highlights the significance of Freudian images of post-therapeutic freedom for Neo-Marxian Critical Theory, for the Structuralist tradition, and impliedly for CLS.[119]

Significantly, David Kennedy's recent study on the roles of Critical Theory and Structuralism in contemporary jurisprudence does not emphasize Marcuse's Freudianism at all, and barely acknowledges Lacan's work. This is neither wrong nor surprising, but rather confirms that the place of Freud in CLS is at present a series of suggestive traces. Not only is there no adoption of psychoanalysis, but not common understanding of Freud's significance for radical social theory emerges.

B. CLS and the Social Freud

"One of the most distinctive derivations from modern Marxism which characterizes critical legal theory has been the shift of focus from economic relations to the focus upon political and cultural relations. Central to this concern is ideology, conceived as a mechanism which forms the consciousness of agents."[120]

CLS has taken many forms in the literature associated with the movement. Some choose to emphasize the implications of CLS for radical practice,[121] and some appear anxious at times to move beyond (rather than digress further into) theoretical concerns.[122] Other emphases include textual concerns and the contemporary debates regarding interpretation, especially of the United States Constitution,[123] the role of CLS in legal education,[124] and specific attacks on traditional or mainstream legal scholars.[125] One unifying theme in the CLS canon, however, is the concern with the ideological role of law in society—legal institutions and processes serve to legitimate hierarchies, to support hegemonic structures, to hide inequalities and oppression. I have argued, elsewhere,[126] that CLS is at its best when viewed as an ideology critique. Nevertheless, Alan Hunt points out that CLS betrays an unfounded assumption that the legal ideology of judges and lawyers is somehow "effective in constructing the perception and consciousness of the dominated in contemporary capitalist societies."[127]

How does legal ideology work to legitimate hierarchical structures? Anthony Chase investigates, and recommends further inquiry into, mass culture images of law and lawyers.[128] A more fundamental question persists, however, in the doubt expressed by some ideology critics as to whether a single invisible ideology exists at all.[129] One might conclude that CLS lacks both a theoretical foundation for its ideology critique and "an empirical demonstration of the connection between legal ideology and the formation of popular consciousness."[130] In the face of these questions, I believe we should reassess Freudian theory and its potential for social criticism.

Charles Lawrence[131] considers several theories of racial inequality in his 1983 book review of David Kirp's *Just Schools: The Idea of Racial Equality in American Education.* Lawrence's exposition of ideology as an unconscious defense mechanism is particularly instructive. Using Freudian terms, Lawrence argues that individuals justify, rationalize or even deny uncomfortable realities—uncomfortable perhaps because of a conflict with what has been taught to them as morally acceptable behavior.[132] "At the societal level, ideology assumes the role of the defense mechanism in the individual psyche."[133] While ideology can be viewed as the result of rational calculation of those in power, Lawrence prefers to view ideology as a symptom—a symbolic outlet for emotional disturbances.[134] The ideology of equal opportunity is developed by academics, judges, politicians and lawyers identified with the socioeconomic order but who feel the tension between that order and their ideals.[135] Lawrence wants to explain not only the illusion of equal treatment advanced by law—a CLS-like exercise—but also why legal scholars react by deluding themselves to avoid anxiety and fear.[136] "This self-mystification occurs on an unconscious level and results in selective perception."[137]

Lawrence developed his views further in his 1987 article on equal protection, specifically the doctrine of discriminatory purpose.[138] In Lawrence's analysis, unconscious racism can be explained by reference to the Freudian theory of repression of guilt and to socio-cognitive psychology's theory of tacit beliefs and preferences transmitted by culture.[139] "Whatever our preferred theoretical analysis, there is considerable commonsense evidence from our everyday experience to confirm that we all harbor prejudiced attitudes that are kept from our consciousness."[140] Lawrence extends his analysis by considering two constitutional theories justifying heightened equal protection scrutiny and then proposing and applying (hypothetically) a new "cultural meaning" test.[141] He concludes that unconscious racism violates antidiscrimination law.

The analogy between the critique of ideology and psychoanalysis is also addressed by Raymond Geuss in his study of Habermas and Critical Theory.[142] In *The Future of an Illusion*, Freud distinguished between error (false factual belief), delusion (false belief that satisfies a wish) and illusion (false *or true* belief that satisfies a wish).[143] Geuss refines the Freudian scheme toward a "wishful thinking" model of *Ideologiekritik*, which proceeds by identifying an illusion, or mistaken belief, and explaining it by reference to Habermas' "interests."[144] Geuss' framework enriches Freud's concepts because mistake may be caused by an institutional context and not just individual psychology.[145] This institutional context might cause agents to make mistakes, thereby serving the interests *of others* as, for example, when statisticians work under conditions that cause them to underestimate unemployment in the service of some powerful group. Such factual errors,. however, are not ideological; thus ideologies might consist of those forms of consciousness with little or no observational content, such as attitudes, preferences and normative beliefs. How, then, can the critic label the agent's belief "false"? Geuss turns to Nietzsche's criticism of Christianity to suggest a critical possibility: Christianity (for Nietzsche) arises in hatred; a Christian can't accept hatred as a motive; Christianity requires that its adherents not recognize their motives; therefore a Christian who recognizes the hatred implied by Christianity can rationally give up his or her belief. Whether Christianity is shown as "false" is not important—the point is that the enlightened agent's own standard of acceptability was sufficient for the critique.[146]

The analogy with psychoanalysis is evident. For both Lawrence and Geuss, Freudian concepts illustrate how individuals might think and act contrary to personal morality (Lawrence) or interests (Geuss) because of a ruling ideology. In Lawrence's example, the ideology is the individual's repressive defense mechanism; in Geuss' example, ideology provides a desire or wish that is false by the individual's own standards.

If the above examples seem inspired by Critical Theory— Geuss by Habermas, and Lawrence, impliedly, by Marcuse ("repression from without has been supported by repression from within")[147]—David Kennedy believes that Lacan's psychoanalytic practice is instructive for legal analysis."[148] While the Lacanian analysis is "neither critical nor constructive," the analyst and analysand venture into the symbolic, through and between conscious and unconscious codes, and "a constituting exchange... permits momentary glimpses of the totality...."[149] Thus, "Lacan's approach suggests the possibility for contextual insight within an awareness of ambiguous signs and unknowable origins."[150] The modesty is striking, but the theoretical promise, perhaps barely, avoids nihilism.

Peter Goodrich, a British scholar who participated in the first Round Table on Law and Semiotics,[151] believes that

> [l]egal education, the institutionalization of the future
> custodians of the law, is an exemplary object of analytical study
> in terms of the classical Freudian categories and languages of
> conscious and unconscious states, of the antinomy of the

pleasure principle and the reality principle, in terms of desire and repression played out in the internalized form of parapraxis [e.g., a slip of the tongue], of transference, complex [e.g., of repressed desires], obligation and censorship.[152]

Goodrich identifies two facets of the disciplinary tradition of law: the positive "idealizations present in and presented to the student of law," and the negative "processes of prohibition and censorship whereby the student of law internalizes the limits of legal argument."[153] Enter psychoanalysis, which

as method, language and voice represents precisely that disordering or denial of unity and of control over meaning that law and doctrine exist to disallow, to cover over.... Psychoanalysis speaks of and intermittently provides a text for that which is inadmissable, constrained or undisclosed in the liberal culture of the individual.[154]

While the psychoanalytical account of legal education will face obstacles not unlike the analysand's defenses in clinical analysis,[155] we have a duty to speak out, despite how unbearable our voice to the institution, in "view of the irreducible damage that law does to our lives, in view of the absence of any limit to its encroachment upon the 'private sphere,' that sphere which appears to have no other function than that of providing a reference point, which is also a vanishing point...."[156] Goodrich's provisional exploration, which (informed by Freud as well as by Lacan, Kristeva, Foucault, Derrida and Irigaray) sees psychoanalysis as a "theory of interpretation and an epistemology of language," implicates law and legal doctrines and institutions generally. His concerns parallel those of CLS—hierarchical training in law schools, hidden discourses or structures of power in law, and the repression of alternatives.

The potential for Freud in CLS is not so much in "opening up new avenues of inquiry," but in explicating and thereby enriching the critique of ideology that is already implied in the CLS canon. In the search for the process or mechanism whereby legal ideology is confirmed or legitimated in society, the psychoanalytic tradition teaches that society introduces

into each individual its own ideological axes, which then become the generative kernels of emotions, attitudes and modes of relating to others....These axes are profoundly unconscious, entering into each of us through our early and most intense contacts with others who already bear the weight of ideology upon them.[157]

C. Freudian Criticism of CLS

Robin West recently explored the relationship between legal liberalism and Freud's "understudied but provocative" notion of the Rule of Law.[158] West's exposition, however, also introduced an implied criticism of leftist legal scholarship based upon Freudian social and political theory.

Briefly, Freud identified a "problem of power" in civilization arising from the aggressive, antisocial instinctual desires of individuals that cannot be neutralized by the capacity for altruism, empathy or love.[159] The Rule of Law, for Freud, was history's solution to the problem, as illustrated by the story of the "father horde." Once the brothers of the horde killed the all-powerful father, their remorse led to collective obedience to the substitute father—the *totem*—and its commands, including a prohibition against killing the totem animal and each other.[160] The Rule of Law, West explains, originates for Freud in this state of artificial equality under the murder taboo.

The potential for eros, the love instinct, to hold civilization together is problematic for Freud (if not Marcuse). Not only does eros struggle against an equally powerful death instinct, but eros is itself ambivalent toward civilization. The fundamental erotic instinct is oriented to relationships between couples, not large social groups. "Protection for the communal unit," therefore, "must be found elsewhere."[161]

Institutionalized guilt, followed by "renunciatory obedience to a protective and impersonal authority," is, for Freud, the historical resolution reflected in both the father horde story and in modern civilization's Rule of Law.[162] West argues that Freud's scheme is instructive for contemporary legal liberalism, as well as law and economics scholarship. Significantly for the present study, West then contrasts the Freudian conception of the Rule of Law with critical and feminist legal scholarship. While acknowledging the aggressive, antisocial element in humanity, the critical tradition challenges Freud's lack of confidence in "communitarian" drives to unify civilization.

> Thus, to the Freudian and liberal promise that law can bring artificial equality and therefore freedom from the tyranny of

unequal power, the feminist and critical scholars answer with their own promise that law at its best can bring an empathic and loving community and, with that, a release from the anguish of alienation and separateness.[163]

The depersonalized Rule of Law, based upon a fear of love, is for the critics "an obstacle to the encouragement of intersubjective unity."[164]

West finds a response to critical scholarship in the early pages of *Civilization and Its Discontents*, where Freud confesses he can find no feeling of "oceanic oneness" in himself.[165] The well-demarcated boundary between self and the world—rejected by critical scholars—is fundamental for Freudian psychology. While romantic love between two individuals "melts away" the boundary between ego and object, universal love—indifferent to reciprocity—disproves any notion of "oceanic" union. Freud attributes the "oceanic feeling" to infantile memories wherein the ego is not yet distinguished from the world. By contrast, the totemic impulse is based upon the "capacity for obedience and the memory of helplessness"; the affection binding social groups together is for the leader, not one another.[166]

West concludes the study by praising Freud's naturalistic method and chides legal liberals for choosing the "path of faith" over the "path of reason." At the same time, West concedes that Freud's description of our nature and history "may well be false." West's point is that legal theorists should defend the authority of law "by reference to naturalistic, and therefore falsifiable, assumptions," to "fact instead of faith."[167]

Such confidence, of course, is at odds with the critical theory that West contrasts with orthodox Freudianism. West clearly identifies the reason why Freud's own theories about law are not compelling at all to the critical and feminist scholars. Not only are Freud's naturalistic assumptions questionable, but the very scientific method West praises is not properly contrasted with faith. For those in the critical tradition, the element of belief is present in all of science, and every scientific enterprise is ideological to the core.[168]

West's exposition also demonstrates that CLS will likely draw its Freudianism from Marcuse or Lacan and not from the "scientific" Freud. Sufficient doubt has been raised concerning the positivistic value of Freud's writings,[169] and even Marcuse, in his attack of Freudian revisionism, prized Freud's anthropological speculation for its symbolic value.

VII. DEFINING AND OVERCOMING IDEOLOGY

"As is well known, the accusation of being in ideology only applies to others, never to oneself...."[170]

Critical Legal Studies is itself the subject of criticism—that CLS is not new, that its critique is useless or non-empirical, and so forth. Again, even if conceived as a useful and liberating critique of ideology, CLS inherits two problems which plague similar social theories. First, what *is* ideology?[171] And second, if it exists as an inevitable perceptual grid or linguistic power structure, how does the critic overcome its effect on his or her own critique?[172]

The implicit role of psychoanalytic theory within CLS begins to answer these questions. In this section, I first return to Lacan in order to explore Althusser's commentary (which analogizes the unconscious and ideology) and Peter Gabel's psychoanalytic critique of legal culture (which is inspired by Lacanian concepts). A definition of ideology emerges that can also serve to define legal ideology. Next, I consider Habermas' early commentary on Freud, which emphasized the self-reflective element in psycho-analysis, keeping in mind that Habermas has substantially altered his theoretical concerns. Finally, I attempt to describe a tentative agenda for radical socio-legal psychoanalysis.

A. Lacan (and Althusser)

"Lacan...made a very successful career out of saying things that just about no one could understand....He seems to have gone to great lengths to prevent people from finding out what he had to say."[173]

Lacanian clinical analysis, which seeks verbalization of the patient's unconscious,[174] is an attempt to escape "normal" (or civil, coherent and rational) communication between analyst and analysand, and thereby "to discover another logic."[175] The controversial "short session" (Lacan's repudiation of the traditional "fifty minute hour") serves to keep the analysand off balance—"the analysand [does] not have time to get his bearings, to establish his sense of being in control of the situation, to get his thoughts in order."[176] In Freudian terms, the short session, which may last only a couple of minutes, frustrates the ego's censorship and explanatory functions:

Almost by definition, the ego can never be the master of the short session.

....

> This ego, however,....asserts itself with a vengeance, not only in trying to control the situation but in offering interpretations....This mode of interpretation is eventually revealed to be the system that holds the neurosis in place.[177]

The analyst, in this conception, ignores the intentions of the ego, and "hears the discourse of the other, the unconscious that slides through the gaps in intentionality."[178]

Louis Althusser's reliance upon Freud (and commentary upon Lacan) is particularly relevant to the question of the place of psychoanalysis in CLS's critique of ideology. Marx's early conception of ideology as "the system of the ideas and representations which dominate the mind of a man or a social group" is later formulated (in *The German Ideology*) in a "plainly positivistic context":

> Ideology is conceived as a pure illusion, a pure dream, i.e. as nothingness. All its reality is external to it. Ideology is thus thought as an imaginary construction whose status is exactly like the theoretical status of the dream among writers before Freud. For these writers, the dream was the purely imaginary....[179]

Althusser's own view of ideology, as the "'representation' of the imaginary relationship of individuals to their real conditions of existence," confirms the material existence of ideologies.[180] However, ideology is eternal, as "individuals are always-already interpellated [hailed, recruited or transformed] by ideology as subjects."[181] Althusser draws support for his thesis from Freud's discovery of the familial ideological configuration into which we are born.[182] This

> configuration is, in its uniqueness, highly structured, and...it is in this implacable and more or less 'pathological'...structure that the [child] will have to 'find' 'its' place....It is clear that this ideological constraint and pre-appointment, and all the rituals of rearing and then education in the family, have some relationship with what Freud studied in the forms of the pre-genital and genital "stages" of sexuality, i.e. in the "grip" of what Freud registered by its effects as being the unconscious.[183]

In this way, the eternity of ideology is related to Freud's eternal unconscious.[184]

Althusser recognizes Lacan's "return to Freud" as an attempt to define rigorously the unconscious and its laws.[185] Recall Lacan's statement that the unconscious is structured like a language. Aided by structural linguistics, Lacan discovered that the transition from birth into human existence "can only be grasped in terms of a recurrent language [of the cure situation]... localized within the law of language in which is established and presented all human order, i.e. every human role."[186] This transition is achieved within the "Law of Culture" (Althusser's term), the determinate ideological formations that have "been lying in wait for each infant born since before his birth, [seizing] him before his first cry, assigning to him his place and role, and hence his fixed destination."[187]

B. Gabel

> "[For Lacan,] psychoanalysis is based on a fundamental split between the subject and the knowledge he has of himself. Psychoanalysis deals particularly with wishes and desires that are unknown to the subject, in the unconscious."[188]

Peter Gabel, whose work is associated with CLS scholarship, clearly employs psychoanalytic language and concepts. One of his most recent essays focuses on the social and intersubjective nature of desire, and the need for those involved In progressive politics to understand the desire for social confirmation. Reagan's economic and social agenda, as well as President Bush's campaign, were responsive to human needs for community and solidarity.[189] In contrast, the job and benefit programs of today's Democrats may be "experienced as psychologically repressive to the degree that...people's emotional context—their sense of unconnectedness and underconfirmation—[is treated] as fixed and inevitable."[190] Both political parties appear to avoid confronting—by offering only "fantasies" or "programs"—"the real alienation and blockage of social desire that is our most serious problem as a people."[191]

"Desire" is nowadays associated with the instinctual forces of the id that must be controlled.[192] Such a model results in the separation of desire from knowledge (as in "dispassionate" social science), and in the "individualization" and "privatization" of desire.[193] The desire for mutual recognition that we experience and perceive in others

> is resisted and even opposed by those around us who have learned...to deny this desire in themselves. The medium of this opposition is well-captured by what...Lacan called "misrecognition," a process by which the parent, instead of confirming the infant in his or her being, "throws" the infant and later the child into a series of roles that...alienate the child...from the centered desire that is the social dimension of the child's soul.[194]

The split between the child's desire and his or her social self will be reproduced in others through familial and social contacts; moreover, the desire may be repeatedly repressed in an effort to maintain the validity of the internalized role.[195]

While the parent-child relationship may be the first locus for alienation, the distance between our desire and our social selves is maintained in schools and workplaces, through the media and in the various social structures that make up the apparently "given" world.[196] At the same time, the "blockage' is maintained by the individual's reciprocal projection of an "outside" world and deference—"in a milieu of misrecognition and collective denial"— to an external agency to ground his or her identity.[197] For Gabel, the circle of underconfirmation is not a problem for clinical psychoanalysis but is rather a. political problem requiring a gradual increase in *public* confidence.[198]

Legal culture, which provides a particularly visible example of mediation between local ("concrete") conflicts or needs and the national or universal (the larger "we") context, tends to reinforce the collective denial identified by Gabel.[199] Lawyers and judges, and legal reasoning itself, are "disembodied" and elevated in our society: "[Law] is made to appear as an authoritative system of thought outside of and above everyone...rather than as a contingent and developing expression of social and political meaning that we actively create and interpret."[200] Legal discourse is thus an embodiment of the dynamic projection of underconfirmed subjects of an externalized source of social authority.[201]

Gabel concludes his analysis by suggesting that progressive lawyers reconstitute legal culture by systematically challenging "the modes of role-based, disembodied interaction" in everyday life, and thereby begin to affirm social desire.[202] Public interest lawyers have too often accepted, Gabel explains, "the confines and assumptions of existing legal discourse and roles," thus relegating their own political and moral aspirations to their "private" lives.[203] The transformative dimension of progressive legal practice will continue to be neutralized unless this ideological contradiction is recognized.

C. Habermas

Habermas' reflections on psychoanalysis, published in *Knowledge and Human Interests*, now belong to history—to the "early Habermas."[205] The theoretical exposition in *Knowledge and Human Interests* has been recognized as flawed, even by Habermas, yet the essays on psychoanalysis are significant for the problems introduced if not the solutions offered.[206] The fact is that Habermas' early work left much to be clarified and justified.

In 1968 Habermas viewed psychoanalysis as "the only tangible example of a science incorporating methodical self-reflection," even though Freud himself misunderstood the scientific aspect of the discipline he discovered.[207] Psychoanalysis thus represented a new version of cultural interpretation directed not at the conscious intentions of language, but at the "*self-deceptions of the author*....inaccessible to him and alienated from him and yet [his] nevertheless."[208] The mistakes in the text of everyday language (or action or bodily expression), normally ignored (or so obtrusive to be called symptoms) and, in any case, incomprehensible to the speaker, are "split-off" parts of a symbolic structure, another language.[209] The dream. provides the pathological model of such a text for Freud, and dream interpretation also illustrates the defense mechanisms so central to psychoanalysis: "The transformation of the latent dream-thoughts into the manifest dream-content...is the first instance known to us of psychical material being changed over from one mode of expression to another...."[210] Freud identified, in the systematic distortion of latent, symbolic "dream-thoughts" in the manifest dream, a restricting agency that even controls everyday thought and action.[211] The defensive or "censorship" agency, representing social repression, is in conflict with unconscious wishes or motivations, and distorts the meaning of ("displacement") or eradicates the offensive passages of the text of the unconscious.[212]

The "object domain" of psychoanalysis is the field of incomprehensible symbols which disrupt everyday language.[213] Significantly, the project is not akin to translation of a text to mediate between people with different languages, but is rather an effort to teach a person to comprehend his or her own self-mutilated language.[214] The act of understanding is self-consciousness or self-reflection, as exemplified in Freud's analytic technique.[215] When the patient's defensive mechanisms "run idl[y]"[216] in the analytic situation, the ego recognizes "itself in its other...as *its own* alienated self and [identifies] with it."[217]

Habermas, in the custom of earlier critical theorists seeking a Freudo-Marxian synthesis, saw structural parallels between the individual psyche and contemporary culture. Collective solutions to the pressures of reality, represented by various institutions of social organization, seemed to resemble individual neurotic "solutions."[218] Cultural tradition was understood as the collective unconscious.[219] And, just as self-reflection in the analytic situation liberates a patient from falsifications and self-deceptions, the critique of ideology sets off a process of reflection upon and discourse concerning the collective illusion of "frozen relations of dependence that can in principle be transformed."[220]

D. Contours of a Psychoanalytic Critique of Legal Ideology

"Lacan shifts the Freudian paradigm from intrapsychic mechanisms to intersubjective relations, and from quasi-biological instincts to language, partially opening psycho-analysis to cultural theory."[221]

Before attempting a summation and outline for the psycho-analytic criticism of legal culture, I should acknowledge again the limited scope of my inquiry. Lacanian theory is much richer in scope and potential than my remarks suggest, Althusser's work on ideology is likewise quite substantial and complex, and Habermas' ever-developing social theory is a major topic in many disciplines. Moreover, I have not explored the work of many other scholars who integrate psychoanalysis and ideology critique, for example, Foucault's disclosure of strategies of power within discourse,[222] and Deleuze and Guattari's work on the Oedipus Complex.[223] The suggestive remarks that follow, therefore, are but further "traces" of the potential for psycho-analytic concepts in critical legal research.

Keeping in mind the revisionistic parallel between the topology of the individual psyche and that of culture, I will focus below on the concepts of socialized *roles*, collective *desire*, and *self*-criticism as essential elements of the critique of ideology. Each involves a glimmer of liberation, the elusive goal of radical social theory.

1. Roles Freud's interpretation of childhood teaches that "the organization of everyday life by the social institution of the restricted family [leaves] a clear imprint on the course of [the] childhood experience...."[224] However, Freud tended to view the child's psyche as a primary function and the social environment as a secondary influence. By contrasts as John Brenkman points out:

Lacan's project has been the attempt to give language and intersubjecjtivity primacy....He recognizes that the *Umwelt*, the environment or outer world, of [the infant] is preeminently social. From birth, the human being is affected by actions, gestures, wishes, and intentions that are already imbued with the symbolic and that occur within the constraints of specific, historically determined institutions.[225]

That is, the subject is "radically dependent on the field of the Other" for identity and for the language that eventually makes interaction possible.[226]   Recall that Althusser sees the family configuration as an ideology which waits for each of us to be born and assigns our respective places or roles.   The family as social and socializing institution "limits the possibilities of interaction which emerge in the experience of speech...."[227]

Many scholars associated with CLS have identified legal institutions and processes as "arrangers" of everyday life, shaping and constraining the situations and interactions we experience.   Further, critics of legal ideology can be conceived as cultural analysts who disclose or bring to the surface hidden or unconscious belief systems concerning the law.   However, while such metaphors are suitable for ideology critique generally, they represent an impoverished conception of psychoanalysis.   Peter Gabel's recent reflections on collective desire provide a richer analogy between the critical-legal and the social-psychoanalytical projects.

2. Desire

> "In Lacanian terms, it is from the Other that the subject receives the signifiers of his or her desire....The Other can refer to the child's mother [who *represents* the community in her initial, exclusive hold on discourse; but what) is radically Other is precisely 'the concrete discourse of [the subject's] surrounding.'"[228]

Gabel's account of social desire, which attempts to move beyond Lacan (who insisted on the unintelligibility of desire and was "as unable to capture what we are alienated *from* as Freud was"),[229] posits a collective desire for social confirmation and mutual recognition.   He suggests that the social self is often alienated or blocked from such real desire by our *privatization* of desire and by collective *denial* of that social dimension.[230]   The alienation or blockage, in Gabel's somewhat ambiguous scheme, is reproduced (by repetitive repression of desire to maintain social roles) and maintained (by deference to "phantom" social structures for identity and by reciprocal projection of that "given" world) in a circle of denial and desire.[231]   Legal culture exemplifies role-based interaction wherein political or moral desire is privatized in subjection to an externalized social authority.[232]

John Brenkman's psychoanalytic theory of culture, another attempt to employ and go beyond Freud and Lacan, is similar in several respects to Gabel's approach. Freud, in his neglect of the social constitution of the ego and the social organization of "reality," grants to the ego only the ability to adjust to reality.[233] Lacan's restatement of Freudianism in social and cultural terms (as a theory of the subject's constitution by and through language) initiates an immanent critique of psychoanalysis that Brenkman incorporates into his own Neo-Marxian critique:

> The critical theory of society and culture requires a theory of subjectivity and lived experience, and in turning to psychoanalysis to develop that, it discovers another task as well: to disclose those points in psychoanalytic theory where historical forms of domination—principally the social division of labor and the social organization of sexual difference—have to become integral and primary elements of that theory itself.[234]

Gabel, too, seeks an enrichment of the critical-legal project by reference to psychoanalytic conceptions. The identification of social desire and its repression illuminates the externalization and maintenance of legal authority.

Brenkman's reassessment of psychoanalysis also inspires hope for social change. Repression of desire, which blocks the "subject's access to his or her own history," is the ego's response to the conflict between desire and, present reality.[235] If reality, however, is essentially social, then a third orientation "toward the future and toward another reality" appears.[236] This critical orientation implies the possibility of renouncing reality "not in the mode of repression, which hampers the possibilities of the present under the impact of an unlived and untold past, but in the mode of a liberation which, comprehending the past and demanding a new future, condemns the present."[237]

Gabel's recognition of the need to reconstitute legal culture by challenging "given" roles and contingent social structures provides an example of Brenkman's "third orientation." Moreover, the problematic questions of the existence and operation of legal ideology are directed by Gabel into a reflection upon the division between desire (experienced and perceived in others) and collective denial, between our privatized ideals and our social selves, and between contingent realities.

3. Cultural Self-Criticism The psychoanalytic project inspired by Lacan's Freud also provides a model of self-criticism for the critic of legal ideology. Althusser's Lacanian conception of the eternity of ideology contrasts sharply with the Marxian notion of ideology as *false* consciousness, a term which suggests that the critic is outside ideology. Indeed, the critic, at best, encourages cultural self-awareness, hence the significance of the early Habermas' picture of psychoanalysis as fundamentally self-reflective and his analogy between a patient's self-consciousness and social liberation. In Brenkman's construction:

> Human knowledge cannot, especially when it pretends to be a scientific knowledge of the forms of everyday cognition, detach itself from the lived experiences out of which genuine subjectivity emerges.
>
> This problematic, in which science is inseparable from politics in the. development of an understanding of human social, psychological, and cultural life, never becomes visible in Freud and never completely breaks into the clear in Lacan.[238]

Gabel, I think, would agree, as he links his social theory directly to politics: "transcendent social knowledge can emerge only from transcendent social experience."[239]

I would go further, avoiding the reduction to politics, and maintain that *all* theory as well as everyday thought, is inseparable from ideology if we take ideology to mean those belief systems that are often hidden (or unconscious) but are subject to self-critical disclosure and discourse. Informed by the psychoanalytic tradition, such belief systems can now be seen to include changeable social desire, repression and reality.

CONCLUSION

One of the most profound criticisms of CLS is that it does not really exist—people "belong" to the movement, conferences are held, symposia are published, but the essential legal theory is often elusive. Those who criticize CLS by attacking Roberto Unger find, to their surprise, that they have only criticized Unger. If the same critics, wisely, reattack Unger, Duncan Kennedy and Morton Horwitz, the critique might be ignored as a harmless, but typically unenlightened, reification of CLS. The critic's difficulty results from the eclectic and disjointed character of a new intellectual movement.

Works such as David Kennedy's exploration of Critical Theory and Structuralism are particularly helpful in giving bearings to CLS adherents and enemies.[240] Jack Balkin's exposition of deconstruction, likewise, was a welcome but belated guide to much that was presumed in the CLS canon.[241] The potential for CLS to be understood, much less to contribute to contemporary legal discourse, is dependent upon studies that seek the connections between CLS scholarship and its methodological forebears. And, just as traces of Marx and Habermas, Lévi-Strauss and Derrida, need to be identified and discussed, adopted or revised, the traces of Freud (and Marcuse and Lacan) have yet undetermined significance.

NOTES

1. Hunt, *The Theory of Critical Legal Studies*, 6 OXFORD J. LEGAL STUD. 1, 3 (1986).

2. *See, e.g.*, Kennedy & Klare, *A Bibliography of Critical Legal Studies*, 94 YALE L.J. 461 (1984). A bibliography of recent CLS-oriented articles, symposia and books appears in each issue of the *Newsletter of the Conference on Critical-Legal Studies* edited by Alan Freeman and Betty Mensch at SUNY Buffalo Law School.

3. *See, e.g.*, Kelman, *Trashing*, 36 STAN. L. REV. 293, 304 (1984); Trubek, *Where the Action Is: Critical Legal Studies and Empiricism*, 36 STAN. L. REV. 575, 607 (1984).

4. *See, e.g.*, Johnson, *Do You Sincerely Want To Be Radical?*, 36 STAN. L. REV. 247, 250 (1984); Trubek, *supra* note 3.

5. *See* H. MARCUSE, EROS AND CIVILIZATION, A PHILOSOPHICAL INQUIRY INTO FREUD (1955).

6. *See* E. FROMM, THE CRISIS OF PSYCHOANALYSIS: ESSAYS ON FREUD, MARX AND SOCIAL PSYCHOLOGY (1970)

7. See *infra* notes 112-19 and accompanying text.

8. West, *Law, Rights, and Other Totemic Illusions: Legal Liberalism and Freud's Theory of the Rule of Law*, 134 U. PA. L. REV. 817 (1986). Of course, Freud's writings are sufficiently ambiguous to inspire various and conflicting interpretations of his theories.

9. *See* P. ROBINSON, THE FREUDIAN LEFT: WILHELM REICH, GEZA ROHEIM, HERBERT MARCUSE (1969).

10. *See generally* Kennedy, *Critical Theory, Structuralism and Contemporary Legal Scholarship*, 21 NEW ENG. L. REV. 209 (1985-86).

11. *See* R. GEUSS, THE IDEA OF A CRITICAL THEORY: HABERMAS AND THE FRANKFURT SCHOOL 12-19 (1981). For an example of such an approach with respect to legal ideology, see M. TIGAR & M. LEVY, REFLECTIONS ON LAW, CAPITALISM, AND LEGAL HISTORY (1977), *reviewed by* Koffler, *Review Essay*, III ALSA FORUM 67 (Dec. 1978).

12. See R. GEUSS, *supra* note 11, at 9-10. Attempts to define ideology continue to appear in sociological and political literature. Lewins suggests that the preoccupation with the *function* of ideology in society, associated with Marxian approaches, has eclipsed questions of the content of ideology. Lewins, *Recasting the Concept of Ideology: A Content Approach*, 40 BRIT. J. SOC. 678 (1989). For a recent functionalist account, see Nielson, *The Concept of Ideology: Some Marxist and Non-Marxist Conceptualizations*, 4 RETHINKING MARXISM 146, 169 (Nov 4, 1989) (The author argues that conceptions of ideology as any set of closely related ideas or beliefs tend to miss "the way in which ideologies...help generate hegemonic, ruling-class ideas which will make people come to accept a social order which sustains the interests of that dominant class.").

13. Kornhauser, *The Great Image of Authority*, 36 STAN. L. REV. 349, 376 (1984).

14. *Id.* at 377-79.

15. D. McLELLAN, IDEOLOGY 73 (1986).

16. J. THOMPSON, STUDIES IN THE THEORY OF IDEOLOGY 5 (1984).

17. *Id.* at 35, 61; *cf.* Kavanagh, *Ideology*, in CRITICAL TERMS FOR LITERARY STUDY 312 (F. Lentricchia & T. McLaughlin eds. 1990) ("[I]deological analysis maintains its edge—that which prevents it from becoming a form of social psychology—only by keeping our eyes on the relations of cultural texts to questions of politics, power, and/or class.").

18. J. THOMPSON, *supra* note 16, at 35, 131; *cf.* Brenkman, *The Other and the One: Psychoanalysis, Reading*, The Symposium, in LITERATURE AND PSYCHOANALYSIS: THE QUESTION OF READING: OTHERWISE 396 (S. Felman ed. 1982).
> Lévi-Strauss' studies of mythic thought and symbolic exchange
> in primitive societies, Barthes' analysis of the cultural products
> and practices of consumer society as a specific mode of
> semiological connotation, and Derrids's deconstructive reading
> of philosophy, which treats "concepts" not as instances of
> consciousness grasping truth or reality but as elements within
> a textual process—all of these researches [sic] have made it
> possible to consider "ideology" as discourse or semiological
> operation or text.

Id. at 445.

19. Hunt, *supra* note 1, at 12.

20. *See* Mujeeb-ur-Rahman, *The Freudian Paradigm*, in THE FREUDIAN PARADIGM: PSYCHOANALYSIS AND SCIENTIFIC THOUGHT 3 (M. Mujeeb-ur-Rahman ed. 1977).

21. *See* R. BOCOCK, SIGMUND FREUD 7–8 (1983) (noting the influence of Freud upon Talcott Parsons and Erik Erikson).

22. *See id.* (noting the influence of Freud upon Horkheimer, Marcuse and Habermas).

23. C. HALL, A PRIMER OF FREUDIAN PSYCHOLOGY 17 (1954); see Meltzer, *Editor's Introduction: Partitive Plays, Pipe Dreams*, 13 CRITICAL INQUIRY 215 (1987). The introduction is to a symposium entitled *The Trials of Psychoanalysis* in which Hall writes:

> Psychoanalysis has infiltrated such diverse areas as literature (to which it owes its myths, linguistics, philosophy, anthropology, history, feminism, psychology, archeology, neurology, to name some. And it is in the notion of "some," perhaps, that Lies the crux of the problem. For there is in psychoanalysis an overt conviction that it exists as the ultimate totality, of which everything else in a part.

Id. at 216.

With respect to literature, see generally Brooks, The Idea of a Psychoanalytic Literary Criticism, 13 Critical Inquiry 334, 336 (1987) (discussing traditional psychoanalytic criticism, which tends to analyze either "the author, the reader, or the fictive persons of the text," and arguing for a return to the text). Brooks asserts:

> [P]sychoanalytic perspectives in literary study must ultimately derive from our conviction that the materials on which psychoanalysts and iiterary critics exercise their powers of analysis are in some basic sense the same: that the structure of literature is in some sense the structure of the mind—not a specific mind, but...the dynamic organization of the psyche, a process of structuration.

Id. at 336–37 (emphasis in original); see also E WRIGHT, PSYCHOANALYTIC CRITICISM: THEORY IN PRACTICE (1987) (discussing criticism of art and literature generally); FRUED AND THE HUMANITIES (P. Horden ed. 1985) (anthology including contributions on biography, art history and classical studies).

On the use of psychoanalysis in historical studies, see generally P. Gay, Freud for Historians (1985) (arguing that psychoanalytic interpretation is essential to historical interpretation). See also LaCapra, History and Psychoanalysis, 13 Critical Inquiry 222 (1987) (arguing that historical analysis is inherently a part of psychoanalysis).

24. *See* Gelman, *Finding the Hidden Freud*, NEWSWEEK, Nov. 30, 1981, at 64 ("[Freud] gave the world more than a theory and a therapy. He provided a world view. His ideas about dreams, religion, creativity and the unconscious motivations underlying all human behavior are so pervasive that it would be difficult to imagine twentieth-century thought without them.").

25 S. FROSH, THE POLITICS OF PSYCHOANALYSIS: AN INTRODUCTION TO FREUDIAN AND POST-FREUDIAN THEORY 1 (1987) (Freudian "concepts of repression, sexual desire and the unconscious [are] often implicit in [our] 'common-sense' understandings of ourselves and each other.").

26. *See, e.g.*, Y. GABRIEL, FREUD AND SOCIETY 2 (1983); A GRÜNBAUM, THE FOUNDATIONS OF PSYCHOANALYSIS: A PHILOSOPHICAL CRITIQUE (1984) (questioning the clinical credentials of psychoanalysis and identifying fallacies in Freudian methodology). *But see* Sachs, *In Fairness to Freud: A Critical Notice of* THE FOUNDATIONS OF PSYCHOANALYSIS by Adolf Grünbaum, 98 PHIL. REV. 349, 351 (1989) (arguing that Grünbaum's study contains "major misreadings of Freud").

In the popular press, a recent issue of *The Atlantic Monthly* included a report on Allan Hobson's challenge to Freud's dream theories. *See* Dolnick, *What Dreams are (Really) Made Of*, ATLANTIC MONTHLY, July 1990, at 41–61.

27. S. FROSH, *supra* note 25, at 1. *See generally* Gilman, *The Struggle of Psychiatry with Psychoanalysis: Who Won?*, 13 CRITICAL INQUIRY 293 (1987) (containing a brief history of the "struggle" with attention to the questions of the "scientific" or medical status of psychoanalysis).

28. Y. GABRIEL, *supra* note 26, at 1; *see* S. FREUD, FIVE LECTURES ON PSYCHO-ANALYSIS 21–28, 40–48 (J. Strachey ed. & trans. 1957) (second and fourth lecture respectively) [hereinafter S. FREUD, FIVE LECTURES]. The second lecture (of five given at Clark University in 1909) describes the concept of repression, while the fourth lecture explains the Freudian emphasis on sexuality. Freud openly acknowledged

> that this assertion of [the predominance of erotic life] will not be willingly, believed. Even workers who are ready to follow my psychological studies are inclined to think that I over-estimate the part played by sexual factors....
>
> ...Unluckily even doctors are not preferred above other human creatures in their personal relation to questions of sexual life, and many of them are under the spell of the combination of prudery and prurience which governs the attitude of most "civilized people" in matters of sexuality.

Id. at 40–41. Of course, critics of Freudianism remind us that Freud did not "discover" the *unconscrous*—a concept pre-dating psychoanalysis, and also that modern schools of psychology place less emphasis on sexuality than did Freud. On the latter point, see D. SCHULTZ, A HISTORY OF MODERN PSYCHOLOGY 356 (3d ed. 1981). Regarding early conceptions of the "Unconscious," see Meltzer, *Unconscious*, in CRITICAL TERMS FOR LITERARY STUDY, *supra* note 17, at 147–48.

29. S. FROSH, *supra* note 25, at 2; *see* S. FREUD, AN AUTOBIOGRAPHICAL STUDY 74–90 (J. Strachey trans. 1952) (originally appeared in a

collection of autobiographical studies, by leaders in medicine, entitled *Die Medizin der Gegenwart in Selbstdarstellungen*; Strachey's translation was first published in the United States in 1927) [hereinafter S. FREUD, AN AUTOBIOGRAPHICAL STUDY]. Freud here explains the method of *free association*, analytical interpretation, transference (an intense emotional relationship between patient and analyst wherein the patient re-experiences repressed emotions), and the importance of dreams and everyday *slips* and mistakes to psychoanalysis. The latter phenomena (dreams, slips and mistakes) of normal life parallel, for Freud, patho-logical symptoms, since explanation of such phenomena requires "the same assumptions—the repression of impulses, substitute-formation, compromise-formation, the dividing of the conscious and the uncon-scious into various psychical systems...." *Id.* at 90. Therefore,

> psychoanalysis was no longer a subsidiary science in the field of psychopathology, it was rather the foundation for a new and deeper science of the mind which would be equally indispensable for the understanding of the normal....[A] path lay open to it that led far afield, into spheres of universal interest.

Id.

30. *See generally* R. BOCOCK, *supra* note 21. *See, e.g.*, S. FREUD, THE FUTURE OF AN ILLUSION (W.D. Robson-Scott trans. & J. Strachey ed. 1964) first appeared in translation in 1927) [hereinafter S. FREUD, THE FUTURE OF AN ILLUSION]; S. FREUD, CIVILIZATION AND ITS DISCONTENTS (J. Strachey ed. & trans. 1961) (first appeared in translation, by J. Fiviere, in 1930) [hereinafter S. FREUD, CIVILIZATION AND ITS DISCONTENTS]. In writing these books, Freud remarked:

> I perceived ever more clearly that the events of human history, the interactions between human nature, cultural development and the precipitates of primaeval experiences (the most prominent example of which is religion) are no more than, a reflection of the dynamic conflicts between the ego, the id, and the super-ego, which psychoanalysis studies in the individual-are the very same processes repeated upon a wider stage.

S. Freud, An Autobiographical Study, supra note 29, at 138 (1935 postscript to the 1929 translation).

Significantly, however, Freud's later writings on society are *not* the primary materials for radical social psychoanalytic theory. Lacan's "return to Freud," discussed below, "is essentially a return to the spirit of the earlier works." R. HARLAND, SUPERSTRUCTURALISM: THE PHILOSOPHY OF STRUCTURALISM AND POST-STRUCTURALISM 34 (1987). "The radical aspect of Freud lies precisely in the clinical origins and usage of his theories," not in his later "philosophic aspirations." P. ROAZEN, FREUD: POLITICAL AND SOCIAL THOUGHT 17–18 (1968).

31. C. HALL, *supra* note 23, at 22-27; see S. FREUD, THE EGO AND THE ID 9-17 (J. Riviere trans. & J. Strachey ed. 1960) (first appeared in translation in 1927) [hereinafter S. FREUD, THE EGO AND THE ID]; S. FREUD, AN OUTLINE OF PSYCHO-ANALYSIS 14-18 (J. Strachey trans. & ed. 1949) (first appeared in translation in 1940) [hereinafter S. FREUD, AN OUTLINE OF PSYCHO-ANALYSIS].

32. C. HALL, *supra* note 23, at 27-31; *see also* Freud, *Formulations Regarding the Two Princinles in Mental Functioning (1911)* (M.N. Searl trans.), in S. FREUD, GENERAL PSYCHOLOGICAL THEORY 21-28 (P. Rieff ed. 1963) [hereinafter S. FREUD, GENERAL PSYCHOLOGICAL THEORY].

33. C. HALL, *supra* note 23, at 31-35. We "see this same ego as a poor creature owing service to three masters and consequently menaced by three dangers: from the external world, from the libido of the id, and from the severity of the super-ego." S. FREUD, THE EGO AND THE ID, *supra* note 31, at 46; *see also* S. FREUD, AN AUTOBIOGRAPHICAL STUDY, *supra* note 29, at 113 ("The super-ego...represents the ethical standards of mankind.").

34. C. HALL, *supra* note 23, at 34. For a discussion of the other elements involved in Freud's theory of personality, including distribution and disposal of psychic energy, instincts, cathexis and anti-cathexis and the various forms of anxiety, see *id.* at 36–71.

35. *Id.* at 85; *see* S. FREUD, AN OUTLINE OF PSYCHO-ANALYSIS, *supra* note 31, at 52–61.
> [The] ego is fighting on two fronts: it has to defend its existence against an external world that threatens it with annihilation and against an internal world that makes excessive demands. It adopts the same methods of defense against [both]....
> ....
> Whatever...the ego [does in efforts of defense,] whether it is repudiating a portion of the external world or whether it seeks to reject an instinctual demand from the internal world, its success is never complete and unqualified....[I]t is only necessary to remark what a small proportion of all these processes become known to us through our conscious perception.

Id. at 111–12, 119.

36. C. HALL, *supra* note 23, at 86; *see* S. FREUD, FIVE LECTURES, *supra* note 28, at 21–28. Freud identified, in his early studies of patients suffering from hysteria,
> a wishful impulse which was in sharp contrast to the subject's other wishes and which proved incompatible with the ethical and aesthetic standards of his personality....[The] idea which had appeared before consciousness as the vehicle of this

irreconcilable wish fell a victim to repression, was pushed out of consciousness with all its attached memories, and was forgotten....[Repressionl was thus revealed as one of the devices serving to protect the mental personality.

Id. at 24.

37. C. HALL, *supra* note 23, at 89-91; *see* S. FREUD, BEYOND THE PLEASURE PRINCIPLE 23 (J. Strachey trans. & ed. 1961) (first translated in 1922 by C.J.M. Hubback).

[A] particular way is adopted of dealing with any internal excitations which produce too great an increase of unpleasure: there is a tendency to treat them as though they were acting, not from the inside, but from the outside, so that it may be possible to bring the shield against stimuli into operation as a means of defence against them. This is the origin of projection....

Id. (emphasis in original).

38. C. HALL, *supra* note 23, at 91–93. Freud wrote:

In the obsessional neurosis, as we know, the phenomena of reaction-formation predominate....

....

The reproaches of conscience in certain forms of obsessional neurosis are just as painful and tormenting [as in melancholia, but it] is remarkable that the obsessional neurotic, in contrast to the melancholic [whose strong super-ego "rages against" the ego], never takes the step of self-destruction: he is as if immune against the danger of suicide....We can see that what guarantees the safety of the ego is the fact that the object has been retained. In obsessional neurosis it has become pos-sible...for the love-impulses to transform themselves into impulses of aggression against the object. Here again the instinct of destruction has been set free and it aims at destroying the object, or at least it appears to have this aim. These tendencies have not been adopted by the ego: it struggles against them with reaction-formations...and they remain in the id.

S. FREUD, THE EGO AND THE ID, *supra* note 31, 75–78.

39. C. HALL, *supra* note 23, at 93-97; *see* S. FREUD, AN OUTLINE OF PSYCHO-ANALYSIS, *supra* note 31, at 27 ("It has been found that in early childhood there are signs of bodily acuvity to which only ancient prejudice could deny the name of sexual, and which are connected with mental phenomena that we come across later in adult love, such as fixation to a particular object, jealousy, and so on."); *see also* Freud, *Three Contributions to the Theory of Sex,* in THE BASIC WRITINGS OF SIGMUND FREUD 553-629 (A.A. Brill ed. & trans. 1938). "All the factors

which injure the sexual development s#ow their effect in that they produce a *regression*, or a return to a former phase of development." *Id.* at 626–27 (emphasis in original).

40. C. HALL, *supra* note 23, at 96.

41. Brill, *Introduction* to THE BASIC WRITINGS OF SIGMUND FREUD, *supra* note 39, at 7.9. Freud recognized that symptoms are over-determined, that is, caused by many psychological events. *See* S. FREUD, FIVE LECTURES, *supra* note 28, at 38.

In his account of one of Breuer's patients, who suffered from "hysteria," Freud observes that when "she was put under hypnosis, it was possible, at the expense of a considerable amount of labor, to recall the scenes to her memory; and, through this work or recollecting, the symptoms were removed." *Id.* at 19. Freud, of course, abandoned hypnotism in favor of the "talking" cure and eventually the process of free association. *See* S. FREUD, AN AUTOBIOGRAPHICAL STUDY, *supra* note 29, at 48–76.

42. Brill, *supra* note 41, at 10. In one of Freud's formulations:
The analyst, who listens composedly but without any con-strained effort to the stream of associations and who, from his experience, has a general notion of what to expect, can make use of the material brought to light by the patient according to two possibilities. If the resistance is slight he will be able from the patient's allusions to infer the unconscious material itself; or if the resistance is stronger he will be able to recognize its character from the associations, as they seem to become more remote from the subject, and will explain it to the patient.... Thus the work of analysis involves an *art of interpretation*....
S. FREUD, AN AUTOBIOGRAPHICAL STUDY, *supra* note 29, at 77 (emphasis in original). Freud also posited a pre-conscious, midway between the conscious and the unconscious,, 'which contains memories of which one is unaware, but which one can eventually recall with some effort." Brill, *supra* note 41, at 13; *see* Freud, *A Note on the Unconscious in Psychoanalysis* (1912), in S. FREUD, GENERAL PSYCHOLOGICAL THEORY, *supra* note 32, at 49–55.

43. Brill, *supra* note 41, at 12; *see* Freud, *Neurosis and Psychosis* (1924), in S. FREUD, GENERAL PSYCHOLOGICAL THEORY, *supra* note 32, at 185–89.

44. *See* S. FREUD, CIVILIZATION AND ITS DISCONTENTS, *supra* note 30, at 28. "[E]ach one of us behaves in some respect like a paranoic, corrects some aspect of the world which is unbearable to him by the con-struction of a wish and introduces this delusion into reality." *Id.*; *see also* S. FREUD, AN AUTOBIOGRAPHICAL STUDY, *supra* note 29.

45. S. Frosh, *supra* note 25, at 2. In "sociology, literature, film studies and philosophy, as well as in Marxist and feminist theory, there has been an enormous burgeoning of interest in psychoanalysis in recent years." *Id.* at 11.

46. For example, Lacan's model of the psyche (from Freud's earlier works), which identifies the conscious, the pre-conscious and the unconscious, does not really correspond to Freud's more developed id/ego/super-ego model. The concept of the super-ego implies a superficial societal influence on a more basic, individual self's id and ego. In Lacan's unconscious, society precedes individuality, and Lacan's ego or pre-conscious is a center of resistance rather than the healthy and rational self. *See generally* R. Harland, *supra* note 30, at 37-38 (citing J. Lacan, Écrits: A Selection 23 (A. Sheridan trans. 1977)).

47. S. Frosh, *supra* note 25, at 2; *see also id.* at 3-5 (discussing ego analysis, object-relations theory, Kleinian theory and Lacanian theory). Robert Wallerstein argues that the various schools of psychoanalysis, including ego-psychology, object-relations theory, self psychology, as well as the Kleinians, Bionians and Lacanians, share a common ground in their clinical methods notwithstanding their obvious theoretical diversity. Wallerstein, *Psychoanalysis: The Common Ground*, 71 Int'l J. Psycho-Analysis 3 (1990).

48. S. Frosh, *supra* note 25, at 11.

49. *See* N. Brown, Life Against Death 3 (1959); H. Marcuse, *supra* note 5, at 11.

50. S. Freud, Civilization and Its Discontents, *supra* note 30, at 44.

51. S. Frosh, *supra* note 25, at 40. *See generally* S. Freud, Civilization and Its Discontents, *supra* note 30.

52. S. Frosh, supra note 25, at 46. Regarding Freud's views on infantile sexuality, see S. Freud, Five Lectures, *supra* note 28, at 40–48.
A child has its sexual instincts and activities from the first; it comes into the world with them; and, after an important course of development passing through many stages, they lead to what is known as the normal sexuality of the adult. There is even no difficulty in observing the manifestations of these sexual activities in children; on the contrary, it calls for some skill to overlook them or explain them away.
Id. at 42.

53. S. Frosh, *supra* note 25, at 46.

54. *Id.* at 46–47.

55. *Id.* at 47. The Oedipus Complex—involving for Freud the incest taboo, desire opposed by authority and internalization of authority—symbolizes the individual encounter with society and describes a possible mechanism by which "social structures are incorporated into individual consciousness and have a formative role on the ordering of the psyche." *Id.* at 48.

56. *Id.* at 52.

57. S. FREUD, CIVILIZATION AND ITS DISCONTENTS, *supra* note 30, at 92.

58. S. FROSH, *supra* note 25, at 60.

59. Y. GABRIEL, *supra* note 26, at 4.

60. *See generally* Restak, *Psychiatry in America*, WILSON Q. 95, 107–12 (Autumn 1983). The American Psychoanalytic Association, founded in 1911, has over 3,000 member analysts, is affiliated with local societies in most major United States cities and accredits over 25 training institutions. *See* AM. PSYCHOANALYTIC ASS'N, ABOUT PSYCHOANALYSIS (1985). The Association publishes the *Journal of the American Psychoanalytic Association* and holds national meetings annually. Another organization, the National Psychological Association for Psychoanalysis ("NPAP"), derives from the denial of full membership to Theodor Reik, a Freudian who held a Ph.D., rather than an M.D., in the American Psychoanalytic Association. The NPAP publishes *The Psychoanalytic Review* and conducts a training institute.

61. *See generally* Y. GABRIEL, *supra* note 26; S. FROSH, *supra* note 25. Both books discuss Freud's followers and revisionists. *See also* E. WRIGHT, *supra* note 23. Wright provides several helpful summaries in the context of literary and art criticism. *Id.* at 56–68 (summarizing ego-psychology); *id.* at 69–76 (summarizing Jungian theory); *id.* at 79–104 (summarizing object-relations theory) *id.* at 107–32 (summarizing structural psychoanalysis); *id.* at 133–56 (summarizing post-structural psychoanalysis); *id.* at 159–74 (summarizing ideology studies in psychoanalysis).

62. *See* Gelman, *supra* note 24.

63. *See generally* M. MOORE, LAW AND PSYCHIATRY: RETHINKING THE RELATIONSHIP (1984); Stone, *Psychiatry and the Law*, in THE HARVARD GUIDE TO MODERN PSYCHIATRY, 651–64 (A. Nicholi, Jr. ed. 1978) (containing a brief but comprehensive catalogue of issues, including civil commitment, the insanity defense, competency, capacity, right to treatment and sexual psychopathology). *See* A. BROOKS, LAW, PSYCHIATRY AND THE MENTAL HEALTH SYSTEM (1974 & Supp. 1980); D. SHUMAN, PSYCHIATRIC AND PSYCHOLOGICAL EVIDENCE (1986 & Supps. 1988 & 1989).

Sally Lloyd-Bostock's recent book summarizes British approaches to the use of and insights from psychology in dealing with witnesses and suspects, acquiring trial persuasion skills, sentencing, the role of children in legal proceedings and employing psychological and psychiatric experts. S. LLOYD-BOSTOCK, LAW IN PRACTICE: APPLICATIONS OF PSYCHOLOGY TO LEGAL DECISION MAKING AND LEGAL SKILLS (1988). The new textbook by Robert Bastress and Joseph Harbauch considers various theories from psychology (including psychoanalytic, person-centered, behaviorist and others) and their use in interviewing, counseling and negotiation. R. BASTRESS & J. HARBAUCH, INTERVIEWING, COUNSELING, AND NEGOTIATION: SKILLS FOR EFFECTIVE REPRESNETATION (1990). For recent examples of more specific studies in law and psychology, see A. FELTHOUS, THE PSYCHOTERAPIST'S DUTY TO WARN OR PROTECT (1989); and W. WAGENAAR, IDENTIFYING IVAN: A CAST STUDY IN LEGAL PSYCHOLOGY (1988) (regarding the trial of John Demjanjuk).

64. Jerome Frank integrates psychoanalytic theory (although rarely mentioning Freud) into his realist critique of law and lawyers. *See* J. FRANK, LAW AND THE MODERN MIND (1930). Frank identifies a basic social myth, unconsciously reinforced by lawyers, that law is precise and coherent, rather than vague and unsettled. *Id.* at 8–9. Acknowledging that his explanation of this myth is partial, Frank analogizes a child's search for security and authority in his or her father with the craving of society for finality and rules in the law, and the role of judges as father-substitutes. *Id.* at 13–31. "[T]he image of the father [is] hidden away in the authority of the law...." *Id.* at 269. Legal language, moreover, creates the appearance of such longed-for definiteness and pre-dictability, thereby hiding the inevitable, non-rational bias in legal decisions and processes. *Id.* at 29–32. Frank acknowledges that "relatively superficial" political bias is obvious, but our

> most compelling biases have deeper roots and are far better concealed from consciousness....To admit their existence would be difficult and painful. Most of us are unwilling—and for the most part unable—to concede to what an extent we are controlled by such biases....We are able...to delude ourselves by giving "reasons" for our attitudes....So we persuade ourselves that our lives are govemed by Reasons.

Id. at 31–32.

The radical implications of Frank's study appear undeveloped in legal scholarship, except in the sense that recent critical legal research inherited the deconstructive (if not the scientific) methods of Legal Realism. Psychoanalysis seems to have been welcomed into law as another "partial" (read "not earthshaking") explanation of law and legal institutions and practices.

65. Franz Rudolf Bienenfeld (1886-1961), an Austrian legal scholar, did not complete his planned book on psychoanalysis and law, but the

partial manuscript was eventually published in two parts. Bienenfeld, *Prolegomena to a Psychoanalysis of Law and Justice*, 53 CALIF. L. REV. 957, 1254 (1965). Professor Ehrenzweig remarks, in a preface to the *Prolegomena*, that the book, if completed, "could well have become the definitive psychoanalytical study of law and justice." *Id.* at 959 (preface). Bienenfeld wanted to go beyond earlier psychoanalytical studies of crime and guilt, which over-emphasized Oedipal aggression, toward an acknowledgment of the Oedipal union. *Id.* at 962 ("marital obligations are not conditioned bn guilt"). The *Prolegomena* investigates family relations (child/child, parent/child) and claims for justice, which parallel the structure of the state. State production of legal systems is then described, emphasizing law as a system of obligations, with particular reference to psychoanalytic research, Gestalt psychology, Jerome Frank's observations and Piaget's experiments. Bienenfeld analyzes relative obligations ("social" (mother/child) law, "criminal" (father/child) law, "constitutional" (husband/wife) law and "contract" (between siblings) law); the absolute obligation to protect life, safety and property; and procedural laws by which obligations are ascertained. Of interest to the present study, Bienenfeld argues that *social* law, "which institutionalizes the rules for survival by support," has been neglected (by identifying law with criminal law) in most accounts of the psychological origin of law:

> The earliest concept of law has its psychological source in the earliest experience of the mother's directions, guidance, and help in nursing. All elements of law are *in nuce* present in this earliest situation. The institutionalization of social law originates from the desire for support and its satisfaction by the mother.

Id. at 967 (emphasis in original).

For a positive assessment of Bienenfeld's significance for attempts to explain the roles of rationality and values in judicial decisionmaking, see Gottschall, *Bienenfeld's Psychodynamic Model and the Judicial Process: Toward a New Paradigm in Law?*, III ALSA FORUM 33, 34 (Dec. 1978) (dynamic model of the human psyche provides "the missing synthesis for the now rigidly antithetical behavioral and rationalistic approaches to the judicial process").

66. Joseph Goldstein explores the potential contribution of psychoanalysis to legal theory, but remarks that the integration "is not close at hand, and the scant beginning has occurred only at a relatively superficial descriptive level." Goldstein, *Psychoanalysis and Jurisprudence*, 77 YALE L.J. 1053, 1054 (1968). The article is relatively short (25 pages), and the author is as interested in challenging as in establishing the "mutual relevance" of psychoanalysis and law. *Id.* at 1055 "[I]t is important to locate the limits of psychoanalytic theory in understanding the dynamics of law as a product of, stimulator of, and regulator for human behavior." *Id.* at 1059. "Law cannot find in psychoanalysis...

the moral, political, or social values upon which to base or evaluate its decisions." *Id.*; *see also id.* at 1060–64 (danger of misuse of psychoanalytic insights in criminal trials); *id.* at 1071 (similar events may have different significances to a person over time and to different people at the same time). Goldstein does suggest a positive role for psychoanalysis in, for example, child custody cases, yet re-emphasizes in his conclusion, that psychoanalysis is just another analytic tool for legal scholars and practitioners. *Id.* at 1076–77. Students expecting a finished or complete psychoanalytical theory will be either "duped or disappointed." *Id.* at 1077.

67. In contrast to Goldstein's emphasis upon psychoanalysis as another partial explanation of legal institutions and processes, *see supra* note 66, Albert Ehrenzweig asserts that "the findings of Freud and of some of his disciples have opened the gate to a new jurisprudence." A. EHRENZWEIG, PSYCHOANALYTIC JURISPRUDENCE: ON ETHICS, AESTHETICS, AND "LAW"—ON CRIME, TORT, AND PROCEDURE 146 (1971) (Ehrenzweig gives this new science a new name: psychosophy); *cf.* Cavell, *Freud and Philosophy: A Fragment*, 13 CRITICAL INQUIRY 386, 388 (1987) (Freud suggested that "philosophy has been fulfilled in the form of psychoanalysis") (citing Freud, *The Interpretation of Dreams*, in 4 THE STANDARD EDITION OF THE COMPLETE PSYCHOLOGICAL WORKS OF SIGMUND FREUD 144, 145 (J. Strachey ed. & trans. 1953–74)) [hereinafter COMPLETE PSYCHOLOGICAL WORKS]; Berthold-Bond, *Freud's Critique of Philosophy*, 20 METAPHILOSOPHY 274 (1989). Ehrenzweig's thesis that the "age of Plato has yielded to the age of Freud," A. EHRENZWEIG, *supra*, at 5, necessitates for him a comprehensive treatment (Part 1) of the history of legal philosophy before turning to psychology and law (Part II). The relationship between aesthetics and law is explored in Part II, and then an effort is made to apply psychoanalytic (or "psychosophic") insights to problems in criminal law, torts and procedure. Ehrenzweig's major theme is that irrational, unconscious feelings at work in the law (*e.g.*, the desire for vengeance in murder and tort cases, and the belief in the effectiveness of adversary proceedings before an "impartial" judge or jury) should be identified as inevitable and then left undisturbed in an effort to reform rational areas of law. *See id.* at 220–21, 258–59, 275. But see Weyrauch, *Taboo and Magic in Law*, Book Review, 25 STAN. L. REV. 782 (1973). In his critical review of *Psychoanalytic Jurisprudence*, Weyrauch writes:

> If desire for vengeance is combined with conscious or unconscious racism, it should not be left undisturbed in the interest of limited law reform even if the cost is backlash.... Professor Ehrenzweig is the last person to deny this aspect of the problem, as his discussion of civil disobedience [in Nazi Germany] clearly indicates.

Id. at 806–07 (citing A. EHRENZWEIG, *supra*, at 87–95). "Backlash" refers to Ehrenzweig's warning that retributionary "aggression, purportedly displaced, may return with a vengeance." A. EHRENZWEIG, *supra*, at 220.

68. C.G. Schoenfeld attempts to synthesize basic Freudian psychoanalysis with law and to suggest applications in constitutional law.   C.G. Schoenfeld, Psychoanalysis and the Law (1973).   Beginning with the warning that psychoanalytic explanations "are at best partial," *id.* at 7 (emphasis in original), Schoenfeld identifies (1) the influence of unconscious motives in the criminal and the judge alike, and in society with respect to the punishment of criminals, *id.* at 12-21, 63-64; (2) the super-ego as the moral and ethical standards that originate in the family, *id.* at 22-24; (3) judges as unconscious parent symbols, *id.* at 40; and (4) examples of self-deceptive rationalization (*e.g.*, in legal opinions). projection (*e.g.*, fear of big business), and identification (*e.g.*, with victims of crime), *id.* at 72-101.   When Schoenfeld turns to several constitutional problems, his arguments are sometimes simplistic, and therefore tentative.   For example, after suggesting that post-Civil War acceptance of judicial review of congressional law might be explained by "the unconscious wish for parental direction" after a traumatic event, he calls his explanation "admittedly speculative" and "at best a limited or partial explanation, since it fails to treat of matters that a sociologist, a political scientist, an historian, an economist, or others, might well deem highly relevant."   *Id.* at 114 (footnote omitted).   Likewise, psycho-analytic insights do not seem promising in solving the judicial-activism-versus-self-restraint debate, except in producing "a greater open-mindedness than now exists."   *Id.* at 136-37.   Literalism in consti-tutional interpretation may be explained by the "unconscious remnants of the childhood stage of the omnipotence of words," *id.* at 154; and the balance of powers may unconsciously symbolize the "balance between the powers of parents and their children," *id.* at 202; but "only a begin-ning has been made," *id.* at 208.   Given the controversies surrounding Freudianism, acknowledged by Schoenfeld, *id.* at 208–09, such a deprecatory attitude is understandable.

Schoenfeld's most recent book is an attempt to demonstrate a role for psychoanalysis in law reform.   C.G. Schoenfeld, Psychoanalysis Applied to Law (1984).   He discusses juvenile delinquency, mental illness, punishment of criminals, heroin addiction, discretion and international law.   In each case he focuses on unconscious emotional needs that may be overlooked when law is approached#s essentially rational and logical.

69. *See infra* notes 158–69 and accompanying text.

70. *See supra* note 63; Richards, *Law, Psychiatry, and Philosophical Analysis* (Book Review), 73 Calif. L. Rev. 1659 (1985).

71. Elizabeth Wright explains that, for Freud, infant sexual instincts are gradually organized into culturally approved adult sexuality: "The match of biological sex with the sexual role determined by society is thus achieved, not given."   E. Wright, *supra* note 23, at 14.   This "bleak

theory of the construction of gender..., as was first pointed out [in J. MITCHELL, PSYCHOANALYSIS AND FEMINISM (1974),] can be used as an ideological weapon for women to fight their own oppression....[It] enables them to demonstrate that gender is symbolic and not biological...." *Id.* at 198. The weapon, however, has another edge: "it constructs woman around the phallic sign." *Id.* Thus feminism in general has viewed Freud and his science "as prime perpetrators of patriarchy." Gallop, *Reading the Mother Tongue: Psychoanalytic Feminist Criticism*, 13 CRITICAL INQUIRY 314, 314 (1987).

Feminist ambivalence toward Freudianism continues, for example, in recent psychoanalytic feminist literary criticism, inspired in part by Lacanian psychoanalysis. *Id.* at 314–15 (Lacan promotes "language to a principal role in the psychoanalytic drama and so naturally offers fertile ground for crossing psychoanalytic and literary concerns."). Lacan, however, is often embraced by feminists as "coolly" as Freud, and debate continues as to "how far [Freud and Lacan] may be said to serve the feminist cause." E. WRIGHT, *supra* note 23, at 198. "Gallop is among those feminists who believe that Lacan's doctrine really does go 'beyond the phallus' in that he provided a theory about human identity-formation having a generality that applies no matter what the power-structure is at a given historical moment." *Id.*; *see also* Kerrigan, *Terminating Lacan*, 88 S. ATLANTIC Q. 993, 997 (1989) ("Lacan's version of psychoanalysis in [sic] unrelievedly biased toward one gender...more so than Freud's, despite the enthusiasm of some feminists for *Encore* [LE SEMINAIRE XX: ENCORE (1975)]."); Miller, *The Death of the Modern: Gender and Desire in Marlowe's "Hero, and Leander,"* 88 S. ATLANTIC Q. 757, 761 (1989) ("[T]he work of Freud and Lacan is equally informed by transferential structures grounded in the principle of paternity.").

With respect to feminist legal criticism of "male" jurisprudence, and Robin West's recent rejection of Peter Gabel's "deeply gendered" account of alienation (which draws on Lacanian psychoanalysis), see *infra* note 195.

72. *See* Brooks, *supra* note 23; *see also* E WRIGHT, *supra* note 23 (surveying, with respect to theories of literature and the arts, classical Freudian (id-psychology) criticism, post-Freudian (ego-psychology) criticism, archetypal (Jungian) criticism, object-relations theory, structural (Lacanian) psychoanalysis, post-structural psychoanalysis (Derrida and Bloom) and the critique of ideology (Deleuze and Guattari)).

73. Freud, *New Introductory Lectures on Psycho-Analysis*, in 22 COMPLETE PSYCHOLOGICAL WORKS, *supra* note 67, at 206.

74. *See generally* M. HORKHEIMER & T. ADORNO, DIALECTIC OF ENLIGHTENMENT (J. Cumming trans. 1972). In 1927, for example, the Russian semiologist V.N. Vološinov harshly criticized Freudianism as a bourgeois ideology that privileged biological (and sexual) explanations

over the socio-historical. V.N. VOLOŠINOV, FREUDIANISM: A MARXIST CRITIQUE 8-10 (I. Titunik trans. & N. Bruss ed. 1976); *id.* at 80 ("Freudian psychical dynamics and its mechanisms are only a projection into the individual psyche of social interrelationships."). On the other hand, Ernesto Laclau has pointed out that Marxism affirmed

> the opaqueness of the social—the ideological nature of collective representations—which establishes a permanent gap between the real and the manifest senses of individual and social group actions. It is easy to see how it is possible...to establish a dialogue with psychoanalysis...[by reference to] the action of the unconscious and to the pluraiity of "systems" established in the various Freudian topographies.

Laclau, *Psychoanalysis and Marxism,* 13 CRITICAL INQUIRY 330, 331 (1987) (A.C. Reiter-McIntosh trans.).

75. *See* M. HORKHEIMER & T. ADORNO, *supra* note 74; M. JAY, THE DIALECTICAL IMAGINATION 86–87 (1973).

76. M. JAY, *supra* note 75, at 91; *see* E. FROMM, *supra* note 6, at 134.

77. J. KLAPWIJK, DIALEKTIEK DER VERLIGHTING 23 (1976).

78. *See* M. JAY, *supra* note 75, at 100-06.

79. H. MARCUSE, *supra* note 5, at 60; see *infra* text accompanying notes 159-60 (Robin West's explication of the primal horde and father).

80. *Id.* at 4, 20; *see also id.* at 17 ("The notion that a non-repressive civilization is impossible is a cornerstone of Freudian theory. However, his theory contains elements that break through this rationalization; they shatter the predominant tradition of Western thought and even suggest its reversal.").

81. *Id.* at 16.

82. *Id.* at xxvii.

83. S. FREUD, THE EGO AND THE ID, *supra* note 31, at 75.

84. H. MARCUSE, *supra* note 5, at 32.

85. *Id.* at 33.

86. *Id.* at 44 (emphasis in original).

87. P. ROBINSON, *supra* note 9, at 195, 210.

88. S Frosh, supra note 25, at 160.

89. E. KURZWEIL, THE AGE OF STRUCTURALISM: LÉVI-STRAUSS TO FOUCAULT ix (1980); *see also* M. BRADBURY, MY STRANGE QUEST FOR MENSONGE:

STRUCTURALIMS'S HIDDEN HERO 2, 4 (1989) (satire of post-modernist criticism). Bradbury writes:

> In fact, and to be honest, there is no doubt that Structuralism-Deconstruction has become, to say the least, chic, and the title 'designer philosophy'...is, though unfair, not totally off target....
>
> ....
>
> [Structuralism and Deconstruction] are, in the realm of cognition, what Texas is to California in the realm of growth potential and property values, but with the added advantage of not being directly oil-related.

Id. at 24 (emphasis in original).

90. E. KURZWEIL, *supra* note 89, at 14.

91. *Id.* at 19.

92. *See id.* at 39–40; *infra* notes 179–87 and accompanying text.

93. *See* E. KURZWEIL, *supra* note 89, at 87–98; *see also* Ricoeur, *A Philosophical Interpretation of Freud*, in THE PHILOSOPHY OF PAUL RICOEUR: AN ANTHOLOGY OF HIS WORK 169 (C. Reagan and D. Steward eds. 1978); *Ricoeur The Question of Proof in Freud's Psychoanalytic Writing*, in THE PHILOSOPHY OF PAUL RICOEUR, *supra*, at 184 (includes a summary of FREUD AND PHILOSOPHY: AN ESSAY ON INTERPRETATION (D. Savage ed. 1970)).

94. *See* E. KURZWEIL, *supra* note 89, at 199–201, 239. *See generally* M. FOUCAULT, MADNESS AND CIVILIZATION: A HISTORY OF INSANITY IN THE AGE OF REASON (R. Howard trans. 1973).

95. *See* Hoy, *Jacques Derrida*, in THE RETURN OF GRAND THEORY IN THE HUMAN SCIENCES 54–55 (Q. Skinner ed. 1985).

96. E. KURZWEIL, *supra* note 89, at 136. Kurzweil notes:

> As Clara Malraux once told me, people who listened to [the Parisian seminars of Lacan (including herself) often did not understand what he was saying....Yet they went to hear him and to observe him: he put on the best show in town. His outrageous behavior provided unexpected excitement, and his statements always left his listeners in intellectual suspense....

Kurzweil, *The Freudians*, 57 PARTISAN REV. 38, 40 (1990) (excerpt from E. KURZWEIL, THE FREUDIANS: A COMPARATIVE PERSPECTIVE (1989)); *see also* E. RAGLAND-SULLIVAN, JACQUES LACAN AND THE PHILOSOPHY OF PSYCHOANALYSIS (1987).

> Anglophone readers...express the hope that someone will explain Lacan to them in their own terms. This is simply impossible. To do so would permit an interlocutor to retain assumed meanings, providing the comfort of resolution, but only the *illusion* of understanding. Lacan intended to bring about a reconceptualization of the conventionally assumed and

unquestioned words by which Western people have come to describe themselves.

Id. at x (emphasis in original).

97. E. KURZWEIL, *supra* note 89, at 137; *see* J. Lacan, *supra* note 46, at 1-7. Commentators on Lacan have identified, in the Lacanian conception of the ego, "an extreme and controversial interpretation of Freud." B. BENEVENUTO & R. KENNEDY, THE WORKS OF JACQUES LACAN: AN INTRODUCTION 60 (1986). Lacan "thought there was not enough emphasis on the ego's function of *méconnaissance*—the refusal to acknowledge thoughts and feelings—and that the later Freud put too much emphasis on the ego's adaptive functions." *Id.* at 52. Parting "company with other analytic schools in his view of the ego," Lacan suggests that "the ego's function is purely imaginary, and through its functions the subject tends to become alienated." *Id.* at 60; *see* J. LACAN, *supra* note 46, at 22:

> Freud seems...to fail to recognize the existence of everything that the ego neglects, scotomizes, misconstrues in the sensations that make it react to reality, everything that it ignores, exhausts, and binds in the significations that it receives from language: a surprising *méconnaissance* on the part of the man who succeeded by the power of his dialectic in forcing back the limits of the unconscious.

Lacan was "opposed to any idea of adjustment to the social environment, and his writings abound with a tireless polemic against such a notion." B. BENEVENUTO & R. KENNEDY, *supra*, at 61 (the "ego's mastery of the environment is always an illusory mastery" for Lacan).

As an aside, it is worth mentioning that Lacan's model of the conscious subject is divided into two parts or functions, the *moi* (roughly, the ego, with indentificatory functions) and the *je* (the speaking subject). *See generally* E. RAGLAND-SULLIVAN, *supra* note 96, at 1-67.

> [T]he terms "ego" or "self" are misleading in understanding Lacan's concept of the subject, since they imply a wholeness or totality that he refuted by his literal reformulation of the Freudian idea of an *Ichspaltung* or a splitting of the subject.

Id. at 2 (emphasis in original). Both the *moi* and the *je*, in the Lacanian scheme, "participate" in both the conscious and unconscious "systems." *Id.* at 42.

98. E. KURZWEIL, *supra* note 89, at 142-43; *see* J. LACAN, *supra* note 46, at 2 (emphasis in original):

> We have only to understand the mirror stage *as an identification*, in the full sense that analysis gives to the term: namely, the transformation that takes place in the subject when he assumes an image....This jubilant assumption of his specular image by the [infant...would seem to exhibit in an exemplary situation the symbolic matrix in which the I is precipitated in

its primordial form, before it is objectified in the dialectic of identification with the other, and before language restores to it, in the universal, its function as subject.

99. *See* T. EAGLETON, LITERARY THEORY: AN INTRODUCTION 165–67 (1983). In another formulation, "[o]nce the child has acquired language, however rudimentary it may be, then all the pre-verbal structures are radically altered to fit in with the language system....For Lacan,...once the child has the capacity for language, there is a qualitative change in the psychical structure—he becomes a subject." B. BENVENUTO & R. KENNEDY, *supra* note 97, at 131 ("In Lacan's view, the father introduces the principle of law, in particular the law of the language system."). Given recent trends in the discipline, many developmental psychologists would find such statements embarrassingly "Piagetian." *See, e.g.*, Gardner, Scherer & Tester, *Asserting Scientific Authority: Cognitive Development and Adolescent Legal Rights*, 44 AM. PSYCHOLOGIST 895, 898 (1989) (citations omitted) ("Adolescent cognitive development is not stage-like....[In the 1960s and early 1970s, Piaget and others] described cognitive development as a series of stages in which children's thought had a homogeneous logical structure across task domains. Recent cognitive development theory however, has turned away from stage theories."). *But see* R. KEGAN, THE EVOLVING SELF: PROBLEM AND PROCESS IN HUMAN DEVELOPMENT 73–109 (1985) (defending, from an object-relations perspective, a neo-Piagetian scheme of child developmental stages, while acknowledging that the "stages" are overlapping and interrelated).

100. T. EAGLETON, *supra* note 99, at 167. Lacan posits the Symbolic, Imaginary and Real orders. J. LACAN, *supra* note 46, at 30–113. Benvenuto and Kennedy explain:

The Imaginary Order includes the field of phantasies and images. It evolves out of the [Prototypical] mirror stage, but extends into the adult subject's relationships with others....

The Symbolic Order is easier to grasp, being concerned with the function of symbols and symbolic systems, including social and cultural symbolism. Language belongs to the Symbolic Order, and in Lacan's view it is through language that the subject can represent desires or feelings, and so it is through the Symbolic Order that the subject can be represented, or constituted. The Real Order, on the other hand, is the most elusive of these categories, and is linked to the dimensions of death and sexuality....Basically, it seems to be the domain outside the subject....[I]t is what the subject keeps "bumping up against."

101. T. EAGLETON, *supra* note 99, at 167. Lacan writes:.
This moment in which the mirror-stage comes to an end inaugurates...the dialectic that will henceforth link the *I* to socially elaborated situations.

It is this moment that decisively tips the whole of human knowledge into mediatization through the desire of the other constitutes its objects in an abstract equivalence by the co-operation of others, and turns the I into that apparatus for which every instinctual thrust constitutes a danger, even though it should correspond to a natural maturation—the very normalization of this maturation being henceforth dependent, in man, on a cultural mediation as exemplified, in the case of the sexual object, by the Oedipus complex.

J. LACAN, *supra* note 46, at 5–6 (emphasis in original).

Lacan draws on Piaget's work on the linguistic development of children—work that is nowadays viewed as dated by the dominant schools of psychology. *See, e.g.,* Gelman & Baillargeon, *A Review of Some Piagetian Concepts,* in 3 HANDBOOK OF CHILD PSYCHOLOGY 167–221 (P. Mussen ed. 1983) (questioning Piaget's broad stages of development, each characterized by qualitatively distinct structures).

102. T. EAGLETON, *supra* note 99, at 168-69.

[The psychoanalyst's] whole experience must find in speech alone its instrument, its context, its material, and even the background noise of its uncertainties.

...[W]hat the psychoanalytic experience discovers in the unconscious is the whole structure of language. Thus...the notion that the unconscious is merely the seat of the instincts will have to be rethought.

J. LACAN, *supra* note 46, at 147.

For a discussion of Lacan's complex reconception of Saussure's linguistic theory, set forth in J. LACAN, *supra* note 46, at 146-78 (essay entitled *The Agency of the Letter in the Unconscious or Reason Since Freud),* see B. BENVENUTO & R. KENNEDY, *supra* note 97, at 103-25, 217-22. *See also* Meltzer, *supra* note 28, at 158–60. For Saussure

a linguistic *sign* unites, not a thing and a name, but a concept [signified) and a sound-image [signifier)....Saussure claimed that meaning is generated by signifiers, not just in relation to their signifieds but also according to their position in the sentence in relation to other signifiers. So, too, Lacan will liken the unconscious to the movement of the signifier....[W]hat matters...is the meaning generated by the position of the signifier, not the dual meaning (signified) associated with it.

Id. at 159 (emphasis in original). Using Saussure's terminology, the "unconscious is just a continual movement and activity of signifiers, whose signifieds are often inaccessible to us because they are *repressed.*" T. EAGLETON, *supra* note 99, at 168 (emphasis in original). The "potentially endless movement from one signifier to another is what Lacan means by desire." *Id.* at 167.

103. T. Eagleton, *supra* note 99, at 169; *see also* B. Benvenuto & R. Kennedy, *supra* note 97, at 56 ("The ego has the illusion of autonomy, but it is only an illusion, and the subject moves from fragmentation and insufficiency to illusory unity."); *id.* at 61 ("[T]he human subject will continue throughout life to look for an imaginary 'wholeness' and 'unity.'").

104. E. Kurzweil, *supra* note 89, at 148.

105. *Id.* at 148J9.

106. *Id.* at 153.

107. T. Eagleton, *supra* note 99, at 170.

108. *Id.*

109. *Id.* (citing L. Althusser, Lenin and Philosophy and Other Essays (B. Brewster trans. 1971)); *see infra* notes 179–87 and accompanying text (discussing Althusser's theory of ideology). *But see* E. Ragland-Sullivan, *supra* note 96, at 272:

> All ideolojcal readings of Lacan miss the point. In the Marxist Louis Althusser's famous misreading of Lacan, the subject and the [exteriorized yet determinative Other] are equated so that the conscious subject is both master of Desire and of language.

110. T. Eagleton, *supra* note 99, at 172.

111. *Id.* (Althusser's view). In Lacan's formulation:

> Symbols in fact envelop the life of man in a network so total that they join together, before he comes into the world, those who are going to engender him 'by flesh and blood'; so total that they bring to his birth...the shape of his destiny; so total that they give the words that will make him faithful or renegade, the law of the acts that will follow him right to the very place where he *is* not yet and even beyond his death.

J. Lacan, *supra* note 46, at 68 (emphasis in original) (footnote omitted) (quoting C. Lévi-Strauss, Les Structures Élémentaires de la Parenté (1949)). Thus the subject, as "the slave of language is all the more so of a discourse in the universal movement in which his place is already inscribed at birth, if only by virtue of his proper name." *Id.* at 148. Frederic Jameson observes:

> Lacan's attention to the components of language has centered on those kinds of words, primarily names and pronouns, on those slots which, like the shifters generally, anchor a free-floating syntax to a particular subject, those verbal joints, therefore, at which the insertion of the subject into the Symbolic is particularly detectable.

Jameson, *Imaginary and Symbolic in Lacan: Marxism, Psychoanalytic Criticism, and the Problem of the Subject*, in Literature and Psychoanalysis, *supra* note 18, at 362.

For a more conventional but similar description of socialization into an already-established family and then culture, see K. Kaye, The Mental and Social Life of Babies: How Parents Create Persons 202–21 (1982) (self concept transmitted to infant through language, child accommodates to social system, self as product of membership in social system).

112. Gabel & Kennedy, *Roll Over Beethoven*, 36 Stan. L. Rev. 1, 45 (1984) (emphasis in original) (Kennedy's response to Gabel) (transcript of a seminar).

113. *Id.* at 29 (Cabel's response to Kennedy).

114. Gabel, *The Phenomenology of Rights-Consciousness and the Pact of the Withdrawn Selves*, 62 Tex. L. Rev. 1563 (1984).

In spite of the many modifications psychoanalytic theorists since Freud have made to his original formulations, only [Lacan and R.D. Laing] have produced theories that enrich the experiential texture of these formulations while retaining their full critical bite....[Lacan's] descriptions of how the child's desire is skewed by cultural conditioning is [sic] a phenomenological advance over the abstractness of Freud 's account, but [his] insistence on the unintelligibility of desire leaves him as unable to capture what we are alienated *from* as Freud was....[R. D. Laing], who has written very good experiential studies of how alienation is mediated through the family,...has never tried to develop a theory of social being comparable in scope to Freud's.
Id. at 1565 n.3 (emphasis in original) (citations omitted).

115. Trubek, *supra* note 3, at 607.

116. *Id.* at 608 (emphasis added).

117. Kelman, *supra* note 3, at 304. Kelman, however, is critical of Peter Gabel's "empty slogans":

He says things like "[t]he project is to realize the unalienated relatedness that is immanent within our alienated situation." But I see too few concrete references to lived experience in this "specification" to know if he is actually describing a blissful state-of-mind or a small household appliance....My mind goes utterly blank when I try to picture Peter's characters [for example, real legal actors behind juridical abstractions] glimpsing liberation by way of unalienated relatedness.
Id. at 343–44 (footnotes omitted) (quoting Gabel & Kennedy, *supra* note 112, at 1).

118. Boyle, *The Politics of Reason: Critical Legal Theory and Local Social Thought*, 133 U. PA. L. REV. 685, 702 n.49 (1985).

119. Heller, *Structuralism and Critique*, 36 STAN. L. REV. 127 132–33, 158–59 (1984).

120. Hunt, *supra* note 1, at 11.

121. *See, e.g.*, Simon, *Visions of Practice in Legal Thought*, 36 STAN. L. REV. 469 (1984).

122. *See, e.g.*, Johnson, *supra* note 4, at 289–91.

123. *See, e.g.*, Tushnet, *Ctitical Legal Studies and Constitutional Law: An Essay in Deconstruction*, 36 STAN. L. REV. 623 (1984).

124. Kennedy, *Legal Education as Training for Hierarchy*, in THE POLITICS OF LAW 40 (D. Kairys ed. 1982).

125. See Hutchinson, Book Review, *Indiana Dworkin and Law's Empire*, 96 YALE L.J. 637 (1987) (reviewing R. DWORKIN, LAW'S EMPIRE (1986)).

126. Caudill, *Disclosing Tilt: A Partial Defense of Critical Legal Studies and a Comparative Introduction to the Philosophy of the Law-Idea*, 72 IOWA L. REV. 287 (1987).

127. Hunt, *supra* note 1, at 11

128. *See* Chase, *Toward a Legal Theory of Popular Culture*, 1986 WIS. L. REV. 527.

129. *See* D. MCLELLAN, *supra* note 15, at 73; J. THOMPSON, *supra* note 16, at 5; *see also* Tushnet, *Perspectives on the Development of American Law: A Critical Review of Friedman's "A History of American Law,"* 1977 WIS. L. REV. 81, 100.

130. Hunt, *supra* note 1, at 13.

131. Lawrence, Book Review, *"Justice" or "Just Us": Racism and the Role of Ideology*, 35 STAN. L. REV. 831 (1983).

132. *Id.* at 841.

133. *Id.*

134. *Id.* at 842 (citing Geertz, *Ideology as a Cultural System*, in THE INTERPRETATION OF CULTURES 201–02 (1973)).

135. *Id.*

136. *Id.* at 843–48.

137. *Id.* at 848; see also R. KOENIGSBERG, THE PSYCHOANALYSIS OF RACISM, REVOLUTION AND NATIONALISM (1977).

138. Lawrence, *The Id, the Ego, and Equal Protection: Reckoning with Unconscious Racism*, 39 STAN. L. REV. 317 (1987) (reconsideration of discriminatory purpose doctrine in Washington v. Davis, 426 U.S. 229 (1976)).

139. *Id.* at 322-23. Thus the requirement of a racially discriminatory purpose to challenge a facially neutral law "ignores much of what we understand about how the human mind works." *Id.* at 323; *see also id.* at 329 ("The law has, for the most part, refused to acknowledge what we have learned about the unconscious.").

140. *Id.* at 339. Lawrence notes that his purpose is not "to defend psychoanalytic theory as the definitive description of psychological processes....Rather, I have drawn upon psychoanalytic theory because it provides a conceptual vocabulary for processes that we have all observed in our everyday lives." *Id.* at 331 n.55.

141. *Id.* at 344-81.

142. R. GEUSS, THE IDEA OF A CRITICAL THEORY: HABERMAS AND THE FRANKFURT SCHOOL (1981).

143. S. FREUD, THE FUTURE OF AN ILLUSION, *supra* note 30, at 47-53 (religious belief as an illusion in Freud's scheme).

144. R. GEUSS, *supra* note 142, at 41; *see id.* at 45 (containing a discussion of Habermas' theory of interests with citations to Habermas' own work).

145. *Id.* at 41.

146. *Id.* at 42-44.

147. H. MARCUSE, *supra* note 5, at 16.

148. Kennedy, *supra* note 10, at 282 n.180.

149. *Id.*

150. *Id*

151. The annual Round Table is held at Penn State-Berks (Reading), and is organized by Roberta Kevelson, the director of the Center for Semiotic Research in Law, Government and Econoics. The papers from the first Round Table are published in 1 LAW AND SEMIOTICS (R. Kevelson ed. 1987).

152. Goodrich, *Psychoanalysis in Legal Education: Notes on the Violence of the Sign*, in LAW AND SEMIOTICS, *supra* note 151, at 200 (footnote omitted).

153. *Id.* Legal "education provides...irrefragable authorities, irrefutable norms, incontestable truths or...it provides...a surrogate father figure; it also "imposes a canon of argument and of correct meanings [that] preclude and denigrate those discourses that are based upon emotive and non-centripetal categories of communicative competence...." *Id.* at 200-01.

154. *Id.* at 195-96.
In raising the question of the manner in which the individual as subject is temporarily and psychically constructed analysis is led eventually to question an order of repression, of motives and of the unconscious, in which the laws governing the forms of discourse, of the possibilities of speech, are inscribed in the very constitution of subjectivity.
Id. at 196.

155. *Id.* at 197, 204.

156. *Id.* at 208; *id.* at 204 (citing Lacan) ("What is monstrous to the educational institution, to the scriveners of the codicils, is the advent of a rhetoric which writes differently, which collapses and inverts the authoritarian hierarchies inscribed in grammar itself....").

157. S. FROSH, *supra* note 25, at 269.

158. West, *supra* note 8, at 818.

159. *Id.* at 822.

160. *Id.* at 823-24 (citing S. FREUD, TOTEM AND TABOO 184–85 (A. Brill trans. 1918)).

161. *Id.* at 834.

162. *Id.* at 835-36.

163. *Id.* at 860-61.

164. *Id.* at 863.

165. *Id.* at 865 (citing, S. FREUD, CIVILIZATION AND ITS DISCONTENTS, *supra* note 30, at 11).

166. *Id.* at 866–68 (citing S. FREUD, CIVILIZATION AND ITS DISCONTENTS, *supra* note 30, at 12–19).

167. *Id.* at 881.

168. *See, e.g.,* Freeman & Mensch, *Religion as Science/Science as Religion: ConstitutionalLow and the Fundamentalist Challenge,* 2 TIKKUN 69 (Nov./Dec. 1987) ("[S]cientific methodology cannot claim any objective, transcendent separation from social and political life. Science is

rooted in the culture within which it operates, and its underlying presuppositions are always a part of that social context.").

169. *See* S. Frosh, *supra* note 25, at 6–9 (summary of scientific criticisms of Freud). For two sympathetic accounts of the "scientificity" of comtemporary psychoanalysis, see generally Eagle, *The Epistemologiccl Status of Psychoanalysis*, 56 Soc. Res. 383 (1989); and Holland, *Scientiflcity and Psychoanalysis: Insights from the Controversial Discussions*, 17 Int'l Rev. Psycho-Analysis 133 (1990). Eagle argues:

> What is known as psychoanalytic theory is a rather hetero-geneous, loosely constructed set of formuiations...[that] range from ones that can reasonably be subjected to empirical test, at least in theory, to those that are quite unsusceptible to empiri-cal evaluation. Hence, any sweeping unqualified statements— such as "Psychoanalysis is a science" or "Psychoanalysis is not a science"—are likely to be inaccurate and incomplete.

Eagle, *supra*, at 386.

Holland argues that Freud's functionalistic, or positivist, perspective was the first of three "contradictory and distorted" paradigms inhabited by Freud (the others designated as the "interpretive" and the "radical humanist"): "All of them wrong and incomplete, but all that he had, and so much more than anybody has enjoyed before or after him." Holland. *supra*, at 142.

170. L. Althusser, *supra* note 109, at 175.

171. *See supra* notes 11–19 and accompanying text.

172. That is, "How did [CLS writers'] souls survive uncorrupted?" Schwartz, *With Gun and Camera Through Darkest CLS-Land*, 36 Stan. L. Rev. 413, 446 (1984).

173. S. Schneiderman, Jacques Lacan: the Death of an Intellectual Hero vi (1983).

174. *Id.* at 57. "All the analyst can do is offer to the patient access to speech. This speech, being described as free association, is not centered on a particular subject; the only subject the analyst recognizes is the subject of the unconscious." *Id.* at 116.

For Lacan, language is "the precondition of the unconscious, and speech is the instrument of cure." Schneiderman, *The Most Contro-versial Freudian Since Freud*, Psychology Today, Apr. 1978, at 56.

175. S. Schneiderman, *supra* note 173, at 118. Lacan "felt that analysis should offer another structure, a structure that was not identical with that of everyday life." *Id.* at 143.

176. *Id.* at 151. "Lacan must have felt that talking too much often was used as a resistance to avoiding the issues." *Id.* at 138.

177. *Id.* at 134. Bringing a neurotic condition into consciousness "does produce some changes in the attitude of the neurotic toward his neurosis, but it does not alter the structure in any fundamental way." *Id.*

178. *Id.* According to another commentator, Lacan acknowledged Freud's discovery that truth manifests itself in the letter rather than the spirit, that is, in the way things are actually said rather than in the intended meaning....The psychoanalyst learns to listen not so much to her patient's main point as to odd marginal moments, slips of the tongue, unintended disclosures.
J. GALLOP, READING LACAN 22 (1985); *cf. supra* note 111, at 338 (Fredric Jameson's remark) (language "constitutes that primary social instance into which the pre-verbal, pre-social facts of archaic or unconscious experience find themselves somehow inserted").

179. L. ALTHUSSER, *supra* note 109, at 159. "In fact, *The German Ideology* does offer us...an explicit theory of ideology, but...it is not Marxist...." *Id.* at 158.

180. *Id.* at 162. Althusser wants to adopt Marx's conception of ideology while avoiding its positivism. Jameson refers to Althusser's definition of ideology—inspired by Lacan—as the "first new and as yet insufficiently developed conception of the nature of ideology since Marx and Nietzsche...." Jameson, *supra* note 111, at 393–94. Ideological representation must "be seen as that indispensable mapping fantasy or narrative by which the individual subject invents a 'lived' relationship with collective systems which otherwise by definition exclude him insofar as he or she is born into a pre-existent social form and its pre-existent language." *Id.* at 394. For recent criticism of Althusser, see Smith, *Ideology and Interpretation: The Case of Althusser*, 10 POETICS TODAY 493, 499-500 (1989) (Althusser "risks substituting one form of [Marxian] determinism for another, linguistic for economic"; moreover, Althusser's post-modernist tendencies lead to nihilism); Nielsen, *The Concept of Ideology: Some Marxist and Non-Marxist Conceptualizations*, 2 RETHINKING MARXISM, Winter 1989, at 146, 157-61; and P. RICOEUR, LECTURES ON IDEOLOGY AND UTOPIA 103–58 (G. Taylor ed 1986).

181. L. ALTHUSSER, *supra* note 109, # 176.

182. *Id.*

183. *Id.*; *see also* R. LAING, THE POLITICS OF THE FAMILY AND OTHER ESSAYS 3-19 (1971). Note, however, that R.D. Laing's theory of the "divided self" is to be distinguished from, and indeed is opposed to, Lacan's topology of the psyche. *See* E. RAGLAND-SULLIVAN, *supra* note 96, at 62:

> Laing (following Winnicott) makes a Rousseauesque division between true and false images of self ("true" belonging to the

natural and good inner self and "false" to the distorting, repressive effects of the social realm)....Lacan's subject, on the other hand, is a paradox of true and false....No final separation exists, therefore, between the inside and outside realms.

For a more conventional treatment of the familial configuration, from the perspective of family, therapy and its basis in systems theory, see Minuchin, *Families and Individual Development: Provocations from the Field of Family Therapy*, 56 CHILD DEV. 289 (1985).

184. L. ALTHUSSER, *supra* note 109, at 161 (emphasis in original) ("*ideology is eternal*, exactly like the unconscious").

185. *Id.* at 199–201.

186. *Id.* at 209.

187. *Id.* at 211; *see also id.* at 211 n.4 (defining "Law of Culture").

188. B. BENVENUTO & R. KENNEDY, *supra* note 97, at 18.

189. Gabel, *Dukakis's Defeat and the Transformative Possibilities of Legal Culture*, 4 TIKKUN 14 (Mar./Apr. 1989) [hereinafter Gabel, *Dukakis's Defeat*] ("Although the moral vision of the conservatives has been to a large degree imaginary...the right's symbolic discourse has recognized the centrality of social desire to politics and has offered at least compensatory fantasies to alleviate, at the intrapsychic level, the alienation of everyday life."). For a similar analysis of the jurisprudence of original intention as an imaginary psychopolitical account of our connection to one another, see Gabel, *Founding Father Knows Best: A Response to Tushnet*, 1 TIKKUN 41 (Mar./Apr. 1986), reprinted in 36 BUFFALO L. REV. 227 (1987).

190. Gabel, *Dukakis's Defeat*, *supra* note 189, at 14.

191. *Id.* at 15.

192. *Id.*

193. *Id.* at 15–16.

194. *Id.* at 16. For a similar analysis of childhood culminating in the divided self, see R. UNGER, PASSION: AN ESSAY ON PERSONALITY 151–65 (1984). Jameson described the Lacanian "Unconscious"

as that reality of the subject which has been alienated and repressed through the very process by which, in receiving a name, it is transformed into a representation of itself.

This production of the Unconscious by way of a primary repression which is none other than the acquisition of language is then reinterpreted in terms of the communicational situation as a whole....[A] distinct dimension of [the above-mentioned linguistic alienation is] the inescapable mediation of other people, and more particularly of the Other...or in other words the parents: yet here the Law represented by the parents, and in particular by the father, passes over into the very nature of language itself, which the child receives from the outside and which speaks [to] him just as surely as he learns to speak it.

Jameson, *supra* note 111, at 363–64.

195. Gabel, *Dukakis's Defeat*, *supra* note 189, at 16. Robin West's recent attack upon Gabel's psychoanalytic account as "deeply gendered" must here be acknowledged. *See* West, *Jurisprudence and Gender*, 55 U. CHI. L. REV. 1, 45 (1988). Feminist scholars have convincingly identified the male perspective in contemporary jurisprudence. *See, e.g.*, O'Donovan, *Engendering Justice: Women's Perspectives and the Rule of Law*, 39 U. TORONTO L.J. 127, 131 (1989) (citing C. Dalton, Remarks on Personhood (Jan. 5, 1985) (paper presented at AALS panel)) (Rawls' theoretical construct—the person who chooses civil libertarianism—"represents the caricature of a 'male' personality type"); Lahey, "...*Until Women Themselves Have Told All That They Have to Tell...*," 23 OSGOODE HALL L.J. 519, 526 (1985) (emphasis in original) ("[T]he male perspective has its own point of view, and...feminists object to treating the male point of view as a *universal* point of view."). West argues that *all* modern legal theory—"liberal legalism" as well as "critical legal theory"—"is essentially and irretrievably masculine" by virtue of a shared "separation thesis." West, *supra*, at 2.

> Liberal legalists, in short, describe an inner life enlivened by freedom and autonomy from the separate other, and threatened by the danger of annihilation by him. Critical legal theorists, by contrast, tell a story of inner lives dominated by feelings of alienation and isolation from the separate other, and enlivened by the possibility of association and community with him....
> Each story...constitutes a legitimate and true part of the total subjective experience of masculinity.

Id. at 5. Women, on the other hand, are not essentially separate, and are distinctively "connected" to one another in the experiences of pregnancy, heterosexual penetration, menstruation and breast feeding. *Id.* at 2–3; *see also id.* at 14 ("Women are actually or potentially materially connected to other human life. Men aren't.").

While women experience, West explains, fear of the unnatural state of separation, it is not the same dread of natural, male alienation identified in the CLS canon. Id. at 40–41. Thus Gabel's story "of attachment, separation, longing, rejection, repression, humiliation"and then alienation is a story of male development, not female." Id. at 45. West is eventually constructive: "Gabel has confused his male experience of separation and alienation with 'human' experience...because women have not made clear that our day-to-day, lived experience...is incommensurable with men's. We need to flood the market with our own stories...." *Id.* at 65.

196. Gabel, *Dukakis's Defeat, supra* note 189, at 106 ("These circular or 'rotating' of denial in which each person passes the same doubt on to the next person for processes often to millions of people at once, as in the case of the newscaster) also account for the phantom phenomena we usually refer to as 'social structures.'").

197. *Id.* at 106–07.

198. *Id.* at 107. Gabel's work parallels the approach of Michael Lerner (editor of *Tikkun*; Gabel is a frequent contributor to, and associate editor of, *Tikkun*). *See* M. LERNER, SURPLUS POWERLESSNESS: THE PSYCHODYNAMICS OF EVERYDAY LIFE...AND THE PSYCHOLOGY OF INDIVIDUAL AND SOCIAL TRANSFORMATION x-xi (1986) (Lerner acknowledges that his ideas were refined through discussions with Gabel). Gabel's recognition of the need for public confidence appears to reflect Lerner's conception of "Surplus Powerlessness"' "[T]he set of feelings and beliefs that make people think of themselves as even more powelress than the actual power situation requires, and then leads them to act in ways that actually confirm them in their powerlessness." *Id.* at ii. Surplus Powerlessness "is the new form by which people are kept enslaved. It is inside our own heads, and it is recreated by us in every thought that assumes that how things are is the equivalent of 'reality.'" *Id.* at 4–5. In addition to *conscious*, misguided assessments of power, Surplus Powerlessness functions most effectively through a Social Unconscious: "shared meanings that most people assume in their daily interactions with others of which they are not aware and which they would resist knowing should they be pointed out." *Id.* at 12. However, and precisely "because denial of our fundamental human needs hurts so much, there is continual hope that we will break through our isolation and connect with each other in a deeper way and find ways to change the larger situation." *Id.* at 16. Significantly, Lerner sees the summary dismissal of religious insights by the Marxian and psychoanalytic traditions as a serious mistake: "As an alternative, the religious worldview helps to challenge the dominant society's attempt to frame reality as 'that which is' at the moment....The religious worldview opens up the social, intellectual and emotional space to imagine a quite different way of approaching reality." *Id.* at 265.

In a recent book, Unger attempts to critique and restate the Christian-romantic view of human identity. *See* R. UNGER, *supra* note 194. Unger there identified "'two connected tasks: the development of a psychology of empowerment and the analysis of the social conditions on which empowerment depends." *Id.* at 72. While we are mentally and socially structured by "'institutional or imaginative assumptions" taken as given, we can break through and revise, or invent new, formative contexts." *Id.* at 7–8. For example,

we are empowered by freeing our understanding of society from superstition....The characteristic form of superstition about

society is the superstition of false necessity: the ease with which
we mistake the constraints imposed by a particular formative
context of social life for the inherent psychological, organizational, and economic imperatives of society.
Id. at 14.

199. Gabel, *Dukakis's Defeat, supra* note 189, at 107–08.

200. *Id.* at 108. The judge's platform and robe, and the attorney's
"glassy-eyed, disembodied power-discourse in spite of the strain
required to keep it up," serve to alienate citizens "from the political
community that the lawyer or judge is supposed to represent." *Id.*

201. *Id.* at 109 ("the categories of legal discourse form a perceptual
grid that is experienced by most people as "the way things are'"); *see
also* Gabel, *A Critical Anatomy of the Legal Opinion*, V ALSA FORUM 5, 10
(Fall 1980) ("[T]he social function of law is not to be found in its direct
effect on socio-economic activity, but rather in its effect on people's
minds.").

202. Gabel, *Dukakis's Defeat, supra* note 189, at 110–11.

203. *Id.* at 110.

204. *See id.* at 111.

205. *See* Bernstein, *Introduction* to HABERMAS AND MODERNITY 12 (R.
Bernstein ed. 1985) ("Habermas soon came to realize that the systematic program sketched in *Knowledge and Human Interests* was
seriously flawed....In [*The Theory of Communicative Action*], and in the
writings leading up to it, one can discern a new systematic synthesis—
which preserves Habermas's earlier insights, corrects its inadequacies,
and points to new directions for research.").

206. Bernstein, supra note 205, identifies four major flaws in
Habermas' theory. First, there "is a radical ambiguity in the basic
concepts of reflection and self-reflection[;]" Habermas failed to
distinguish between Kantian "self-reflection of reason upon the
conditions of its employment" and the emancipatory self-reflection "that
aims at freeing a subject...'from ideological frozen forms of dependence
that can in principle be transformed.'" *Id.* at 12 (quoting Kant's
Critique); *see also infra* note 220 and accompanying text. The second
major flaw involves a failure to show "how we can at once justify the
claim that there are unavoidable necessary universal conditions of
communicative action and rationality, and maintain that these can be
discovered and warranted in a scientific manner." Bernstein, *supra* note
205, at 13. Thirdly, Habermas obscured "the intrinsic intersubjective
and dialogical character of communicative action." *Id.* at 14. Finally,
no critical social science was systematically articulated. *Id.* at 14–15.

Bernstein argues that Habermas' recent work substantially addresses these four shortcomtngs.

With respect to Habermas' retreat from Critical Theory's synthesis of Freud and Marx, see Whitebook, *Reason and Happiness: Some Psychoanalytic Themes in Critical Theory*, in HABERMAS AND MODERNITY, *supra* note 205, at 140–60 (Adorno and Marcuse as id-psychologists). *See also* LaCapra, *supra* note 23, at 249 (Habermas' ego-psychological perspective) (citing M. JAY, MARXISM AND TOTALITY: THE ADVENTURES OF A CONCEPT FROM LUKAS TO HABERMAS 480–81 (1984)) (discussing Habermas).

> [W]hereas the patient and analyst shared an a priori interest in relieving the patient's neurotic symptoms, in society no such consensus could be assumed. Indeed, insofar as certain men or classes benefited from the maintenance of ideological distortion and exploitative power relations, there was no reason to assume they would willingly enter the process of dialogic enlightenment suggested by the psychoanalytic model. Nor would their improved understanding of reality necessarily generate a desire to transform it.

La Capra, *supra* note 23, at 249.

207. Habermas, *Self-Reflection as Science: Freud's Psychoanalytic Critique of Meaning*, in J. HABERMAS, KNOWLEDGE AND HUMAN INTERESTS 214 (J. Shapiro trans. 1971) (First published in 1968).

208. *Id.* at 218 (emphasis in original).

209. Habermas, *Peirce's Logic of Inquiry: The Dilemma of a Scholastic Realism Restored by the Logic of Language*, in J. HABERMAS, *supra* note 207, at 110–11; *see* C. ALFORD, NARCISSISM: SOCRATES, THE FRANKFURT SCHOOL, AND PSYCHOANALYTIC THEORY 166 (1988):

> In key respects Habermas's view Of psychoanalysis resembles that of Lacan. Both see it as hermeneutics....
>
> Yet the views of Lacan and Habermas are hardly identical....For Habermas, the goal of analysis...is the reestablishment of the autonomous individual on a new basis....For Lacan, the goal is to show that the very idea of rational individuality is a veil....

210. Freud, *On Dreams*, in 5 COMPLETE PSYCHOLOGICAL WORKS, *supra* note 67, at 642. Habermas explained that three "layers" appear in drum interpretation, namely the patient's rationalized elaboration, the manifest dream comprised of the "day's residues" and the "depth layer with the symbolic contents that resist the work of interpretation." J. HABERMAS, *supra* note 207, at 221.

211. *See* Freud, *New Introductory Lectures on Psycho-Analysis*, in 22 COMPLETE PSYCHOLOGICAL WORKS, *supra* note 67, at 14. The censorship (or repression) of unconscious motives is "slackened" in sleep

and the motives thereby find a language. J. HABERMAS, *supra* note 207, at 224 ("The text of the dream can be conceived as a compromise... between a substitute social censorship contained in the self and unconscious motives....[U]nder the exceptional conditions of sleep, unconscious motives push forward into the material of the preconscious which can be publicly communicated....").

212. J. HABERMAS, *supra* note 207, at 223–24.

213. *Id.* at 226.

214. *Id.*

215. *Id.* at 228. Note that for Freud the patient does not suffer from ignorance, but from resistances which cause and maintain this ignorance. Freud, *"Wild" Psycho-Analysis,* in 11 COMPLETE PSYCHOLOGICAL WORKS, *supra* note 67, at 225.

216. J. HABERMAS, *supra* note 207, at 232.

217. *Id.* at 235–36 (emphasis in original); *see also id.* at 242 ("Freud conceived the defensive process as the reversal of reflection...analogous to flight, through which the ego conceals itself from itself.").

218. Habermas, *Psychoanalysis and Social Theory: Nietzsche's Reduction of Cognitive Interests,* in J. HABERMAS, *supra* note 207, at 276 ("Like the repetition compulsion from within, institutional compulsion from without brings about a relatively rigid reproduction of uniform behavior that is removed from criticism....").

219. *Id.* at 282.

220. Habermas, *Knowledge and Human Interests: A General Perspective,* in J. HABERMAS, *supra* note 207, at 310.

221. J. BRANKMAN, CULTURE AND DOMINATION x (1987).

222. *See, e.g.,* M. FOUCAULT, THE ORDER OF THINGS: AN ARCHEOLOGY OF THE HUMAN SCIENCES (1970).

223. *See* G. DELEUZE & F. GUATTARI, ANTI-OEDIPUS: CAPITALISM AND SCHIZOPHRENIA (1977).

224 J. BRENKMAN, *supra* note 221, at 149.

225. *Id.* at 152. With respect to the ego's function, "there are no reality-altering actions that are not already situated in and affected by the social network of a human community." *Id.* at 155.

226. *Id.* at 152. For an empirical psychoanalytic-oriented inquiry into the self-other relationship, in support of Brenkman, see Pipp, *Sensorimotor and Representational Internal Working Models of Self,*

Other, and Relationship: Mechanisms of Connection and Separation, in
THE SELF IN TRANSITION: INFANCY TO CHILDHOOD (D. Cicchetti & M. Beeghley
eds. 1990). *See generally* Keil, *Constraints on Knowledge and Cognitive
Development,* 88 PSYCHOLOGICAL REV. 197 (1981) (regarding the constraints of language).

227. J. BRENKMAN, *supra* note 221, at 174.

228. *Id.* at 146 (quoting and translating J. LACAN, *supra* note 46, at
319).

229. *See supra* note 114; *see also supra* text accompanying note 97.
Gabel's (and Brenkman's) attempt to go beyond Lacan will, of course, be
viewed by Lacanians as superficial. *See, e.g.,* E. RAGLAND-SULLIVAN,
supra note 96, at 66–67:

> Psychologists...who look for truth in "resolution" are...destined
> to be disenchanted....Even the Other's Desire, which makes up
> the unconscious discourse, is not a *Dasein* (being or existence),
> for it can only ever be partially captured, and even that
> indirectly, intersubjectively, and transindividually....
>
> ...The subject [of identifications and objectifications-the
> *moi*] is...an unbridgeable gap between a person's perceptions
> and alienation in relation to an external *Gestalt,* an internal
> discourse, and Desire.

Therefore, for Lacanians,

> Lacan's picture of the human subject accurately conveys the
> tragedy of natural being. We are faced with a choice between
> individuation through psychic Castration (that is, learning
> difference by alienation into language, social conventions, and
> rules) or failure to evolve an identity adequate to social
> functioning.

Id. at 273.

230. *See supra* notes 193–94 and accompanying text.

231. *See supra* note 196.

232. *See supra* notes 200–01.

233. *See* J. BRENKMAN, *supra* note 221, at 166–68.

234. *Id.* at 150.

235. *Id.* at 167–68.

236. *Id.* at 168.

237. *Id.*

238. *Id.* at 160–61.

239. Gabel, *On Passionate Reason: Transcending Marxism and Deconstruction*, 4 TIKKUN 9, 11 (Nov./Dec. 1989). Gabel confirms "the centrality of engaged, intuitive comprehension to the construction of psychoanalytic knowledge," then explains:

> The kind of critical social thought that I'm talking about here demands that people passionately throw themselves forward into the lived experience of social   phenomena that surround them and attempt to illuminate through evocative description, rather than detached analysis or "explanation," the universal realizations and distortions of social desire that these diverse phenomena share across the cultural richness of their differences.

Id. at 11.

240. *See* Kennedy, *supra* note 10.

241. Balkin, *Deconstructive Practice and Legal Theory*, 96 YALE L.J. 743 (1987).

2

MARIE ASHE _____

Mind's Opportunity: Birthing a Poststructuralist Feminist Jurisprudence

INTRODUCTION

In recent years there has developed in the United States a body of writing that has come to be designated as "feminist jurisprudence."[1] The identifying features of this work have been its central concern with the universal cultural reality of female subordination and its refusal to accept that subordination as necessary or accidental. Writing in this area, during its beginnings in the 1970s, often focused on issues of sex discrimination in employment, developing a critique that coincided with the influx of large numbers of women into the workplace.[2] Since its early concentration on issues of female "equality" and "inequality" in the public areas of cultural life, feminist jurisprudence has broadened to explore what the law is, should, and might be, in the many areas where law explicitly or implicitly effects a differential impact on women and on men.[3]

Feminist jurisprudential work has taken shape against the backdrop of a developing body of law which, in contribution and in response to social change, has defined and redefined the regulation of female activity in the public and private areas of our culture. Since its initial emergence in the form of extensive commentary on the proposed Equal Rights Amendment to the United States Constitution, feminist jurisprudence has touched on a broad range of issues implicated in either judicial pronouncement or legislative policy-making. Commentary has addressed, for example, the United States Supreme Court's analysis of the equal protection clause[4] and of title VII of the Civil

Rights Act of 1964[5] in their relation to sex discrimination in employment;[6] the Court's treatment of female reproductive freedom in the series of abortion cases that commenced with Roe v. Wade;[7] the implications of the amendment of the Civil Rights Act of 1964 by addition of the Pregnancy Discrimination Amendment in 1979;[8] and the likely ramifications of various state statutory schemes providing for pregnancy disability leave from employment.[9] Writing has also focused on issues not yet defined by legislation or adjudication—comparable worth or pay equity,[10] the permissibility of regulation based upon perceptions of "fetal vulnerability" in the workplace[11] and so called "surrogate" motherhood.[12] Feminist scholars have initiated and contributed to discussion of pornography as a form of sex discrimination,[13] and to discussion of the anti-female bias which is claimed to be inherent in criminal sexual assault statutes.[14] Writing has also addressed the changed and changing nature of female activity in the "private" area of the family, with recent work evaluating the erosion of presumptions favoring women in child custody contests as well as the developments in law relating to distribution of marital property and awards of alimony upon dissolution of marriage.[15]

The feminist jurisprudence of the last several years has emerged within the context of awareness of the worsening of economic conditions of women throughout the world.[16] Much writing, motivated by awareness of that reality, has proposed law reform measures to arrest or to reverse trends in the direction of the feminization of poverty and continued marginalization of women. Its reformist concern is perhaps responsible for the location of most feminist jurisprudence within the structure of the liberal philosophical heritage that defines American political and legal theory. A significant amount of the theoretical work done to date has consisted of attempts to formulate or to reformulate consititutional and common law doctrine to accommodate enhancements of the status of women. A reformist commitment has characterized writings advocating expanded constitutional interpretation that would favor the breakdown of gender-based barriers,[17] as well as some writing that has proposed new normative directions.[18]

The most recent intensive efforts of this kind have been attempts to define a coherent "equality theory." In addressing issues of gender or sex differences and how they should be treated, feminist jurisprudence has had to confront fundamental questions concerning the nature and scope of such differences. While reflecting a common commitment to the labor of altering or reshaping structures in order to empower women, liberal feminist contributions to legal theory have reflected deep and fundamental disagreements concerning how best to formulate issues of gender difference, i.e., how to think about "difference." Variations in the selection of a logic of difference have dictated striking divisions among feminist legal theorists concerning what the law should be. Differences on the question of how the law ought to treat pregnancy and childbirth have been most markedly profound.[19] They have, in fact, so clearly disclosed the lack of consensus among feminists as to create a present crisis for feminism and for feminist jurisprudence, throwing into question whether the current women's movement is, or might become, capable of defining a coherent, normative vision susceptible of transformation into "legal meaning."[20]

The internally divided colloquy of liberal theorists of equality has not constituted the entire field of feminist jurisprudence. There has appeared some writing from a "leftist" perspective outside of liberal legalism that has sought to avoid the contradictions and paradoxes implicit in "equality theory" by focusing on the material realities of female lives. This commentary has often proceeded through a kind of phenomenological methodology, defining the material effects of legal doctrine and disclosing the operation of ostensibly objective and neutral legal doctrine as an element of a social structure extremely oppressive of women.[21] Such writing has disclosed the operation of arbitrary power beneath the surface of a legs discourse ostensibly characterized by doctrinal determinacy.

"Leftist" writing has, more consciously and precisely than liberal writing, taken its own bearings and explicitly located itself with reference to the prevailing intellectual movements of American and European feminism, of modern political theory, and of critical theory.[22] Much of this radically critical work has pointed in the direction of a fuller and more materially based examination of the actual condition of women in contemporary society and to that extent, has avoided what one writer has called feminism's "idealist error."[23] The undertakings in this area operate to illuminate our understanding of the enormity and recalcitrance of female subordination in every culture, and may contribute toward the articulation of sounder rationales for public policy directly addressing the manifestations of that condition. This work marks a limited departure from the impasse of contradictory liberal analyses of gender differentiation. As presently developed, however, it provides something less than a fully adequate exit from that impasse.

Formulations of feminist legal theory by leftist writers have not satisfactorily advanced the halting and uncertain movement of feminist thought because they have not been able to resolve the precise issues which have foiled liberal thought. While attempting to bypass the contradictions inherent in liberal thought, leftist writing confronts, at the end of its detour away from liberal theory the very issue that confounds liberal theory: the question of how to think about difference. The leftist exposure of the subordinating reality of legal structures leaves undone the reconstructive task which must commence with that question.

I believe that the fundamental question of difference cannot ultimately be avoided, that it demands confrontation. To abandon the project of speaking meaningfully of "difference" is to abandon the project of speaking meaningfully of "women." The limitation of leftist contributions, at their present stage of development, is twofold. First, the end points proposed (when they are proposed) by leftist writers are not more persuasive or less divisive than the various models proposed by liberal equality theorists.[24] Second, while the leftist critiques take us to points from which we can view with some clarity the material conditions of women in society, they are not notably more successful than liberal theory in giving us a clear view of the motivations or operations that give continuing momentum to processes exclusive of women.[25]

While feminist writers speak in differing and seemingly opposed voices on major foundational issues, they do express a common conviction that gender-based societal barriers work a twofold harm: they threaten individuals who are frustrated in their attempts to move out of narrow and restrictive ranges; and they infuse into every institution of modern culture a malaise that affects and clouds all areas of our lives. I share that certainty, as well as an urgent conviction that no broadly significant and lasting changes in the status of women will be accomplished without continued, deep, and difficult public exploration of the obdurate issues of sex discrimination. I believe that there are definable reasons why the public discourse at this point has reached a kind of impasse. Further, I believe that there does exist a possibility of escape from that impasse. I see that exit located in the thought characteristic of major poststructuralist writers who have been for some time deeply involved with the issues of difference and of differentiation that so plague feminist jurisprudential theory. Poststructuralist critical theory has addressed, in their most general and profound terms, the fundamental issues underlying the feminist jurisprudential crisis, exploring them as issues of knowledge as well as of power.

The exit afforded by poststructuralist theory has become more generally accessible to American readers and writers with the renewed discussion of the intersections of law and philosophy apparent in recent American jurisprudential publication. Branching out of such intersections, poststructuralist theory locates itself in a plane of discourse distinctly removed and quite different from the one in which most American jurisprudence has thus far engaged. European critical theory, as embodied in the poststructuralism of Foucault,[26] Lacan,[27] Derrida,[28] and especially as it appears in the "semiotic" work of Julia Kristeva,[29] may constitute the most profoundly original and promising direction in theory addressing the deepest questions of gender differentiation. I propose that engagement with that work is essential for America legal theorists grappling with related issues.

This Article is intended to sketch out what I discern of the new avenues opened up at the intersections of American feminist jurisprudence and poststructuralist thought. Section I provides an overview of American feminist equal rights theory. Defining the divisions that have brought liberal jurisprudential development to an impasse, section II is devoted to examination of the failure of liberal feminist jurisprudence to provide the sustaining narrative and nomos that might support significant change in the area of gender relations. Section III examines the parallel failure of non-jurisprudential American feminist thought. Section IV touches briefly on the contributions of leftist feminist legal theorists and attempts to define with some particularity the contribution which poststructuralist methodology and epistemological inquiry might offer for that work as well as for liberal equality theory. The section is devoted largely to examination of representative themes expressed in the work of Michel Foucault and Julia Kristeva. I attempt to define the increase in strength and the expansion of scope that characterizes feminist theory elaborated upon a poststructuralist fabric. The Conclusion proposes what I see of the new and demanding directions apparent from the perspectives of poststructuralist theory, which may constitute, for feminism, its only possible alternative to silence and defeat.

I. EQUALITY THEORY OF LIBERAL FEMINIST JURISPRUDENCE

The concentration upon "equal rights" or "equality" theory that has been the dominant feature of feminist jurisprudence can be accounted for in various ways. Freedman has seen the primacy of the "equal rights" doctrine within the feminist movement as derivative of the critical functions of litigation and legal argument in reform politics in general.[30] The concept has also been defined as a "borrowing" of the doctrine that informed and constituted the "legal meaning" of the civil rights struggle of the 1950s and beyond.[31]

Whatever the reasons for its valorization, the emphasis on "equal rights" was intended by both liberal and radical feminists to facilitate a shift in public policy away from gender differentiation based on "naturalistic" or "biologistic" assumptions."[32] Equality theory was invoked as a doctrine that might break down the gender-based stereotyping that restricted women to marginal positions in society, and, particularly, in the "public" sphere. During the 1970s, "equal rights" terminology was incorporated into federal and state legislation intended to increase female access to the public arena,"[33] and was, to some degree, utilized in adjudication of constitutional issues involving differential treatment of the sexes.[34]

The invocation of equality doctrine in the area of sex discrimination law, as in race discrimination issues, has disclosed the nondeterminative nature of that doctrine. Westen, in a critique of equality theory as "empty," has observed that the concept does not in itself define norms, and that it becomes meaningful only as it is informed or completed by a normative imagination.[35] That reality, perhaps most dramatically manifested in the changed conceptions of "equality" reflected in the process from *Plessy v. Ferguson*[36] to *Brown v. Board of Education*,[37] has also been exemplified in the application of equality theory to issues of sex discrimination.

The invocation of "equal rights" for women has proven no less problematic than was its invocation as a remedy for race discrimination in the "separate, but equal" period. While it has been intended to encourage a movement away from biologistic, "anatomy-is-destiny" assumptions surrounding gender differentiation, in fact equality theory has not successfully facilitated such a movement. The reason for this failure resides in the fact that the public imagination has failed to contribute "legal meaning" to equality doctrine by reason of its failure to articulate a coherent normative definition of the nature of sexual or gender difference.

The "emptiness" of the equality concept becomes clear when we consider that while "equality theory" can be understood as requiring the equal treatment, without regard to gender, of equally positioned persons, it does not by itself define the degree to which the sexes can properly be viewed as "equally positioned"—that is, it does not answer the question: to what extent should public policy adopt a perspective of "gender blindness." The deficit in informing imagination has been apparent in both adjudication and legislation. The United States Supreme Court's attempts to define the issue have been widely critiqued as reductionist and inadequate."[38] Congressional and state legislative acts based on "equal' rights" theories disclose, in their legislative histories and in their applications, a dependence upon uncertain, confused, and often contradictory notions of the extent to which gender differences should be regarded either as natural or as cultural.[39]

While the underlying uncertainties and contradictions operative in adjudication and in legislation are not entirely surprising, it has been striking and problematic to find similarly confused and contradictory approaches articulated in contributions to "feminist jurisprudence." In their efforts to fill the "empty vessel" of equality theory, feminist writers have expressed profoundly divided and divisive visions of the reality of sexual difference. Unsurprisingly, these divisions have been particularly apparent in discussions of the law's treatment of pregnancy. The phenomenon of pregnancy has posed particular challenges to equality theory for two reasons: first, it is the apparent capacity for pregnancy (past, present, or future), suggested by the external genitalia, that "marks" particular bodies as "female" from the point of their entrance into the human community; and second, it is in the actuality of pregnancy that the female body seems least "the same" or "to be treated the same" as that of the male. Thus, the potentiality and actuality of pregnancy pose for equality theory directly and unavoidably, two fundamental issues: (1) to what degree sex differences are natural and necessary and to what degree they are cultural and susceptible to change; and (2) whether the realities of pregnancy and childbirth establish a basis for non-invidious discrimination on the basis of sex or gender.

These are difficult questions. They have been addressed by recent feminist jurisprudence and have received conflicting and contradictory answers.[40] The division within feminist legal theory over the fundamental issue of how to think about sexual difference appears at this point so profound as to preclude the possibility of feminism achieving the kind of normative organization that might facilitate broad and deeply significant change affecting the status of women. It becomes urgent at this time to examine and to define the inadequacies of equality theory—on its face and as applied—and to inquire whether other concepts may be invoked to mediate the divisions, or to undo the paradoxes, implicated in "equal right" formulations.

At present, there appear to be three major threads in feminist equality jurisprudence, each defining its own particular pattern in elaboration on the nature of sexual difference and sexual equality. Each of these threads of legal discourse is worked upon the larger fabric of American feminist writing according to designs defined by the philosophical presuppositions of American political and social theory. These major lines have been extensively discussed in recent years. I have defined these three as the "assimilationist," the "respect-for-differences," and the "limited-differences" models.[41] I sketch out in the following subsections a simple account of each.

A. Assimilationism — the "Sameness" Model

Early in the present stage of the American women's movement, well-developed formulations appeared urging the application of equal rights theory to sex discrimination issues. The "assimilationist" position that characterized those formulations became visible in stances taken by the advocates of the Equal Rights Amendment in the 1970s.[42] The "assimilationist" model, it has been suggested, amounted to the position that there are no real, significant, or important differences between females and males. While that formulation may, to some degree, overstate the position, it is certainly true that assimilationist doctrine placed no significant emphasis on "real, biological" differences between the sexes, and made no attempt to provide explicitly for differential treatment of those differences by the law. As noted above, the reasons for invoking this model probably lay, in part, in the promise that the "equal rights" approach seemed to have offered in the movement for civil rights for Blacks.

The "egalitarian" doctrine embodied in the assimilationist approach can be viewed as valorizing the achievement of a "gender-blind" society. This model of sexual equality, thus, resembles the model of racial equality that advocates a "color-blind" society.[43]

Perhaps the chief exponent of the assimilationist model has been Wendy W. Williams. Williams has made major contributions to both American feminist jurisprudential theory and sex discrimination litigation, and has advocated an assimilationist approach in both contexts.[44] Her adoption and development of that position have been supported by her deeply-rooted wariness, based on outcomes of earlier "protective legislation," of schemes that purport to treat the sexes differently in order to protect women.[45] Williams and other exponents of the assimilationist model tend to believe that the harm done by continuing and contributing to stereotypes that define women as more vulnerable and weak than men will always outweigh any possible immediate, short-term benefits to particular women.

While assimilationism has been applied to achieve favorable results for women in a number of major title VII cases,[46] its recent invocation in pregnancy disability cases in California and Montana[47] has brought to the surface some significant dissatisfaction with the model, tied precisely to its avoidance of the "real, biological" differences alluded to above. The dissatisfaction of some American feminist theorists with the "equal rights" approach, so evident in the California and Montana cases, has been apparent in the evolution by feminist jurisprudence of two models other than the "egalitarian-feminist" one. Both these other models are rather more radical than assimilationism in their rejection of what they see as a male standard implicitly adopted by that model. They differ from assimilationism, urging explicit legal recognition of what they perceive as peculiarly female realities.

B. The "Respect-for-Differences" Model

An approach very different from that of the assimilationists has been articulated by Elizabeth Wolgast,[48] and has most recently found support in the increasingly well-known work of Carol Gilligan.[49] Essentially, this approach recognizes the reality of certain habits or ways of being—natural or culturally ingrained—

that tend, on the average, to distinguish men from women. In Wolgast's view, the two sexes have different "strengths, virtues, distinctive tendencies and weaknesses, neither being fully assimilable to the other...," and the proper role of law is to value and protect these differences.[50] Wolgast argues that "egalitarianism leads to sexual uniformity and this means the suppression of whatever does not conform to some neutral or masculine norm."[51] She finds implicit in the egalitarian perspective a devaluing of "whatever marks a female as uniquely female" (e.g., pregnancy and childbirth), and argues that that devaluation will have strong negative consequences for the whole society.[52] While not insistent that sexual differences in behavior are biologically (rather than culturally) based Wolgast does not discount the possibility that they may be. She proposes, for example, alluding to the perennially plaguing mind-body problem of philosophy, that perhaps the differences between male- and female-sexed bodies imply the reality of deeper and more profound (other than purely physical) sexual differences.[53]

Carol Gilligan has advanced, on the basis of empirical data, a definition and interpretation of certain differences in thought and in moral development that appear to distinguish women from men.[54] Gilligan has argued that the theory of moral development stated by Lawrence Kohlberg (and anticipated by Erikson and by Freud) devalues female thought and moral judgment by its implicit adoption of a male standard against which female experience is measured.[55] Gilligan has proposed that different types of "reasoning" characterize males in general and females in general.[56] The predominant "male" mode, referred to as "justice reasoning," is distinguishable from the 'care reasoning" characteristic of females.[57] While both modes exist and operate in both sexes, Gilligan proposes that the "reasoning" one is more preferred by males, and the "care" mode more preferred by females.[58]

Gilligan proposes that the dominance of apparently objective, neutrality-referent, "masculine" moral judgment in our culture—particularly evident in legal reasoning—has caused the "voice" of the "feminine" mode to be silenced or unheard as a public voice.[59] Her work departs from that of predecessor developmental theorists in proposing as a model of high moral development a full integration and expression of modes of thought and judgment traditionally regarded and devalued as "feminine." Gilligan proposes that our public ethic is inadequate to the degree that it fails to include and value the "feminine" perspectives of care and responsibility.[60] Gilligan's work can be regarded as "fleshing-out" the Wolgast "respect-for-differences" approach by its clear definition of certain attributes, modes of thought, and decision-making that characteristically mark one or the other sex, and by its advocacy of a stronger sounding of the "feminine" themes of care and responsibility within the general discourse.

It should be noted that Gilligan's work, like that of other major American psychologists addressing issues of gender differentiation and gender inequality—most notably, Nancy Chodorow[61] and Dorothy Dinnerstein[62]—is located within the parameters of the "ego psychology" that has dominated the American elaboration of psychological developmental theory. That work generally speaks with some confidence about the possibilities for individual movement out of stereotyping strictures that have been imposed by our culture on the basis of biology. Chodorow and Dinnerstein propose that significant change may occur when ink ants and young children begin to be cared for equally by members of both sexes, rather than exclusively or predominantly by females.[63] Gilligan appears less clear about how change might be elected to permit the clearer sounding of the "different" voice. All three focus, in their analyses, on the dynamics of individual families. While all have speculated about the ramifications of the processes which devalue "feminine" experience, none has explicitly extended her analysis to question whether that operation silences other "different" voices; more precisely, none has defined the "feminine" as including *ipso facto* the members of all non-dominant social groups.[64]

The clear implication of Gilligan's work, like that of Wolgast, is that our public policy should operate to protect the "different" features characteristic of "feminine," generally female, expression, without regard to whether those differences originate in biology or in culture. Recent writing by Nel Noddings,[65] which I see as strongly reiterating Gilligan's themes and as falling within the large "respect-for-differences" category, has attempted to undo some of the contradictions inherent in all the "equal rights" theories by replacing those formulations with a variation of the "responsibility" or "care" model of moral judgment described by Gilligan.

C. The "Limited-Differences" Model

A third model of equality theory, which departs from both the assimilationist and the "respect for differences" models discussed above, has been articulated most clearly by Sylvia Law.[66] Law's sympathy for the suspicion of "protective legislation" expressed by Williams[67] leads her to steer away from policies that would reinforce stifling stereotypes, and therefore, precludes her support for any broad "respect-for-differences" policy. On the other hand, Law levels against the pure assimilationist model the criticism that it is reductive and simplistic. She notes:

> [T]he reality of sex-based physical difference poses a significant problem for a society committed to ideals of individual human freedom and equality of opportunity. To the extent that constitutional doctrine shapes culture and individual identity, an equality doctrine that denies the reality of biological difference in relation to reproduction reflects an idea about personhood that is inconsistent with people's actual experience of themselves and the world.[68]

As an alternative to either of the two models already discussed, Law proposes a principle that would recognize and provide for the "limited differences" defined by the biological differences relating to reproduction. She urges:

> Laws governing reproductive biology should be scrutinized by courts to ensure that (1) the law has no significant impact in perpetuating either the oppression of women or culturally imposed sex-role constraints on individual freedom, or (2) if the law has this impact, it is justified as the best means of serving a compelling state purpose. Given how central state regulation of biology has been to the subjugation of women, the normal presumption of constitutionality is inappropriate and the state should bear the burden of justifying its rule in relation to either proposition.[69]

II. NORMATIVE AND NARRATIVE FAILURES OF EQUALITY THEORY

In assessing the variations of equality theory discussed above, I take as my standard for measurement the degree to which each model might facilitate movement toward a more broadly integrated society in which women would no longer occupy or be allocated to marginal status. I posit that any such movement, which might create a new "legal meaning" for the doctrine of equality in the area of sex discrimination, would presume that feminism has articulated a nomos and an underlying, sustaining narrative supportive of that nomos.[70] Thus, my critique inquires into the adequacy of equality theory to the task of creating legal meaning.

The advocates of each of the three models discussed above have propounded their theories with full awareness of the other positions being advanced. Thus, some of the limitations of each theory have been pointed out by proponents of competing theories. The "assimilationist" model, for example, has been stringently criticized for its failure to take account of and provide for the reality of biological differences between the sexes. As noted above, the model has been characterized as reductionist and simplistic in its failure to respect—in every sense of that word—those differences.[71] Sylvia Law's indictment of the model sums up the nature of the criticisms generally leveled. That criticism takes as a "given" the reality of biological differences apparent in pregnancy and in childbirth.

As noted above, the division of feminist commentary surrounding two major pregnancy disability cases that reached the United States Supreme Court docket in 1986 and 1987[72] pointed up the inability of the assimilationist model either to generate feminist consensus or to persuade a reluctant judiciary. In those cases, the egalitarians, unwilling to accord "preferential" treatment to pregnant employees on the basis of a biological difference, did not support the positions advanced by a number of groups representative of large numbers of female employees.[73] While the egalitarians were not hostile to the provision of pregnancy disability leave by state statutes, they found themselves unable to consistently support such benefits except within a framework extending disability leave benefits to all workers for all types of physical disabilities. That position demanded a broad judicial ruling mandating extension of benefits.[74] It did not prove persuasive in *Guerra*, where the Court's ruling was limited to a parsing of the language of possibly contradictory federal and state statutory provisions.[75]

Stated most succinctly, the egalitarian approach has struck many women as involving a denial or rejection of the particular realities of pregnancy and childbirth, and for that reason has tended to exclude from its normative universe persons who have valued those experiences. Beyond its failure to provide for the specific biological differences characterizing women and men, the assimilationist model, it has been suggested, effectively sets up a male standard and advantages women only to the degree that they approximate a male norm.[76] In its imaginary construction of a society in which the roles of women and men would be indistinguishable, assimilationist theory fails to resonate with the full range of women's experience, which includes both memories and expectations of pleasure in functions unique to women. The society implied by the assimilationist model seems to some women to broaden, as well as to echo, the notion that "the two shall be as one" and that the "one" shall be male.[77]

Like assimilationist theory, the "respect-for-differences" model has also been widely criticized within feminist juris-prudence, most strenuously by those who see that model as encouraging a return to old, fettering stereotypes.[78] While Wolgast has argued that law which does not protect broad differences between the sexes will operate to devalue those differences, critics see her proposals as inviting valuations of men and women based upon their manifesting particular behaviors that may bear little relationship to their true poten-tialities.[79] Gilligan's account of "masculine" and "feminine" modes of thought and of moral judgment, and her valuation of an ethic of "responsibility" or "caring"—characterized as "feminine"—has been criticized for its failure to inquire whether the "caring" behavior, to which she attaches high value, may in fact be a behavior learned through the experience of subor-dination.[80] It is suggested that Gilligan's exoneration of that "feminine" mode may encourage women to value the dominated status that gives rise to the behavior. Further, the assumptions underlying this model may be susceptible to criticism for the relative superficiality and naive optimism of the ego psychology theory which they express.[81]

Sylvia Law's "limited differences" model has been subjected to criticisms similar to those raised against the broader "differences" theories. The advocates of assimilationism have been persuaded that a model that limits protection to the "real, biological" differences characterizing women might have the same negative effects as the models advocating protection of broad differences. They believe that the "limited differences" model would contribute to a perpetuation of the stereotyping of women, and to an overvaluation of pregnancy and maternity that, in the long run, would cut back on any progress which may have been made in gaining recognition of women's capacities for participation in a full range of public activity.[82]

The colloquy about equality theory, thus, is clearly beset with contradiction, uncertainty, and paradox. The advocates of the various theories appear, additionally, to be locked in a situation where no clear common exit exists. It appears that on the question of sexual difference there is an utter lack of "nomos" in feminist jurisprudence, and no indication that equality theory is adequate to the task of creating "legal meaning."

Robert Cover has extensively discussed the process of creation of legal meaning, examining the "jurisgenerative" operations of norm-forming groups.[83] Cover has seen in the American women's movement an attempt at "redemptive Constitutionalism," aspiring to deep transformations consistent with a vision of gender justice.[84] He has proposed that the process of creating new legal meaning depends upon a sustaining narrative that permits the objectification of values to which redemptive groups commit themselves.[85] That narrative defines both the vision of the jurisgenerative group and the place of the group in the work of making the alternative world real, something other than merely utopian.[86] Cover has also discussed the role of law within the tension that operates between reality and vision.

> By themselves, the alternative worlds of our vision—the lion lying down with the lamb, the creditor forgiving debts each seventh year, the state all shrivelled and withered away—dictate no particular set of transformations or efforts at transformation. But law gives a vision depth of field, by placing one part of it in the highlight of insistent and immediate demand while casting another part in the shadow of the millennium.[87]

The question arises at this point whether there exists any body of narrative—of the kind that Cover defines as essential—that could undo the contradictions of equality theory by embodiment of a coherent feminist vision of gender justice.

III. AMERICAN FEMINIST NARRATIVES OF SEXUAL DIFFERENCE

One of the most extraordinary aspects of the current women's movement is its having given birth over the last twenty-five years to a powerful body of varied and original writing in almost every traditional discipline. In philosophy,[88] theology,[89] science,[90] social science,[91] literary criticism,[92] poetry,[93] and the novel, female writers have "broken silence." They have done pioneering work in exploring central female experiences, and in structuring forms and styles most suited to those explorations. The writers discussed in the foregoing sections have been, to varying degrees, influenced by those broad developments of feminist thought. Indeed, the emergence of feminist jurisprudence during the last several years can be characterized as an extension of the engagement of female reflection and speech to one more area of discourse. The question thus arises whether there exists—anywhere in American feminist thought—narrative that tells the story of women in our present culture in a way that is persuasive and compelling; in a way that defines an equilibrium of the sexes to whose validity or desirability women might consent so unequivocally as to provide the basis for political activity capable of effecting significant change.

If wealth of narrative by itself were sufficient to establish nomos, one would certainly not expect to find in feminist jurisprudence the division discussed in the preceding sections. However, an examination of feminist writing discloses that the broad body of thought has by no means escaped ambivalence and apparent contradiction on the precise issues that have thwarted feminist jurisprudence. And even in those areas where feminist thought has disentangled itself to some degree from the paradoxes of liberalism, it has not done so in ways that might facilitate an interweaving of narrative and nomos. Specifically, I propose that there has been an absence—or an aborted development—in American feminist thought of the kind of epistemological inquiry which might define the soundness and legitimacy of the critical base upon which feminism poises itself.

Division within non-jurisprudential feminist thought on issues of gender differentiation has received much commentary within feminist literature. Divisions on the question of female identity and on the valuation to be attached to uniquely female functions and activities have been particularly noted.[94] Those divisions in colloquy parallel the divisions among liberal legal equality theorists. At one end of the range of general feminist theory are voices, that, echoing those of assimilationist legal theorists, seem to deny or to devalue female uniqueness; at another extreme are voices that claim an essentialist and superior female culture, and support a separatist distancing from dominant norms.[95]

Recognizing those internal contradictions within feminist thought, some writers have attempted to avoid or to undo them. Their attempt has involved two parts: first, an affirmation of those aspects of femaleness traditionally characterized as negativities; and, second, an attempt to infuse that potentially transformative voice of affirmation into the public discourse of the culture. Women's poetry of the last two decades has embodied particularly striking instances of this kind of writing.[96]

While women's writing has been successful in its strong affirmation of traditionally devalued female realities, it has been much less successful in extending its affirmative voice into the dominant public register. Indeed, while much women's writing appears to be of precisely the sort that might be "world-creating" in Cover's sense, it has often been marked by features that frustrate attempts to transpose it into the common discourse of the law. These themes have been discussed in depth in literary theory, and limitation of space precludes any extensive discussion here. They include, however, the articulation by women's literature of a notion of "self" as fluid or divided; an articulation of various "selves," all of which claim female identity—for example, selves that are heterosexual, lesbian, or asexual; and an articulation whose imagery is highly implicated with female bodily reality.[97]

These features establish obvious obstacles to the incorporation of feminist theory into common public speech—barriers which neither American feminist thought in general nor feminist jurisprudence in particular have yet overcome. The notion of "self" or "selves" expressed in feminist literature, for example, appears utterly at odds with the notions of individual autonomy and personhood valued as fundamental in the liberal legal tradition. And the "body language" characteristic of women's writing cannot easily be transposed into a public discourse in which the ostensibly neutral terminologies of science and medicine prevail. The assertions and affirmations embodied in feminist writing seem best definable as counter-narratives to the dominant narrative. Feminism, at this point, finds itself in a troubled position that seems implicated in relativism and skepticism. That is, feminism seems unable to support its counter-narratives with any truth-claim stronger than the claim of the narrative that it has confronted and exposed. Feminism has not succeeded in shaping its counter-narrative as an affirmative narrative.

I believe that it is the concern to avoid being stranded or lost in relativism that has led most feminist jurisprudence to commit itself to the structure of discourse defined by dominant liberal ideology. That commitment to liberalism may have initially allowed some appearance of objectivity and some credibility based on that appearance. At the same time, however, it has entailed a failure to translate into that master language the strongest world-creating features of feminist thought. At this time, the contradictions which have arisen from that commitment make clear that the concept of equality reified within the dominant legal language cannot do justice to the varieties of female experience. At this impasse, it seems to me, the alternatives are a return to public silence, or such a restructuring of the house of legal liberalism as will permit the narratives told in feminist "rooms of our own"[98] to be heard in the common areas.

The effort of alteration and restructuring is one at which feminist writers have begun to labor. The task has been well defined as that of creating a new "common language."[99]   Olga Broumas, for example, has written of the urgency of that work:

> I am a woman committed to
> a politics
> of
> transliteration...
> like amnesiacs
> in a ward on fire, we must
> find words
> or burn.[100]

The pressing task for feminist jurisprudence at this time is the task of transliteration. That task poses great difficulty. For jurisprudence, as for feminist thought in general, the nature of the labor is definable—the birthing of a different and world-creating language. But the process by which that transliterative effort will be accomplished remains uncertain. While feminist theory may recognize the need to "find words" that will be heard, it is uncertain how a new and powerful common discourse will take shape—language at once true to female realities and able to withstand motions to dismiss it as "merely" female.

The present stage of feminism's long labor is ill-defined by the confusions of liberal theory. Exhausted by uncertainty and division, feminism appears, from some perspectives, incapable of transition into a stage of greater coherence, greater energy, and greater promise.

IV.   POSTSTRUCTURALIST PERSPECTIVES ON GENDER DIFFERENTIATION

The inability of feminist narrative, thus far, to generate a coherent nomos raises the question whether other narratives may offer more promise in their treatment of sexual differentiation. This article is written in the belief that European critical theory, particularly as exemplified in the work of Michel Foucault[101] and the post-Lacanian writings of Julia Kristeva,[102] constitutes a "counter-narrative" that is immediately and precisely pertinent to the present crisis in feminist theory and action. I propose that poststructuralist theory, with its focus on the general question of differentiation and on the particular issue of gender differentiation, is uniquely capable of supporting the nomos of resistance and reformation presently undeveloped in feminism and in other liberation movements.

The field of American feminist jurisprudence has not been totally occupied by liberal theorists, and the influence of European critical theory has begun to be apparent in the work of certain American legal scholars who have directly confronted the contradictions to which equality theory and other liberal legal doctrines have given rise. These writers have explicitly taken their own bearings and have more or less precisely positioned their work in relation to liberalism, in relation to American and European feminist theory in general, and in relation to poststructuralist critical theory. While some of this work is vaguely Marxist in approach, other writings are clearly deconstructive in methodology and in implication;[103] still other work can be characterized as reconstructive in the sense defined by current hermeneutic theory.[104] Both approaches have advanced the discourse of feminist jurisprudence away from the silence—or the frustrating contradiction—characteristic of equality discourse.

These writings vary greatly in the degree of their direct engagement with larger critical theory. They have in common, however, several features consistent with poststructuralist perspectives. These include: (1) an insistent naming of the underlying contradiction and arbitrariness of liberal ideology; (2) a precise accounting of the differential, material injuries imposed upon women and men by that ideology; (3) a willingness to name their own perspective as feminine; and (4) a recognition that turning away from ideology necessitates grappling with foundational issues, which have barely begun to be addressed by jurisprudential theory.

Variation among these writers is apparent in the degree to which their work clearly spells out its own implications about what we can know. Another way of expressing that is to say that these writers differ from one another in their definitions of the limit points beyond which they will cease to ask questions of differentiation.

Recognizing that it has become impossible for feminism to rest on the contradictions of equality theory, I believe that it is equally impossible to rest on Jocasta's advice to "inquire no further."[105] I am convinced that feminist theorists concerned to state a clear validity-claim for women's voices have no alternative except to press their inquiry to its most extreme limits. I am also persuaded that poststructuralist critical theory offers to feminism the possibility of an engagement in which movement in that direction becomes possible.

As is well known, structuralism and poststructuralism refer to the major European philosophical and literary process, which, over the last two decades, has evolved a profoundly critical theory across a broad range of disciplinary and interdisciplinary endeavors. John Sturrock has proposed that the critical identifying feature of all work properly classified as structuralist or poststructuralist is that it takes as its foundation the theoretical work of the Swiss linguist Ferdinand de Saussure (1857–1913).[106] Certainly even superficial reading discloses a thorough preoccupation with linguistic theory in the major writings of structuralism and poststructuralism, as well as in their texts precedent: in the work of Marcel Mauss[107] and Claude Levi-Strauss[108] in structural anthropology; in that of Roman Jakobson,[109] Jacques Derrida,[110] and Roland Barthes[111] in philology and semiotics; in that of Freud[112] and Lacan[113] in psychoanalysis; in the work of Michel Foucault[114] and Julia Kristeva[115] in critical theory relating to all those human sciences.

While classifications of European critical theory as structuralist or as poststructuralist tend to be loosely made, it can perhaps be generally asserted that poststructuralism is distinguished from structuralism by virtue of its critique of metaphysical tendencies—whether latent or clearly apparent—in structuralist theory. Structuralist work, such as that of Lacan, and poststructuralist contribution, such as that of Foucault, Derrida, and Kristeva, have relevance for the contradictory and internally divided state of liberal social and jurisprudential theory. Both confront and address fundamental issues of the limits and constraints of knowledge, asking the following question: What is possible in linguistic and cultural structuring? Poststructuralism, however, more assiduously attempts to avoid metaphysics, while at the same time saying whatever can be said of the structures of culture and of language.

The remainder of this article will focus on certain themes in the writings of Foucault and Kristeva, whose poststructuralist theoretical work may have the most immediately apparent implications for liberal jurisprudence in general and for feminist jurisprudence in particular. I will focus primarily on those features of their work that manifest their approach to fundamental issues of differentiation—including gender differentiation—that liberal theory has been unable to treat with adequacy.

A. Michel Foucault: Inquiry into "Other-ness"

In the work of both Foucault and Kristeva, a focus on language motivates inquiry into what the "privileged discourses" of psychoanalysis, ethnology, and linguistics can disclose about epistemological possibilities—the conditions and limits of knowing.[116] Among Foucault's major themes is his notion that operation within a particular structure of discourse permits certain kinds of "truth," while utterly precluding others.[117] Foucault's methodology involving detailed and precise examinations of the structures of institutions within discrete historical periods, supports his argument that there is nothing essentially "true" about the classification systems according to which modern societies operate. What in fact gives those classifications their stability and endurance is not any intrinsic truth value, but rather, the operation of power Foucault argues that we are subjected to the production of truth through power, and that we cannot exercise power except through the production of truth.[118]

Much of Foucault's work is devoted precisely to articulating the relationship of truth to power. He argues that in modern societies the control and discipline of populations takes place through the sanctioning of the knowledge-claims and practices of the human sciences. Foucault sees the human sciences (biology, economics, philology, psychoanalytic theory, ethnology) as creating a structure, which defines normality and *ipso facto* defines for surveillance and control the area of deviation. In his view the claim of the human sciences to superior knowledge and expertise, and the general acceptance of that claim, are the conditions that have made possible the particular pattern of domination characteristic of this era, a pattern which Foucault discloses in his expositions of the development of the prison;[119] the development of the medical clinic;[120] the history of the treatment of madness;[121] and the history of discourse relating to sexuality.[122] Necessarily implied in that pattern of domination is the adoption by the modern human sciences of a posture that has allowed an objectification of "man."

The methodology utilized by Foucault involves a focus on members of non-dominant, deviant groups—on the "Other." He defines his work as "a history of the Other,...of that which, for a given culture, is at once interior and foreign....whereas the history of the order imposed on things would be the history of the Same.[123] In Investigating the "Other-ness" embodied in individuals designated as "criminal," "mad," or "sexually deviant," Foucault rejects the claims to superior authority of the "master narratives" enunciated through the human sciences. This is apparent throughout Foucault's work, but most dramatically, perhaps, in *I, Pierre Riviere*,[124] in which Foucault gives an account of a multiple murder through the voice and perspective of the murderer, as well as through those of various professional observers—lawyers, doctors, and psychiatrists. The claim that is clearly asserted by that work is that there is no authoritative meta-narrative; that, in fact, every stated narrative is subject to interpretation and demystification by other narratives; and that, particularly, the master narratives of a culture are susceptible to the challenge and resistance expressed by first person narratives in the voices of individual subjects, narratives that the master discourse silences by defining them as lacking validity.

The nature of the "subject" as in some sense unbounded—that is, as perhaps better defined in terms of process than as a fixed, whole, separate, and contained entity—has been highly developed in structuralist work in psychoanalytic theory, ethnology (structural anthropology), and linguistic theory.[125] Foucault and other poststructuralists regard these three as "privileged" among the human sciences in their ability to shed new light on the nature of the "subject,"

Foucault characterizes both psychoanalysis and ethnology as distinctive for the reason that they operate on the "perpetual principle of dissatisfaction, of calling into question, of criticism and contestation of what may seem, in other respects, to be established.[126] Psychoanalysis is singularly critical because of its unique relationship to the unconscious. Foucault suggests that because it takes the unconscious as its object, psychoanalysis directly encounters the questions of language and of meaning, "the relation of representation and finitude."[127] In its direct and deliberate movement toward what is by definition unrepresentable, Foucault proposes that psychoanalysis reveals that the very possibility of representation arises in the realities of death, of desire, and of "a language which is at the same time Law."[128]

That is to say, psychoanalytic theory discovers, in the relationship of transference, that objective meaning and language arise out of the experiences of loss and separation, and that language itself constitutes a structure that the subject cannot control. Death, desire, and the law-language are, thus, the "forms of finitude"[129] that define the transference relation.

What psychoanalysis is to the human subject, ethnology is to human culture. Ethnology spans the whole region of knowledge available through the other human sciences, and moves towards the "boundaries" of knowledge. Its singular scope derives from the unique historical sovereignty of European thought and the posture which allows that thought to come "face to face with all other cultures as well as with itself."[130] This position allows ethnology to break out of the "circular system of actions and reactions proper to historicism."[131] The knowledge made possible because of the relation of Western rational thought to other cultures goes beyond the historic account which people of any culture may give of themselves and pierces through such self-representations to uncover norms and rules.

Foucault's position, as suggested above, is profoundly skeptical, and he cautions that the valorized positions of psychoanalytical theory and ethnology do not imply that either is able to offer any "pure speculative knowledge or a general theory of Man."[132] Indeed, psychoanalytic theory is not concerned, ultimately with "Man," but with the conditions that make "Man" possible. Movement toward that original ground is in fact movement toward the end of Man, and "nothing is more alien to psychoanalysis than anything resembling a general theory of man or of anthropology."[133] While psychoanalysis may bring to consciousness—through transference—the affects that surround the human experiences of separation and loss, and may inscribe those experiences into language, neither psychoanalysis nor the language to which it gives rise can ever exhaust the reality of those experiences.

Psychoanalysis and ethnology are defined as "counter-sciences" relative to the other human sciences. Because of their boundary-reaching natures, they lead the other sciences "back to their epistemological basis and...ceaselessly 'unmake' that very Man who is creating and recreating his positivity in the human sciences."[134]

Linguistic theory, in Foucault's view, complements psychoanalysis and ethnology as a third "privileged" counter-science.

Further, it presents itself as a possible linkage between ethnology and psychoanalysis.[135] The area of intersection of linguistic theory with psychoanalysis and with ethnology has been extensively explored and mapped by Julia Kristeva and will be discussed in the following subsection. Before moving to that discussion, however, I wish to consider some of the implications of Foucault's writing for American feminist theory.

Foucault's work is clearly deconstructive and iconoclastic, rather than positive or reconstructive, in intent as well as in method. He speaks of "restoring to our silent and apparently immobile soil its rifts, its instabilities, its flaws."[136] In attacking the "totalizing discourses" or narratives, Foucault intends a rupturing, which will permit a rediscovery of fragmented, subjugated, local and specific knowledges.[137] He nowhere suggests that his own work, or the voices that may surface through the ruptures, will articulate a new and more satisfactory "grand theory," but he does suggest that the space opened up by the ruptures will allow for the emergence of resistance by those oppressed by the master discourse.

While Foucault's work is, of course, susceptible to the criticism that his own discourse can have no knowledge-claim superior to those of the "master" discourses that he challenges, it is by no means the case that Foucault's work implies the kind of relativistic stance that would deny validity to political action. On the contrary, what Foucault argues for, and exemplifies, is the entry of competing voices into the arena of discourse. While Foucault's work has not concentrated primarily on the specific issue of female subjection, his focus on the "Other" both models and supports the silence-breaking in which feminist writers in Europe and America have been engaged during the last twenty years—the "Other" to which Foucault refers being always that which might oppose the inherently unstable and ultimately vanishing fiction of the rational, whole, unified, and normal modern Man. Foucault's peculiarly European challenge to the "essentiality" of categories or classifications opens an area of discourse much broader than the one within which the American liberal theory discussed in the preceding sections has taken shape. To be persuaded by Foucault's work is to recognize a demystification of power—something which liberation movements, including feminism, welcome. At the same time, however, it is to recognize a demystification of truth, including the truth defined by those same movements. Foucault forces a confrontation with the proposition that the operation of power may always implicate the differentiation and oppression of some "Other" by the force of a dominant discourse—a proposition that must challenge the self-definitions of feminist, as well as other purported liberation movements.

It is my belief that that challenge to its self-definition is one that feminism must meet, and that engagement with that challenge opens up new possibilities that can move feminism—and feminist jurisprudence—from its present, critically threatened position. The strength and freedom that a feminism—or even a "post-feminism"[138]—derives from poststructuralist perspectives is particularly apparent in the work of Julia Kristeva.

B. Julia Kristeva: Explorations of Feminist "Otherness"

The writings of Julia Kristeva may manifest, more than any other, the degree to which post-metaphysical structuralism offers to the peculiarly feminist voice of the "Other" a public space and a place of a kind unavailable within the structure of American political and social theory. Sharing the common structuralist (and peculiarly Lacanian) preoccupation with language and meaning, Kristeva's work has included psychoanalytic, ethnological, and linguistic themes, and has recast these concerns into a unified research by exploring the relationships among them.

Kristeva's "Other" advances the "gynesis"[139] characteristic of much structuralist and poststructuralist thought; that is, she figures the "Other" as peculiarly "feminine." That notion of "feminine" does not restrict itself to definition of only that which is biologically female, but includes all that has been defined by the dominant Western, white male culture as "Other." Nonetheless, it implies recognition that whatever has been silenced as "Other" has been taken to be in some sense "feminine." Thus Kristeva's work represents a striking instance of the intermingling of feminist and poststructuralist concerns. The immediacy of its relevance for liberal feminist jurisprudence is apparent not only in its concern with those silences by the master discourse, but also in its particular inquiry into the motivation and conditions of the oppression of women, and its pressing exploration of the structure, conditions, and alterability of gender differentiation.

The focus of most of Kristeva's work is what she defines as "analytical semiology," an inquiry into the signifying process.[140] The methodology of that research involves inquiry into the "speaking subject" of Saussure and of Lacan as it emerges through "Other-ness." Resembling Foucault in her attentiveness to "Other" discourses, Kristeva shares Foucault's skepticism concerning the possibility of a totalizing discourse or a "master narrative." Writing of her inquiries into the "Other" language manifested in art and literature, Kristeva observes:

> [While] no belief in an all-powerful theory is tenable, there remains the necessity to pay attention to the ability to deal with the desire for language, and by this I mean paying attention...to the art and literature of our time, which remain alone, in our world of technological rationality, to impel us not toward the absolute but toward a quest for a little more truth, an impossible truth, concerning the meaning of speech concerning our condition as speaking beings.[141]

While eschewing any totalizing discourse, Kristeva affirms the possibility of an ethic. Reflecting upon observations made in psychoanalytic practice, she expresses the conviction:

> [If] the overly constraining and reductive meaning of a language made up of universals causes us to suffer, the call of the unnameable, on the contrary, issuing from those borders where signification vanishes, hurls us into the void of a psychosis.... Within that vise, our only chance to avoid being neither master nor slave of meaning lies in our ability to insure our mastery of it (through technique or knowledge) as well as our passage through it (through play or practice).[142]

Kristeva's work is complex and profound, and obviously cannot be treated fully in this article. I would like, however, for purposes of bringing home her relevance for American feminism—and for American jurisprudence—to focus on three central themes, which, I think, are closely related to the themes of American feminist literature discussed above in section III. These are Kristeva's notion of the "speaking subject," her recognition of the validity of a language rooted in the body, and her rejection of female "essentialism." I believe that these central Kristevan themes relate to American feminist literature's reference to a "self" that is fluid or divided,[143] its strong attachment to female bodily imagery,[144] and its inclusion of different and varying voices all claiming identity as "female."[145] Focus on these three themes will, I believe, at once establish their resemblance to those of American feminist writing and manifest the way in which the peculiarly poststructuralist cast of Kristeva's work operates to make its truth-claim cognizable.

1. The "Self" and the "Subject" Like Lacan, Kristeva has taken up in her work the task of weaving together the fibers of psychoanalytic theory and of linguistic theory. Like Lacan, Kristeva expatiates upon "Other-ness," giving that concept a peculiarly "feminine" characterization.[146] Central to Kristeva's integration of psychoanalytic, ethnological, and linguistic theory is an inquiry into the psychoanalytic, ethnological and linguistic structures that make culture possible, an inquiry implicating the concept of the "speaking subject."

Kristeva follows Lacan in the effort to restore to psychoanalytic theory—through a profound reading of Freud—a radical concept of the Unconscious, recognizing the strength, uncontrollability, and subversive power of the Unconscious over the Ego. The notion of the "subject" becomes central in that restoration. Kristeva, like other structuralists, sees the human being as "always, already" implicated in intersubjectivity by virtue of implication in language. Thus, she rejects concepts of "ego" and "self," which carry connotations of autonomy, atomistic individuality, and separateness that belie the reality of intersubjective experience.[147]

The notion of the "subject" is intended to refer to a being that is maintained only through interactive exchanges within a social order. The "subject" is decentered, in that its coherence is continually vulnerable to disturbance or undermining by the Unconscious. It comes into being at the juncture of the Unconscious with the social linguistic structure. Like that of Lacan, Kristeva's "subject" is distinct from the ego, and is definable as "whoever is speaking."[148]

This notion of the "subject" is further defined by the Lacanian reworking of the Freudian theory of "Oedipal stage," that period of human development during which the human child achieves "ego formation" through the definition of sexual identity within the family triad that includes the child and both parents.[149] In Lacanian and Kristevan reformulation, interpretation of the "Oedipus complex" departs from the Freudian emphasis on the drama of the individual family, and transposes the theme into a key in which the larger culture is viewed as necessarily and inevitably implicated.

Essentially, the completion of the "subject" is seen as amounting to the child's mastery of—or submission to—the symbolic function. The Oedipal phase is characterized not so much by the child's submitting to the rule of the actual, familial father, but by submission to the "Law" constituted by the social forces that operate to structure the role defined for the "subject." The passage through the Oedipal period involves the child's acquisition of language, as well as the incorporation of the incest taboo. The totality of the surrounding social forces that impose upon the child through the structure of language constitute a "Law," denominated by Lacan as the "Nom-du-Pere."[150] Through continuing participation in linguistic structures, the "subject" internalizes the culture's values. Thus, entry into the symbolic system marks the source of gender identity. Males and females receive their gender identities by the operation of the sociolinguistic conventions imposed by the cultural context.

A key feature of the "subject" is its continuing desire. Desire exists in language, and is made intelligible by reference to the Saussurean distinction between "signifier" and "signified."[151] That distinction emphasizes the non-representational nature of language. That is, it emphasizes that a word (signifier) does not represent a physical entity to which the word is "attached" by a speaker. Rather, the "signified" is in fact a mental process that takes its physical expression in the spoken, or perhaps, written, word. This distinction establishes a gap, a space, a separation— a non-identity of "signifier" and "signified."[152] Desire is the affective experience of that separation, and clearly discloses itself in the transference relationship of psychoanalysis.

The Kristevan notion of "subject," then, bears strong resemblance to the broken, divided, fragmented, or fluid self of feminist writing. Like that "self," the Kristevan "subject" is very different from the free, stable, and autonomous individual presupposed by liberal political and legal theory.[153] The Kristevan "subject," like the feminist "self," resembles a process more nearly than it does a bounded entity. The difference between the "subject" and the "self" of feminist writing is perhaps most clearly understandable as a difference in positioning. While the feminist "self" is comprehensible in the poetic language of feminist literature, it has not been translatable into the public, common discourse. Kristeva's "subject," on the other hand, escapes that limitation, and operates in the public domain of linguistic and psychoanalytic theory. It is the drastic alteration of perspective achieved by the poststructuralist *episteme* that permits entry of that concept of "Other-ness" into the common discourse.

2. Valorization of Language of the Body   The invocation by feminist writing of female bodily imagery has been discussed above in section III. For women writers, reclaiming the value of female bodily experience has been an essential element of the claiming of identity. It has also been observed that particular transliteration problems arise when the attempt is made to formulate in ostensibly objective and neutral public language the insights incorporated in bodily imagery. Kristeva's work manifests an extraordinary success in that attempt. She in fact accomplishes an expansion of the boundaries of her own language such that it is at once thoroughly preoccupied with the most fundamental processes of bodily reality and operative at the highest levels of generality. In an idiom that echoes feminist literature's focus on corporeal reality, Kristeva defines her effort as that of carrying theory "to that point where apparent abstraction is revealed as the apex of...concreteness."[154]

That effort is apparent in many areas of Kristeva's work. Her understanding of gender differentiation as a socio-linguistic, rather than a biological event does not deter her pressing inquiry into the primitive bodily processes, whose regulation gives rise to culture. In *Semiotics of Biblical Abomination*,[155] Kristeva discloses the aversion toward the abjection of the female body operating at the root of the proscriptions set out in *Leviticus* and *Deuteronomy*. Kristeva's analysis uncovers linkages between dietary prohibitions and the fear of incest and undifferentiation, the fear of death, implicated in a vision of female bodies as defiled. In *Stabat Mater*,[156] Kristeva focuses on the peculiarly female bodily experiences of childbirth and maternity. Both those works manifest an expanded relevance that attaches to particularly female concerns by virtue of their elaboration within a post-structuralist modality.

In her inquiry into the phenomena of childbirth and maternity, Kristeva finds occasion for elaboration of the "semiotic" theory—the proposition that the instinctual drives are organized in the context of the mother/child relationship prior to accession to the Symbolic stage (the stage of entry into the dominant linguistic structure). Kristeva further advances the proposition that the experience of maternity, which involves a unique relationship with an "Other" who was once "the Same," might give rise to a new ethic.[157] Beyond that, she locates in the experience of the semiotic relationship of mother and child, an experience accessible in memory to both men and women, a reality of sustenance and of comfort.[158]

Kristeva's theoretical work on the semiotic phase of human development, like her ethnological and linguistic inquiry into the roots of taboo, moves the focus on female bodily experience apparent in feminist literature to a different plane of discourse. Her discourse may be said to "objectify"[159] the valuation of that experience in the sense that it speaks of it in terms as accessible to men as to women. Beyond that, Kristeva's language and focus are broadly inclusive and healing. These strengths, again, depend upon the "rootedness" of her analysis in poststructuralist ground. That "rootedness" enables Kristeva to say things which have not been said in our memories, about the gaps, the differentiations, and the separations that divide and conceal.

3. Avoiding Essentialism: Woman and Women   Reference has been made to a particular problem of liberal feminism—that of establishing the validity of any particular voice or voices in a poly-vocal field. I have suggested that it may well be the concern to escape relativism that has motivated the reduction of radical feminist insight in order to fit it into the narrow shoe of liberal theory.

For Kristeva, as for Foucault, the rejection of absolutes, of totalizing discourses, does not necessarily result in paralyzing relativism. On the contrary, the fact that a particular voice cannot claim total truth does not reduce the reality that the first-person voice of the oppressed "Other" can claim at least as great a validity as that of any voice speaking of her or his condition.

Kristeva's work insists upon the validity of female voices, which have tended to be silenced not only by the master discourse but by feminism unable to deal with the paradoxes posed by polyvocalism. She undoes those apparent paradoxes by honoring the truth embodied in Lacan's formulation: "There is no Woman; there are only Women."[160]   What this notion emphasizes—cryptically and aphoristically—is that what has been taken to be a commonality, "Woman," is in fact a definition of male negativity, of Otherness. That insight opens up the possibility of turning confidently away from a focus that has given rise to the divisions within feminism. It allows a feminist turn toward recognition of the bases of female commonality and the commonality of all "Others."[161]

In this area, again, Kristeva's work is marked by a strength and freedom derived, in large part, from its structuralist foundation—a strength attached to the rigor of its interdisciplinary methodology; a freedom visible in the originality of its ventures.

Her work reveals to a feminist jurisprudence mired in contradiction the possibility of explorations at untouched depths and heights.

CONCLUSION: POSTSTRUCTURALIST FEMINIST CRITIQUE

Feminist jurisprudence has, for some time, recognized in our law, beneath the surface of a discourse based on rights, the operation of power in limitation and constraint of female language and action, of peculiarly female acts of verbal and physical differentiation. We inhabit a world in which the definition of human gender has been made in a male-dominated discourse that has permitted our understanding of that phenomenon only in terms of sameness and of utter difference. The realities of uniquely female bodily experience, on the one hand, and of apparently contradictory voices all claiming female identity, on the other, have posed impossible challenges to the categories of sameness and difference.

It is not accidental that pregnancy and childbirth have proven to be the sites of major divisions within liberal feminism—indeed, it is at those sites that the ordinary categories of identity, the "self" and the "not-self," break down. They become the locales in which the arbitrariness and ultimate inadequacy of the logic of differentiation stand most exposed. In their defiance of "sameness" and "difference" categorizations, they both demand a different discourse and manifest the deep rootedness of every discourse in precisely those gender-based concepts of differentiation. The task of feminism, and of feminist jurisprudence, in addressing these issues becomes that of pressing for deeper inquiry, moving jurisprudence beyond the abortive philosophical inquiry into gender differentiation with which it has heretofore been satisfied, and exploring the possibilities of alternative differentiation. But even the commencement of that task can be undertaken only as part of the larger labor that questions every differentiation and appreciates the limitation of every narrative.

While pregnancy and childbirth have perhaps posed the most divisive problem for liberal feminism, the limitations of its classifications have become apparent in other areas as well. In the "semiotic" experiences of separation and differentiation that occur in the pre-verbal periods of our lives and resonate and echo in later experience, we inhabit spaces that the boundaries of our ordinary categorizations do not include. For both men and women, a law of "reason" ill fits such experiences.

The events and challenges of the present time present not merely an invitation to feminism to engage in insistent philosophical inquiry, but an imperative to do so. Unless broad change occurs, the labor of self-definition, the naming of female selves well advanced in feminist literature, will never reach the common areas of our public and political lives. What structuralism offers to American feminism, and to feminist jurisprudence, is a valorization of our naming-work and an altered public structure providing hearing room for "Other" narratives.

Recognizing the universal reality of female subordination, we have long known that legal reforms can alter the status of women only to the degree that they cause, or are accompanied by new ways of thinking about gender differentiation. It has been tempting, however, at times when, in every part of the world, the material conditions of women are worsening, to commit to successions of programs seeking to alter those conditions. The notion of changing "how people think" has seemed amorphous, vague, impossible, and irrelevant in the face of women's material realities—something scheduled for the millennium. Now, however, at this time in our history, strangely and unaccountably, such a transformation of thought appears not utopian vision but present possibility. Or even, in some sense, present reality. That transformed thought appears in poststructuralist critical theory, which has taken the central insights of psychoanalysis, ethnology, and linguistics, and demonstrated—by its methodology of "throwing into question"—the limitations of the thought by which power operates to structure our culture.

The immediate implications of the poststructuralist *episteme* seem paralyzingly relativistic, but they are not so. Like Wittgenstein, poststructuralism recognizes that our everyday discourse may not reflect the uncertainties and rifts that we discover when we turn critical eyes upon the fabric of ordinary language—that we operate, in general, according to the ordinary "forms of life."[162] The great relevance of poststructuralism for jurisprudence, however, is that it throws into question the categories and classifications upon which law has uncritically supported exercises of power that have silenced and opposed in the name of nature or in the name of practical necessity. At the non-ordinary occasion of the confrontation of the "speaking subject" with the power of law, poststructuralism forces us to entertain the possible non-necessity of our customary categories. Inquiring at a depth not reached by liberal investigation, poststructuralism proposes inquiry into the alterability of the most fundamental structural components of legal theory. The implications of this kind of inquiry for women, and for other subordinated subjects, are enormous and profound. Law's recognition of its own limitation may open its ears to hearing the namings, the self-definitions, and the claims of oppressed persons, and more significantly, may permit Law's recognition that its customary namings and classifications have no greater claim to validity than do the self-narratives of those whom it has kept in silence.

This Article has been written to urge a commingling of poststructuralist and feminist efforts. The gift of feminism to structuralism, already apparent in Kristeva's work, is the gift of voices asserting the truth-claims of female bodies. Those multiple voices offer to poststructuralism not only an otherwise lacking fullness and richness, but also a promise of the recurring renewals that life to thought. Reviving the Platonic understanding that societies stagnate by exclusion of "poetic language," feminism contributes the broader understanding that the stability of societies rests on repression of death; that all those repressions relate to one another; and that all have implicated repressions of women. Feminism represents an insistence upon continuous and recurring confrontation of all those represseds, inviting alterations in our gendered ways of being.

To feminism, poststructuralist theory offers not only a place of discourse, but also a place in which internal and external threats can fall away. It permits feminism's removal from the locale of liberal ideological discourse, in which it is beset by internal contradictions on the issue of equality, and in which it is threatened externally to the degree that it appears to be merely one among many "power-seeking" ideologies.[163]

An intermingling with poststructuralism would presuppose feminism's surrender of any claim to "totality" of vision or of narrative, its recognition of the "common castration" of the human condition, and its avoidance of "essentialist" notions that perpetuate the errors of the present dominant discourse. Such an intercourse might bring feminist jurisprudence to new possibilities, to active labors of critique and reconstruction.

Such labors would deliver feminist jurisprudence from its present confinement in the structures of liberal ideology, in the structures of "sameness" and "otherness" defined other than by women-selves as "speaking subjects."

Such labors might give shape to theory disclosing the commonality of women with every "Other;" might shape a body of feminist theory broader and fuller than theory focused within perspectives of class, of race, of ethnic identification, or of local culture. The courage and determination necessary to support such labor will develop precisely to the degree that feminism directly confronts the human realities of contradiction, finitude, and death, the realities repressed by the dominant discourse that defines as "Other" the representatives of those realities. To the degree that feminism welcomes those three attendants as its midwives, feminism may move through confusion, pain, and division, to occasions of celebration, to pleasures of renewal, to strengths of giving birth.

NOTES

1. Perhaps the first self-conscious usages of the term "feminist jurisprudence" occurred in Scales, *Towards a Feminist Jurisprudence*, 56 IND. L.J. 375 (1981), and MacKinnon, *Feminism, Marxism, Method, and the State: Toward Feminist Jurisprudence*, 8 SIGNS: J. WOMEN IN CULTURE & SOC'Y 635(1983).

2. *See* Frug, *Securing Job Equality for Women: Labor Market Hostility to Working Mothers*, 59 B.U.L. REV. 55, 55–61 (1979) (discussion of the changing proportion and status of females in the workforce in the 1960's and 1970's); *see also* GELPI, WOMEN AND POVERTY (1986) (discussion of the current situation of women in low-paying, low-status employment); Brown, Emerson, Falk, & Freedman, *The Equal Rights Amendment: A Constitutional Basis for Equal Rights for Women*, 80 YALE L.J. 871 (1971) (an early contribution to feminist theory).

3. *See infra* notes 30–100 and accompanying text.

4. *See* U.S. Const. amend. XIV.

5. *See* Civil Rights Act of 1964, tit. VII, 42 U.S.C. §§ 2000e to -17 (1982). Among the major achievements of feminist jurisprudence has been the definition of sexual harassment as a form of sex discrimination under title VII and the equal protection clause. See C. MACKINNON, SEXUAL HARASSMENT OF WORKING WOMEN: A CASE OF SEX DISCRIMINATION (1979) (describing sexual harassment as "the first legal wrong to be defined by women"); *see also Introduction, Symposium on Sexual Harassment*, 10 CAP. U.L. REV. 1 (1981).

For analysis of current title VII and equal protection doctrine, *see* Freedman, *Sex Equality, Sex Differences and the Supreme Court*, 92 YALE L.J. 913, 922 (1983). Freedman argues that the Supreme Court "has been unable to agree on the nature of sex differences, their relationship to legitimate goals, and the correct standards for deciding cases involving these issues." *Id.*; *see also* Law, *Rethinking Sex and the Constitution*, 132 U. PA. L. REV. 955 (1984) (discussion of the Court's avoidance of analysis in terms of sexual equality).

6. *See* Bartlett *Pregnancy and the Constitution: The Uniqueness Trap*, 62 CAL. L. REV. 1532 (1974) (discussions of the Court's equality analyses in Geduldig v. Aielio, 417 U.S. 484 (1974)); *see also* Comment, Geduldig v. Aiello, *Pregnancy Classifications and the Definition of Sex Discrimination*, 75 COLUM. L. REV. 441 (1975).

7. *See* Roe v. Wade, 410 U.S. 113 (1973); Doe v. Bolton, 410 U.S. 179 (1973): Planned Parenthood v. Danforth,428 U.S.52 (1976); Harris v. McRae, 448 U.S.297 (1980); Akron v. Akron Ctr. for Reproductive Health, 462 U.S. 416 (1983); Thornburgh v. American Coll. of Ob. & Gyn., 476 U.S. 747 (1986).

8. *See* 42 U.S.C. § 2000e(k) (1981) (amending 42 US.C. § 2000e (1964)); *see also* Johnson, *The Legal Background and Implications of Pregnancy Benefits*, 35 LAB. L.J. 352 (1984); Oliver, *Finding a Solution for Pregnancy Discrimination: Did the Pregnancy Discrimination Act Fall Short of the Goal?*, 30 J. URB. & CONTEMP. LAW 171 (1986); Ossian, *Interpretation of the Pregnancy Discrimination Act and the EEOC Guidelines: Conflicting Federal Responses and Analogous Confusion at the State Level*, 1984 DET. C.L. REV. 77; Wald, *Judicial Construction of the 1978 Pregnancy Discrimination Amendment to Title VII: Ignoring Congressional Intent*, 31 AM. U.L. REV. 591 (1982).

9. *See* Kreiger & Cooney, *The* Miller-Wohl *Controversy: Equal Treatment, Positive Action, and the Meaning of Women's Equality*, 13 GOLDEN GATE U.L. REV. 513 (1983); Note, *The State of California Has Determined that Pregnancy May be Hazardous to Your Job*, 16 GOLDEN GATE U.L. REV. 515 (1986).

10. *See* Becker, *Barriers Facing Women in the Wage-Labor Market and the Need for Additional Remedies*, 53 U. CHI. L. REV. 934 (1986); Brown, Baumann, & Melnick, *Equal Pay for Jobs of Comparable Worth: An Analysis of the Rhetoric*, 21 HARV. C.R.-C.L. L. REV. 127 (1986); Flick, *Understanding the Women's Movement*, 12 HUM. RTS. 26 (1984); Scales-Trent, *Comparable Worth: Is this a Theory for Black Workers?*, 8 WOMEN'S RTS. L. REV. 51 (1984); Comment, *Comparable Worth and the Courts: How Fear of the Marketplace is Changing the Face of Title VII*, 23 HOUS. L. REV. 1185 (1985).

11. *See generally* Wright v. Olin Corp,, 697 F.2d 1172 (4th Cir. 1982); *see also* Accurso, *Title VII and Exclusionary Employment Practices: Fertile and Pregnant Women Need Not Apply*, 17 RUTGERS L.J. 95 (1985); Becker, *From* Muller v. Oregon *to Fetal Vulnerability Policies*, 53 U. CHI. L. REV. 1219 (1986); Timko *Exploring the Limits of Legal Duty:*

A Union's Responsibilities with Respect to Fetal Protection Policies, 23 HARV. J. ON LEGIS. 159 (1986); Weinberger, *A Maternal Duty to Protect Fetal Health?*, 58 IND. L.J. 531 (1982–83); Williams, *Firing the Women to Protect the Fetus: The Reconciliation of Fetal Protection with Employment Opportunity Goals under Title VII*, 69 GEO. L.J. 641 (1981).

12. On surrogacy and on issues relating to technology and reproduction, see TEST-TUBE WOMEN: WHAT FUTURE MOTHERHOOD? (R. Arditti, R. Duelli-Klein, & S. Minden eds. 1984). For an application of perspectives expressed in this Article to issues of surrogacy and reproductive technology, see Ashe, *Law-Language of Maternity: Discourse Holding Nature in Contempt*, 22 NEW ENG. L REV. 521 (1988).

13. Major contributions in this area are those of Catharine MacKinnon and Andrea Dworkin. *See* Amicus Curiae Brief for Linda Marciano and Estate of Dorothy Stratten, American Booksellers Assoc., Inc. v. Hudnut, 771 F.2d 323 (7th Cir. 1985) (No. 84.3147) (written by C. MacKinnon and A. Dworkin); A DWORKIN, PORNOGRAPHY: MEN POSSESSING WOMEN (1981); Dworkin, *Against the Male Flood: Censorship, Pornography and Equality*, 5 HARV. WOMEN'S L.J. 1 (1985); MacKinnon, *Not a Moral Issue*, 2 YALE L. & POL'Y REV. 321 (1984); MacKinnon, *Pornography, Civil Rights and Speech*, 20 HARV. C.R.-C.L. L. REV. 1 (1984).

14. *See* S. ESTRICH, REAL RAPE (1987); MacKinnon, *Feminism, Marxism, Method and the State: An Agenda for Theory*, 7 SIGNS: J. WOMEN IN CULTURE & SOC'Y 515 (1982); Olsen, *Statutory Rape A Feminine Critique of Rights Analysis*, 63 TEX. L. REV. 387 (1984).

15. For discussion of the ambiguous consequences of may recent changes in the law in these areas, see Olsen, *The Family and the Market: A Study of Ideology and Legal Reform*, 96 HARV. L. REV. 1497 (1983); Olsen, *The Politics of Family Law*, 2 LAW & INEQUAL. 1 (1984). For general discussion of the issues, see *also* Glendon, *Fixed Rules and Discretion in Contemporary Family Law and Succession Law*, 60 TUL. L. REV. 1165 (1986); Krauskopf, *Maintenance: A Decade of Development*, 50 MO. L. REV. 260 (1985).

16. *See* GELPI, *supra* note 2.

17. *See* Williams, *The Equality Crisis: Some Reflections on Culture, Courts & Feminism*, 7 WOMEN'S RTS. L. REP. 175 (1982); *see also* Law, *supra* note 5.

18. *See* Freedman, *supra* note 5.

19. *See supra* notes 69–87 and accompanying text. These divisions within the American Women's movement have most recently been apparent in the contradictory positions asserted on the issue of

pregnancy-disability leave for female employees. The controversy over "equal treatment/positive action" has developed over several years, having been apparent in debate at the 1982 Annual Conference on Women and the Law. *See* Kreiger & Cooney, *supra* note 9, at 515–16: *see also supra* note 11 and accompanying text. For general discussion of feminist positions on that issue in the context of pregnancy disability, see Williams, *supra* note 17.

20. The concept of "legal meaning" is borrowed from Cover, *Nomos and Narrative*, 97 HARV. L. REV. 4 (1983).

21. For major writing of this kind, reflecting a departure from liberal analysis, see Cornell, *Toward a Modern/Postmodern Reconstruction of Ethics*, 133 U. PA. L. REV. 291 (1985); Dalton, *An Essay in the Deconstruction of Contract Doctrine*, 94 YALE L.J. 997 (1985); MacKinnon, *supra* notes 1, 13, 14; Minow, *When Difference Has Its Home: Group Homes for the Mentally Retarded, Equal Protection and Legal Treatment of Difference*, 22 HARV. C.R.-C.L. L. REV. 112 (1987); Olsen, *supra* notes 14, 15; Scales, *The Emergence of Feminist Jurisprudence: An Essay*, 95 YALE L.J. 1373 (1986).

22. *See infra* notes 101–15 and accompanying text

23. *See* McCloud, *Feminism's Idealist Error*, 14 REV. L. & SOC. CHANGE 277 (1986).

24. *See infra* notes 100–15 and accompanying text

25. Writers of this group appear to share many of the ego psychology assumptions characteristic of American developmental psychology and do not probe so deeply as, for example, Julia Kristeva, into thee depth, recalcitrance, and possible ineradicability of gender differentiation. *See infra* notes 138–61 and accompanying text

26. Foucault's major works in English translation include: M. FOUCAULT, THE ARCHAEOLOGY OF KNOWLEDGE (1970); M. FOUCAULT, THE ORDER OF THINGS: AN ARCHAEOLOGY OF THE HUMAN SCIENCES (1970); M. FOUCAULT, MADNESS AND CIVILIZATION: A HISTORY OF INSANITY IN THE AGE OF REASON (1971); M. FOUCAULT, THE BIRTH OF THE CLINIC: AN ARCHAEOLOGY OF MEDICAL PERCEPTION (1973); M. FOUCAULT, DISCIPLINE AND PUNISH: THE BIRTH OF THE PRISON (1977); M. FOUCAULT, THE HISTORY OF SEXUALITY, VOL. I (1978); M. FOUCAULT, I, PIERRE RIVIERE, HAVING SLAUGHTERED MY MOTHER, MY SISTER AND MY BROTHER...(1978); M. FOUCAULT, POWER/KNOWLEDGE (1980).

27. Lacan's major works in English translation include: J. LACAN, ECRITS: A SELECTION (1977); J. LACAN, SPEECH AND LANGUAGE IN PSYCHOANALYSIS (1986). For other samplings of his writing and commentary, see Lacan, *French Freud*, 48 YALE FRENCH STUDIES (1972);

Lacan, *Literature and Psychoanalysis*, 55/6 YALE FRENCH STUDIES 11
(1977); *see also* S. SCHNEIDERMAN, RETURNING TO FREUD (1980). For useful
analyses of Lacan's work, see J. GALLOP, THE DAUGHTER'S SEDUCTION:
FEMINISM AND PSYCHOANALYSIS (1982); J. GALLOP, READING LACAN (1985); S.
SCHNEIDERMAN, JACQUES LACAN (1983).

28. *See* J. DERRIDA, OF GRAMMATOLOGY (1976); J. DERRIDA, WRITING
AND DIFFERENCE (1978). For an accessible introduction to Derrida, see
PAUL DE MAN, BLINDNESS AND INSIGHT; ESSAYS ON THE RHETORIC OF
CONTEMPORARY CRITICISM (1971).

29. Julia Kristeva's major works in English translation include: J.
KRISTEVA, ABOUT CHINESE WOMEN (1977); J. KRISTEVA, STABAT MATER (1977);
J. KRISTEVA, DESIRE IN LANGUAGE: A SEMIOTIC APPROACH TO LITERATURE AND
ART (1980); J. KRISTEVA, POWERS OF HORROR: AN ESSAY ON ABJECTION
(1980); Kristeva, *Women's Time*, 7 SIGNS: J. WOMEN IN CULTURE & SOC'Y 1
(1981).

30. *See* Freedman, *supra* note 5, at 916.

31. For arguments that the "assimilationist" model is less appro-
priately applied to problems of sexually inequality than to problems of
racial inequality, see Kay, *Models of Equality*, U. ILL. L. REV. 39 (1985).

32. Varieties of "anatomy-is-destiny" theory are discussed in J.
MITCHELL, PSYCHOANALYSIS AND FEMINISM 5–131 (1974).

33. *See* B. BROWN, A. FREEDMAN, H. KATZ, & A. PRICE, WOMEN'S RIGHTS
AND THE LAW: THE IMPACT OF THE ERA ON STATE LAWS (1977).

34. *But see* Freedman, *supra* note 5 (arguing that judicial ambivalence and uncertainty has limited application of the equality doctrine).

35. *See* Westen, *The Empty Idea of Equality*, 95 HARV. L. REV. 537
(1982).

36. 163 U.S. 537 (1896).

37. 347 U.S. 483 (1954).

38. *See* Freedman, *supra* note 5; Law, *supra* note 5.

39. The history of the Pregnancy Discrimination Act is a case in
point. Review of that history discloses utter lack of consensus in
Congress as to the appropriate range of freedom of reproductive
function in women. Supporters of the amendment ranged from
legislators concerned to remedy what they regarded as a "handicap" of
women in the work force to those who supported the amendment as an
anti-abortion measure. *See* H.R. REP. No. 948, 95th Cong., 2d Sess.,
reprinted in 1978 U.S. CODE CONG. & ADMIN. NEWS 4749; H.R. REP. No.
1786, 95th Cong., 2d Sess. *reprinted in* 1978 U.S. CODE CONG. & ADMIN.
NEWS 4756.

40. *See supra* notes 30–39 and accompanying text.

41. For discussion of the three models, see Kreiger & Cooney, *supra* note 9: Law, *supra* note 5; McCloud, *supra* note 23.

42. *See* Brown, Emerson, Falk, & Freedman, *supra* note 2.

43. *See Plessy*, 163 U.5. at 559 (Harlan, J., dissenting).

44. *See* Williams, *supra* note 17; *see also* Amici Curiae Brief of Nat'l Org. for Women; NOW Legal Defense & Educ. Fund; Nat'l Bar Ass'n, Women Lawyers' Div., Wash. Area Chapt.; Nat'l Women's Ctr.; Women's Law Project & Women's Legal Defense Fund, California Fed. Saving & Loan Ass'n v. Guerra, 107 S. Ct. 683 (1987) (No.85–494) (written by W. Williams, K. Keegan, S. Deller Ross, S. Burns, & J. Meier).

45. *See supra* note 44.

46. *See, e.g.,* Wengler v. Druggists Mutual Ins. Co., 446 U.S. 142 (1980); Califano v. Goldfarb, 430 U.S. 199 (1977); Hartford Accident & Indem. Co. v. Insurance Comm'r, 65 Pa. Commw. 249. 442 A.2d 382 (1982); Darrin v. Gould, 85 Wash. 2d 859, 540 P.2d 882 (1975).

47. *See* California Fed. Savings & Loan Ass'n v. Guerra, 107 S. Ct. 683 (1987); *see also* Miller-Wohl Co. v. Commissioner of Labor & Indus., 692 P.2d 1243 (Mont. 1984), *vacated,* 107 S. Ct. 919 (1987).

48. *See* E. WOLGAST, EQUALITY AND THE RIGHTS OF WOMEN (1980).

49. *See* C. GILLIGAN, IN A DIFFERENT VOICE (1982).

50. *See* WOLGAST, *supra* note 48, at 137.

51. *Id.* at 107.

52. *See id.*

53. *See id.* at 110.

54. *See* GILLIGAN, *supra* note 49.

55. *See id.* at 11–23.

56. *See id.* at 151–74.

57. *See id.*

58. *See id.*

59. *See id.*

60. *See id.*

61. *See* N. CHODOROW, THE REPRODUCTION OF MOTHERING: PSYCHO-ANALYSIS OF THE SOCIOLOGY OF GENDER (1978).

62. *See* D. Dinnerstein, The Mermaid and the Minotaur: Sexual Arrangements and Human Malaise (1976).

63. *See* Chodorow, *supra* note 61, at 173–80; Dinnerstein, *supra* note 62, at 33–34, 41–82. For a discussion of the limitations of Chodorow's perspective, see Lorker, Coser, Rossi, & Chodorow, *On the Reproduction of Mothering: A Methodological Debate*, 6 Signs: J. Women in Culture & Soc'y 482 (1981).

64. Neither intends the notion of the "feminine" to match the extent of that concept's range in French critical theory. *See infra* note 139 and accompanying text.

65. *See* N. Noddings, Caring, A Feminine Approach to Ethics and Moral Education (1984).

66. *See* Law, *supra* note 5.

67. *See* Williams, *supra* note 17; *see also supra* notes 44–46 and accompanying text.

68. Law, *supra* note 5, at 955.

69. *Id.* at 1008–09.

70. *See supra* note 20.

71. *See supra* notes 67–68 and accompanying text.

72. *See* California Fed. Savings & Loan Ass'n v. Guerra, 107 S. Ct. 683 (1987); Miller-Wohl Co. v. Commissioner of Labor and Indus., 692 P.2d 1243 (Mont. 1984), *vacated,* 107 S. Ct. 919 (1987).

73. *See Miller-Wohl,* 692 P.2d at 1253. Among the Montana groups that advocated upholding of the state statutory scheme providing particular disability leave benefits for pregnant employees, were the Women's Law Section of the Montana State Bar and the Montana Education Association, the largest teachers' union in the state, an overwhelming proportion of whose membership is female. *See id.*

74. *See* Amici Curiae Brief of Nat'l Org. for Women; NOW Legal Defense & Educ. Fund; Nat'l Bar Ass'n, Women Lawyers' Div., Wash. Area Chapt.; Nat'l Women's Ctr.; Women's Law Project & Women's Legal Defense Fund, California Fed. Savings & Loan Ass'n v. Guerra, 107 S. Ct. 683 (1987) (No. 85-494) (written by W. Williams, K. Keegan, S. Deller Ross, S. Burns, & J. Meier); *see also* Amici Curiae Brief of American Civil Liberties Union, League of Women Voters of the United States, League of Women Voters of Calif., Nat'l Women's Political Caucus, & Coal Employment Project, California Fed. Savings & Loan Ass'n v. Guerra, 107 S. Ct 683 (1987) (No. 85-494) (written by Bertin, Pinzler, Kannar, & Simms; advocating extension of disability leave benefits to all employees).

75. *See Guerra,* 107 S. Ct. at 694–95.

76. *See* WOLGAST, *supra* note 48, at 107.

77. *See* 1 W. BLACKSTONE, COMMENTARIES *442.

78. *See supra* note 66 and accompanying text.

79. *See* Williams, *supra* note 17; Law, *supra* note 5.

80. *See* MacKinnon, *Feminist Discourse, Moral Values and the Law—A Conversation,* 34 BUFFALO L. REV. 11 (1985).

81. *See* S. SCHNEIDERMAN, JACQUES LACAN 105–56 (1983) (discussion of the differences between American "ego psychology" and European psychoanalytic theory); *see also* A. JARDINE, GYNESIS 63 (1985) (examining the question whether "feminist theory as a search for the female self (most characteristic of Anglo-American criticism) [is] in complete contradiction with the, strictly speaking, antifeminist insistence in France on the potentiality of losing the self"); Malcolm, "J'Appelle Un Chat Un Chat," NEW YORKER, April 20, 1987 at 84–102.

82. *See supra* note 79 and accompanying text

83. *See* Cover, *supra* note 20.

84. *See id.* at 33–35.

85. *See id.* at 11–44.

86. *See id.* at 44.

87. *Id.* at 9.

88. *See* M. DALY, BEYOND GOD THE FATHER: TOWARD A PHILOSOPHY OF WOMEN'S LIBERATION (1973); M. DALY, GYN/ECOLOGY: THE METAETHICS OF RADICAL FEMINISM (1978); S. GOULD & M. WARTOFSKY, WOMEN AND PHILOSOPHY: TOWARDS A PHILOSOPHY OF LIBERATION (1976); S. GRIFFIN, WOMAN AND NATURE: THE ROARING INSIDE HER (1978).

89. *See* C. CHRIST, DIVING DEEP AND SURFACING: WOMEN WRITERS ON SPIRITUAL QUEST (1980); C. CHRIST & J. PLASKOW, WOMENSPIRIT RISING: A FEMINIST THEOLOGICAL RECONSTRUCTION OF CHRISTIAN ORIGINS (1983); M. STONE, WHEN GOD WAS A WOMAN (1978).

90. *See* S. HARDING, THE SCIENCE QUESTION IN FEMINISM (1986); S. HARDING & M. HINTIKKA, DISCOVERING REALITY: FEMINIST PERSPECTIVES IN EPISTEMOLOGY, METAPHYSICS, METHODOLOGY AND PHILOSOPHY OF SCIENCE (1983); E. FOX KELLER, REFLECTIONS ON GENDER AND SCIENCE (1985).

91. *See* P. CHESLER, WOMEN AND MADNESS (1st ed. 1972); S. FIRESTONE, THE DIALECTIC OF SEX: THE CASE FOR FEMINIST REVOLUTION

(1970); B. Friedan, The Feminine Mystique (1963); A. Rich, Of Woman Born: Motherhood as Experience and Institution (1976); M. Rosaldo & L. Lamphere, Women, Culture and Society (1974); *see also supra* notes 49, 61, 62.

92. *See* S. Gilbert & S. Guber, The Madwoman in the Attic: The Woman Writer and The Nineteenth Century Imagination (1979); E. Showlater, A Literature of Their Own: British Women Novelists from Bronte to Lessing (1976); E. Showlater, The New Feminist Criticism: Essays on Women, Literature and Theory (1985).

93. For an extensive bibliography of women's poetry, see A. Ostriker, Stealing the Language (1986).

94. For a clear account of the divisions within the women's movement, see A. Snitow, C. Stansell, & S. Thompson, *Introduction,* Powers of Desire (1983).(1983).

95. *See id.*

96. *See* Ostriker, *supra* note 93, at 7 (providing a detailed account of the emergence and development of women's poetry in America). Ostriker proposes that American women's poetry constitutes a literary movement "comparable to Romanticism or modernism in our literary past." *See id.*

97.

98. *See* V. Woolf, A Room of One's Own (1929).

99. *See* A. Rich, The Dream of A Common Language: Poems (1st ed. 1978).

100. *See* O. Brouman, *Artemis,* Beginning with O (1977).

101. *See supra* note 26.

102. *See supra* note 29.

103. Catharine MacKinnon's work manifests a preoccupation with Marxist theory. *See supra* notes 1, 5, 13, 14. Clare Dalton explicitly reflects reliance upon Derridean theory and methodology. *See supra* note 21. The works of Fran Olsen and Martha Minow also embody deconstructive approaches, as does that of Ann G. Scales. *See supra* notes 14, 15, 21.

Catharine MacKinnon's engagement with Marxist theory implicates an attempt to avoid liberalism's contradictory equality theory by an articulation of gender that privileges concepts of hierarchy, rather than concepts of biology. *See* MacKinnon, *supra* note 1. Seeking to "extract the truth of women's commonalities out of the lie that all women are the same," MacKinnon has discovered that commonality in female subordination, steadily emphasizing the persistent reality that—whatever advances have been made to benefit particular women or groups of women—women remain subordinate in our society and in every culture. *See id.* at 639.

MacKinnon distinguishes her approach from Marxism, as well as from liberalism, claiming that it avoids the scientific strain inherent in Marxism, as well as the Kantian moral imperative implicated in liberal theory. She asserts that while her approach does not claim universality, it does not reduce to relativism either.

MacKinnon has proposed as the standard for assessing whether legislation is invidiously sex-discriminatory the inquiry "whether the policy or practice in question integrally contributes to the maintenance of an underclass or a deprived position because of gender status." *See* MacKINNON, *supra* note 5, at 117. She has urged the application of that standard in calling for an understanding of sexual harassment in the workplace, for a fine balancing of legislation that would define a cause of action affording some remedy for provable harms occasioned by pornography without abridging first amendment rights, and for redefinition of criminal sexual assault. *See id.*; *see also* MacKinnon, *Not a Moral Issue*, *supra* note 13; MacKinnon, *Pornography, Civil Rights and Speech*, *supra* note 13.

MacKinnon stands out as perhaps the most brilliantly original, tireless and prolific laborer in the area of sex discrimination issues. Her work has been consistently challenging and disturbing, even when it has not proven fully persuasive. Her proposals are radical in their deconstruction of legal institutions that embody and conceal profoundly anti-female operations, and her phenomenological account of women's subordinate position is most persuasive. There is, however, a lack of underpinning in, or explicit relationship to, psychological theory that makes her contribution ultimately somewhat less than compelling. She does not, for example, venture beyond a phenomenological account of female material subordination to inquire into the motivations of sexual oppression. I believe that her work, in its exclusive emphasis on the subordinated status of women, implies a gender polarization, which, perhaps, could be avoided by a clearer recognition of the great depth and complexity of the powerful irrational processes of gender differentiation that cripple both women and men.

Clare Dalton has undertaken a deconstructive effort in an analysis of contract doctrine. *See* Dalton, *supra* note 21. Her analytic method echoes both Derridean textual analysis and the social analysis of Foucault—that is, she works to lay bare the structure concealed by the rational and ostensibly objective discourse of legal doctrine. Dalton has noted the parallels between the "liberal" world depicted by legal scholars, the "rational" world depicted by Derrida, and the "male" world depicted by feminists. *See id.* at 1095. She has viewed the central issues of contract doctrine as issues of both power and knowledge. *See id.* Dalton has exposed the indeterminacy of contract doctrine and its operation in subordination and suppression of women. *See id.* The non-legal, poststructuralist traditions of scholarship upon which Dalton has relied appear as strong stepping stones for the movement away from the contradiction of liberal theory.

Fran Olsen has applied a deconstructive analysis to the traditional "public/private" distinction that has characterized the ideology of family and marketplace, and has examined that doctrine's contribution to a perpetuation of the material oppression of women. *See supra* notes 14, 15. Olsen's work is strenuous in its insistent pointing out of ambiguities and contradictions inherent in liberal law reform efforts intended to benefit women. In this respect, it demonstrates an entry into the stream of poststructuralist theory discussed in this article. Her entry into that stream, however, seems hesitant. While she expresses a keenly insightful critique of the limitations inherent in the male/female dualism, Olsen offers in lieu of that dualism a concept of "androgyny" as a model of "wholeness." *See* Olsen, *The Family and the Market, supra* note 15, at 1577–78. Reliance upon that concept would seem to lead back into the contradictions of liberal theory. Numerous feminist writers have dealt with that concept and found it inadequate. *See, e.g.,* WOLGAST, *supra* note 48, at 125–37.

Martha Minow has contributed to the deconstructive strain apparent in Dalton and Olsen a clear recognition of the relatedness of all "Others" oppressed by processes of differentiation. *See* Minow, *supra* note 21. Her work, thus avoids the exclusiveness of liberal feminist theory, and gives account of a vision of greater breadth and depth.

Ann C. Scales has emphasized the Wittgensteinian themes implicit in feminist jurisprudence and its critique of objectivity. *See* Scales, *supra* note 21.

104. *See, e.g.,* Cornell, *supra* note 21. This author has attempted a "reconstruction" of ethics in an engagement with the hermeneutic theory of Jurgen Habermas. Cornell appears to espouse the notion of an ethic founded on dialogism. Her contribution in this area adds to the contemporary and growing colloquy on interpretation and hermeneutics that has emerged in American legal theory. *See, e.g., Interpretation Symposium,* 58 So. CAL. L. REV. (1995).

Cornell's work appears susceptible to the charge that the ethic of dialogism may operate to provide only procedural—and not substantive—sustenance to women and other "Others." The definition of an ethic of dialogism having reference to an "ideal speech situation" leaves unanswered the following questions: In whose language will the dialogue occur? How can the "hermeneutic moment" be recognized? And will the recommendation of compromise directed toward achievement of consensus operate to veil a reality of domination?

105. *See* A. SEXTON, TO BEDLAM AND PART WAY BACK (1960). "It is the courage to make a clean breast of it in the face of every question that makes the philosopher. He must be like Sophocles' Oedipus, who, seeking enlightenment concerning his terrible fate, pursues his indefatigable enquiry, even when he divines that appalling horror awaits him in the answer. But most of us carry in our heart the Jocasta who begs Oedipus for God's sake not to inquire further." *Id.* (quoting Schopenhauer, letter to Goethe, Nov., 1815).

106. *See* J. STURROCK, STRUCTURALISM AND SINCE: FROM LEVI-STRAUSS TO DERRIDA (1979).

107. *See* M. MAUSS, THE GIFT: FORMS AND FUNCTION OF EXCHANGE IN ARCHAIC SOCIETIES (Eng. trans. 1954); M. MAUSS & E. DURKHEIM, PRIMITIVE CLASSIFICATION (Eng. trans. 1963); M. MAUSS, A GENERAL THEORY OF MAGIC (Eng. trans. 1972).

108. *See* C. LEVI-STRAUSS, THE SAVAGE MIND (1966); C. LEVI-STRAUSS, THE ELEMENTARY STRUCTURES OF KINSHIP (1969).

109. R. JAKOBSON, FUNDAMENTALS OF LANGUAGE (Eng. trans. 1956); R. JAKOBSON, CHILD LANGUAGE, APHASIA AND PHONOLOGICAL UNIVERSALS (Eng. trans 1968).

110. *See supra* note 28.

111. *See* R. BARTHES, MYTHOLOGIES (1972); R. BARTHES, THE PLEASURE OF THE TEXT (1976); R. BARTHES, WRITING DEGREE ZERO (1977); R. BARTHES, A LOVER'S DISCOURSE, FRAGMENTS (1978).

112. *See* S. FREUD, TOTEM AND TABOO: RESEMBLANCES BETWEEN THE PSYCHIC LINES OF SAVAGE AND NEUROTICS (Eng. trans. 1946); S. FREUD, THE STANDARD EDITION OF THE COMPLETE PSYCHOLOGICAL WORKS OF SIGMUND FREUD (Eng. trans. 1953); S. FREUD, THREE ESSAYS ON THE THEORY OF SEXUALITY (Eng. trans. 1962).

113. *See supra* note 27.

114. *See supra* note 26.

115. *See supra* note 29.

116. *See* M. FOUCAULT, THE ORDER OF THINGS, *supra* note 26, at 344–87.

117. *See* M. FOUCAULT, THE DISCOURSE ON LANGUAGE (1972).

118. *See* M. FOUCAULT, POWER/KNOWLEDGE, *supra* note 26, at 131.

119. *See* M. FOUCAULT, DISCIPLINE AND PUNISH, *supra* note 26.

120. *See* M. FOUCAULT, BIRTH OF THE CLINIC, *supra* note 26.

121. *See* M. Foucault, Madness and Civilization, *supra* note 26.

122. *See* M. Foucault, History of Sexuality, *supra* note 26.

123. *See* M. Foucault, The Order of Things, *supra* note 26, at xxiv.

124. See M. Foucault, I Pierre Riviere, *supra* note 26.

125. *See id.* at 373–87; *see also* J. Kristeva, Desire in Language, *supra* note 29, at 91 n.17. Leon Roudiez, in his introduction to *Desire in Language*, notes that the "speaking subject" is always "a split subject—divided between unconscious and conscious motivations, that is, between physiological processes and social constraints. It can never be identified with anything like Husserl's transcendental ego. The activities and performances of the speaking subject are the result of a dialectical process..." Kristeva, Desire in Language, at 6.

126.

127. *See id.* at 374.

128. *See id.* at 375.

129. *Id.*

130. *See id.* at 376–77.

131. *Id.* at 377.

132. *See id.* at 376.

133. *Id.*

134. *Id.* at 379.

135. *See id.* at 381.

136. *Id.* at xxiv.

137. See M. Foucault, Power/Knowledge, *supra* note 26, at 81–83.

138. *See* Jardine, Gynesis, *supra* note 81, at 20–21. Jardine notes that: the major new directions in French theory over the past two decades—those articulated by both men and women—have, by and large, posited themselves as profoundly...anti- and/or post-feminist. Feminism, as a concept, as inherited from the humanist and rationalist eighteenth century, is traditionally about a group of human beings in history whose identity is defined by that history's representation of sexual decidability. And every term of that definition has been put into question by contemporary French thought.
Id. *See also* J. Kristeva, Powers of Horror, *supra* note 29, at 208. Kristeva seems to reflect that reality in her observation that a feminism "that is jealous of conserving its power—the last of the power-seeking

ideologies" will fail to approach the deepest riddles of sexual identity and the oppressions to which it gives rise. *See id.*

139. *See* JARDINE, GYNESIS, *supra* note 81, at 25. Jardine designates the meaning of the neologism "gynesis: as:

the putting into discourse of 'woman' as that process diagnosed in France as intrinsic to the condition of modernity; indeed, the valorization of the feminine, woman, and her obligatory, that is, historical connotations, as somehow intrinsic to new and necessary modes of thinking, writing, speaking. The object produced by this process is neither a person nor a thing, but a horizon, that toward which the process is tending...

Id.

140. *See* J. KRISTEVA, DESIRE IN LANGUAGE, *supra* note 29, at 1–20. Kristeva sometimes refers to this notion as "semanalysis." Leon Roudiez' useful Introduction to *Desire in Language,* clarifies the meanings of these terms. *Id.*

141. *Id.* at ix.

142. *Id.* at x.

143. *See supra* note 97 and accompanying text.

144. *See id.*

145. *See id.*

146. That is, Kristeva contributes to "gynesis." *See supra* notes 138–39.

147. *See supra* notes 81, 125, 138.

148. *Id.*

149. *See* S. FREUD, THREE ESSAYS, *supra* note 112.

150. *See* J. GALLOP, THE DAUGHTER'S SEDUCTION, *supra* note 27. Gallop has observed that "[w]hereas Freud's Oedipal Father might be taken for a real, biological father, Lacan's Name-of-the-Father operates explicitly in the register of language. The Name-of-the-Father: the patronym, patriarchal law, patrilineal identity, language as our inscription into patriarchy." *Id.* at 47.

151. *See* J. KRISTEVA, DESIRE IN LANGUAGE, *supra* note 29, at 128.

152. *See id.*

153. *Id.* at 127–28; *see also* M. FOUCAULT, I, PIERRE RIVIERE, *supra* note 26, at 373–87.

154. *See* J. KRISTEVA, DESIRE IN LANGUAGE, *supra* note 29, at x.

155. *See* J. KRISTEVA, POWERS OF HORROR, *supra* note 29, at 90–112.

156. *See* J. KRISTEVA, STABAT MATER, *supra* note 29, at 117.

157. *See id.*

158. *See id.* at 111.

159. *See* Cover, *supra* note 20, at 42. My usage of this term follows R. Cover's emphasis on the necessity of "objectification" as a feature of nomos-creating narrative, and as an element of "legal meaning." "Narrative is the literary genre for the objectification of value." *Id.*

160. *See generally supra* note 27.

161. *See* A. JARDINE, GYNESIS, *supra* note 81. This recognition is, of course, apparent in the figuration of the "other" as feminine, discussed by Jardine. *See id.*

162. *See* L. WITTGENSTEIN, PHILOSOPHICAL INVESTIGATIONS (1968); *see also* H. PITKIN, WITTGENSTEIN AND JUSTICE 132–39 (1972).

163. *See* J. KRISTEVA, POWERS OF HORROR, *supra* note 29, at 208.

3

Foucault and (the Ideology of) Genealogical Legal Theory

> The assumption of one single subject is perhaps unnecessary;
> perhaps it is just as permissible to assume a multiplicity of
> subjects, whose interaction and struggle is the basis of our
> thought and our consciousness in general?...My hypothes[i]s:
> The subject as multiplicity.
>
> —Nietzsche, *The Will to Power*

> VI:...But the human essence is no abstraction inherent in each
> single individual. In its reality it is the ensemble of the social
> relations.
>
> —Marx, "Theses On Feuerbach"

PREFACE: NIETZSCHE, MARX, FOUCAULT...

The main body of this text was written in 1989/90. Some minor
changes have been made in an attempt to bring the basic
movement of my discussion into line with more recent work in
contemporary critical theory. The essay was originally produced
under the pressure of a conflict which of course still traverses
the *politics* of critical cultural/legal studies: the contestation over
the theory of social, juridical, and cultural "power" coming all the
way up from Nietzsche and Marx. The work of Michel Foucault
is, I believe, a more or less perfect expression of this critical
division over radical "materialist" theory and the very meaning
and practice of "ideology critique" as something stronger than a
vaguely random and generalist acknowledgment of "differences."
The notion of the "political economy of knowledge," in Foucault's

archaeological and genealogical writings, has its own uneven and split descent into Nietzsche and Marx. Thus, the dialectical principle of an unstable "unity of opposites"—centered on the question of power but fundamentally divided over an historical account of the uses of power, its development and its trans-formations—informs my (re)reading of Foucault as a thinker to be taken very seriously, to learn from, but not simply to "celebrate" or "accept" word for word.

THE DISCOURSE OF POWER

In his "Two Lectures"[1] Foucault addresses the question of the analysis of power[2] by first (re)presenting two widely held conceptualizations which, for Foucault, function as the all too familiar props and counter-positions to be attacked and displaced. These are, namely, the liberal or juridical conception of power, on the one side, and the instrumental Marxist conception on the other.[3]

The liberal theory of power is essentially constituted by three aspects. First, it is fundamentally "based on the idea that the constitution of political power obeys the model of a legal trans-action involving a contractual type of exchange.[4] Secondly, "power is taken to be a right, which one is able to possess like a commodity"; thus, power 'is that concrete power which every individual holds." Lastly, since political power obeys the model of a legal transaction, a contract or an exchange, and also because every individual holds a certain share of this power, "one can in consequence transfer or alienate [this power], either wholly or partially, through a legal act or through some act that establishes a right, such as takes place through cession or contract."[5] The outcome of all this, as Foucault puts it, is that the "partial or total cession [of power held individually] enables political power or sovereignty to be established."[6] By contrast, in the general Marxist conception, "power is conceived *primarily* in terms of the role it plays in the maintenance simultaneously of the relations of production and of a class domination which the development and specific forms of the force of production have rendered possible."[7]

According to Foucault, what becomes evident in the com-parison of the liberal and the Marxist conceptions of power is that the two models are deeply economistic in nature. In other words, the common point of liberalism and Marxism is found in "an economism in the theory of power."[8] With the liberal conception, the formal mode of political power is "discoverable in the process of exchange, the economic circulation of commodities."[9] Power, in other words, is modelled exclusively on the commodity. And with the Marxist conception, the "historical raison d'etre of political power and the principle of its concrete forms and actual functioning, is located in the economy."[10] Power, then, is conceived to always function in a subordinate relation to the economy. Power serves and realizes, answers to and for, maintains and reproduces "the relations appropriate to the economy and essential to its functioning".[11] The problem of both of these dominant understandings of power is thus a theoretical reductionism: In liberal theory, power looks like the economy, and in Marxist theory, power obeys the economy.

Given that both of these dominant theoretical models appear now so similar in their aspect of reductivity—the theoretical totalization by means of economism—Foucault suggests that what is needed for the analysis of power is a *variety of tools*, which would include, for instance, a non-economic analysis of power. Nonetheless, Foucault concedes that such an analysis would still "allow that it effectively remains the case that the relations of power do indeed remain profoundly enmeshed in and with economic relations and participate with them in a common circuit."[12]

Foucault's analysis of power begins, then, by displacing both the liberal and the Marxist models with the following two assertions. The liberal conception is displaced by the claim that "power is neither given, nor exchanged, nor recovered, but rather *exercised*, and that *it only exists in action*."[13] The Marxist conception is displaced by the claim that "power is not *primarily* the maintenance and reproduction of economic relations, but is above all *a relation of force*."[14]

Given these fundamental claims concerning power, one would not analyze the operations of power in terms of contractual change (the liberal model), nor would an analysis of power be adequate to the task if it proceeded primarily in terms of power's functional role in the maintenance of the relations of production. If power is understood as the way in which relations of forces are deployed and given concrete expression,[15] then, as Foucault argues, the analysis of power should proceed primarily in terms of struggle, conflict and war. Thus, we come to (re)conceptualize political power relations as a continuation of war by other means, and this being, as Foucault points out, a theoretical inversion of the Clausewitzian formulation of war as politics continued by other means.[16]

Several theoretical consequence follow from this conception of political power. First, "it implies that the relations of power that function in a society such as ours essentially rest upon a definite relation of forces that is established at a determinate, historically specifiable moment, in war and by war."[17] Second, political power only "puts an end to war" to the extent that it puts an end to the "disequilibrium of forces that was displayed in war."[18] Thus, political power does not suspend the effects of war. Rather:

> The role of political power...is perpetually to reinscribe this relation [of warfare and the disequilibrium of forces] through a form of unspoken warfare; to reinscribe it in social institutions, in economic inequalities, in language, in the bodies themselves of each and everyone of us.[19]

This indeed appears as the most striking and disturbing mark of Foucault's analysis of power that is, as he puts it, to see politics as sanctioning and upholding the disequilibrium of forces that was displayed during war. Thus, none of the phenomena of the political society, not even in the long durations of "civil peace," should be understood except as a continuation of war, violent struggle and hostile conflict.

To summarize, Foucault has (re)presented two conceptualizations of power, the liberal or juridical paradigm, on the one side, and the Marxist paradigm on the other. It would seem as though his conception of power works to entirely reject the former and dismantle the hierarchy of the latter. This is to say, Foucault's analytic of power relations works to displace the liberal power model, which is, as he puts it, the "contract-oppression"[20] schema. According to this representation of power—which is, clearly, that which is taken as true for the mainstream of American legal culture—sovereignty is made possible by virtue of each and every individual's contractual exchange of her natural and original power/right. And in turn, this power that is contractually "given up" to the sovereign (or any other freely contracting individual) "risks becoming oppression whenever it over-extends itself, whenever-that is-it goes beyond the terms of the contract."[21] Thus, in this liberal or juridical conception, power is contractually exchangeable, and oppression is the transgression of the contractually agreed-upon limit of that power.

Foucault's approach to the analysis of power is radically more concrete than this liberal conception, which is essentially a mythologizing narrative of the Great Origin of Western Rationality, Law and Order. Instead of conceptualizing political power as the end of warfare relations, Foucault maintains that political power is none other than the continuation of war by other means; that is to say, the "other means" of a vast and proliferating array of institutional structures and apparati, the language and imagery of (post)modern science, technology and mass media, and the knowledge(able) discourses made possible by the subtle inmixing and linkage of psychiatry, medicine and law. Thus, the subjugation of groups and classes is not to be understood as the "transgression of the limits of a contractually exchanged power," but as none other than "the mere effect and continuation of a relation of domination."[22] Relations of subjugation, or more extreme and intense relations of domination, are, as Foucault puts it, "none other than the realization, within the continual warfare of this pseudo-peace, of a perpetual relationship of force."[23] Finally, then, in opposition to the liberal paradigm's contract-oppression schema wherein the mystified debate centers on the opposition of "legitimacy" to "illegitimacy," Foucault's defamiliarizing discourse of power establishes the *war-domination* schema, for which the pertinent opposition is *struggle* and *submission.*[24]

THE RULE OF LAW

We now have the proposition that political power is not a matter of commodity exchange and contractual obligation, with some set of reasonably and freely agreed-upon limits, the transgression of which would signify oppression and abuse of power. Political power also does not primarily function as the handmaid of the economy and the relations of production. Rather, as Foucault formulates it, political power is the continuation of war by other means. It is, in other words, an unspoken warfare, or a warfare conducted by means of silent, invisible, diffuse mechanisms and tactics of control, subjugation and domination. Likewise, political power constitutes a deployment of forces speaking a language of reason, logic and fairness, not a language of open combat. The unspoken warfare of politics is only, as Foucault writes it, "the endlessly repeated play of dominations."[25]

In Foucault's "Nietzsche, Genealogy, History" we find specific articulation of his understanding of the Rule of Law and its relation to the analytics of power and domination elaborated in "Two Lectures." In the first place, acts of political subjugation must avoid the possibility of being identified as such; that is to say, such acts must avoid the "localization" of the public gaze, or, as Foucault puts it (following Nietzsche), domination must occur at a "non-place."[26] To put it another way, such political acts must even avoid the appearance of a "relationship" of domination. Such an open appearance would run directly counter to the dominant order's need to disguise and occlude from critical inspection the violence at stake in political conflicts and confrontations—that is to say, the violence which is constantly at stake in the maintenance and reproduction of the existing order of relations. As Foucault puts it, "This relationship of domination is no more a 'relationship' than the place where it occurs is a place; and, precisely for this reason, it is fixed, throughout its history, in rituals, in meticulous procedures that impose rights and obligations."[27]

Rules of law are, on this analysis, inseparable from the rights and obligations which arise from the rituals of political dominations. This is, indeed, an understatement. Such rules are, as Foucault puts it, by no means designed to temper violence "but rather to satisfy it."[28] This understanding of the rules of law is, of course, consistent with Foucault's conceptualization of power—that is, as war continued by other means. Foucault's conceptualization of the Rule of law—understood in a more general sense than the particular rules or rule systems—is also consistent with his notion of politics as war. Just as power relations—or, in other words, the political life of culture—only sustain and in fact instigate the unspoken warfare of civil pseudo-peace, "it would be false to think that total war exhausts itself in its own contradictions and ends by renouncing violence and submitting to civil laws."[29] For Foucault quite the contrary is the case:

> [L]aw is a calculated and relentless pleasure, delight in the promised blood, which permits the perpetual instigation of new dominations and the staging of meticulously repeated scenes of violence. The desire for peace, the serenity of compromise and the tacit acceptance of the law, far from representing a major moral conversion or a utilitarian calculation that gave rise to the law, are but...[the law's] result and, in point of fact...[the law's] perversion: "guilt, conscience, and duty had their threshold of emergence in the right to secure obligations; and their inception, like that of any major event on earth, was saturated in blood."[30]

The subtlety of Foucault's thought can not be underestimated. I think, specifically, that one should be cautious of oversimplifying the conceptualization of the relation between the Rule of Law and power. Law and power do not become identical at that point of emergence of the "civil society," where open warfare takes the form and character of political "diplomacy" and institutionalization. In "Power and Strategies" Foucault identifies law as a partial, complex and non-monolithic instrument in relation to power. Law, writes Foucault, "is neither the truth of power nor its alibi. *It is an instrument of power which is at once complex and partial.* The form of law with its effects of prohibition needs to be restrained among a number of other, non-juridicial mechanisms."[31]

Foucault claims, for instance, that the penal system should not merely be analyzed "*purely and simply* as an apparatus of prohibition and repression of one class by another, nor as an alibi for the lawless violence of the ruling class."[32] Though these *negative functions* are undeniably true, the penal system should also, and more importantly for Foucault, be analyzed as making possible "a mode of political and economic management which exploits the difference between legality and illegalities."[33] Thus, by analogy, in order to conceptualize the Rule of Law as not purely and simply a negative and prohibitive effectivity, but also as a *productive* mechanism of power, I would substitute the "legal system" for Foucault's "penal system," and substitute "legitimacy and illegitimacies" for his "legality and illegalities." I would then come out with this formulation: The *legal system* should be analyzed as making possible a mode of political and economic management which exploits the difference between *legitimacy and illegitimacies.*

This non-identical relation of law and power can be further elaborated by a consideration of Foucault's work on law and "power/knowledge" relations in his *Discipline and Punish.* From "Power and Strategies" we have the formulation that law is not identical with power, but is "an instrument of power which is at once complex and partial."[34] And as Foucault writes in the famous passage from *Discipline and Punish:*

> Perhaps...we should abandon a whole tradition that allows us to imagine that knowledge can exist only where the power relations are suspended and that knowledge can develop only outside its injunctions, its demands, and its interests. Perhaps we should abandon the belief that power makes people mad and that, by

the same token, the renunciation of power is one of the conditions of knowledge. We should admit, rather, that power produces knowledge (and not simply by encouraging it because it serves power or by applying it because it is useful); that power and knowledge directly imply one another; that there is no power relation without the correlative constitution of a field of knowledge nor any knowledge that does not presuppose and constitute at the same time power relations. These "power-knowledge relations" are to be analyzed, therefore, not on the basis of a subject of knowledge who is or is not free in relation to the power system; but, on the contrary, the subject who knows, the objects to be known, and the modalities of knowledge must be regarded as so many effects of these fundamental implications of power-knowledge and their historical transformations. In short, it is not the activity of the subject of knowledge that produces a corpus of knowledge, useful or resistant to power, but power-knowledge, the processes and struggles the traverse it and of which it is made up that determines the forms and possible domains of knowledge.[35]

This passage, I think, is crucial for a (re)conceptualization of the Rule of Law in relation to political power, for it allows the "instrumentality" conception of law to be taken one step further. That is to say, law may be (re)understood as *a discourse of power/knowledge*: a complex apparatus or mechanism of power which in a myriad of ways produces (and is produced by) the hegemonizing knowledge and truth necessary for the existing order of culture.

The Rule of Law does not purely and simply function as that which says no. On the contrary, law is much more importantly engaged in positive acts of (re)production. In other words, just as power produces knowledge (and is produced by knowledge), the law, as an instrument of power and as a discursive apparatus of power/knowledge, also produces knowledge (and is produced by knowledge) and constitutes a *regime of truth*. The kind of knowledge and truth that the law produces is that of its "own"—that is, the power/knowledge system of which it is a part—legitimacy and illegitimacies. The law is positioned precisely in order to produce the discourse of its own legitimacies and illegitimacies. Simultaneously, the law must exploit this very discourse in the name of the Rule of Law's lofty promises of justice.

Also, as the law produces this knowledge and truth of its legitimacy and illegitimacy, and as it is constrained to perpetually reach beyond itself for some apparent fulfillment of its promises, the law also (re)produces and circulates another, similar kind of discourse of knowledge and truth, namely the discourses of "discipline." The law perpetually and increasingly seeks that discourse which provides the knowledge and truth of a "disciplinary society," or a society of normalization[36]—that is, the knowledge of normalization, (ab)normalities, control. The discourses of legitimation which are produced with the enunciative apparati of the Rule of Law are not identical with the discourses of the disciplines of the so-called human sciences. However, these latter discourses, knowledge, techniques and procedures of normalization "come to be ever more constantly engaged in the colonisation of those [discourses, knowledge, techniques and procedures] of law."[37] As Foucault writes it:

> Modern society, then, from the nineteenth century up to our own day, has been characterized on the one hand, by a legislation, a discourse, an organization based on public right, whose principles of articulation is the social body and the delegative status of each citizen; and, on the other hand, by a closely linked grid of disciplinary coercions whose purpose is in fact to assure the cohesion of this same social body....Hence these two limits, a right of sovereignty and a mechanism of discipline, which define, I believe, the arena in which power is exercised. But these two limits are so heterogenous that they cannot possibly be reduced to each other. The powers of modern society are exercised through, on the basis of, and by virtue of, this very heterogeneity between a public right of sovereignty and a polymorphous disciplinary mechanism....The disciplines may well be the carriers of a discourse that speaks of a rule, but this is not the juridicial rule deriving from sovereignty, but a natural rule, a norm. The code they come to define is not that of law but that of normalisation.[38]

"Discipline," then, signifies two interrelated mechanisms. On the one side are the discourses of normalization, and on the other are the proper *effects* of such discourses: the practices, techniques and procedures made possible by the construction of a norm. To put the finger on it, the power-effect of the knowledge apparati centered around normalization is precisely that of regimentation, order, hierarchy, control. And to return to the question of the relation between law and power, one can readily see that "the power of law" must be grasped not merely as *power-instrumentality*, but simultaneously as a system of knowledge, or a *truth machine*.

The law is, in a sense, precisely the relation of interchange and (dis)appearance which is signified by *power/knowledge*. Law is the always incomplete instrument of a power dispersed in discourse, knowledge and truth. Incomplete, that is, in the sense that the law is always obligated to re-legitimate its illegitimacies by a constant production and circulation of new forms of knowledge and truth. As Foucault writes in *Discipline and Punish*, "Today, criminal justice functions and justifies itself by this perpetual reference to something other than itself, by this unceasing reinscription in non-juridical systems."[39] Law, in other words, is none other than an instrument of the unceasing function of political power, a "non-place" which is always already stretched out beyond itself in order to deliver up the discourse of its own legitimacy: "Its fate is to be redefined by knowledge."[40]

LEGAL RULES AND INTERPRETATION

As I have implied above, the intricate and multitudinal sets of *rules* of law are inseparable from the similarly diverse forms of legal rights and obligations, all of which are constituted within the rituals of political struggle. These rules of law should be understood, then, as cultural signifiers of power struggles. The use of particular legal rules, or the more generalized resort to legal rule systems in the effort to derive some set of principles embodied in them, is a concealed deployment of political force. These legal rules and their use are therefore not designed to temper violence, but, on the contrary, to satisfy it.[41] As Foucault puts it: "Humanity does not gradually progress from combat to combat until it arrives at universal reciprocity, where the rule of law finally replaces warfare; humanity installs each of its violence in a system of rules and thus proceeds from domination to domination."[42] At least a partial answer to the genealogical enquiries into the historical processes of political violences, therefore, would lie precisely in this properly critical identification of the radical contingency, malleability and interpretability of the rules themselves—that is to say, in a theory of the opacity of language.[43]

Thus we have the proposition that the particular rules of law are, at a single stroke, the disguises of violent struggle and the "tools" (critically understood) or instruments of that struggle. As Foucault writes in 'Nietzsche, Genealogy, History":

> Rules are empty in themselves, violent and unfinalized; they are
> impersonal and can be bent to any purpose. The successes of

history belong to those who are capable of seizing these rules, to replace those who had used them, to disguise themselves so as to pervert them, invert their meaning, and redirect them against those who had initially imposed them; controlling this complex mechanism, they will make it function so as to overcome the rulers through their own rules.[44]

It goes almost without saying that an oppositional politics is concerned with this "play of dominations,"[45] as Foucault puts it, which constantly rumbles beneath the surface of appearance in legal(istic) culture. But it is no less true that those political collectivities which currently exercise hegemony/dominance must also, at some level of consciousness, know the threatening pressure at stake in the question of interpretation as Foucault's work (re)presents it—that is to say, the exposure of an essential indeterminacy in the existence of rules, and thus an obstinate contingency at the heart of culture's order and organization. The threatening position of a genealogical legal theory, in other words, is that reading is always already political; or to put this same proposition on a more general level, that power insinuates itself into the fabric of not only what we claim to understand, but also what is (re)presented as the unknown and mysterious. What goes by the name of "interpretation," then, under Foucault's analytic of power/knowledge, is in fact a series of actions which are profoundly dangerous and potentially uncertain: "the violent or surreptitious appropriation of a system of rules, which in itself has no essential meaning, in order to impose a direction, to bend it to a new will, to force its participation in a different game, and to subject it to secondary rules."[46]

The critical insight running through Foucault's analyses of political power, law and interpretation is that the knowledge(able) practices inscribed in such cultural operations constitute, at bottom, a silent warfare, a play of dominations, a constant tug of war over the organization of culture and the (re)presentation of its historical formation. That this is indeed a constant struggle and not a natural given, or a "once and for all" event, is doubtless of most importance for the forces of opposition, for as Foucault reminds us in the interview "Body/Power," "the impression that power weakens and vacillates...is in fact mistaken; power can retreat here, re-organise its forces, invest itself elsewhere...and so the battle continues."[47] This understanding of political struggle as conquest, displacement, reversal, re-conquest, etc., can of course be situated in the context of juridical struggles over rules of "right" by recalling the legal apparatus as a massive field of discursive productions—involved in producing, namely, the truths of legitimacy. The effect of this discursive *machination* is that, just as oppositional forces effectively expose legal illegitimacies to the dangerous extent that the dominant legal consciousness must acknowledge crisis and the concomitant necessity of reform(ation) (of the same system), the dominant regime's seemingly innocent interpretation of a new set of rules or "rights" effectively works to recoup the losses of the crisis-moments in order to reinscribe but another form of hegemony. As Robert Gordon has written, the doctrinal "victories" tend always to peak all too early; just as an apparently promising line of rules is opened up, they become qualified (interpreted) before becoming truly threatening to the existing order.[48]

A large part of the problem for opposition to the legal hegemony, then, lies in this awareness that this massive network of the dominant juridical apparatus vigorously works at once—at the level of social appearances—to recognize its operations and acts of interpretation as illegitimate, and at a deeper, critical level to produce ever more subtle plateaus of cultural legitimacy. To put it another way, as oppositional discourses effect real crisis consciousness at the social level—or, in other words, as opposition intervenes in the hegemonic system of signification—the juridical apparatus (among other system-maintaining apparati of culture) responds essentially in the way of a "crisis management" to re-articulate the terms (the appearance of "new" rules and rights) of the same macropolitical structure. As Gordon puts it, 'The official legal establishment ha[s] been compelled to recognize claims on its utopian promises. But these real gains have deepened the legitimacy of the system as a whole."[49] But as Foucault insists, what is taking place in these contestations is not so much a "recuperation" as the "usual strategic development of a struggle....One has to recognise the indefiniteness of the struggle—though this is not to say it won't some day have an end...."[50]

CONCLUSION: PRAXIS?

After all: Why read Foucault? I would like to conclude briefly by suggesting that the general question of a radical/oppositional legal praxis may provide at least one possible footing for an investigation of Foucault's work. For example, I think that it is possible to read in Foucault's discourses on power a political metanarrative which profoundly resembles the tensions of praxis which currently threaten to fracture and therefore paralyze leftist legal movements today. In other words, to put it schematically, Foucault's (re)presentation of power is founded on a privileging of the radical specificity of power, its dispersion, diversity and local existence(s). Such an understanding of power relations makes necessary, as Foucault writes in "Intellectuals and Power," his privileging of an understanding of theory as "local and regional, ...not totalizing."[51] To read Foucault's discourses on power/ theory as a political metanarrative would mean that, however much these discourses resist, as Gilles Deleuze puts it, "the indignity of speaking for others,"[52] they can not conceivably avoid the inevitability of generating a narrative of the macro-structural space of culture—precisely within which such discourse must emerge, and by which such a consciousness is produced. Also, this inevitable production of cultural metanarrative may be "read" or identified precisely to the extent that the discourses and (re)presentations of culture operate *un*-consciously with respect to their enabling conditions. In other words—and in fact to use Foucault's own formulations from *The Order of Things*— the political metanarrative of the discourses of culture finds its conditions of possibility precisely in that which it excludes: the *unthought* of history, or history's Other.[53] For Foucault's discourses, this is identifiable in the extent of his (micro)concentration on the polymorphous and heterogeneous diversity/ difference of power mechanisms at the exclusion of the global space within and against which such differences and tactics must be registered in the first place. In other words, as Fredric Jameson puts it, difference must ultimately be "understood as a relational concept, rather than as the mere inert inventory of unrelated diversity....[O]ne cannot enumerate the differences between things except against the background of some more general identity."[54]

To my mind then, it would appear useful to draw the parallel between Foucault's discourses on power and the sort of self-rupturing which currently marks the space of contemporary leftist movements in law. These fractures of the possibility of a radical collectivity, in other words, are identifiable not only in the tensions polarizing radical lawyers, on the one side, and critical theorists on the other, but also in the violent splits occurring along race and gender axes. My partial (that is, both "limited" and "committed")[55] response to the question, Why read Foucault?, finally, is by no means an answer to, or resolution of, this problematic configuration of the left in contemporary legal opposition, but is modestly a suggestion that a truly radical praxis is profoundly disabled to the extent that a narrowly theorized heterogeneity takes precedence over collectivity and the linkage of forces. Speaking in terms of a more general cultural praxis, I understand Jameson's remarks in his "Postmodernism, or The Cultural Logic of Late Capitalism" to be making a similar point, and implying a similar call for a refiguring of the space of our current resistance: "If we do not achieve some general sense of a cultural dominant, then we fall back into a view of present history as sheer heterogeneity, random difference, a coexistence of a host distinct forces whose effectivity is undecidable."[56] In other words, an un(macro)critical praxis essentially amounts to no real praxis at all, in that its emblems of heterogeneity, diversity and dispersion tend to operate, symptomatically, as the vertiginous fragmentation, alienation and estrangement from which we seek to break away, and politically, as the system-maintaining logic of a vacuous pluralism. Finally, I would also suggest that a truly effective praxis within the apparati of law must also work to transgress the boundaries of its own limited regionality. That is to say, we must continue to transgress and overthrow the cultural domination inscribed in what is inno-cently known as our discipline(s) of specialization. I hope my work here figures to do just this.

NOTES

1. See Michel Foucault, "Two Lectures," in Power/Knowledge: Selected Interviews and Other Writings 1972–1977, ed. Colin Gordon, New York: Pantheon, (1990): 79–108.

2. For (a later) Foucault's very precise articulation of the "subject" in his work, see Foucault, "The Subject and Power," in Hubert L. Dreyfus and Paul Rabinow, *Michel Foucault: Beyond Structuralism and Hermeneutics*, 2nd ed., Chicago: University of Chicago Press (1983): 208–28.

3. Foucault's career-long war against "Marxism" is, in all of his work, an assault on a deeply caricatured "Marxism." The intellectual-political legacy of Foucault's always very simplifying polemic has been, and continues to be, that any historical materialist analytics, drawing upon the work of Marx, which doesn't bow down to Foucault's analytics of "power," is itself quickly branded "simple," "reductive," "economistic," "crude" and so forth. When a different text of mine, for instance, which

explicated and strongly critiqued Foucault's conceptualizations of "the history of systems of thought," was rejected from the American journal, *Rethinking Marxism*, David Ruccio, one of the journal's "Marxist" referees, found it quite easy to make the following conclusive statement: "Finally, given the fact that the [my] essay has been submitted to *R[ethinking] M[arxism]*, the author should at least acknowledge that there is nothing obvious about the identity between Marxism and the primacy of the economic (either in terms of social explanation or transformation)." To re-state the main point of this extraordinarily telling and symptomatic comment, what *is* quite "obvious" after Foucault is that any "acceptable"—i.e., compromised—Marxist position must identify itself as a *pluralist* analytics with no "crude" *prioritization* of any kind in the theorization of social contradictions and cultural change.

4. "Two Lectures" at 88.

5. Ibid.

6. Ibid.

7. Ibid. at 88–89, emphasis added.

8. Ibid. at 88.

9. Ibid. at 89.

10. Ibid.

11. Ibid.

12. Ibid.

13. Ibid., emphasis added.

14. Ibid., emphasis added.

15. Ibid. at 90.

16. Ibid.; see also Foucault, "Truth and Power," in *Power/Knowledge*, 109–33.

17. "Two Lectures," at 90.

18. Ibid., emphasis added.

19. Ibid.

20. Ibid. at 91–92.

21. Ibid. at 91.

22. Ibid. at 92.

23. Ibid.

24. Ibid. In "Two Lectures" Foucault does not actually designate his analytic of power relations as that of "war-domination," but variously (and only suggestively) as "domination-repression," "war-repression" and "struggle-repression." I am supplying the term "war-domination" in light of Foucault's cautious hesitancy regarding the notion of "repression," and also in view of his later, more extended and detailed studies of the concept—what he defamiliarizes as the (psychoanalytical) "repressive hypothesis" in *The History of Sexuality. Vol. I: An Introduction*, trans. Robert Hurley, New York: Random House, Vintage Books (1978). In "Two Lectures," for instance, Foucault remarks: "The need to investigate this notion of repression more thoroughly springs... from the impression I have that it is wholly inadequate to the analysis of the mechanisms and effects of power that it is so pervasively used to characterise today" (92). The critique of the politics of the psycho-sexual concept of "repression" is far more thoroughly waged in *The History of Sexuality. Vol. I*. To whatever extent Foucault has problematized the concept of "repression," his interrogations have clearly remained at the level, as I suggested above, of politico-*sexual*/-erotic discourses and non-discursive practices of subject-formation. Foucault largely ignores the possibility of an *ideological* theorization of "repression" as the repression of *class-conscious*, revolutionary subject-positions. In this case, one would need to inquire not only into the question of *what* subject-positions or "identities" are repressed in the dominant culture, but far more importantly *why* such modes of repression are historically significant and signs of crisis in the reproduction of the existing order.

25. Foucault, "Nietzsche, Genealogy, History," in *The Foucault Reader*, ed. Paul Rabinow, New York: Pantheon (1971): 76–100. There are two texts which are in my view indispensable for understanding Foucault's genealogical project: first, "Nietzsche, Genealogy, History," which I am largely dealing with here, the full text of which may be found in Foucault, *Language, Counter-Memory, Practice: Selected Essays and Interviews*, ed. Donald F. Bouchard, Ithaca, New York: Cornell University Press (1977): 139–64; and second, a seldom-discussed text of Foucault's, "History, Discourse and Discontinuity," *Salmagundi*, trans. Anthony M. Nazzaro, no. 20 (1972): 225–48. A helpful, if largely uncritical, explication of Foucault is Jack L. Amariglio, "The Body, Economic Discourse, and Power: An Economist's Introduction to Foucault," *History of Political Economy*, vol. 20:4 (1989): 583–613. See also Rosemary Hennessy, "Materialist Feminism and Foucault: The Politics of Appropriation," *Rethinking Marxism*, vol. 3:3–4 (Fall-Winter 1990): 252–74.

26. "Nietzsche, Genealogy, History" at 85.

27. Ibid.

28. Ibid.

29. Ibid.

30. Ibid.; Foucault is quoting from Nietzsche, *On the Genealogy of Morals*, trans. Walter Kaufmann and R.J. Hollingdale, New York: Random House, Vintage Books (1969), 65.

31. Foucault, "Power and Strategies," in *Power/Knowledge*, at 141, emphasis added.

32. Ibid., emphasis added.

33. Ibid.

34. Ibid.

35. *Discipline and Punish: The Birth of the Prison*, trans. Alan Sheridan, New York: Random House, Vintage Books (1979), 27–28.

36. See "Two Lectures" at 107.

37. Ibid.

38. Ibid. at 106.

39. *Discipline and Punish* at 22.

40. Ibid.

41. See "Nietzsche, Genealogy, History" at 85.

42. Ibid.

43. For a (post)modern critique-al theory of "meaning," see Mas'ud Zavarzadeh and Donald Morton, "Theory Pedagogy Politics: The Crisis of 'The Subject' in the Humanities," in Morton and Zavarzadeh, eds., *Theory/Pedagogy/Politics: Texts for Change*, Urbana: University of Illinois Press (1991). In "Theory Pedagogy Politics," Zavarzadeh and Morton write:

> Meaning emerges not as the result of certain stylistic maneuvers...but as a mode of cultural and political behavior. In this semantic space opened up by the demystifying critique, the learner...recognizes close affinities between the way she reads a Shakespearean sonnet (the so-called aesthetic experience) and the way she "reads" and understands events that take place in South Africa/Nicaragua/her domestic life. A critique re-locates "reading" in the humanities curriculum and problematizes it by indicating that it is not the outcome of a simple connection between two independent consciousnesses

(of author and reader) but a mode of producing significations, of making the world intelligible.

...(Post)modern critical theory understands language not as a simple tool, a transparent means through which already formulated meanings are transmitted, but as a system of differentiation. Theory constructs the world in the sense that it provides a grid of intelligibility for it...Meaning, in other words, is shown to be an effect of frames of intelligibility, which themselves are boundaries of ideology. These limits of ideology and boundaries of allowable meaning are constantly contested by various social classes through the types of writing they put forth as most significant (7–8).

44. "Nietzsche, Genealogy, History" at 95–96.

45. Ibid. at 85.

46. Ibid. at 86.

47. Foucault, "Body/Power," in *Power/Knowledge* at 56.

48. See Gordon, "New Developments in Legal Theory," in David Kairys, ed., *The Politics of Law: A Progressive Critique*, New York: Pantheon (1992), 281–93. See generally also the following: Robert Gordon, "Unfreezing Legal Reality: Critical Approaches to Law," *Florida State Univ. Law Review*, vol. 15 (1997): 195–220; Kimberlé Crenshaw, "Race, Reform, and Retrenchment: Transformation and Legitimation in Antidiscrimination Law," *Harvard Law Review*, vol. 101 (1988): 1331–397; Alan Freeman, "Truth and Mystification in Legal Scholarship," *Yale Law Journal*, vol. 90 (1981): 1229–237; "Legitimizing Racial Discrimination Through Antidiscrimination Law: A Critical Review of Supreme Court Doctrine," *Minnesota Law Review*, vol. 62 (1979): 1049–119; Karl Klare, "Judicial Deradicalization of the Wagner Act and the Origins of Modern Legal Consciousness, 1937–1941," *Minnesota Law Review*, vol. 62 (1978): 265–339; and Mark Tushnet, "An Essay on Rights," *Texas Law Review*, vol. 62 (1984): 1363–383.

49. See Gordon, "New Developments in Legal Theory."

50. "Body/Power" at 56–57.

51. Foucault (with Gilles Deleuze), "Intellectuals and Power: A Conversation between Michel Foucault and Gilles Deleuze," in *Language, Counter-Memory, Practice*, at 208.

52. Ibid. at 209.

53. See Foucault, *The Order of Things: An Archaeology of the Human Sciences*, trans. Alan Sheridan-Smith, New York: Random House (1970).

54. Jameson, *The Political Unconscious: Narrative as a Socially Symbolic Act*, Ithaca, New York: Cornell University Press (1981), 41–42.

55. See Donald Morton, "The Politics of the Margin: Theory, Pleasure, and the Postmodern *Conférance*," *The American Journal of Semiotics*, vol. 5:1 (19871: 95–114. See V. I. Lenin, "Parties in Philosophy and Philosophical Blockheads," as excerpted in Robert C. Tucker, ed., *The Lenin Anthology*, New York: W.W. Norton and Co. (1975): 644–47.

56. Jameson, "Postmodernism, or The Cultural Logic of Late Capitalism," *New Left Review*, vol. 146 (1984): 53–92. I do not engage in a critique of Jameson's work here. See Leonard, "Transgressive Postmodernism: Prolegomenon to a Radical Legal Studies," *Legal Studies Forum*, vol. 15:4 (1991): 367–406. See also the following: Douglas Kellner, ed., *Postmodernism/Jameson/Critique*, Washington, D.C.: Maisonneuve Press (1993): Mas'ud Zavarzadeh, *Pun(k)deconstruction and the (Post)Modern Political Imaginary*, Washington, D.C.: Maisonneuve Press (1994).

Dossier II

THE SIGN

4

GAYATRI CHAKRAVORTY SPIVAK_____

Constitutions and Culture Studies

I wrote this paper in response to a hundred-odd manuscript pages of Bruce Ackerman's book *We the People.*[1] Fleshing it out, I have come to sense that the paper shares some of the occupational weaknesses of the new and somewhat beleaguered discipline of a transnational study of culture, especially if that study steps back from what is perceived as contemporary. Conceptual schemes and extent of scholarship cannot be made to balance. Once again, then, the following pages must be offered as possible directions for future work.

Here is a summary of my understanding of what I read in Professor Ackerman's manuscript pages:

A dualist view of U.S. political practice is true to American political philosophy and history. Legitimizing it in terms of foreign (read European) models is incorrect. The dualism is between normal everyday politics where We the People are not much involved. Contrasted to this are the great changes in political practice—constitutional politics—where We the People are mobilized and involved in the process of change through higher lawmaking. Professor Ackerman is aware that by thus naming the Letter and the Spirit of the law, so to speak, as *normal* and constitutional, he is taking the view that the role of We the People in the American polity is activated in "exceptional" cases.

Ackerman's historical account discloses that these revolutions in the law are also managements of crisis. Although We the People were mobilized at the time of Reconstruction, it was the crisis of a possible impeachment of the President that brought the Constitutional amendments. Similarly, in spite of the electoral mobilization of We the People, it was the crisis of a possible court-packing that brought in the welfare state of the New Deal. Thus the changes from a federalist division of powers through a nationalist separation of powers to the consolidation of Presidential power can be inserted into a continuation of *normal* political practice. Indeed, if I understand right, Professor Ackerman comes close to suggesting that, in the modern context at least, the electoral mobilization of We the People provides an alibi for crisis-management among the powers by allowing the party to claim "A People's Mandate."

We are, in other words, hearing the story of the gradual constitution (small c), normalization, and regularization of something called the People (capital P) as a collective subject (We) in the interest of crisis-management. Professor Ackerman acknowledges that "the Constitution presupposes a citizenry," and calls this process the "popular cultivation of the arts of liberal citizenship." And, if you will forgive a slightly tendentious phrase, "the ideological state apparatus" does work to this end.

Here is the making of a collective "We the People" in the high school classroom:

> Mr. Bower's American Government class has been studying the U.S. Constitution. He has designed a rich multiple-ability groupwork task to help his students understand the relationship among the three branches of the federal government. To reach his objectives, he wants to challenge the students to think metaphorically and to produce insights that allow students to use their critical thinking skills....The task will require many different abilities. Some students will have to be good conceptual thinkers; some will need to be good artists; at least one person will have to be able to quickly find the relevant passages in the Constitution; and someone will need to have strong presentation skills....[This] example...demon-strate[s] the advantage of groupwork that may be gained with the proper preparation and structure necessary for success.[2]

Mr. Bower is preparing a General Will where the signifier "People," seemingly remaining constant as a referent, is being charged with a more and more distanced and mediated signification, as actual agency passes from the popularly elected House of Commons model to today's electoral securing of the noun implicit in the adjective "Popular" in "Popular Mandate." I do not question the astuteness of Professor Ackerman's analysis or the efficiency of the gradual reconstitution of the signifying phrase "We the People." I do, however, question the conviction that this reading gives America back to the people in the American way. I dare to say this because such an unexamined view of the academic's social task is currently laying waste our own field of humanistic education—the proper field of the production of something called a "People."[3]

If we move from the techniques of knowledge production to the techniques of the electoral securing of the People's Mandate, this becomes even clearer. Editorials in all major newspapers have commented extensively on the fact that, under media management, candidates at all levels are becoming detached from local or popular constituencies. Jean Baudrillard has called this the electronic production of the "hyper-real," which is simulated by agencies of power as the Real itself. "Simulation" here means declaring the existence of something that does not exist. Attention to the details of meaning-making might describe the mechanisms of securing a higher law as a spectacular and seamless exercise in simulation.[4]

I have taken a dualist, exceptionalist, and crisis-management reading of the Constitution as instrument of higher lawmaking through Popular Mandate to its logically rather unsettling consequences to highlight an obvious point: A constitutional victory operates within a calculus that does not correspond to the possibility or even the guarantee of justice in the name of any personalized picture of a collection of subjects called "We the People." In fact, as I will insist later in this paper, a constitution can operate only when the person has been coded into rational abstractions manipulable according to the principle of reason. The presupposed collective *constitutional* agent is apart from either the subject, or the universal-in-singular ethical agent.

Yet the narrative guarantee of justice in the name of a collection of subjects is perennially offered as legitimation to the people who will secure the "Popular Mandate." And the authority behind this narrative legitimation—the Constitution as the expression of the general will to justice exercised in time of crisis—is itself secured with reference to an origin-story: the original documents left by the Founding Federalists, Reconstruction Republicans, and New Deal Democrats.

It seems to me that an innovative and flexible text for use such as the U.S. Constitution can only be given what Jean-Francois Lyotard has called a paralogical legitimation.[5] In other words, it provides occasion for morphogenetic innovation—innovations leading to new forms.

Strictly speaking, paralogical legitimation is not teleological. Yet the legitimizing debates at times of crisis impose closure by claiming faithfulness to original intent, even if only the intent to keep the document historically flexible, and thus restoring its origin by gaining its end. The more "accurate" guarantee, not of justice as the expression of a general will of We the People, but of a persistent critique of originary legitimations, by the very people who supply the Popular Mandate for the electoral machinery, can be precariously fabricated if the paralogical is kept in mind.

One of the counter-narratives that can help as a reminder of the paralogical is of the contingency of origins. Let me give you an example.

Professor Ackerman correctly states that the American origin was not simply "an escape from old Feudalism," as de Tocqueville would have it, but a new start. Is it banal to remind ourselves that this new start or origin could be secured because the colonists encountered a sparsely populated, thoroughly pre-capitalist social formation that could be managed by pre-political maneuvers? Robin Blackburn's recent compendious book *The Overthrow of Colonial Slavery* has argued that the manipulation of chattel slavery as an item of political economy was also effective in securing a seemingly uninscribed slate in a space effectively cleared of political significance in the indigenous population. No discussion of the historical development of the mode of operation of the Constitution can afford altogether to ignore this rusing at the origin:

> The key slogan in the struggle against the British had been "no taxation without representation."...The acceptance that slaves as wealth should entitle Southern voters to extra representation built as acknowledgement of slavery into the heart of the Constitution....The text of the Constitution resorted to shame-faced circumlocution rather than use the dreaded words "slave" and "slavery": "Representatives and direct Taxes shall be apportioned among the several states which may be included within this Union, according to their respective Numbers, which shall be determined by adding to the whole Number of free Persons, including those bound to Service for a Term of Years, and excluding Indians not taxes, three fifths of all other persons."[6]

Later in this essay I will present Derrida's discussion of the originary hypocrisy that produces all signatories: the politics of the proper name. Here the origin of the "Good People" of these colonies guaranteeing as they are guaranteed by the signatories is secured by staging the hypocrisy in a theater of violence.

Since I am an Indian citizen, let me offer you a bizarre narrative of what, in Professor Ackerman's vocabulary, may be called a "failed originary moment." "After much hesitation... Elizabeth [I]...granted a charter of incorporation on December 31st 1600" to the East India Company. As is well known, there was increasing conflict between the British Government and the Company until, by Pitt's India Act of 1784, "the control of the Company was brought under the House of Commons."[7] Of course it is absurd to offer a fable as fact, or attempt to rewrite history counterfactually. But let us remember that Professor Ackerman has the integrity to admit that he too is retelling a story. Let us also remember that in the eighteenth century, economists such as Adam Smith, functionaries of the East India Company, as well as the British popular press, were exercised by the failed parallel between the American and Indian examples.[8] Let me, therefore, ask you to imagine that, because the East India Company was incorporated, and because India was not a sparsely populated, thoroughly pre-capitalist social formation easily handled through pre-political maneuvers and the manipulation of chattel slavery; in other words, because it was not possible for a group of British merchants to establish a settlement colony there, no apparent origin could be secured and no Founding Fathers could establish the United States of India, no "Indian Revolution" against Britain could be organized by foreign settlers.

I admire the United States greatly, so much so that I have made it my second home, lived and worked here over half my life. Speaking as a not-quite-not-citizen, then, I would submit to you that Euramerican origins and foundations are also secured by the places where an "origin" is violently instituted. In the current conjuncture, when so much of the identity of the American nation-state is secured by global economic and political manipulation, and when the imminent prospect of large-scale fence-mending beckons and recedes, it is not disrespectful of the energy of We the American people to insist that domestic accounts that emphasize America as a self-made giant illegally wrenching the origin of freedom from merely a moribund Europe have their own political agenda.

Constitutional talk is normally a tale of transactions between Europe and America. In my opinion, Transnational Culture Studies must put this transaction in an international frame. If, for example, the project of recovering or discovering the true structure of the national discourse from ideas of foreign manufacture is taken as a general principle of the study of constitutions, the enterprise would become productively problematic as soon as we move outside Euramerica. One cannot substitute "native" for "national" in that undertaking. A transnational study of culture will not neutralize or disciplinarize the problem by defining it away as "comparative" work, assimilate it by considering the last great wave of imperialism as basically a part of metropolitan history, or yet, however implicitly, bestow upon colonialism what Professor Bernard Williams has called "moral luck" in the context of ethical philosophy.[9]

Turkey is a most interesting case in point. If we take the Conquest of Istanbul (1453) as a dividing line, we can see parallel but highly differentiated formations developing in Mediterranean and Western Europe on the one hand and the Ottoman Empire on the other.[10] What characterizes the latter is the extraordinarily active and vastly heterogeneous diasporic activity that is constantly afoot on its terrain.

There is still an unfortunate tendency, in the "comparativist" arena, to represent the Ottoman Empire as governed by the static laws of something like "the Asiatic Mode of Production," with its change-inhibiting bureaucratic hierarchy and absence of private property in land.[11] If, however, Western Europe is not taken as a necessary norm, the successes and vicissitudes of the Ottoman Empire can be seen as an extraordinary series of experiments to negotiate questions of ethnicity, religion, and "national" identity upon a model rather different from the story of the emergence of nationalism in the former space. (I am of course not interested in legitimizing the Eurocentric model by endorsing the "Islamic Revival.") It has been argued by contemporary scholars that the economic formations of late 18th century Western Europe began to shift the balance within the Ottoman Empire so that its Muslim component began increasingly to slip or remain contained into a pre-capitalist mode.

Professor Kemal Kerpat has argued that what was a curiosity about the West was gradually recoded as the necessity to imitate.[12] Religious nationalism began to grow as "the ideal of impartiality which insulated the bureaucracy" began to break down.

The Ottoman trade monopoly on the Black Sea came to an end in 1774. The Mediterranean trade had been dominated by the West. Now "for the common good of the two Empires," Russia stepped into the Black Sea trade. In 1798 Napoleon invaded Egypt, threatening the British trade route to India. "The Ottoman economy gradually entered a period of total submission to the industrial giants of Europe." In this transforming society, religious difference gradually gets politically re-coded as majorities and minorities, until, in a century's time, "the Ottoman government [is] increasingly called 'Turkish,' and 'Turkish' [now] means a dominant Muslim majority."

This is not merely a demographic change imposed from without. It is a discursive shift, making possible certain kinds of statements, ultimately making possible a Turkish nationalist who "finds it 'in vain to offer resistance' to European civilization," the "visionary mimic man as father of the nation," Mustafa Kemal Ataturk.[13]

We are speaking of the same period—1774, 1798—as in the cases of the U.S. and India. But the narrative is different again. In the case of the United States, an originary claim is secured. In the case of India, colony and Empire step forth as place-holders for "a failed originary movement." Here the question of origin is settled differently.

Let us consider secularism without the moralistic fervor with which we contemplate its "organic development" in the West, just as we thought of "nation"-s a moment ago without necessarily checking them against the story of the rise of nationalism in the West.[14] In a practically multi-national empire like the Ottoman, the separation of Church and State was practically effective in the interest of the overarching State. This secularism was not the name of the socializing of Western Christianity, which has something like a relationship with the rise of industrial monopoly capitalist imperialism. It was rather a pre-capitalist practical (not philosophical) secularism which was given loose ideological support by a communitarianist universalism taken to be present in the Islamic *umma*. (Any suggestion that this can be suddenly injected into "Islamic" polities today is to work in the "naive conviction that the Muslim masses are still living in the religious atmosphere of the Middle Ages.")[15]

The impact of a shift in world trade begins to reconstitute the habitus (Pierre Bourdieu's term) of the region into the Western European discursive formation at the end of the 18th century In other words, things begin to "make sense" in Western European terms. The Ottoman example is now a "deviation." And now, in a reconstituted Muslim-majority Turkish State, it is possible for Western Europe to *offer* an *originary* model. Turkey begins to constitute itself as a nation-state. The Constitution of 1876 is its first inscription, the general "balkanization" of the Empire after the First World War its necessary military-political consolidation.[16]

I have argued at length elsewhere that the peculiar play of contingency in the narrativization of history should not be construed as the Laws of Motion of History. My argument has been developed in the context of presenting a contrast between the circumstances contingent upon two great monotheisms— Christianity and Islam—in the possibility of their reinscription as secularism as such.[17] This is not the moment to repeat that argument in detail. As an example I will refer to something from recent Indian history, without necessarily connecting it to my previous mention of the Indian case.

The Khilafat movement (1918-1925) in India, launched in the name of a multi-national unitarian universalist Islam supporting the Ottoman Caliphate, was out of joint with the times.[18] It was in fact an anti-imperialist nationalist attempt at the consoli- dation of the minority rights of Islam in India. Here, too, the reconstitution of the Imperial Mughal State and the independent principalities of India through (more direct) contact with industrial monopoly capitalist imperialism had established a new habitus: majority-minority. In the sphere of decolonization it was European-style nationalism that was on the agenda. (In fact, that was the subtext of the Khilafat movement.) Thus, although the Khilafat movement lent support to the rise of Mustafa Kemal, the creator of "modern Turkey " it was by Kemal's Constitution, in early 1924 that the actual Khilafat or Caliphate was abolished. For the Indians, after a negotiated Independence, in 1947, Western European codes and English Common Law offered models of origin. The constitution of the secular state of India was launched under the auspices of Lord Mountbatten, although the voice of Islam and a semitized Hinduism as alternatives to the European Enlightenment were still heard.[19]

Let us look now at the question of origin in the Turkish case. A simulated alien origin or source, from which to draw "modernization" and constitutionality appears, politically and philosophically cognizable, facing a terrain re-territorialized in response to the global release of industrial Capital. The teleological vision of a Turkish "nation" now effaces the incessantly negotiated multi-nationality that was the Ottoman Empire because that can no longer be recognized as multi-"nation"-ality. The gap can be measured by the distance between Midhat Pasha's Constitution of 1876 and Mustafa Kamal's Constitution of 1924.

> 1876: Art. 1. The Ottoman Empire comprises present countries and possessions and semi-dependent provinces. It forms an indivisible whole, from which no portion can be detached under and pretext whatever....Art. 8. All subjects of the Empire are called Ottomans, without distinction, whatever faith they profess; the status of an Ottoman is acquired and lost, according to conditions specified by law.[20]
>
> 1924: Art. 2. The Turkish State is republican, nationalist, populist, etatist, secular and reformist....Art. 68. Every Turk is born free, and free he lives.[21]

Whatever the discrepancy in the U.S. or in Turkey, "between constitutional norms and political realities," between Empire and Nation, by 1924 "the free Turk" is coded into constitutional rationality as a person, as opposed to the Ottoman."[22] "The free American," comparably coded, can disavow the contingent securing of his origin, and present his felicitous connection with world trade at the moment of origin (compounded by domestic simple commodity production with "organic" links to industrial capitalism) as *only* a bold rupture."[23] "The free Turk" is obliged to a perennial acknowledgement of European debt.

As for the Republic of India, which is now attempting to consolidate central power in the place of a loose federalist model, the most horrifying dissension is arising there from the lack of fit between the constitutional presupposition of a "People" and a heterogeneous electorate not "organically" deduced from it, blindly seeking other channels to national agency. The national agency of "foreign" provenance still remains the shaky alibi for federal policy.[24]

The Japanese Constitutions from 1889 to 1947, the latter (though this, is at issue at the moment) drafted by staff members of General Douglas MacArthur, would provide another, quite different, set of manipulations of narratives of origin and end. In the interest of balance, I will not proliferate examples here.

I should, however, like to look at the "free Turk" in a sharper focus.

In the brief first section, entitled "Declarations of Independence," of *otobiographies*, Derrida points out that "the good People of these Colonies" in whose name the representatives sign the American Declaration of Independence do not, strictly speaking, exist. As such they do not yet have the name and authority before the Declaration. At the same time, they are required to produce the authority for a Declaration which gives them being.

"This outrageous thing [is] quotidian."[25] That fact does not, however, authorize us to ignore it as trivial.

> This undecidability between what we might call a performative and a constative structure [is] *required* for the production of the desired effect....The signature [on the Declaration] invents the signatory [the name and authority of the Good People]...in a sort of fabulous retroactivity....This fabulous event [is only]... possible in truth by a present's inadequation to itself....The constitution...guarantees...your passport...marriages... checks....[by] the signature of each American citizen [which] depends, in fact and by right, upon this indispensable confusion....[The Good People] sign in the name of ["the laws of Nature and of Nature's God"]...and therefore all the play that must insist on presenting performative utterances as constative.[26]

This confusion guarantees the identity of the national agent—passport, marriage, check. But this originary "hypocrisy," entailing the involvement of the laws of nature, guarantees/produces the national agent *as such*, who is also the guarantor of the guarantee. The first is seen in the constative/ performative in "every Turk is *born* free" (1924). The second is seen in the guarantor/guaranteed in the self-inadequate present of "the system *is* based on the principle that the people per- sonally and effectively *direct* their own destinies" (1921).

If the series of Turkish constitutions are read with Derrida's extraordinary attention to detail, we would, again and again, trace this disclosure/effacement of the trace, at the origin of the founding of modern constitutions. Undecidability secures the agent's ability to decide as a free national agent.

Why do we need to remember this? So that the possibility of agency is not taken to guarantee the self-proximity of the subject; and national or ethnic *identity* do not become fetishized. Nationalism in the context of metropolitan countries can then become the justification for the founding racist ideology of imperialism and neo-colonialism, "the end of history," declaring "the triumph of the West," predicated upon being "turned off by [the] nihilistic idea of what literature was all about [taught by] Roland Barthes and Jacques Derrida."[27] In the context of the Third World, if the undecidable and slippery founding of agency is seen to be the birth of a new man/woman, the act of the founding, celebrating political independence, comes to be seen as an end in itself. Responding to the U.S. reception of his *Islam and Capitalism*, so staunch a Marxist as Maxime Rodinson is obliged to renounce both economics as the last instance and access to scientific truth:

> I merely hold that the translation of the popular will into political decisions requires something else than free parliamentary elections, quite other arrangements differing according to the social condition of the population under consideration.... My struggle [is] precisely against faith in the panacea of political independence. That does not mean that I scorn political independence, that I renounce my support of the struggle for decolonization....Just as it is important to perceive, behind the scenes in the representative institutions, the reality of the forces of economic pressure, so too is it necessary to understand that a world of independent political units, each with an equal voice at the U.N., even endowed with representative institutions, does not, in itself, make a "free world." That is undoubtedly obvious to the most naive observer of the international political game, but the ideology that sacralizes political institutions impedes acknowledgement of all the consequences....The whole truth is no more accessible to man than full freedom or complete harmony of social relations.[28]

In the mid-sixties, writing for a French rather than U.S. audience, Rodinson had told his readers that "there remain[ed] a very large area of the field of learning that can and must be explored with...philosophical presuppositions provisionally suspended...and the positivist procedure is the one to follow."[29] The American Preface, quoted above, shows the suspension of assurances of positivism as well. Activist thinkers of the Third or any world, not merely anxious "to shine in some salon, lecture-theatre or meeting-hall," repeatedly come up against the call to suspension when questions of originary justification for labels of identity confront them.[30]

Having acknowledged that basing collective practice on the ground of identity begs the question in the very house of self-evidence, how do we re-open the distinction between the U.S. and Turkish cases? It is in the area of the origin from which the new nation separates itself, an issue, as we have noticed in Professor Ackerman's discussion, that is not without a certain importance: "Under the circumstances it was necessary to efface another signature of state by 'dissolving' the lines of colonial paternity or maternity."[31] As the Declaration states: "it becomes necessary for one people to dissolve the political bands which have connected them with another." It is here that the laws of God and Nature provide the necessary last instance that can accommodate "the hypocrisy indispensable to a politico-militaro-economic coup de force."[32] And stand behind the Constitution as pre-text.

Like the U.S. Declaration, what the Turkish Constitution separates itself from is its own past, or rather it secures a separation already inaugurated by the Ottoman Constitution of 1876. In terms of the access to agency, the earlier constitution had not yet fully coded a *coup* (blow) as a *coupure* (cut). The irreducible performative/constative confusion sustaining Art. 3 (1924): "sovereignty belongs *unconditionally* to the nation," depends on the abolition of the Caliphate.

And this is not declared in the name of the Good People of Turkey; merely in the unwritten name of Europe. The "national" is already catachrestic, "wrested from its proper meaning" (OED).[33]

It might, therefore, be politically useful to consider whether Euro-American origins are also not catachrestic, secured by *other* places; to consider, in Derrida's words, "the politics of the proper name used as the last instance." God/Nature in the case of the United States, Europe in the case of Turkey. The two must be read side by side. Turkey is especially interesting because it is not a case of decolonization, but rather an obligatory self-deimperialization. For a transnational study of culture, the "comparative" gesture cannot be docketed in a comfortable academic sub-division of labor; but rather, the inexhaustible taxonomy of catachreses—*how* a constitution begs the question of origin—must at least be invoked at every step.[34] Culture

Studies must, therefore, constantly risk (though not flaunt) is a loss of specialism.

In a provocative sentence in "The Laugh of the Medusa," Helene Cixous writes, "as subject *for* history, woman always occurs simultaneously in several places."[35] I have discussed elsewhere the implications of such a statement for feminism in decolonization.[36] To summarize here, let me propose that Cixous is not speaking of woman as world-historical subject, or as subject *of* history. In her view and mine all historizing is narrativizing—putting in the form of a story. (This view does not assert that truth is fiction in the narrow sense.) Cixous is speaking, I think, of how woman must be presupposed so that she would be appropriate for a new story—a new narrativizing. Cixous is fortunate that the history of the French language offers her this double sense in the ordinary use of the word *histoire*. "Herstory," billed as tendentious, has not caught on.

Let us hold on to the idea of an alternative history/story *for* which woman must be newly imagined as pluralized subject. The new story will make visible what, in the old figurations of the pluralized woman (as mother, wife, sister, daughter, widow female chattel, whore, exceptional stateswoman or public woman with femininity re-coded, and so on) was excluded as historical narratives were shored up, in many different ways, with the representative man as its subject. (The Turkish or Indian accounts given above, for example, would have to be broken up if women were the subject *for* history.)[37]

In this context, *we are* speaking of a subject, broader than the intending person, with outlines that are overdetermined by the many networks (psycho-sexual, familial, political, legal—to *name* a few) in which it puts itself together.

The notion of "woman's history" as one of the levers for deconstructing the discipline of history is one of immense theoretical and practical interest. The scope of the venture is far-reaching, and can be surmised through the more empirical work of, say, the History Workshop in Britain, *Signs* in the U.S., and the feminist contingent of the Subaltern Studies Collective in India. In this paper I am concerned with the legitimation of the normative and privative idiom of constitutions. I must, therefore, restrain my interest in plurality and recall my earlier remark: "the constitutional agent is apart from either the subject or from the universal-in-singular ethical agent."

What I am now going to write can easily be misread as "postmodern modesties replac[ing] Marxist certitudes," as anti-libertarian anti-feminist irresponsible dream talk.[38] This is the risk that one must run in order to understand how much more complicated it is to realize the responsibility of playing with or working with fire than to pretend that what gives light and warmth does not also destroy.

U.S. women must of course use the Constitution to guarantee the possibility of securing the paralogical legitimation of what is defined as "women's rights," because "abortion in the U.S. hovers tenuously in a repressive political climate and a dominant antifeminist culture."[39] Yet, as the writer of these important words, Rosalind Petchesky rightly insists,

> to deny that there will always be a residual conflict between...the idea of concrete individuality, or subjective reality—and that of a social and socially imposed morality of reproduction seems not only naive but dismissive of an important value.[40]

I am pointing at the confusion underlying the conflict and suggesting that, *residually*, we must remember while we are in struggle that, just as a computer codes language production into rationally manipulable bits on the model of artificial intelligence(s), so also must constitutional law code the woman's presupposed self-proximity to her body into abstractions manipulable on the model of simulated person(s). What is compromised or effaced by this is the affective-cognitive-political-social-historical plurality (to *name* a few strands) of "woman" seized as a springboard for a critique of homogenizing reason. Woman's involvement with the Constitution is thus not an unquestioned teleological good but a negotiation with enabling violence. Perhaps this will make clear the structural import of the post-colonial negotiation with the originary discourses of constitutionality.

If we present the urgency of the negotiation as an unques-tioned teleological good, we disavow the fact that the best and the worst in the history of the Feminist movement also entail capitalism and imperialism. In this divided terrain, as woman is normalized into the discursive constitution (both small *and* large C) of "We the People," through struggle over both the instruments that Professor Ackerman helps us to understand anew, *both*, that is to say, "transformative opinions" *and* "constitutional amendments," both Roe v. Wade *and* the ERA, how are we to deal with this defining of ourselves into part of a General Will by way of articles of "foreign"—that is to say gender-alienated—manufacture? The negotiative precariousness of the enterprise comes particularly clear if we notice that the issue of reproductive rights is edging into constitutional rationality by way of the most public (constitutional) framing of the area marked "private."[41] This is indeed a precarious simulation of "privacy" in the narrow sense that can never be adequate to the area where the very notion of privacy is contested in the most general sense. To identify the two is to confuse the subject with the agent by way of a pragmatic notion of the person. As if, after a constitutional victory there is nothing left to do but, to protect the right and train more lawyers. The present of the subject is not adequate to itself. The agent in its constitution both effaces and discloses it.

By contrast, I am suggesting that U.S. women, if they are attentive to the importance of frame-narratives, are in a unique and privileged position to continue a *persistent* critique of mere apologists for their Constitution, even as they use its instruments to secure entry into its liberating purview. Favorite sons and daughters who refuse to sanctify their father's house have their uses. Persistently to critique a structure that one cannot not (wish to) inhabit is the deconstructive stance.

I have given equal time to Professor Ackerman's new telling of the U.S. constitutional narrative, on the one hand, and, on the other, to the two frame discourses. I say this in conclusion because I have become accustomed to the usual benevolent universalist dodge: the Third World (obvious phrase) and women are of course very important issues, but they are not relevant to the topic at hand, and would distract from the seriousness of the debates intrinsic to it. A Transnational Culture Studies would parry that dodge every time.

NOTES

1. Bruce Ackerman, *We the People* (Cambridge: Harvard University Press, 1991).

2. Elizabeth G. Cohen and Joan Benton, "Making Groupwork Work," *American Educator* 12, no. 3 (Fall 1988): 11–12.

3. E. D. Hirsch, *Cultural Literacy: What Every American Needs to Know* (New York: Vintage Books, 1987), and the recent directive for a

50-hour curriculum by Lynn Cheney, the Director of the National Endowment for the Humanities are two tremendously influential examples.

4. Jean Baudrillard, "The Precession of Simulacra," in *Simulations*, tr. Paul Foss et al (New York: Semiotext(e), 1983).

5. Jean-Francois Lyotard, *The Postmodern Condition: A Report on Knowledge*, tr. Geoff Bennington (Minneapolis: Univ. of Minnesota Press, 1984).

6. Robin Blackburn, *The Overthrow of Colonial Slavery 1776–1848* (London: Verso, 1988), 123–24.

7. Arthur Berridale Keith, *A Constitutional History of India: 1600–1935*, 2nd ed. (London: Methuen, 1937), 1.

8. Adam Smith, *An Inquiry into the Nature and Causes of the Wealth of Nations* (Chicago: Univ. of Chicago Press, 1976), 2:150–51. Ranajit Guha, *A Rule of Property for Bengal: An Essay on the Idea of Permanent Settlement*, 2nd ed. (New Delhi: Orient Longman, 1981), 62 n. 2, 45, 75, 76.

9. Bernard Williams. "Moral Luck," in *Moral Luck: Philosophical Papers*, 1973–1980, (Cambridge: Cambridge Univ. Press, 1981). See also Spivak, "Poststructuralism, Postcoloniality, Marginality, and Value," in *Literary Theory Today*, ed. Peter Collier and Helen Geyer-Ryan (Cambridge: Polity Press, forthcoming).

10. This section relies on Maxime Rodinson, *Islam and Capitalism*, tr. Brian Pearce (Austin: Univ. of Texas Press, 1978) and Kemal H. Kerpat, *An Inquiry into the Social Foundations of Nationalism in the Ottoman State: From Social Estates to Classes, From Millets to Nations* (Princeton University: Research Monograph No. 39, 1973). I have followed through their English-language documentation as far as possible. I am also grateful to Dr. Aysegul Baykan and Dr. Mehmet Ali Dikerdem.

11. Two impassioned exhortations against such tendencies are Perry Anderson, "Appendix," *Lineages of the Absolutist State* (London: Verso, 1974) and Edward W. Said, *Covering Islam* (New York: Pantheon, 1981).

12. Kerpat, *Inquiry*, 52. See also p.57f. Quotations in the following paragraph are from pp. 55, 92.

13. Extract from a speech by Ataturk, quoted in Rodinson, *Islam*, 127.

14. The moral fervor itself has often served as alibi. "It [the pursuit of happiness] was developed into a supra-national secular ideology first

in the form of the 'liberal-humanitarian' ideology (to use Mannheim's terminology), with mobilizing forms such as French Jacobinism, in a number of countries (including in the East) and in a variety of periods.... But the use made of this ideology to provide cover for domination by the powers of money, and especially by American 'Big Business,' and also to disguise domination by Europe, has done it a very great deal of harm," Rodinson, *Islam*, 234. This is of course rather an obvious point. I am always surprised to note how often it bears repeating. My source here is Rodinson because I am using him as one of my main secondary texts.

15. Rodinson, *Islam*, 231.

16. At this writing, the *New York Times* for Sunday, November 12, 1989, offered a series of rough maps of the area around East Germany in order to clue the reader into the nationalist-political movements after *glasnost*. It is interesting to watch the emergence and disappearance of the word "Ottoman" between the explanation material of the second and third frames (1933 to 1943!). If at all noticed, it stands in for a barely noticed pre-history for the U.S. reader careful enough to notice.

17. Spivak, "Reading *The Satanic Verses*," *Public Culture* 2.1 (Fall 1989).

18. See Gail Minault, *The Khilafat Movement: Religious Symbolism and Political Mobilization in India* (New York: Columbia Univ. Press, 1982).

19. See Maurice Gwyer and A. Appadorai, eds., *Speeches and Documents on the Indian Constitution* (New York: Oxford Univ. Press, 1957). See also Granville Austin, *The Indian Constitution: Cornerstone of A Nation* (Bombay: Oxford Univ. Press, 1972).

20. *Turkey*, No. 2 (1877): Correspondence Respecting the Conference at Constantinople and the Affairs of Turkey, 1876–77 (London: Harrison and Sons, 1877).

21. Helen Miller Davis, *Constitutions, Electoral Laws, Treaties of States in the Near and Middle East* (Durham: Duke Univ. Press, 1953).

22. Bert P. Blaustein and Gisbert H. Flanz, eds., *Constitutions of the Countries of the World* (New York: Oceana, 1976), 4.

23. For a discussion of the paired modes of production, see Samir Amin, *Unequal Development*, tr. Brian Pearce (New York: Monthly Review Press, 1976), 21. The link is also between Virginia and New England.

24. For a study of communalism in India, see Bipan Chandra, *Communalism in Modern India* (New Delhi: Vikas, 1984). The following remark appeared in "The Week in Review," *New York Times*, 15 Oct.

1989: "Many Indians say the legislature's importance has been declining for two decades, first under Prime Minister Indira Gandhi and now under her son Rajiv....A leading social scientist, Rajni Kothari, said in a recent interview that the five years of Mr. Gandhi's Government 'have been, institutionally, the worst in Indian history.'" The *New York Times* is not a scholarly organ, but it does reflect ideological trends. And Mr. Kothari is indeed a social scientist of stature.

25. Jacques Derrida, *otobiographies: l'enseignement de Nietzsche et la politique du nom propre* (Paris: Galilee, 1984), 23.

26. Derrida, *otobiographies*, 21–25. I have rearranged the word order slightly in order to make coherent extrapolations.

27. James Atlas, "What is Fukuyama Saying?," *New York Times*, 22 Oct. 1989, Sunday Magazine, 38–39.

28. Rodinson, *Islam*, xxiii, xxv, xxvi.

29. Rodinson, *Islam*, xv.

30. Rodinson, *Islam*, 2. I write these words in some bitterness because my calls to scrupulous suspension at one point gave rise to bizarre document: Biodun Jeyifo and anonymous colleague, "'Race' and the Pitfalls of Ventriolquial Deconstruction: Gayatri Chakravorty Spivak's Regressive Monologue on Africa," unpublished but very widely circulated by authors.

31. Derrida, *otobiographies*, 24.

32. Derrida, *otobiographies*, 27.

33. For the argument that the political claims of decolonized nations are catachrestic, see Spivak, "Poststructuralism, Postcoloniality, Marginality, and Value," in *Literary Theory Today*, ed. Peter Collier and Helga Geyer-Ryan (Cambridge: Polity Press, forthcoming).

34. For a somewhat schematic view on this from the disciplinary perspective of history, see Charles Bright and Michael Gyer, "For a Unified History of the World in the Twentieth Century," *Radical History Review* 39 (1987): 69–91.

35. Helene Cixous, "The Laugh of Medusa," in *New French Feminisms*, ed. Elaine Marks and Isabelle de Courtivron (Amherst: Univ. of Massachusetts Press, 1980), 252.

36. "French Feminism Revisited: Ethics and Politics," in *Feminists Theorize the Political*, ed. Joan Scott and Judith Butler (forthcoming).

37. See Aysegul Baykan, "Modernism, Fundamentalism and the Women in Between" (Paper presented at the 1989 ASA Conference); and

Spivak, "Woman in Difference: Mahasweta Devi's 'Douloti the Beautiful,'" (Paper presented at Nationalisms and Sexuality Conference, Harvard Univ., 16–18 June 1989).

38. Jeffrey C. Goldfarb, "The Age of Dissent: Democracy Crashes Party," *Village Voice Literary Supplement* (October, 1989).

39. Rosalind Pollack Petchesky, *Abortion and Woman's Choice: the State, Sexuality, and Reproductive Freedom* (London, Verso, 1986), vi.

40. Petchesky, *Abortion*, 395.

41. The Fourteenth Amendment offers the most hospitable text for the insertion of reproductive rights into the Constitution. The rational and abstract formula that can guarantee "privacy" is: "Nor shall any State deprive any person of...liberty...without due process of law." Petchesky's impressive suggestion, that abortion be re-territorialized from "right to privacy" to "social need" is crucial as a displacement of the right to control reproduction, still within the code. For a recent text which provides documentary access to a good deal of the literature on reproductive ethics and law see Zillah Einstein, *The Female Body and the Law* (Berkeley: Univ. of California Press, 1988).

5

NANCY FRASER _____

Sex, Lies, and the Public Sphere: Some Reflections on the Confirmation of Clarence Thomas

INTRODUCTION

The recent struggle over the confirmation of Clarence Thomas and the credibility of Anita Hill raises in a dramatic and pointed way many of the issues at stake in theorizing the public sphere in contemporary society. At one level, the Senate Judiciary Committee hearings on Hill's claim that Thomas sexually harassed her constituted an exercise in democratic publicity as it has been understood in the classical liberal theory of the public sphere. The hearings opened to public scrutiny a function of government, namely, the nomination and confirmation of a Supreme Court justice. They thus subjected a decision of state officials to the force of public opinion. Through the hearings, in fact, public opinion was constituted and brought to bear directly on the decision itself, affecting the process by which the decision was made as well as its substantive outcome. As a result, state officials were held accountable to the public by means of a discursive process of opinion and will formation.

Yet that classical liberal view of the public sphere does not tell the whole story of these events.[1] If we examine the Thomas confirmation struggle more closely, we see that the very meaning and boundaries of the concept of publicity was at stake. The way the struggle unfolded, moreover, depended at every point on who had the power to successfully and authoritatively define where the line between the public and the private would be drawn. It depended as well on who had the power to police and defend that boundary.

Consider how those issues underlay many of the questions that were explicitly debated: Was the public disclosure on 6 October 1991 of Anita Hill's accusations against Clarence Thomas a leak that represented a breach of proper procedure and confidentiality, or was it an act of whistle-blowing that exposed a cover-up? Was Anita Hill's failure to go public with her accusations prior to 6 October grounds for doubting her account, or was it consistent with her story? Should the behavior Hill ascribed to Thomas be considered innocent comraderie or abuse of power? Is such behavior "normal" or "pathological"?

Moreover, do men and women have different views of these issues, and are they positioned differently with respect to privacy and publicity? Did the efforts of Thomas's supporters to undermine the credibility of Anita Hill constitute an invasion of her privacy or a proper exercise of public scrutiny? Were there significant differences in the ability of Thomas and Hill respectively to define and defend their privacy?

Was the injection of the issue of race by Clarence Thomas a mere smoke screen, or did the convening of an all-white public tribunal to adjudicate on television a dispute between two blacks signal the existence of real racial-ethnic differences in relation to privacy and publicity? Is "sexual harassment" a figment of the fevered imagination of puritanical, sexually repressed, elite white feminists or an instrument of gender, race, and class power? Does the vindication in this case of a black man's ability to defend his privacy against a white-dominated public represent an advance for his race or a setback for black women?

Did the hearings themselves constitute in unseemly circus that degraded the democratic process, or were they a rare exercise in democratic publicity, a national teach-in on sexual harassment? Was the airing in public hearings of the charge of sexual harassment another case of the American obsession with the private lives of public figures, an obsession that displaces real politics onto questions of characters? Or was it instead a historic breakthrough in an ongoing struggle to achieve a more equitable balance in the social relations of privacy and publicity?

Finally is democratic publicity best understood as a check on the public power of the state, or should it be understood more broadly as a check against illegitimate "private" power as well? And what is the relationship between various publics that emerged here: for example, the official public sphere within the state (the hearings); the extragovernmental public sphere constituted by the mass media; various counterpublics associated with oppositional social movements like feminism and with ethnic enclaves like the black community (the feminist press, the black press); various secondary associations active in forming public opinion (interest groups, lobbies); the ephemeral but intense constitution of informal public spheres at various sites in everyday life—at workplaces, restaurants, campuses, street corners, shopping centers, private homes, wherever people gathered to discuss the events? In each of those public arenas, whose words counted in the conflict of interpretations that determines the official public story of what "really" happened? And why?

Underlying all these questions are two more general problems that are centered on power and inequality: Who has the power to decide where to draw the line between public and private? What structures of inequality underlie the hegemonic understandings of these categories as well as the struggles that contest them?

GENDER STRUGGLE

The first phase of the struggle was played out as a gender struggle, and it laid bare important gender asymmetries concerning privacy and publicity. These were not the familiar orthodoxies of an earlier stage of feminist theory, which protested women's alleged confinement to the private sphere. Rather, the asymmetries here concerned women's greater vulnerability to unwanted, intrusive publicity and lesser ability to define and defend their privacy.

These issues first emerged when the public at large learned of a struggle that had been waged behind closed doors for several weeks between Anita Hill and members of the Senate Judiciary Committee over the handling of her accusations against Clarence Thomas. In her first public news conference after her charges had been publicly reported, Hill focused on what she called her lack of "control" over the routing, timing, and dissemination of her information. She was already having to defend herself against two apparently contradictory charges: first, that she had failed to make public her allegations in a timely fashion, as any bona fide victim of sexual harassment supposedly would have; but second, that in making these charges she was seeking publicity and self-aggrandizement. Hill sought to explain her actions, first, by insisting that "control" over these disclosures "had never been with me," and second, by acknowledging her difficulty in balancing her need for privacy against her duty to disclose information in response to the committee's inquiry.[2] As it turned out, she never succeeded in fully dispelling many Americans' doubts on these points.

For its part, the committee's initial decision not to publicize her sexual harassment charges against Thomas represented an effort to delimit the scope of the first round of public hearings in September and to contain public debate about the nomination. Once Hill's charges were made public, however, the committee lost control of the process. Instead, its members became embroiled in a public struggle with feminists who objected to the privatization of an important gender issue and accused the senators of "sexism" and "insensitivity."

The gender struggle was widely reported in the media in counter-point with a counterdiscourse of outrage over "the leak." These two themes of "The Senate and Sexism" and leaks were for a time the two principal contenders in the battle for preeminence in interpreting the events, as the struggle over whether or not to delay the Senate vote on the nomination was being waged.[3] The vote was of course delayed, and the feminists succeeded in broadening the space of the official national political public sphere to encompass, for the first time, the subject of sexual harassment.

Getting an issue on the public agenda, however, does not guarantee success in controlling the discussion of it. Even as it was being decided that the vote on Thomas's nomination would be delayed and that public hearings on the sexual harassment charges would be held, there began a fierce backstage contest to shape the public debate over the issues. While public debate focused on the question of the Senate's "insensitivity," White House strategists worked behind the scenes to shape the focus of the hearings and the interpretation of events.

As it turned out, the administration's plan to shape public debate and limit the scope of the hearings had three crucial features. First, the White House sought to prevent or marginalize any new allegations of sexual harassment by other victims in order to shape the hearings as a he-said-she-said affair. Second, they sought to rule off-limits any interrogation of what was defined as Thomas's "private life," including what the *New York Times* called his "well-documented taste for watching and discussing pornographic movies while he was at Yale Law School."[4] Third, and last, they sought to exclude expert testimony about the nature of sexual harassment and the characteristic responses of victims, so that, in the words of one administration spin doctor, they could "prevent this from turning into a referendum on 2000 years of male dominance and sexual harassment."[5]

Together these three moves cast Clarence Thomas and Anita Hill in very different relations to privacy and publicity. Thomas was enabled to declare key areas of his life "private" and therefore off-limits. Hill, in contrast, was cast as someone whose motives and character would be subjects of intense scrutiny and intrusive speculation, since her "credibility" was to be evaluated in a conceptual vacuum. When the Senate Judiciary Committee adopted these ground rules for the hearings, they sealed in place a structural differential in relation to publicity and privacy that worked overwhelmingly to Thomas's advantage and to Hill's disadvantage.

Once these ground rules were in place, the administration could concentrate on its hardball attempt to undermine Hill. They sought to insure, as Senator Alan K. Simpson presciently predicted, that "Anita Hill will be sucked right into the maw, the very thing she wanted to avoid most. She will be injured and destroyed and belittled and hounded and harassed, real harassment, different from the sexual kind."[6]

While open season was being declared on Hill, Clarence Thomas was attempting to define and defend his privacy. His attempts had a certain ironic flavor, to be sure. Given his insistence in the first round of hearings on substituting his life story—or at least his version thereof—for discussion of his political, legal, and constitutional views. Having first tried to make his private character the public issue, he was nearly undone by the focus on his character when Hill's accusation was made public.

In the second round of hearings, Thomas responded to Hill's charges by trying to define what he thought was or should be his private life. He refused to accept questions that breached his privacy as he defined it. And he objected to "reporters and interest groups...looking for dirt" as un-American and Kafkaesque.

I am not here...to put my private life on display for prurient interests or other reasons. I will not allow this committee or anyone else to probe into my private life....I will not provide the

rope for my own lynching or for further humiliation. I am not
going to engage in discussions nor will I submit to roving
questions of what goes on in the most intimate parts of my
private life, or the sanctity of my bedroom. These are the most
intimate parts of my privacy and they will remain just that,
private.[7]

Certainly, Thomas was not entirely successful in enforcing
his definitions of privacy and publicity, as the mere airing of
Hill's charges attested. Yet within the limits imposed by the fact
of the hearings, he was more successful than not. His ques-
tioners on the committee generally accepted his definition of
privacy and their questions did not trespass on that space as he
had defined it. They didn't inquire into his sexual history or his
fantasy life, and he was not in fact questioned about his practice
of viewing and discussing pornographic films. The one time
when this subject was broached, at the session of 12 October
1991, Thomas successfully repulsed the inquiry:

> [Senator Leahy]: Did you ever have a discussion of pornographic
> films with...any other women [than Professor
> Hill]?
>
> [Thomas]: Senator, I will not get into any discussions that
> I might have about my personal life or my sex
> life with any person outside of the workplace.[8]

The question was not pursued. Later, after the Senate confirmed
the nomination, Democratic members of the Judiciary Committee defended their failure to cross-examine Thomas vigorously
by saying that he had put up a "wall" and refused to answer
questions about his private life.[9]

The relative success of Thomas's efforts to define and defend
his privacy can be seen in the fact that while the country was
awash in speculation concerning the character, motives, and
psychology of Anita Hill, there was no comparable speculation
about him. No one wondered, it seemed, what sort of anxieties
and hurts could lead a powerful and successful self-made black
man from a very poor background to sexually harass a black
female subordinate from a similar background.

Anita Hill also sought to define and defend her privacy, but
she was far less successful than Thomas. Events constantly
eluded her efforts to keep the focus on her complaint and on the
evidence that corroborated it. Instead, the principal focus soon
became *her* character. During the course of the struggle, it was
variously suggested that Hill was a lesbian, a heterosexual

erotomaniac, a delusional schizophrenic, a fantasist, a vengeful spurned woman, a perjurer, and a malleable tool of liberal interest groups. Not only the Republican hit men, Arlen Specter, Orrin Hatch, and Alan Simpson, but even her female coworkers from the Equal Employment Opportunity Commission tarred her with many of the classical sexist stereotypes: "stridently aggressive," "arrogant," "ambitious," "hard," "tough," "scorned," "opinionated." Nor did any of the Democratic committee members succeed, or for that matter even try, to limit the scope of inquire into her "privacy."[10]

Hill's lesser success in drawing the line between public and private testifies to the gendered character of these categories and to the way their constitution reflects the asymmetry or hierarchy of power along gender lines. That asymmetry is reflected in the phenomenon of sexual harassment as well. Consider the following account by Hill in response to the questioning of Howell Heflin, who first read to her portions of her own opening statement:

> "I sense[d] that my discomfort with [Thomas's] discussion [of pornography] only urged him on as though my reaction of feeling ill at ease and vulnerable was what he wanted."

Then, in response to Heflin's request for elaboration, Hill replied: "It was almost as though he wanted me at a disadvantage...so that I would have to concede to whatever his wishes were....I would be under his control. I think it was the fact that I had said no to him that caused him to want to do this."[11] As Hill saw it, then, Thomas's behavior had been an assertion (or reassertion) of power, aimed simultaneously at compensating himself and punishing her for rejection. She herself had lacked the power to define the nature of their interaction; he, in contrast, had had the power to inject what liberals consider private sexual elements into the public sphere of the workplace against her wishes and over her objections.

Given the gender differential in ability to define and protect one's privacy, we can understand some of the deeper issues at stake in Thomas's insistence on avoiding the "humiliation" of a "public probe" into his "privacy." This insistence can be understood in part as a defense of his masculinity; to be subject to having one's privacy publicly probed is to risk being feminized.

Women's difficulty in defining and defending their privacy is also attested by an extremely important absence from the hearings: the non-appearance of Angela Wright, a second black woman who claimed to have been sexually harassed by Thomas and whose testimony to that effect was to have been corroborated by another witness, Rose Jordain, in whom Wright had confided at the time. Given that disbelief of Hill was often rationalized by the claim that there were no other complainants, the non-appearance of Wright was significant. We can speculate that had she testified and proved a credible witness, the momentum of the struggle might have shifted decisively. Why then did Angela Wright not appear? Both sides had reasons to privatize her story. Thomas's supporters feared a second accusation would be extremely damaging and threatened to discredit her by introducing information concerning her personal history. Thomas's opponents may have feared that a woman described in the press as presenting "a more complex picture than Professor Hill"[12] would appear to lack credibility and undermine Hill's as well. Thus, the silencing of a complainant who was thought to lack Hill's respectability was a crucial and possibly even decisive factor in the dynamics and outcome of the struggle.

THE STRUGGLE OVER RACE

During the first, gender-dominated phase of the struggle, the issue of race was barely discussed, despite repeated, but unelaborated references to the Senate as an all-white body.[13] The relative silence about race was soon shattered, however, when Thomas himself broached the issue. Moving quickly to occupy an otherwise vacant discursive terrain, he and his supporters managed to establish a near-monopoly on "race" talk, and the result proved disastrous for Hill.

Thomas claimed that the hearings were a "high-tech lynching" designed to stop "uppity Blacks who in any way deign to think for themselves."[14] He also spoke repeatedly about his defenselessness before charges that played into racial stereotypes of black men as having large penises and unusual sexual prowess.[15]

Here it is important to note that by combining references to lynching with references to stereotypes about black men's sexual prowess, Thomas artfully conflated two stereotypes, which, although related, are far from identical. The first is the stereotype of the black man as sexual stud, highly, desired by women and capable of providing them great sexual pleasure. This was the figure that emerged from Hill's testimony, according to which Thomas bragged to her about his heterosexual virtuosity. The second stereotype is that of the black man as rapist, a lust-driven animal, whose sexuality is criminal and out of control. There was no hint of that stereotype in Hill's testimony.

It is possible that at an unconscious level there are affinities between these two stereotypes. But they differ importantly in at least one crucial respect. While both have been embraced by white racists, the first, but not the second, has also been embraced by some black men.[16] Thus, while it may be inconceivable that Thomas would have elected to affect the persona of black man as rapist, it is not inconceivable that he would have affected the persona of the black male sexual stud. Yet by conflating these two stereotypes, Thomas was able to suggest that Hill's reports of his behavior as a would-be stud were equivalent to southern white racist fabrications of criminal sexuality and rape. This turned out to be a rhetorical master stroke. The Democrats on the committee were too cowed by the charge of racism to question the nominee's logic. Many leading black liberals seemed caught off guard and unable to respond effectively; most simply denied that race had any relevance in the case at all.

The mainstream press contributed to the confusion. For example, the *New York Times* printed solemn quotations from Harvard psychiatrist Alvin Poussaint about the effects of Hill's charges on black men:

> "Black men will feel [her allegations] reinforce negative stereotypes about them as sexual animals out of control....It will increase their level of tension and vulnerability around charges of this type....There's a high level of anger among black men...that black women will betray them; that black women are given preference over them; that white men will like to put black women in between them to use them. Black men feel that white men are using this black woman to get another black man."[17]

I have no way of knowing whether or to what extent Poussaint is accurately reporting the views and feelings of black men. What is clear, however, is the lack of any comparable discussion of the effects of the case on black women. In the absence of such discussion, moreover, the fears ascribed to black men seem to acquire legitimacy. They are not contextualized or counter-pointed by any other perspective. The press coverage of the racial dimensions of the struggle generally slighted black women. It focused chiefly on questions such as whether or not all black

men would be tarred in the eyes of white America, and whether
or not another black man would get a shot at a seat on the
Supreme Court.

One of the most important features of the entire struggle was
the absence from the hearings and from the mainstream public
sphere debate of a black feminist analysis. No one who was in a
position to be heard in the hearings or in the mainstream mass
media spoke about the historic vulnerability of black women to
sexual harassment in the United States and about the use of
racist-misogynist stereotypes to justify such abuse and to malign
black women who protest.[18] As a result, black women were yet
again "asked to choose...whether to stand against the indignities
done them as women, sometimes by men of their own race, or to
remember that black men take enough of a beating from the
white world and to hold their peace."[19] In other words, there was
no widely disseminated perspective that persuasively integrated
a critique of sexual harassment with a critique of racism. At this
stage the struggle was cast as either a gender struggle or a race
struggle. It could not, apparently, be both at once.

The result was that it became difficult to see Anita Hill as a
black woman. She became, in effect, functionally white. Certainly, Thomas's references to lynching had the effect of calling
into question her blackness. The lynching story requires a white
woman as "victim" and pretext. To my knowledge, no black man
has ever been lynched for the sexual exploitation of a black
woman. Thomas's charge thus implied that Hill might not really
be black. Perhaps because she was a tool of white interest
groups. Or perhaps because she had internalized the uptight,
puritanical sexual morality of elite white feminists and had
mistaken his lower class, black courting style for abuse, a view
propounded by Orlando Patterson.[20] Or perhaps most ingen-
iously of all, because, like Adela Quested, the white female
protagonist of E. M. Forster's *A Passage to India*, Hill was an
erotomaniacal spinster who fantasized abuse at the hands of a
dark-skinned man out of the depths of her experiences of rejection and sexual frustration, a view apparently originated by John
Doggett, but more effectively—because less self-servingly—
presented by Hatch and other Thomas supporters.

Whichever of these scenarios one chose to believe, the net
effect was the same: Anita Hill became functionally white. She
was treated, consequently, very differently from the way that
Angela Wright would probably have been treated had *she*

testified. Wright might very well have been cast as Jezebel, opposite Hill's Adela Quested, in a bizarre melodramatic pastiche of traditional and nontraditional casting.

The "whitening" of Anita Hill had much broader implications, however, since it cast black women who seek to defend themselves against abuse at the hands of black men as traitors or enemies of the race. Consequently, when the struggle was cast exclusively as a racial struggle, the sole black protagonist became the black man. He was made to stand synecdochically for the entire race, and the black woman was erased from view.

A recent development holds out some hope for redressing this erasure and for overcoming the definition of the struggle as either a gender or a race struggle. This is the founding of a group called African American Women in Defense of Ourselves, whose inaugural statement is worth quoting at some length:

> Many have erroneously portrayed the allegations against Clarence Thomas as an issue of either gender or race. As women of African descent, we understand sexual harassment as both. We further understand that Clarence Thomas outrageously manipulated the legacy of lynching in order to shelter himself from Anita Hill's allegations. To deflect attention away from the reality of sexual abuse in African American women's lives, he trivialized and misrepresented this painful part of African American people's history. This country, which has a long legacy of racism and sexism, has never taken the sexual abuse of Black women seriously. Throughout U.S. history Black women have been sexually stereotyped as immoral, insatiable, perverse; the initiators in all sexual contacts—abusive or otherwise. The common assumption in legal proceedings as well as in the larger society has been that Black women cannot be raped or otherwise sexually abused. As Anita Hill's experience demonstrates, Black women who speak of these matters are not likely to be believed.
>
> In 1991, we cannot tolerate this type of dismissal of any one Black woman's experience or this attack upon our collective character without protest, outrage, and resistance....No one will speak for us but ourselves.[21]

What is so important about this statement is its rejection of the view, held by many supporters of Anita Hill, that race was simply irrelevant to this struggle, apart from Thomas's manipulation of it. Instead, the statement implies that the categories of privacy and publicity are not simply gendered categories; they are racialized categories as well. Historically, blacks have been denied privacy in the sense of domesticity. As a result, black women have been highly vulnerable to sexual harassment at the hands of masters, overseers, bosses, and supervisors. At the same time, they have lacked the public standing to claim state protection against abuse, whether suffered at work or at home. Black men, meanwhile, have lacked the rights and prerogatives enjoyed by white men, including the right to exclude white men from "their" women and the right to exclude the state from their "private" sphere.

Perhaps, then, it is worth exploring the hypothesis that in making his case before the white tribunal, Clarence Thomas was trying to claim the same rights and immunities of masculinity that white men have historically enjoyed, especially the right to maintain open season on black women. Or perhaps he was not claiming *exactly* the same rights and immunities as white men. Perhaps he was not seeking these privileges vis-à-vis all women. After all, no white woman claimed to have been sexually harassed by him. Is that because in fact he never sexually harassed a white woman, although he married one? And if so, is *that* because he felt less of a sense of entitlement in his interactions with his white female subordinates at work? If so, then perhaps his references to lynching were not *merely* a smoke screen, as many people assumed. Perhaps they were also traces of the racialization of his masculinity. In any event, we need more work that theorizes the racial subtext of the categories of privacy and publicity and its intersection with the gender subtext.[22]

CLASS STRUGGLE?

Sexual harassment is not only a matter of gender and racial domination but one of status and class domination as well. The scene of harassment is the workplace or educational institution; the protagonists are bosses, supervisors, or teachers, on the one hand, and employees or students, on the other; the effect of the practice is to maintain the power of the former over the latter.[23] Sexual harassment, therefore, implicates the classic issues of workers' power in the workplace and student power in the school. It should be high on the agenda of every trade union, labor organization, and student association.

Yet the class and status dimensions of the struggle over Thomas's confrontation were not aired in the public sphere debates. No trade unionist or workers' or students' representative testified in the hearings. Nor did any publish an op-ed piece in the *New York Times*. In general, no one in a position to be widely heard articulated support for Anita Hill grounded in class or status solidarity. No one foregrounded the accents of class to rally workers and students to her side.

The absence of a discourse of class conflict in the United States is no surprise. What is surprising perhaps was the deployment in the final phase of the struggle of a counter-discourse of class resentment to mobilize support for Thomas.

On the day before the Senate confirmation vote, the *New York Times* printed an op-ed piece by that longtime friend of labor, former speech-writer for presidents Reagan and Bush, Peggy Noonan. Noonan predicted victory for Thomas based on a "class division" between the "chattering classes" supporting Hill and the "normal humans," who believed Thomas. She also glossed this as a division between the "clever people who talk loudly in restaurants and those who seat them":

> You could see it in the witnesses. For Anita Hill, the pro-fessional, movement-y and intellectualish Susan Hoerchner, who spoke with a sincere, unmakeupped face of inherent power imbalances in the workplace. For Clarence Thomas, the straight-shooting Maybellined J.C. Alvarez, who once broke up a mugging because she hates bullies and paid $900 she doesn't have to get there because she still hates 'em....Ms. Alvarez was the voice of the real, as opposed to the abstract, America: she was like a person who if a boss ever sexually abused her would kick him in the gajoobies and haul him straight to court.[24]

Here Noonan appealed in familiar terms to the "real American" workers (tough and macho, even if wearing eyeliner) to resist the effeminate (albeit make-up-free) intellectuals who impersonate them and feign concern for their interests, but whose American-ness is suspect (shades of Communism). The scenario thus appeared to oppose "the real worker," J. C. Alvarez, to "the intel-lectual," Susan Hoerchner. Yet Alvarez here actually represented Thomas, the boss, while the actual aggrieved subordinate, Anita Hill, disappeared altogether behind the representation of Hoerchner. Moreover, by painting "the worker" as a Maybellined tough guy, Noonan simultaneously updated and perpetuated masculinist stereotypes. It became hard to see most women, who do not repay sexual harassment with a kick to the groin, as "workers."

Noonan's rhetoric mobilized class resentment in support of Thomas by disappearing Anita Hill as a worker. A similar tack was taken by Orlando Patterson, whose own *New York Times* op-ed piece appeared the following week in the guise of a more analytical postmortem. Although Patterson acknowledged Hill's lower class origins, he nonetheless treated her as an instrument of "elitist" (read: "bourgeois") forces. In his scenario she was a tool, not simply of whites or of feminists, but of elite, upper-class white feminists bent on using the law to impose a class-specific sexual morality on poor and working-class populations with different, less repressive norms. Workers were in effect called to defend their class culture—by siding with the boss against his assistant.[25]

Both Noonan and Patterson in effect bourgeoisified Anita Hill, just as Thomas had earlier whitened her. Her actual social origins in rural poverty, which she had stressed in her opening statement to the committee, had by the end of the affair become so clouded by the rhetoric of class resentment that to many she was just another yuppie. The way, once again, was paved by Thomas. Very early on, even before the sexual harassment story broke, he staked out a strong claim to the discourse of impoverished origins. And as in the case of race, here too he retained a near-monopoly.

The "class struggle" in this affair, then, was largely a matter of manipulating the signifiers of class to mobilize resentment in the interests of management. But was class not relevant in any other sense? Were there no class differences in the way Americans viewed these events and in the way they chose sides?

Some news reports following closely on Thomas's confirmation portrayed white working-class women and women of color of all classes as unsympathetic to Hill. For example, in a story titled "Women See Hearing from a Perspective of Their Own Jobs," the *New York Times* reported that blue-collar women were put off by her soft-spokenness and what they construed as her inability to take care of herself. The story contrasted this "blue-collar" view with the views of female "lawyers, human service professionals, and politicians," who strongly sympathized with and believed Hill.[26] Despite the title of the article, the *Times* did not consider the possibility that these putative class differences could be rooted in different class work cultures. It could be the case, for example, that working-class people who felt that Hill should simply have told Thomas off and quit and found another job were not attuned to professional career structures, which require cultivation of one's reputation in the profession via networking and long-term maintenance of relationships.

There was another sense in which class affected this struggle, but it remained largely unspoken and implicit. Polls taken on the last night of the hearings showed that party affiliation was the most statistically significant factor distinguishing Thomas's supporters from Hill's.[27] This suggests that a large part of what was at stake in the confirmation of this and other recent Supreme Court nominees was the continuation—or not—of the Reagan-Bush agenda, broadly conceived. For a moment, the question of sexual harassment became the condensation point for a host of anxieties, resentments, and hopes about who gets what and who deserves what in America. In our current political culture, those anxieties, resentments, and hopes are often articulated in terms of gender and race, but they are also necessarily about status and class. Noonan and Patterson notwithstanding, class remains the great unarticulated American secret. As such, it remains highly susceptible to manipulation and abuse.

CONCLUSION: SOME MORALS OF THE STORY

This extraordinary series of struggles proves the continuing importance of the public sphere in relation to state power. However, it also shows the need to revise the standard liberal view of the public sphere, since the categories of publicity and privacy are multivalent and contested, and not all understandings of them promote democracy.

For example, male-supremacist constructions enshrine gender hierarchy by privatizing practices of domination like sexual harassment. They enforce men's privacy rights to harass women with impunity in part by smearing in public any woman who protests. As a result, women are in effect asked to choose between quiet abuse in private and noisy discursive abuse in public.

However, the gendered character of the categories publicity and privacy cannot today be understood in terms of the Victorian separate-spheres ideology, as some feminists have assumed. It is not the case now, and never was, that women are simply excluded from public life; nor that men are public and women are private; nor that the private sphere is women's sphere and the public sphere is men's; nor that the feminist project is to collapse the boundaries between public and private. Rather, feminist analysis shows the political, ideological nature of these categories. And the feminist project aims in part to overcome the gender hierarchy that gives men more power than women to draw the line between public and private.

Yet even that more complicated view is still too simple because the categories of public and private also have a racial-ethnic dimension. The legacy of American slavery and racism has denied black women even the minimal protections from abuse that white women have occasionally managed to claim, even as their disadvantaged economic position has rendered them more vulnerable to sexual harassment. That same legacy has left black men without white men's privacy rights; they have sometimes tried to claim them in ways that endanger black women. That suggests the need to develop an antiracist project that does not succeed at black women's expense, one that simultaneously attacks the racial and gender hierarchy embedded in hegemonic understandings of privacy and publicity.

Recognizing how these categories become defined by gender and race points up several inadequacies of the liberal theories of the public sphere. For one thing, it is not correct to view publicity as always and unambiguously an instrument of empowerment and emancipation. For members of subordinate groups, it will always be a matter of balancing the potential political uses of publicity against the dangers of loss of privacy. Likewise, it is not adequate to analyze these categories as supports for and challenges to state power exclusively. Rather, we need also to understand the ways in which discursive privatization supports the "private" power of bosses over workers, husbands over wives, and whites over blacks. Publicity, then, is not only a weapon against state tyranny, as its bourgeois originators and current eastern european devotees assume. It is also potentially a weapon against the extrastate power of capital, employers, supervisors, husbands, fathers, among others. There was no more dramatic proof of the emancipatory potential of publicity in relation to "private" power than the way in which these event momentarily empowered many women to speak openly for the first time of heretofore privately suffered humiliations of sexual harassment.

Yet these events also show that publicity as a political weapon cannot be understood simply in terms of making public what was previously private. They demonstrate that merely publicizing some action or practice is not always sufficient to discredit it; that is only the case where the view that the practice is wrong is already widely held and uncontroversial. Where, in contrast, the practice is widely approved or contested, publicity means staging a discursive struggle over its interpretation. Certainly, a key feature of the Thomas-Hill confrontation was the wider struggle it sparked over the meaning and moral status of sexual harassment.

The way that struggle played out, moreover, reflected the current state of American political culture. The drama unfolded at a point at which a feminist vocabulary for naming and interpreting the behavior ascribed to Thomas had already been created in the feminist counter-public sphere and disseminated to a broader public. Not only was that vocabulary thus available and ready to hand, but it was also even encoded in law. However, the feminist interpretation of sexual harassment was neither deeply rooted nor widely accepted in the culture at large. Consequently, it was contested and resisted throughout these events despite its official legal standing. In fact, it was precisely the disjuncture between its official legal acceptance, on the one hand, and the widespread popular resistance it met, on the other, that helped determine the shape of the struggle. Much of the disbelief of Anita Hill may well have been a disguised rejection of the feminist view of sexual harassment as a wrong, a rejection that could not easily be openly expressed and that was displaced onto doubts about Hill. Moreover, because the feminist understanding had legal legitimacy before it had widespread popular legitimacy, it could become a target for the expression of class, ethnic, and racial resentments. While it is not the case, in other words, that the feminist perspective is elitist, white, upper class, and so forth, it was vulnerable to being coded as such. Consequently, people with any number of a range of class, ethnic, or racial resentments, as well as those with gender resentments, could express them by disbelieving Hill.[28] Yet the result was a sharpening and broadening of the battle of interpretation.

If one result of this struggle was some increased consciousness-raising about sexual harassment, another was the fracturing of the myth of homogeneous "communities." "The black community," for example, is now fractured into black feminists versus black conservatives versus black liberals versus various other strands of opinion that are less easy to fix with ideological labels. The same fracturing holds for "the women's community." This struggle showed that women don't necessarily side with women just because they are women. Rather, the polls, for what they are worth (and it may not be much), showed that a plurality of women in every age, income, and education group said they believed Clarence Thomas more than Anita Hill.[29] Perhaps these events should lead us to consider replacing the homogenizing, ideological category of "community" with the potentially more critical category of "public" in the sense of a discursive arena for staging conflicts.

This last point suggests that if these events expose some weaknesses in the liberal theory of the public sphere, they also point in the direction of a better theory. Such a theory would need to take as its starting point the multivalent, contested character of the categories of privacy and publicity with their gendered and racialized subtexts. It would have to acknowledge that in highly stratified late capitalist societies, not everyone stands in the same relation to privacy and publicity; some have more power than others to draw and defend the line. Further, an adequate theory of the public sphere would need to theorize both the multiplicity of public spheres in contemporary late capitalist societies and also the power differentials among them. It would need to distinguish, for example, official governmental public spheres, mass-mediated mainstream public spheres, counter-public spheres, and informal public spheres in everyday life; and it would have to show how some of these publics marginalize others. Such a theory would certainly help us better understand discursive struggles like the Clarence Thomas-Anita Hill confrontation. Perhaps it could also help inspire us to imagine, and to fight for, a more egalitarian and democratic society.[30]

NOTES

1. See Jürgen Habermas, *The Structural Transformation of the Public Sphere: An Inquiry into a Category of Bourgeois Society*, trans. Thomas Burger (Cambridge, Mass., 1989).

2. "Excerpts of News Conference on Harassment Accusations against Thomas," *New York Times*, 8 Oct. 1991, p. A20.

3. Maureen Dowd, "The Senate and Sexism," *New York Times*, 8 Oct. 1991, p. A1.

4. Dowd, "Image More Than Reality Become Issue, Losers Say," *New York Times*, 16 Oct. 1991, P. A.14. The mainstream press frequently referred to Thomas's alleged porn habit. See Michael Wines, "Stark Conflict Marks Accounts Given by Thomas and Professor," *New York Times*, 10 Oct. 1991, p. A18, for an account by one of his fellow Yale law school students.

5. "Bush Emphasized He Backs Thomas in Spite of Uproar," *New York Times*, 10 Oct. 1991, p. B14

6. Alan K. Simpson, *Congressional Record-Senate*, 102d Cong. 1st sess., 1991, 137, pt. 143:14546.

7. Clarence Thomas, "Hearing of the Senate Judiciary Committee," 11 Oct. 1991, morning sess., in Nexis Library, FEDNWS file, Federal News Service.

8. "Excerpts from Senate's Hearings on the Thomas Nominations," *New York Times*, 13 Oct. 1991, p. A30.

9. Quoted in Dowd, "Image More Than Reality Became Issue, Losers Say," p. A14.

10. Dowd, "Republicans Gain in Battle by Getting Nasty Quickly," *New York Times*, 15 Oct. 1991, p. A18.

11. "Excerpts from Senate's Hearings on the Thomas Nomination," *New York Times*, 12 Oct. 1991, p. A14.

12. Peter Applebone, "Common Threads between the 2 Accusing Thomas of Sexual Improprieties," *New York Times*, 12 Oct. 1991, p. A11.

13. See Anna Quindlen, "Listen to Us," *New York Times*, 9 Oct. 1991, P. A25. These references rendered invisible the Asian-Americans in the Senate, thereby attesting to the American cultural tendency to turn race into the stark opposition of white versus black.

14. "Thomas Rebuts Accuser: 'I Deny Each and Every Allegation,'" *New York Times*, 12 Oct. 1991, p. A1.

15. See Richard L. Berke, "Thomas Backers Attack Hill; Judge, Vowing He Won't Quit, Says He Is Victim of Race Stigma," *New York Times*, 13 Oct. 1991, p. A1.

16. In a roundtable discussion on a local Chicago television talk show, three black male journalists, Salim Muwakkil (*In These Times*), Ty Wansley (WVON radio), and Don Wycliff (*Chicago Tribune*) agreed with the suggestion of black political satirist Aaron Freeman (author or the play "Do the White Thing") that many black men embrace the stereotype of the sexual stud.

17. Alvin Poussaint, quoted in Lena Williams, "Blacks Say the Blood Spilled in the Thomas Case Stains All," *New York Times*, 14 Oct. 1991, p. A16.

18. The one exception was Ellen Wells, a witness who corroborated Hill's version of events by testifying that Hill had told her that Thomas was harassing her at the time. In the course of her testimony, Wells

explained why Hill might have nonetheless maintained contact with Thomas:

> My mother told me, and I'm sure Anita's mother told her. When you leave, make sure you leave friends behind, because you don't know who you may need later on. And so you do at least want to be cordial. I know I get Christmas cards from people that I...quite frankly do not wish to [see]. And I also return their cards and will return their calls. And these are people who have insulted me and done things which perhaps have degraded me at times. But these are things that you have to put up with. And being a black woman you know you have to put up with a lot. And so you grit your teeth and you do it. ["Questions to Those Who Corroborated Hill Account," *New York Times*, 14 Oct. 1991, p. A13]

19. Quindlen, "The Perfect Victim," *New York Times*, 16 Oct. 1991, p. A25.

20. See Orlando Patterson, "Race, Gender, and Liberal Fallacies," *New York Times*, 20 Oct. 1991, p. E15.

21. "African American Women in Defense of Ourselves," advertisement, *New York Times*, 17 Nov. 1991, p. A19.

22. A good beginning has been made in two important articles that appeared shortly after the end of the struggle. See Nell Irvin Painter, "Who Was Lynched?" *The Nation*, 11 Nov. 1991, p. 577, and Rosemary L. Bray, "Taking Sides against Ourselves," *New York Times Magazine*, 17 Nov. 1991, pp. 56, 94–95, 101.

23. There is in addition another variety of sexual harassment, in which male workers harass female coworkers who are not formally under their supervisory authority. This sort of harassment is frequent when very small numbers of women enter heavily male-dominated and masculinized occupations such as construction, fire fighting, and military service. Women in these fields are often subject to harassment from coworkers who are technically their peers in the occupational hierarchy—in the form, for example, of the display of pornography in the workplace, sexual taunts, noncooperation or sabotage, and even having male coworkers urinate in front of them. This sort of "horizontal" harassment differs significantly from the "vertical" variety discussed in the present essay, which involves harassment of an occupational subordinate by a superordinate. "Horizontal" harassment merits a different sort of analysis.

24. Peggy Noonan, "A Bum Ride," *New York Times*, 15 Oct. 1991, p. A15.

25. Patterson, "Race, Gender, and Liberal Fallacies," p. E15.

26. Felicity Barringer, "Women See Hearing from a Perspective of Their Own Jobs," *New York Times*, Midwest ed., 18 Oct. 1991, p. A1.

27. See Elizabeth Kolbert, "Most in National Survey Say Judge Is the More Believable," *New York Times*, 15 Oct. 1991, pp. A1, A20.

28. Perhaps this helps explain the otherwise surprising fact, disclosed in polls, that large numbers of people who claimed to believe Hill nonetheless supported Thomas's confirmation, either minimizing the seriousness of her accusations, or judging her to be too prudish, or insisting that she should have handled the situation herself by simply telling him where to get off.

29. See *New York Times*, 15 Oct. 1991, pp. A1, A10.

30. For an attempt to develop such a theory, see Nancy Fraser, "Rethinking the Public Sphere: A Contribution to the Critique of Actually Existing Democracy," *Social Text*, no. 25/26 (Fall 1990): 56–80.

6

COSTAS DOUZINAS AND RONNIE WARRINGTON _____

"A Well-Founded Fear of Justice: Law and Ethics in Postmodernity

> "Does he know his sentence?" "No" said the officer. "He doesn't know his own sentence?" "No" the officer said again; he was still for a moment as if expecting the traveller to volunteer some reason for his question, then he said, "There would be no sense in telling him. He experiences it on his own body."
>
> Kafka, *In the Penal Colony*

INTERPRETATION AND ACTION

Legal judgments are both statements and deeds. They both interpret the law and act on the world. A conviction and sentence at the end of a criminal trial is the outcome of the judicial act of legal interpretation. But it is also the authorisation and beginning of a variety of violent acts. The defendant is taken away to a place of imprisonment or of execution, acts immediately related to, indeed flowing from the judicial pronouncement. Again as a result of civil judgments people lose their homes, their children, their property, or they may be sent to a place of persecution and torture.

The recent turn of jurisprudence to hermeneutics, semiotics and literary theory has focussed on the word of the judge and forgotten its force.[1] The meaning-seeking and meaning-imposing component of judging is analysed as reasoned or capricious, principled or discretionary, predictable or contingent, shared, shareable or open-ended according to the political standpoint of the analyst. But as Cover has reminded us, in our obsession with hermeneutics we forget that "legal interpretation takes place

197

in a field of pain and death.[2] The main if not exclusive function of many judgments is to legitimise and trigger off past or future acts of violence. The word and the deed, the proposition and the sentence, the constative and the performative are intimately linked.

Legal interpretations and judgments cannot be understood independently of this inescapable imbrication with—often violent—action. In this sense, legal interpretation is a practical activity other-orientated and designed to lead to effective threats and—often violent—deeds. This violence is evident at each level of the judicial act. The architecture of the courtroom and the choreography of the trial process converge to restrain and physically subdue the body of the defendant. From the latter's perspective, the common but fragile facade of civility of the legal process expresses a recognition "of the overwhelming array of violence ranged against him and of the helplessness of resistance or outcry."[3] But for the judge too, legal interpretation is never free of the need to maintain links with the effective official behaviour that will en-*force* the statement of, the law. Indeed the expression "the law is enforced" recognises that force and its application lies at the heart of the judicial act. Legal sentences are both propositions of law and acts of sentencing.[4] Judges, whatever else they do, deal in fear and pain and death. If this is the case, any aspiration to coherent and shared legal meaning will flounder on the inescapable and tragic line that distinguishes those who mete out violence from those who receive it.

This necessary distinction and linkage between the constative and performative aspects of legal judgments has passed without much comment in jurisprudence. Hermeneutically orientated legal theory assumes that the rightness, fairness or justice of the interpretative enterprise will bestow its blessing on the active component of the judgment and justify its violence. Theory and practice, word and deed are seen as belonging to the same field, as successive points on an unproblematic continuum. A just interpretation and statement of the law is accepted without more as just action. But is this assumption justified? Does the correct interpretation of the law—if it exists—and the "right answer" to a legal problem—if we can find it—lead to moral and just praxis? Is the law law because it is just or is the law just because it is the law?

To do justice to such questions we turn to some paradigmatic tests which explicitly or impliedly address ethics and the problem of justice. Our reference will be three recent cases from the canon of postmodern philosophy and another three judgments from the British House of Lords and the Court of Appeal. The stakes behind the confrontation are high. Can there be a postmodern ethics that while accepting the pragmatic, epistemological and ontological critiques of modern moral philosophy, is not condemned to cynicism or passivity?

THE ETHICS OF POSTMODERNITY

The Face of the Other

> Driven out of Abraham's house, Hagar and Ishmael wandered in the desert. When their water supply was spent, God opened Hagar's eyes and she saw a well and gave drink to her dying son. But the angels who know the future and the law protested: "Wilt thou bring up a well for one will one day make Israel suffer?" "What does the end of the history matter" replied God. "I judge each for what he is now and not for what he will become."

"I judge each for what he is now." If postmodernity recognises the exhaustion of all attempts to pound action upon cognition and reason or some a priori stipulated conception of the Good, it also marks the beginnings of an ethical awareness steeped in the "now" and the event. Emanuel Levinas, the Jewish philosopher of alterity, stands as the figure of the other of Greek archaeology—the ethics of the *arche*, of principles and origins, and of *logos*, reason and logic.[5] The ethics of alterity on the contrary, are based on the shifting relationships between self and Other. It is the unique encounter with the living Other, in his present and unrepresentable corporeality, that opens up the field of ethics.

The Other is not the self's *alter ego*, nor its extension. Nor is the Other the negation of self in a dialectical relation that can be totalized in a future synthesis. Heidegger correctly emphasizes the historical and social nature of self since "the word is always one I share with the Other."[6] But the Other is not similar to self; self and Other are not equal partners in a Heideggerian "we" in which we share our world; nor is it the threatening externality and radical absence of Sartrean existentialism that turns self into an object.

The Other comes first. (S)he is the condition of existence of language, of self and of the law. The Other always surprises me, opens a breach in my wall, befalls the ego. The Other precedes me and calls upon me: where do you stand? Where are you now and not who you are. All "who" questions have ended up in the foundational moves of (de)ontology. Being or the I of the Cartesian *cogito* and the Kantian transcendental subject start with self and create Other as *imitatio* ego. In the philosophy of alterity the Other can never be reduced to the self or the different to the same. Nor is the Other an instance of Otherness or of some general category, an object to a subject that can become a move in dialectics. The of another is the face.

The face is unique. It is neither the sum total of facial characteristics, an empirical entity, nor the representation of something hidden, like soul, self or subjectivity. The face eludes every category. It brings together speech and glance, saying and seeing in a unity that escapes the conflict of senses and the arrangement of the organs. Nor is the face the epiphany of a visage, or the image of a substance. Thought lives in speech, speech is (in) the face, saying is always addressed to a face. The Other is her face. "Absolutely present, in his face, the Other— without any metaphor—faces me."[7]

Defying all categorising, the face is more unique than the leaf of a tree in the spring, more concrete than the species of a genus, more particular than the instance of an essence, more singular than the application of a law. In its uniqueness, the face gets hold of me with an ethical grip "myself beholden to, obligated to, in debt to, the other person, prior to any contract or agreements about who owes what to whom."[8] In the face-to-face, I am fully, immediately and irrevocably responsible for the Other who faces me. A face in suffering issues a command, a decree of specific performance: "Welcome me," "Give me Sanctuary," "Feed me". The only possible answer to the ethical imperative is "an immediate respect for the other himself...because it does not pass through the central element of the universal, and through respect, in the Kantian sense for the law."[9]

The demand of the Other that obliges me is the "essence" of the ethics of alterity. But this "essence" is based on the non-essence of the Other who cannot be turned into a concept or the instance of a law. "The other arises in my field of perception with the trappings of absolute poverty, without attributes, the other has no place, no time, no essence, the other is nothing but his or her request and my obligation."[10] As the face of the Other turns on me, (s)he becomes my neighbour. But (s)he is not the neighbour of the principle. As absolute difference and otherness, my neighbour is at the same time most strange and foreign. Closer than the air I breathe and further away than the starry sky, the Other calls on me, but the encounter can be never fully consummated. Our relationship is necessarily non-symmetrical and non-reciprocal. Equity is not equality but absolute dissymmetry.

The ontology of alterity too is based on the absolute proximity of the most alien. When self comes to constitute itself, it faces before the *I*, *I*'s relationship with the Other. The Other has always and already been within self, (s)he dispossesses and decentres self. The face is a trace of otherness inscribed on the "ground" of self. And if such is the case, all return to self from otherness is exposed to this exteriority which leaves its trace but can never be fully internalised. Self is always followed by the Other's demand, never able to return home fully, always in internal exile. I am always persecuted by the refugee and seek asylum from the exile, but (s)he always comes back, always before me, a step behind or a step in front, the not yet which is the always has been.

Asylos is (s)he who is not subjected to *syle*, the act and the right of seizure, of plundering and of reprisals, (s)he who is not stripped of her arms, deprived of her possessions, robbed of her due. Asylum is the place that offers sanctuary to the *asylos* from the *syle*. Do we enjoy asylum from the Other? Not in the postmodern ethics of alterity. Πανταχοῦ ουλωμένων ἡμῶν, despaired the Greeks. Wherever we go, we are being plundered. Such is the position of self. The Other persecutes me, puts me in passivity, asks me for sanctuary as (s)he persistently refuses it to me. And if this is the law of ethics, does the law heed its call?

The Justice of Sentences

The recent writings of Lyotard and Derrida have been answering the call of the Other. In Lyotard's *The Differend*, the singularity of the ethical relationship with the Other becomes the example of a postmodern philosophy of events and sentences—and of justice. Derrida in the Force of Law declares that justice concerns singularity, individuals, irreplaceable groups, events and lives, "the other or myself as other."[11] Both Derrida and Lyotard seem to share a number of positions on the nature of ethics and the action of justice. As Lyotard's narrative is the more analytical of the two, we will start from his story, and we will try to weave into it the tales of law and Derrida's aphorisms.

The linguistic mode of ethics is the imperative or, in Lyotard's terminology, the prescriptive sentence.[12] An ethical command cannot be derived from a theory, a concept or a descriptive sentence nor from a general prescription or law, like the Kantian categorical imperative. The demand "Welcome me" of a stranger asks me to act but offers no criteria of choice. The specificity of the ethical moment is that self feels obligated, and acts in response to an inescapable order—"You must." I must act, I am not free not to act, I cannot do otherwise.[13] Criteria of judgment on the other hand follow theoretical and deductive models and attempt to ground ethical action either on the description of a state of affairs to be achieved or on the calculation of consequences.

The specifity and urgency of the ethical command, however, befalls and obligates me before any possibility and without any need for reasons or justifications. Indeed for Lyotard, every sentence is a unique event that happens now. When it occurs, the sentence-event presents a "universe" upon which its four poles or instances and their unique relationship, their "situation," are placed: a sentence first presents its referent, that of which it is about; secondly, the meaning of the case which the sentence presents; the sentence then presents that to which or to whom this meaning is addressed (the receiver), and finally that in whose name the meaning signifies (the sender or addressor). Thus sentences position both subjects and realities and open up worlds of possibilities.

Sentences belong to various incommensurable "regimes." They are descriptive, prescriptive, normative, interrogative. Sentences from the various regimes link together and create "genres" of discourse—science, philosophy, poetry, law, etc. Every sentence is a radically unique occurrence, but it is always followed by another sentence. Linking between sentences is necessary, but what type of linking actually occurs is contingent. Genres act like a gravitational force: they try to attract sentences towards those linkages that promote the function of the genre, e.g., to know, persuade, seduce, amuse, be just, etc. "One will not link unto *To Arms!* with *You have just formulated a prescription*, if the stakes are to make someone act with urgency. One will do it if the stakes are to make someone laugh."[14]

The characteristic of descriptive sentences is that their sender and addressee are potentially interchangeable. They find themselves in a position of equivalence because the referent of the sentence is "reality." Prescriptives on the other hand place addressor and addressee in a situation of radical dissymmetry. Lyotard here follows closely Levinas's ethics of alterity. An ethical command turns the *I* of the addressee into its *you* as the sender of the command becomes master and takes the other's *I* hostage. Self experiences this displacement into the receiver's pole, the "*You*," that the command imposes, as a loss of freedom, knowledge and pleasure. The *I* is tempted to explain or justify his dispossession. New sentences are produced that will transport the *I* back to the under position; their stake will be to give persuasive reasons for the command and the obedience. For the ethics of alterity, this urge to explain is due to the blindness of the *I*, ego's infatuation with knowledge which, as we saw, presents the Other as symmetrical to self. "The blindness of transcendental illusion resides in the pretension to found the good or the just upon the true, or what ought to be upon what is."[15] But this epistemological narcissism has no object. The *I* cannot put itself in the position of the Other and discover her intentions or deduce them from the sense of the command. To be obligated by an order because self can fully understand its sense would be a crime against ethics. It would both reduce the Other into self and would violate the autonomous underived sense of obligation that ethical prescriptives create. More generally no theory of the good society nor account of justice can furnish criteria for ethical action. Theories are descriptions of determinate states of affairs while the ethical response is indeterminate, something to be done rather than something said.

Kantian philosophy accepts this dissymmetry between prescriptive and constative sentences. According to Kant the data of experience and the metalanguage of scientific principles are homologous, making the passage from observation to theory unproblematic. But in ethics, the object language (*You must...*) and the metalanguage are not isomorphic. The Good is not given and cannot be apprehended in experience nor are moral judgments the affective reactions of moral agents to empirical properties. The knowledge of a state of affairs cannot be the basis of moral knowledge and action. In a move that resembles the operations of the aesthetic in the Third Critique, Kant tries to deduce the ethical command by analogy, *as if* it were a fact of nature amenable to reason. "The 'you must' of obligation is assimilated, via what Kant calls the 'type' (i.e. the form of conformity to the law in general) to the 'I know' of knowledge and the 'I can' of freedom."[16]

The categorical imperative asks us to act as if the maxim of our will may become a principle of universal legislation. The recognition of will's involvement in action is a typically modern move which distinguishes practical from pure reason. But the injunction to universalize the maxim of the will presents the world as a totality. To act on principles that would be acceptable and willed by all rational people is to assume that self's desires and actions are compatible and coherent with those of all others. The radical first step of the Kantian moral philosophy comes to an end in the assertion that we live in a totalisable community of reason. Furthermore, the categorical imperative installs self as both legislator and subject, sender of the law and its addressee. This is of course the typically modern conception of autonomy or self-determination, the other side of will's enthronement. Within the legal system, laws from now on will be considered just if they are prescribed by those who will have to obey them.

The philosophy of sentences and the ethics of alterity refutes these assumptions. "There is no point in formally distinguishing will from understanding, will from reason, when you decide at once to consider as good will only the will which adheres to clear ideas, or which makes decisions only out of respect for the universal."[17] Similarly the split *we* of the legislator/subject cannot become the horizon of the ethical relationship of the *Thou/I*. The Other cannot be turned into an integral element of a totality or into a monad of an empirical consensus. If the obligation of the ethical command cannot be derived or explained cognitively, neither is it the outcome of autonomy willing the universal law. Without the safe anchorage of a concept and without law, postmodern ethics is left only with responsibility. Indeed with a responsibility for the responsibility created by the suffering face of my neighbour.

THE REFUGEES CASES

Our first two cases are very similar.[18] They involved a number of Tamils seeking asylum in Britain. The refugees were fleeing Sri Lanka in 1987 as a result of an offensive by the majority Sinhalese government and the Indian army against the guerilla Tamil forces in the north of the islands.[19] According to the court, parts of the country "have been in a serious state of civil disorder, amounting at times to civil war. The authorities have taken steps [which] have naturally resulted in painful and distressing experiences for many persons innocently caught up in the troubles...[The] Tamils are the people who have suffered most" (1:198).

In both cases the applicants were refused asylum by the immigration authorities and challenged the refusal in proceedings for judicial review. In the first case the material question was under what circumstances is someone a refugee entitled to asylum; in the second, what can one do to challenge the decision that refused him/her refugee status.

Under Art.1 of the U.N. Convention on the Status of Refugees, a refugee is someone who "owing to well-founded fear of being persecuted for reasons of race, religion, nationality, membership of a particular social group or political opinions, is outside the country of his nationality and is unable or, owing to such fear, is unwilling to avail himself of the protection of that country." In the first case, the sole point for consideration before the House of Lords was the proper basis for the determination of a "well-founded fear of persecution." The Court of Appeal had held that the test for a "well-founded fear" was qualifiedly subjective. It would be satisfied by showing (a) actual fear and (b) good reason for this fear, looking at the situation from the point of view of one of reasonable courage. Unless an applicant's fear could be dismissed as "paranoid," "fear is clearly an entirely subjective state and should be judged accordingly" (1:195).

The House of Lords reversed, reinstated the immigration decisions and as a result the refugees were sent back to Sri Lanka. The Court held that a genuine fear of persecution could not suffice. The fears should have an "objective basis" which could be "objectively determined" (1:196). Such fears to be justified should be based on "true", "objective facts" that could be ascertained by an objective observer like the Home Secretary or the immigration Officers and not solely "on the basis of the facts known to the applicant, or believed by him to be true" (1:200). Once that was accepted the Secretary of State was entitled to have regard to facts "unknown to the applicant" in order to assess whether "subjective fear was objectively justified." The Secretary indeed had taken into account such "unknown facts", reports of the refugee unit of his department compiled from press articles, "journals and Amnesty International publications, and also information supplied to him by the Foreign Office and as a result of recent visits to Sri Lanka by ministers" (1:198). He had concluded that the army activities, "that amounted to civil war" and "occurred principally in areas inhabited by Tamils" "do not constitute evidence of persecution of Tamils as such" (1:199), "nor of any group of Tamils." As no "real risk" of persecution of the group in general existed, nor a risk "on the balance of possibilities," the Secretary was justified to conclude that none of the applicants had been or was likely to be subjected to persecution.

Lord Goff rounded off by assuring the UN High Commissioner for Refugees who had intervened in favour of the applicants that he need have "no well founded fear that, in this country, the authorities will feel in any way inhibited from carrying out the UK's obligations under the convention by reason of their having to make objective assessments of conditions prevailing in other countries overseas" (1:203). The U.K. would continue to apply the law and give sanctuary to refugees. The objective test was necessary to ensure that this country— regarded as a suitable haven by many applicants for refugee status—would not be "flooded" with persons who objectively experienced no fear of persecution (1:201).

The second case involved four applicants who were refused asylum by the immigration authorities and wanted to challenge that decision. They claimed that they met the criteria for asylum and that they should not be removed to a country where they feared persecution unless they had exercised a right of appeal against the initial refusal. Now, under the Immigration Act 1971, illegal entrants and those refused leave at a port of entry have a right of appeal against refusal to the immigration adjudicator and further to the Immigration Appeals Tribunal but only after they had left the country. With the beginning of the troubles in Sri Lanka, a visa requirement was imposed upon all those arriving from that country.[20] Both those without visa and those refused refugee status at a port of entry should leave the country and appeal against the refusal from abroad. One suspects that people fleeing persecution will experience some difficulty in acquiring genuine travel documents and visas.

The appellants had been designated illegal entrants because they had obtained temporary leave to enter on various grounds and later applied for refugee status. They claimed that under the U.N. Handbook on Refugee Determination Procedures, they had a right to appeal against refusal and that their removal—a precondition for appealing under the Act—would frustrate that right. The House of Lords ruled first that the Handbook had "no binding force in either municipal or international law" (2:946). It went on to endorse the applicants designation as illegal entrants. At the time of arrival they had misrepresented to the immigration authorities the "true nature and purpose of their visit...by making statements—which they knew to be false or did not believe to be true" (2:947). Such being the case, to allow the applicants to stay, while all visitors denied leave to enter could appeal after leaving "would be plainly untenable" (*ibid.*). It was prohibited by law, and it would discriminate in favour of illegal entrants.

CRITERIA OF (IN)JUSTICE (I): FEAR AND TRUTH

"Before the Law stands a doorkeeper. To this doorkeeper there comes a man from the country who begs admittance to the Law. But the doorkeeper says that he cannot admit the man at the moment. The man, on reflection, asks if he will be allowed, then, to enter later. "It is possible," answers the doorkeeper, "but not at this moment."

Kafka, *Before the Law*

The Tamils cases are (legal) judgments on (administrative) judgments. Are the judgments just? Can we judge their justice? Can we ever be just when facing the refugee? Justice requires that we must read the judgments carefully and justly, do justice to their word.

A foreigner comes along to the house of the law. He says: "I am in fear." He asks to be admitted and to be given sanctuary. The immigration officer/judge demands: "Justify your fear, give reasons for it." He answers: "My father has been killed by the police of my country. My two sisters have been harassed. One of my cousins was arrested, taken to a barracks where he died of injuries. Before dying he gave particulars of my friends and relatives including myself. My other cousin has since been arrested and killed."[21] "Ah," says the judge "you must accept that fear is valid when it is based on the facts. And facts being what they are I can find them out as well as you can. Indeed better. I know the true facts from my newspapers and from reports by my agents and informers on 'the current political, social and law and order position at present pertaining'" (2:949) in your country. Let us have a look at the facts. People are being killed in your part of the world, some Tamils in particular. But then people are always killed in your part of the world. On the basis of the true facts as I know them I can find no systematic persecution of Tamils or of any group amongst you.

There is no objective basis for your fear as you are under no 'real and substantial risk'. I cannot admit you at the moment."

In this encounter with the refugee the role of the judge has gradually changed. He started as the recipient of the refugee's request but in asking for grounds and reasons and in stating the facts he now claims to be on the same plane as the refugee able to understand his predicament. In other words, the past pain of the refugee and his fear of future torture have been translated into an interpretable, understandable reality that like all reality is potentially shareable by judge and victim. But if interpretation is the possibility of constructing interpersonal realities in language, pain, death and their fear bring interpretations to an end.

> For the person in pain [or fear of pain], so incontestably and unnegotiably present is it that "having pain [or fear of pain]" may come to be thought as the most vibrant example of what it is "to have certainty" while for the other person it is so elusive that hearing about pain [or its fear] may exist as the primary model of what it is to "have doubt." Thus pain [and fear of pain] comes unsharably into our midst as at once that which cannot be denied and that which cannot be confirmed. Whatever pain [and its fear] achieves, it achieves through its unshareability, and it ensures this unshareability in part though its resistance to language.[22]

The claim that fear and pain can be rationalised through the shared understanding of their cause puts the victim in a double bind. Either he is in fear or he is not. If he is, he should be able to give facts and reasons for it which, as they belong to the genre of truth, should match up to the assessment of the judge. If they do not, the refugee is lying. If, on the other hand, he cannot give "objective" justifications for his fear the refugee is again lying. Similarly, when the refugee is inarticulate and cannot explain the "objective basis" of his fear, he is not in fear. But when he can do so, the immigration officer "formed the view that the Applicant, who appeared in good health, was alert and confident at interview, was moving away from Uganda because a better life awaited him somewhere else and that this was not a genuine application for asylum" (2:949).

In the idiom of cognition, fear is either reasonable and can be understood by the judge or is unreasonable and therefore non-existent. In the first instance it is the excess of knowledge and reason on the part of the judge that disqualifies the fear, in the second it is the excess of fear that disqualifies itself. But this translation of fear into knowledge and of the *syle* into reasons and causes assumes that the judge can occupy the place of the refugee and share his pain. Fear, pain and death, however, are radically singular; they resist and at the limit destroy language and its ability to construct shared worlds.

Lyotard has called this violent double bind an ethical tort (*differend*); it is an extreme form of injustice in which the injury suffered by the victim is accompanied by a deprivation of the means to prove it.

> This is the case if the victim is deprived of life, or of all liberties, or of the freedom to make his or her ideas or opinions public, or simply of the right to testify to the damage, or even more simply if the testifying phrase is itself deprived of authority...Should the victim seek to bypass this impossibility and testify anyway to the wrong done to her, she comes up against the following argumentation, either the damage you complain about never took place, and your testimony is false; or else they took place, and since you are able to testify to them, it is not an ethical tort that has been done to you.[23]

When an ethical tort has been committed the conflict between the parties cannot be decided equitably because no rule of judgment exists that could be applied to both arguments. The genre and the rules used to judge such cases will not be those of the genre judged and the outcome will be necessarily unjust. The violence of injustice begins when the judge and the judged do not share a language or idiom. It continues when all traces of particularity and otherness are reduced to a register of sameness and cognition mastered by the judge. Indeed all legal interpretation and judgment presuppose that the Other, the victim of the language's injustice, is capable of language in general, is man as a speaking animal, in the sense that we, men give to the word language. And as Derrida reminds us "there was a time, not long ago and not yet over, in which 'we, men' meant 'we adult white male Europeans, carnivorous and capable of sacrifice.'"[24] But our communities have long lost any aspirations to a common idiom. We should not forget, therefore, that justice may turn out to be impossible, just a shibboleth.[25]

CRITERIA OF (IN)JUSTICE (II): THE LAW OF EXCLUSION AND ABSTRACTION

> The Law, the man from the Country thinks, should be accessible for every man and at all times, but when he looks more

closely at the doorkeeper in his furred robe, with his huge, pointed nose and long, thin, Tartar beard, he decides that he had better wait until he gets permission to enter. The door-keeper often engages him in brief conversation, asking him about his home and about other matters, but the questions are put quite impersonally, as great men put questions, and always conclude with the statement that the man cannot be allowed to enter yet.

The first type of injustice reduced the feeling of fear and pain of the Other to objective facts which the judge could allegedly ascertain. A different form of injustice accompanies the Kantian assertion that the principle of morality is to be discovered in the universalisable maxim of the will of the rational agent. To understand why, let us take another brief look at the philosophy of sentences.

Substantive provisions of statutes and other legal rules are formally normative sentences. Norms are the meta-language of commands. Normatives can be seen as prescriptives or com-mands put in inverted commas that give them authority. The prescriptive says "x should carry out y." Its normative reformu-lation adds "it is a norm (or z decrees) that 'x should carry out y.'" In a democratic polity political and legal legitimacy are allegedly linked with the fact that the addressor of the norm (the legislator) and the addressees of the command (the legal sub-jects) are one and the same. The essence of freedom is that the subjects who make law are also law's subjected. As our third case puts it: "The first law is the law of the land...[T]he final arbitrator of the public interest can only be Parliament...[others] may not agree with it, but it is society's answer given through the mouth of Parliament."[26] As we have seen ethical prescriptions are felt as obligatory without any further authorisation other than the immediate call to obedience they give rise to. But the normative restatement of the various commands in legal form elevates their addressees to legal subjects who are at the same time metaleptically declared to be its legislators and therefore free and equal before the law.

But the law of the nation-state, despite its generality, excludes from the community of its subjects foreigners, immigrants and refugees. Aliens, not themselves the addressees of the legal norm, are given notice that if they come in contact with the state, the authority of its law will be engaged. There is a dissymmetry between the addressees of the law (subjects, citizens, the nation) and those others, its secondary addressees, who should be aware, however, of its effects. If they come to the gates of the state and put themselves before the law, they will be the addressees of the law's commands but not its subjects.

International and supranational law, the international treaties and principles of human rights, for example, are instances of a law that potentially addresses all states and all human persons *qua* human. Similarly, imperial law extends its authority beyond the territorial boundaries of a nation-state and tries to address an ever-expanding group, to speak *urbi et orbi*. In all these instances the (potential) audience of the order (*you ought to...*) and of the norm (*it is authoritatively decreed that you ought to...*) are co-extensive. At the other end of the spectrum, national law excludes non-nationals from the community of its addressees and reduces them to a subordinate pole, as barbarians to the "Greeks" alien, non-patrial, refugees, people who have no claims under the law but may be arraigned before it.

This process of inclusion/exclusion and the legitimation claims linked with it is closely followed in the judgments. National law is demarcated both from international law and from the principles of human rights. The U.N. High Commission for Refugees Handbook on Procedures for Determining Refugee Status "is of no binding force in either municipal or international law" (2:946). Domestic law does not give a right of appeal to refugees refused asylum. The invocation of international law and the requests under it that decisions should be reached with the cooperation and approval of the High Commission are therefore "plainly untenable" (2:997). Furthermore, whilst the Court admits that "the most fundamental of all human rights is the individual's right to life" (2:952) it adds that applications for refugee status "do not in general raise justiciable issues. Decisions under the [Immigration] Act are administrative and discretionary rather than judicial and imperative" (2:955). But at the same time the court asserts for the national system the legitimacy of the supranational law whose validity, however, is denied. The authorities of Britain which is regarded as "a suitable haven by many applicants for refugee status...will [not] feel in any way inhibited from carrying out the United Kingdom's obligations under the [international refugees] convention" (1:201, 203).

Immigration law is a prime and symbolic space for the construction of the asymmetrical relationship between "we" and the "others." The "we" of "we decree as a norm" and the "you" of the "you ought to obey" are radically external to each other. The "you" can never become "we" because it never enters into a dialogue with the "I." The use of the Other is to underpin the superiority of the law (and) of belonging. The fairness, worth and justice of this law is proved and its attractiveness "as a haven" justified even when—especially when?—it turns the refugee away and sends him back to his fate. "Where the result of a flawed decision may imperil life or liberty a special *responsibility lies on the court in the examination of the decision-making process*" (2:956). The dignity of the process should be protected at all costs. Its integrity will both defend those inside and explain why the outside wills the—national—law.

Immigration law then acts as a passage from the international to the national, from the universal to the general, as a line of closure and of opening up, a boundary like the borders, the checkpoints and the patrols that await immigrants and refugees. To come to the law, the refugee comes to the port of entry, the physical space of entrance into the country but also the metaphorical door of the law. But to face the law and challenge the legality of the refusal to grant asylum, the refugee must leave both the country and its law. To come before the law the refugee must go. The coming is a departure, the law is present and makes its presence felt only to the absent. The refugee is brought to the law in his violent removal.

This removal is doubly violent: it both shuts the door at the face of the refugee and it may send him "to the country where, contrary to the view formed by the Secretary of State, he is in fact in danger of persecution" (2:956). In doing so, the judgment suspends the need for legal interpretation. The refugee may appeal to the law from the country of his—potential—persecution but he is unlikely to do so.[27]

And if, as jurisprudence claims, it is the interpretative moment of judgment which belongs to the horizon of justice, the Tamils cases show that the time of justice is never fully present, but always still to come in a promised but deferred future. If a legal judgment is both word and deed, constative and performative, in this instance the act precedes the interpretation and endlessly defers it. It may be objected of course that this precedence of violent performance over legal interpretation is rather exceptional. But it is exactly this "exception" that indicates the nature of normal cases. In every act of judging there is a moment of saying and a moment of doing and justice cannot be identified exclusively with what is said.

In the refugees cases the deferral ensures that the law will not come face to face with the Other. Could it be that one of the reasons for the exclusion of the refugee from the process of law is to avoid the call of her face? A face in fear or pain cannot be explained by "true facts" nor be reduced to "objective reasons." It cannot be subsumed to the generality of the norm nor the uniformity of application that asks immigrants to leave before they can come before the law. Neither the object of cognition nor the instance of a rule, the face of suffering comes in its singularity to haunt its neighbours as much as its persecutors. Is not this the reason why the firing squad blindfolds their victim? The executioner covers the head of the hanged as a defence against the face upon which suffering gets indelibly and indescribably inscribed and persecutes the persecutor.

Similarly the face of the refugee in fear calls for a singular, underived and underivable answer to its call. "An expression like *Welcome the alien* must be able to be valid, not because it can be inferred from statements previously admitted, not because it conforms to older statements, but by the sole fact that it is *an order having in itself its own authority*."[28] And yet the law in its generality can only answer by subjecting the fear to procedures of truth, or by subsuming the alien under categories and concept or finally by applying the norm. "Neither Tamils generally nor any group of Tamils were being subjected to persecution" (1:199). Despite the recognition that a "flawed decision may imperil life or liberty" (*ibid.*) no mention whatsoever is made of the circumstances of the individual applicants. The arguments and objections of the refugees to the conclusions of the immigration officers are not dealt with judicially at all but are summarily dismissed: "It appears that the Secretary of State... considered whether any individual applicant had been subjected [to persecution] and decided that none of them had been" (*ibid.*). Even when he comes to the law the refugee is treated as a faceless entity.

From the applicant to groups of Tamils to Tamils generally. In this process of abstraction and generalisation the individual is sacrificed to the concept, in a display of another common type of violence that the law and judgments deal in. The law is about rules and universals. Its categories and concepts, self-enclosed and auto-referential, form a normative grammar that multiplies endlessly according to its internal logic. But the justice of the abstract code must be tested in its applications. The nonreferential code must create its own instances of application and be seen to work on the world. In its performative aspect the judgment abstracts the particular, generalises the event, calculates and assesses individuals and distributes them along normative and normal(ised) paths under a rule that subjects the different to the same and the Other to the self.

> The most tenacious subjection of difference is undoubtedly that maintained by categories...Categories organise the play of affirmations and negations, establish the legitimacy of resemblances within representation, and guarantee the objectivity and operations of concepts. They suppress the anarchy of difference, divide differences into zones, delimit their rights, and prescribe their task of specification with respect to individual beings...They appear as an archaic morality, the ancient decalogue that the identical imposed upon difference.[29]

This ancient decalogue that denies difference lies at the heart of law. The gist of the rule of law, the modern concept of legality *par excellence*, is a demand for equality in abstraction and for repetition. Concrete individuals are turned into legal subjects, unique and changeable characteristics are subsumed under (ideal?) types and roles, singular and contingent events are metamorphosed into model "facts" and scenes in impoverished narratives constructed according to the limited imagination of evidence and procedure. And as the law ascribes fixed and repeatable identities, and transparent and calculable intentions to those brought before it, it necessarily negates the singularity of the Other. "Within law we are fated to be 'unfaithful' to otherness, as we are forced to make comparisons which inevitably call for an analogy of the unlike to the same. Law classifies, establishes the norms by which difference is judged. If classification in and of itself is thought to be violence against singularity, then law inevitably perpetuates that violence."[30]

Kant had realised that applying a rule to a particular case or an example would be to act legally but not necessarily in accordance with justice. In such a case, the justice of the decision would depend on the justice of the rule and to determine that one would have to turn to the origins of the rule and the law, a process that would be all the more loyal to its aim the more removed it would be from the immediate call to justice of the case in hand. The justice of a straightforward rule-application resembles the efforts of the refugee and of Kafka's man of the country to come before the law. The closest you come to your end the furthest away you find yourself from it. But as Derrida reminds us in his apophantic tenor the aporia of justice goes further. "If I were content to apply a just rule, without a spirit of justice and without in some way inventing the rule and the example for each case, I might be protected by law, my action corresponding to objective law, but I would not be just. I would act, Kant would say, *in conformity* with Duty but not *through* duty or *out of respect* for the law."[31]

Justice addresses the Other as irreplaceably unique, judges the refugee in his own language and idiom. "How are we to reconcile the act of justice that must always concern singularity, individuals, irreplaceable groups and lives, the other or myself *as* other, in a unique situation, with rule, norm, value or the imperative of justice which necessarily have a general form, even if this generality prescribes a singular application in each case?"[32] If law is similarity and repetition, justice is dis-symmetry, inequality and contingency.

Immigration law then in policing the borders and marking the property and propriety of the inside repeats endlessly the violence of exclusion and silencing. And if the law needs this exclusion in order to present and demarcate its own territory and subjects, the principle of exclusion stands in and before the law. It is the founding violence upon which every legal system rests, what Benjamin calls the "mystical foundation of authority." This violence is none other than the exclusion, deportation, the *sylein* of the refugee. And if this analysis is not completely misguided we should be able to find traces of the fear of the Other through-out the law.

CRITERIA OF (IN)JUSTICE (III): ETHICS AND THE WHOLE

Anyway the machine still works and is its own justification.

Nothing could be more removed from the world of refugees than that of the protagonist of our third case. From Sri Lanka to the square mile, from fear and torture to high finance and insider information, from the demands of sanctuary from persecution to those of personal honour and professional deontology, the difference is total. And as it was the world of the City that exemplified the cultural—postmodern?—moment of the eighties, it is no wonder that the Court came to consider and expound its theory of ethics and justice in this case.

Mr. Goodwin, the defendant, a journalist with a specialist magazine owned by Morgan-Grampian, the other defendants, was given confidential information by an unidentified source as to the business plans of the plaintiff company. There was a suggestion that the information was based on a draft plan stolen from the company. When Mr. Goodwin contacted the plaintiffs in order to check the information with a view to writing an article about them, he was faced with a deluge of legal actions. *Ex parte* injunctions were issued against the magazine restraining them from publishing the information and an order against the journalist requiring him to disclose his source of information. The Court of Appeal varied the order asking the journalist to disclose the notes of his conversation with the source which would allegedly help the plaintiffs identify that source and take action against him. The journalist refused to comply with the orders, and he and the publishers appealed against them.

For the Master of the Rolls the case was about the relationship between personal and professional ethics and the rule of law. Goodwin's refusal to reveal his sources was based either on an explicit promise given to that effect or/and more generally on professional deontology and the NUJ code of journalistic conduct that ensures the protection of the sources of investigative journalism. Lord Donaldson's resolution of the "conflict" was logically quite neat and simple—almost simplistic.

The court started from a rather bland reiteration of outdated constitutional doctrine. "Parliament makes the law and it is a duty of the Courts to enforce the law, whether or not they agree with it...That is what parliamentary democracy and the rule of law is all about...[The law] is society's answer given through the mouth of Parliament, and who are journalists, victims or judges to set themselves up as knowing better? In a parliamentary democracy personal and professional honour surely equates with the acceptance of and obedience to the rule of law" (3:621, 622). Through a series of metaphors and metonymies society is equated with Parliament, Parliament with law, the law with the Courts that "enforce" it and finally individual morality and honour with the duty to obey the courts.

What is the place and force of ethics against this all-encompassing edifice? The court accepted that occasionally conflicts arise between "the first law [which] is the law of the land" and "the second [which] is a moral imperative, usually, but not always of religious origin" (3:623). But the moral imperative does not excuse breaches of the law and anyone who contemplates such a course "would be well-advised to re-examine his conscience." The judge could not "over-emphasize the rarity of the moral imperative" (*ibid.*). If the journalist's moral dilemma was the result of his own promise to the source "it is of his own making [and] he is deserving of no sympathy." If on the other hand it was the result of his professional ethics, there is "more honour and morality in conforming to the democratically evolved laws of the land rather than to the private self-imposed rule of the profession to which he belongs" (3:624).

While the "rare" moral imperative is often attributable to religious feelings, it is the law that resembles religion most: "if any secular relationship is analogous to that between priest and penitent, it is that between lawyer and client" (3:622). The imagery of the law as the "mouthpiece" of society's wishes and the embodiment of social interests now moves onto a quasi-divine plane. Law's representatives, the courts, are not just the repositories of legality but arbiters of morality, too. When those rare conflicts between law and ethics arise "the answer must be [with] the courts" (3:621).

Goodwin's claim to decide the moral dilemma for himself is, therefore, a challenge to morality and justice. "The adminis-tration of justice in a parliamentary democracy depends in the last analysis on a general acceptance of the authority of the Courts as representing society as a whole. No challenge to that authority can be ignored" (3:625). Goodwin's challenge was so fundamental that in an unprecedented move the court denied Goodwin and his arguments a hearing for this contempt of its order.[33]

Could this not be seen as a display of the semi-priestly power that the judges had just asserted for themselves? The rebellious penitent is silenced and removed from the proceedings. Although more civil that those well-known instances of physical gagging of defendants by American courts, the Court of Appeal action is as effective.[34] If the body of those arraigned before the law is under the control of the court, their faculty of speech too is law's gift to be withdrawn from dissidents and contemnors. The journalist's insistence to act ethically in the only possible way, that is according to his own lights, makes "his interests not worthy of consideration" (*ibid.*). Like the refugees and Kafka's man from the country, the journalist comes to the law as he is kept outside its doorway. Access to the law, law's (in)accessibility, appears to be implicated in all our cases. But law's (in)accessibility has always been associated with justice. Let us have a final look at the rela-tionship between law and justice.

The *Morgan-Grampian* judgment is more unusual for its effects than for its reasoning and may be critically analysed from a number of perspectives. What interests us here is the way it links law with ethics. The law as expounded by the courts is proclaimed to be the main, if not the exclusive, source of moral duty. Ethics is consistently underrated and is referred to through a series of slightly derisory paraphrases and epithets: "professional ethics," "personal and professional honour," "rare moral imperative," "quaintly called 'iniquities,'" "self-made moral dilemmas deserving of no sympathy." The tenor and rhetoric of the judgment keeps repeating that ethics is secondary, that its demands are valid only if formally legislated and that it is for the court and not the individual to resolve according to the law any conflict between legality and morality.

The argument of the court resembles a well-known philosophical gambit associated with Hegelian metaphysics. Society, the "real," and law, the "normative," are presented as co-eval or homologous through a succession of substitutions. Society speaks through Parliament, Parliament speaks through law, the law speaks through the courts, the courts define morality, and individuals must accept their definition. And as society is the all-inclusive figure of reality, the law too is actual and total. If society is ever-present, society's mouthpiece, the law, is fully synchronised with society and matches it up as a re-presentation of society's presence. But the law is also a totality: it brings together and unifies legality and ethics, is and ought, the subject and his moral duty. There is no outside to the law, as law and reality are co-extensive. What exists is legal, and what contradicts the law cannot be real and does not count. The law "imposes its sentence by proclaiming itself as a totality, which informs its own truth and by so doing makes itself a fact."[35]

The truth of the law, which according to Lord Donaldson's simple equation is revealed in judicial pronouncements, is at the same time the essence of ethics. But as Levinas and Derrida have reminded us, there is always a remainder, "something" that cannot be assimilated by systems of representation and objectification.[36] It may be the otherness of ethics or the face of the refugee, but the remain(s) will deny and endlessly defer the promised closure of the (legal) system.

THE MOMENTARY PRINCIPLE OF JUSTICE

"What do you want to know now?" asks the doorkeeper, "you are insatiable." "Everyone strives to attain the Law," answers the man, "how does it come about, then, that in all these years no one has come seeking admittance but me?" The doorkeeper perceives that the man is nearing his end and his hearing is failing, so he bellows in his ear: "No one but you could gain admittance through this door, since this door was intended for you. I am now going to shut it."

Drucilla Cornell has eloquently argued in a series of important essays against the tendency to present the deconstruction of philosophy "as the complete loss of the Good."[37] Cornell usefully summarises Levinas's critique of ontology and Derrida's discussion of the remainder that destabilises all systems of representation. But she goes on to rescue elements of the Hegelian position and to argue that "in law, reason is a 'practical faith' we are called upon to exercise as an essential task of elaborating principles of justice." These principles are seen in Dworkinian terms not as rules but as "guiding lights" that appeal to the "universal" within concrete legal systems.[38] In a highly typical call to law teachers, Cornell reminds us that "to heed the call to responsibility within the law is both to remind our students of the disjuncture between law and the ideal and to affirm our responsibility to make the promise to the ideal, to aspire to counter the violence of our world in the name of universal justice."[39]

For Cornell only legal positivism can be accused of the type of ontological imperialism we encountered in the *Morgan-Grampian* case. Positivism imposes the order of the same upon the Other and the different by proclaiming the Being of what is as the Truth of the Whole and as the realisation of the Good. "Positivism attempts to fill the legal universe. The individual subject gobbled up in the system has significance only as a cog through which the legal machine works."[40]

While agreeing with Cornell's call to responsibility, we should immediately add that although positivism may be an extreme instance of ontological imperialism gone mad, other less positivistic approaches are not entirely innocent of the indictment.

These approaches emphasize practical reasoning and the principled and interpretative nature of legal decision-making. In so doing they open legal judgments to considerations and materials, including moral philosophy, not immediately available or ascertainable from within the strict confines of legal rules. Their aim, however, is still to present legal *interpretation* as more creative, or more flexible, or as value orientated. They address exclusively the constative part of the legal sentence and edge its justice according to the "rightness" of the expanded conception of what it is to interpret. The field from which the "right answer" is to emerge has been considerably and admirably extended; but it is still from within this past field of law-worked-by-principle and its interpretation that the sentence will act upon the Other. The translation from theory (the right answer according to the legal facts and principles) to ethics (the demand for and performance of just action) remains unexamined.

We can conclude that the justice of the judgment is inscribed and suspended in the space between the statement of the law (what *exists* legally) and the invocation of an ideal state of affairs (what *ought to be* according to some principles or conception of morality). It is the space where the Other brought before the law is acted upon, where violence is inflicted or justice is done. "For a decision to be just and responsible, it must, in its proper moment if there is one, be both regulated and without regulation: it must conserve the law and also destroy it or suspend it enough to have to reinvent it in each case, rejustify it, at least reinvent it in the reaffirmation and the new and free confirmation of its principle."[41]

The time of justice too differs from the time of interpretation. Interpretation turns to the past or measures up to the future as they inhabit the ever-present, its time is synchronic. The time of action—violence or justice—on the other hand is diachronic. It addresses the Other here and now and in each here and now and answers or denies her call. This is the pure ethical time, the time of what Levinas calls "*il y a*"—it is happening.

Interestingly the two opposing conceptions of time were discussed by the courts in the first refugee case. It will be recalled that the Court of Appeal had adopted there a subjective definition of fear. The Master of the Rolls illustrated the text by means of an allegory. "A bank cashier confronted with a masked man who points a revolver at him and demands the contents of the till could without doubt claim to have experienced a 'well-founded fear.' His fears would have been no less well-founded if, one minute later, it emerged that the revolver was a plastic replica or a water pistol."[42] The House of Lords, however, dismissed the analogy in summary fashion. An "objective observer" of the robbery would accept the cashier's fear as well-founded only until he discovered the truth. Before that he could not have been an "objective" observer in any case. The objective observer must reserve judgment until such time when all the relevant facts are in. According to the Lords, immigration officers and judges should also act as objective observers. From that position the refugees' fears were not "of instant personal danger arising out of an immediate predicament" and the official response should be determined after "examining the *actual* state of affairs in [the refugees'] country" (1:196, 197).

We can draw a parallel here between the time of fear and pain and the time of justice. When fear, pain or justice are dealt with as "real" entities, that can be verified or falsified according to objective criteria, their time or the time of the response to them is the time of constancy and omnitemporality of descriptions, theories and institutions. Truth is atemporal, and theory is all-seeing. Fear and pain, on the other hand, are individual feelings experienced as temporal responses to stimuli. In treating the time of fear as non-instant and non-immediate, the House of Lords is also violating the time of ethics. To recollect the Biblical story, God who knows that Ishmael will in the future shed innocent blood, still gives him water now because he is dying of thirst and, therefore, suffering injustice now.

Violence or justice can only happen at the moment of their occurrence. They are the performative aspects of the legal judgment. Nothing that happened earlier—a reading of the law or a commitment to principle—and nothing that anticipates the future—a promise or a vision of what should happen—can account fully or preempt the uniqueness of the response. And as in the robbery analogy the response of he who is obligated can only be instant and immediate. We can now understand why for Derrida the instant of the just decision is a madness and has an urgency that obstructs knowledge. Justice, like the robber and his fear, cannot wait for all relevant facts. Even if the addressee of justice had all the information and all the time in the world "the moment of decision, as such, always remains a finite moment of urgency and precipitation...since it always marks the interruption of the juridico- or ethico- or politico-cognitive deliberation that precedes it."[43]

The urgency of the call and of the answer to justice can be compared with the formal structure of performative speech acts. The performative says and does, saying what it does by doing what it says. Similarly, the justice of the legal judgment can be judged according to the way it acts. The action of the judgment is neither the continuation of the legal interpretation nor its opposite. There is an imperceptible fall from interpretation to action, an invisible line that both fissures and joins the legal sentence.

This trait divides and separates the constative from the performative. But at the same time, as the space and time of action and of the encounter with the Other, the trace is where the interpretative part of the judgment is brought before the law of its performance. This trace is justice. A judgment is just if it follows and creates its momentary principle. The paradox of a "momentary principle" best paraphrases just action which *qua* action resists and denies all paraphrase.

The trace is a principle in so far as it answers the call of the suffering of the Other; but it is only fleeting as the encounter with the Other is always concrete and unrepeatable. Justice is the momentary and principled response to the Other's concrete generality. This is the law of justice, of "whose subject we can never say 'there it is,' it is here or there. It is neither natural nor institutional; one can never attain to her, and she never arrives on the grounds of an original and proper taking place."[44] This momentary principle of justice, inscribed at the heart of the judgment but always before the law is what in other contexts has been called *différance* or even deconstruction.

Finally, can we aspire with Cornell to discover this principle in the legal system? We should not be surprised to find instances where the "right" legal answer violates—the momentary principle of—justice. The refugee cases are clearly such examples. But in other instances the performative part of judgments can be seen to act ethically against the grain of the interpretative moment. The courts themselves came to consider the role of justice in legal proceedings in our third case. The technical context of the discussion was s.10 of the Contempt of Court Act 1981 under which a court may not force journalists to disclose their sources unless it is necessary in the interest of justice. Lord Donaldson visualised the "interests of justice" as a doorway, law's door and judges as the doorkeepers. Plaintiffs must "squeeze" or "barge through" before they can get law's protection. But when the court comes to discuss the "shape, colour and dimensions" of this doorway, it repeatedly asserts that justice "is not used in a general sense as the antonym of 'injustice' but in the technical sense of the administration of justice in the course of legal proceedings in a court of law."[45] It is just to say that justice can only be talked about in figures,

paraphrases, allegories, justice's "antonyms." But in immediately identifying justice with court procedure, the Court like
Kafka's doorkeeper shuts the door.

Could this not be judged as a well-founded fear of justice?

NOTES

1. The linguistic and interpretative aspects of the law were always a
part of legal theory. They were neglected during the heyday of legal
positivism, but they have now returned to the forefront of jurisprudence.
Law is seen as an exclusively linguistic and meaningful construct and
various types of hermeneutics and literary theory are being adopted to
explain and justify the operations of the "prison house of legal
language." In orthodox jurisprudence R. Dworkin, *Law's Empire*
(London: Fontana, 1986); S. Levinson and S. Mailloux, eds., *Interpreting
Law and Literature: A Hermeneutic Reader* (Evanston: Northwestern
University Press, 1988), and S. Fish, *Doing What Comes Naturally*
(Cambridge: Cambridge University Pres, 1990), are clear examples of the
linguistic turn. For a more critical approach see P. Goodrich, *Legal
Discourse* (London: Macmillan, 1987); P. Goodrich, *Languages of Law*
(London: Weidenfeld, 1990), and C. Douzinas and R. Warrington (with
S. McVeigh), *Postmodern Jurisprudence: The Law of Text in the Texts of
Law* (London: Routledge,1991). There is no doubt that the importation
of literary theory and hermeneutics into jurisprudence has immensely
helped a field plagued by the largely irrelevant and irredeemably boring
debates of the 60s and 70s between positivism, analytical moral
philosophy and various shades of sociology of law. The present essay is
not directed at the linguistic and meaning constructing nature of the
law but against some types of uncritically imported literal theory which
completely forget the violent nature and unjust character of much legal
action.

2. Cover, "Violence and the Word", *Yale Law Journal* 95 (1986),
1601.

3. *Ibid.*, at 1607.

4. For a more detailed look into the linguistics and pragmatics of
sentences as applied to legal tests see C. Douzinas and R. Warrington,
"Suspended Sentences", in *Postmodern Jurisprudence, supra* n. 1, at
197–271.

5. Levinas is the major 20th century philosopher who introduces a
post-rational ethics as a first philosophy that is not dependent upon
cognitive claims and does not lead to totalising systematisations. His
most influential books in English are *Otherwise than Being*, transl. A.
Lingis (The Hague: Nijhoff, 1981), and *Ethics and Infinity*, transl. R. A.
Cohen (Pittsburgh: Duquesne University Press,1985). A good intro-

duction to Levinas' occasionally inscrutable work that owes both to European phenomenology and to the Jewish theological tradition is *The Levinas Reader*, ed. S. Hand (Oxford: Blackwell,1981).

6. M. Heidegger, *Being and Time* (New York: Harper & Row, 1962), 145.

7. Levinas quoted by Derrida in "Violence and Metaphysics" his famous, discussion of Levinas' theory in *Writing and Difference* (London: Routledge, 1978), 100.

8. R.A. Cohen, "Absolute Positivity and Ultrapositivity: Husserl and Levinas," in *The Question of the Other*, ed. A. Dallery and C. Scott (New York: State University of New York Press,1989), 43.

9. *Op.cit.* at 96.

10. J.F. Lyotard, *The Differend: Phrases in Dispute* (Manchester: Manchester University Press, 1988), 111.

11. "Force of Law: The 'Mystical Foundation of Authority'" *Cardozo Law Review* 11 (1990), 919, at 949.

12. The sentence is for Lyotard the basic unit of all discourse and action, the minimum constituent of our world. As such it is a unique event that just happens. The economy of sentence that *The Differend* analyses is one of pure happenings that combine to create meanings and reality. The translator of *The Differend* opts for the English word phrase as the best translation of the French "phrase." We will prefer here with Bennington (*Lyotard: Writing the Event* (Manchester: Manchester University Press,1988)) the word "sentence." We feel that the ambiguously singular nature of a legal sentence best encapsulates Lyotard's ambition to theorise the irreducibly unique.

13. For an ordinary language analysis of the "idea of obligation" see H.L.A. Hart, *The Concept of Law* (Oxford: Clarendon, 1979), 79–88. Hart bases his "internal point of view" on the linguistic distinction between "being obliged,' and "having an obligation." Hart rightly points out that "having an obligation" to do something does not depend on beliefs, motives or the prediction of sanctions. But Hart goes on to identify the feeling of obligation with rule-based behaviour. As we will see in this essay this identification often leads to violations of the ethical demand.

14. Lyotard, *supra* n. 10, at 84.

15. *Ibid.* at 108.

16. Bennington, *supra* n. 12 at 139.

17. Levinas quoted by Lyotard in *The Lyotard Reader*, ed. A. Benjamin, (Oxford: Blackwell,1989).

18. *R.* v. *Secretary of State for the Home Department, ex parte Sivakumaran* and conjoined appeals [1988] 1 All E.R. 193 H.L. (herein after cited in text as 1:); *Bugdaycay* v *Secretary of State for the Home Department* and related appeals [1987] 1 All E.R. 940 H.L. (hereinafter cited in text as 2:).

19. A recent Amnesty International report paints a harrowing picture of many thousands of extrajudicial executions and disappearances and of extensive torture of Tamils in the last 4 years. See *Sri Lanka* (London: Amnesty International Publication, 1990). But despite the well-documented evidence of persecution against Tamils, the British Government adopted a "street fighting approach" towards Tamil refugees seeking asylum in Britain. David Waddington, a Home Office Minister in 1987, described their claims as "manifestly bogus" and Tory MPs called them "criminals" (Hansard 17.2.8). The political resolve to refuse asylum was also evident in the tough legal tactics adopted. Mrs. Thatcher announced in February 1987 that airlines could be penalized for carrying immigrants into the country without proper documentation, and in March Mr. Hurd, the then Home Secretary, introduced the necessary legislation. (Immigration (Carriers' Liability) Act 1987). Furthermore, under new arrangements the Government severely restricted the right of refugees to seek independent legal advice and limited the traditional power of MPs to intervene in individual cases in favour of immigrants. See, U.K.: *Deficient Policy and Practice for the Protection of Asylum Seekers* (London: Amnesty International British Section,1990) and D. Burgess, "Asylum by Ordeal," *New Law Journal* (Jan. 18th 1991), 50.

20. Visa requirements were introduced in 1985 for Sri Lankans; in 1986 for nationals of India, Pakistan, Nigeria, Ghana and Bangladesh; in 1989 for nationals of Turkey as a result of an increasing number of Kurds fleeing persecution and in 1990 for nationals of Algeria, Morocco, Tunisia and Somalis. The Immigration (Carriers' Liability) Act 1990 imposes on airlines a £1000 fine per passenger brought into the U.K. without proper documentation. As the visa requirements and carrier sanctions do not distinguish between refugees and what the government calls "economic migrants," it is hard to imagine how a refugee could ever legally reach this country. Mr. Justice Schiemann resisted the further step of the Government which argued that 6 Lebanese had used fraud to travel to this country and claim asylum while on transit. The judge aptly described the Catch-22 facing refugees: "He who wishes to obtain asylum in this country, short of prior contact with the Home Secretary offering him asylum, has the option of lying to the UK authorities in [his] country in order to obtain a tourist or some other visa; obtaining a credible forgery of a visa; or obtaining an airline ticket to a third country with a stopover in the UK." *R* v. *Secretary of State for the Home Department ex parte Yassine and others, The Times,* 6 March 1990.

21. This is taken almost verbatim from the second refugees case. It describes the experience of a Ugandan refugee who had been refused asylum and was being deported to Kenya, "a safe country," from where he had arrived in the U.K. The House of Lords quashed the decision on *Wednesbury* grounds accepting that the Home Secretary had not taken into account the fact that Kenya had returned Ugandan dissidents to Uganda in the past despite serious fears for their safety. This is the only instance in which an appellant won in these cases and, interestingly, it is also the only instance in which the House of Lords discussed the evidence produced by a refugee to support his claim of being a victim of persecution.

22. E. Scarry, *The Body in Pain* (Oxford: Oxford University Press, 1987), 4.

23. Lyotard, *supra* n. 10, at 5.

24. Derrida, *supra* n. 11, at 951.

25. See our "The Books of Judges: The Shibboleths of Justice," in *Postmodern Jurisprudence, supra* n. 1, at 183.

26. *X Ltd* v. *Morgan-Grampian (Publishers) Ltd and others* [1990] 1 All E.R. 616, C.A. at 623, 622 (hereinafter cited in text as 3:).

27. The extraordinary legal odyssey of the 5 applicants of the first case did not come to an end with their defeat in the House of Lords. Following their expulsion to Sri Lanka in February 1988 their lawyers launched an appeal against the refusal of asylum. On return to Sri Lanka, three of the five were subjected to torture and the Adjudicator found that all five were entitled to political asylum and directed that they should all be returned to the UK with the minimum delay. The Home Office appealed but the Immigration Appeals Tribunal upheld the findings of the Adjudicator. (*Secretary of the State for the Home Department v. Sivakumaran and others,* [1988]) Imm. A.R. 147). Never to be disheartened by a defeat and fighting both for governmental policy and, one suspects, the honour of the House of Lords, indirectly rebuked by the two administrative tribunals, the Home Office sought judicial review of the Immigration Appeals Tribunal ruling. Interestingly, the ruling of the Tribunal was revealed only a month later at the High Court hearing because of the danger to the lives of the Tamils still in Sri Lanka (*The Independent,* 13 April 1990). Both the Divisional Court and the Court of Appeal rejected the application on procedural grounds; the Home Office had failed to address their appeal to the Tribunal correctly. (*R.* v *Immigration Appeals Tribunal* and an *Immigration Appeals Adjudicator ex parte the Secretary of State for the Home Department* [1990] Imm. A.R. 429). At this point, the Home Office finally gave in and the five were returned to the UK in October 1989. In the meantime,

their lawyers had launched an application with the European Commission of Human Rights alleging violations of art. 3 of the ECHR (torture and inhuman or degrading treatment) and art. 13 (lack of effective remedies to challenge the asylum refusal). On May 8, 1990 the Commission fund no breach of Art. 3 on the President's casting vote but by a 13-1 vote a breach of Art. 13. The Commission ruled that "in matters as vital as asylum questions it is essential to have a fully effective remedy providing the guarantees of a certain independence of the parties, a binding decision-making power and a thorough review of the reasonableness of the asylum seeker's fear of persecution". Judicial review of asylum refusals is not an adequate remedy since the Courts "are concerned with the way in which a decision is taken and not with the merits of the decision." *Vilvarajah and others* v. *UK* (8 May 1990), Appl. No. 13163/87. These cases are now before the Court of Human Rights and a judgment is expected in 1991. Most of the arguments in the text apply also to the recent deportations of Iraqi nationals and Palestinians during the Gulf War. The Court of Appeal thought that the total lack of any procedural safeguards did not violate natural justice. For the Master of the Rolls the non-statutory advisory panel (the "three wise men") that could hear the representations of the deportees without legal representation, any knowledge of the allegations against them, or any reasons given for their expulsion was an "independent quasi-judicial scrutiny." The problem existed only for "the insular and blinkered eyes of those who regard the adversarial system of justice as the only one worthy of the name." "The Court was entitled to assume," the Master of the Rolls concluded, "in the absence of evidence to the contrary, that [the Home Secretary] took account of all relevant circumstances which were brought to his attention." *Ex parte Cheblak, The Guardian*, February 6,1991. One marvels at the newly-found judicial enthusiasm for non-statutory administrative panels or at the benevolent "assumption" about the Home Secretary's probity. During World War 11, Lord Atkin stated, in a case not dissimilar to the present, what "I view with apprehension the attitude of judges who...when face to face with claims involving the liberty of the subject show themselves more executive minded than the executive." *Liversidge* v *Anderson* [1942] A.C. 206 per Lord Atkin dissenting at 244.

28. Lyotard, *supra* n. 17, at 286.

29. M. Foucault, *Language, Counter-Memory, Practice* (Oxford: Blackwell, 1977),186.

30. D. Cornell, "Post-structuralism. the Ethical Relation. and the Law," *Cardozo Law Review* 9 (1988), 1587, at 1591.

31. Derrida, *supra* n. 11, at 949.

32. *Ibid.*

33. [1990] 1 All E.R. 616 at 624–625. On appeal, the House of Lords accepted that courts have a discretion to decline to entertain the appeal of contemnors who defy the court's authority. But in the present case the Court of Appeal was "incongruous." It entertained Goodwin's appeal, dismissed it, gave leave to appeal to the Lords but in the process declined to hear his arguments in support of the appeal. The House of Lords heard argument from Goodwin's counsel but dismissed his appeal, [1990] 2 All E.R. 1 at 12.

34. The best known instance is that of Bobby Seale, one of the defandants in the Chicago 6 trial, who was bound and gagged during proceedings. See *Illinois* v. *Allen*, 397 US 337 (1970).

35. D. Cornell, "From the Lighthouse: The Promise of Redemption and the Possibility of Legal Interpretation," *Cardozo Law Review* 11 (1990), 1689 at 1693.

36. For Derrida's exquisite reading of the remain(s) in Hegel, see *Glas* (Lincoln: University of Nebraska Press,1986).

37. *Supra* n. 35, at 1697.

38. *Ibid.* at 1705, 1704.

39. Cornell, *supra*, n. 30, at 1628.

40. Cornell, *supra* n. 35, at 1693.

41. Derrida, *supra* n. 11, at 961.

42. [1987] 3 W.L.R. 1053. Interestingly, Hart uses the gunman analogy repeatedly to distinguish the meaning of "being obliged" from that of "having an obligation." Only the latter is supposed to be the correct response to normative, in particular legal, commands. Lord Donaldson, in accepting that the fear is necessarily an individual and unshareable feeling and in responding to it, is in this instance following the "principle" of justice of the ethics of alterity. His judgment in *Morgan-Grampian*, on the other hand, shows that this principle is momentary. It is neither a generalisable rule nor does it derive from the consistent and coherent action of a prudent judge.

43. Derrida, *supra* n. 11, at 967.

44. J. Derrida. "Devant la Loi." in *Kafka and the Contemporary Critical Performance: Centenary Readings*, ed. A. Edoff (Bloomington: Indiana University Press, 1989), 141.

45. While broadly agreeing with Lord Donaldson the House of Lords slightly extended the definition of the "interests of justice" to mean that "persons should be enabled to exercise important legal rights and to protect themselves from serious legal wrongs whether or not resort to

legal proceedings in a court of law will be necessary to attain these objectives" [1990] 2 All E.R. 9, 13. The identification of—a wider concept of the—law with justice is, however, still upheld.

7

DRUCILLA CORNELL _____

Time, Deconstruction, and the Challenge to Legal Positivism: The Call for Judicial Responsibility

INTRODUCTION

The central purpose of this essay is to show why the deconstruction of the traditional conception of time, a conception which privileges the present, permits an effective challenge to Niklas Luhmann's systems theory. As we will see, this deconstruction of the privileging of the present helps give us a correct understanding of the relationship between law, justice, and the phenomenology of judging.

The traditional conception of time defines the past and the future as modifications or horizons of the "now." By time, I am not evoking chronology, but the privileging of the present as it is understood to be necessary to the establishment of a legal system. Without this present there would be no legal system that could be grasped as simply there for its participants, whether they be lawyers or judges. We find the deconstruction of the traditional conception of time worked through in Jacques Derrida's discussions of *différance*. I will specifically focus on how the diachronic view of time implicit in the explanations of *différance* undermines the very possibility of a positivist conception of law as Luhmann conceives of it.

Legal positivism, when left unchallenged, creates a system, a kingdom which reigns over possibility and excludes the dream of a truly different future. Deconstruction, however, exposes the presumption of a determinant certitude of a present "justice" as

231

defined by any current legal system, including legal positivism. But in so doing, deconstruction is hardly the nihilistic language exercise claimed by many critics. In the movement through the aporias of justice, deconstruction protects the divide between law and justice. This exposure of the aporias of justice is in and of itself ethical. The aporias, or more precisely, justice conceived as aporia is an uncrossable limit which continually returns us to an inherent and ultimately irresolvable paradox. Justice so conceived resists its own collapse into law.

As we will see, this ethical resistance to positivism is crucial for the development of an adequate conception of legal interpretation. First, it allows us to understand why legal interpretation always involves both "discovery" and "invention." Interpretation is not an activity separable from the other two. Indeed, deconstruction emphasizes precisely the necessity of "invention" in interpretation. But this process of invention and restatement of legal norms also entails a judge's "responsibility toward memory." This responsibility is not to an accurate repetition through the recollection of legal norms, but to a refutation of the belief that what has been can *ever* be conflated with justice. Invention is inescapable if legal norms cannot be discovered purely through their mere recollection. We cannot escape appeals to redemptive perspectives projected into the future as the "truth" of the past in justifying legal norms. The judge is responsible for his or her projection of the legal truth or appeal to the normative rightness of the past.

I use the word "redemption" deliberately, even if it sounds foreign in the context of the secularized vocabulary of modern, liberal jurisprudence. I have chosen "redemption" because I wish to emphasize the inevitability of the projection of a "different" and "better" future, an inevitability which is essential to the justification of legal principles if such justifications are not to be reduced to a positivist appeal to convention. Moreover, it is a "projection," not simpy a recovery of the past or the inevitable fulfillment of the *telos* of history. We can only maintain a critical resistance against the pull of the logic of recursivity through projections of the "future." It is the turn toward the future, once it is properly understood, that deconstruction demands of us.

Is this simply a restatement of the Kantian insistence that justice is an ideal of political-historical reason, and as such is irreducible to the actual conventions of any existing legal system? In Kant's later writings the idea of justice or the totality of reasonable beings functions as the "as if" which is an ethical condition for the future that we must postulate if we are to present practical judgment from being a mere appeal to convention. Deconstruction does not, as it is often interpreted, reject out of hand the Kantian project. But deconstruction refuses to reduce the aporias of justice to a horizon. To analyze why, we will have to discuss how an ethical horizon has traditionally been conceived. The question of whether one can or should project a horizon of justice is itself addressed through the recognition that there is a historical specificity of types of horizons associated with the project of a horizon as an ideal. Do we idealize a 'totality' of multiple language games, as in Jean-François Lyotard's paganism, or the totality of reasonable beings in Kant's own Kingdom of ends? Would we instead project an ideal speech situation as does Jürgen Habermas? The questioning of the very concept of horizon as itself a reaction of historical specificity is just that—a questioning.

The Kantian ethical suspicion of consensus as a "reality" which dresses up convention as truth is undoubtedly evidenced in deconstruction. Like Kantianism, deconstruction rejects the identification of the ethical with reality. This affinity does not, of course, mean that deconstruction does not challenge the metaphysical premises that underlie the Kantian split between the phenomenal and the noumenal realms. Deconstruction undermines this rigid dichotomy as it does all others.

Deconstruction operates within the reality of the legal system by breaking it open and showing us that there can be no legal system that is just there. The Derridean deconstruction of the present also reminds us of the responsibility of judges, lawyers, and law professors for what the law "becomes." Moreover, this responsibility is connected with the very idea of judgment. Judgment is only judgment, and not mere calculation or recollection, if it is "fresh."[1] The judge is called upon to do just that, judge. As we will see, Derrida's remarkable insight into the limits of memory is connected to his deconstruction of the traditional conception of the modalities of time in which the present is privileged. The unique Derridean contribution to legal interpretation is to show us why the act of memory in judging involves the seemingly contradictory notion that the judge, in his or her decision, remembers the future.

Deconstruction, in other words, helps us to correct recent misdescriptions of the process of legal interpretation which either appeal to the established conventions of the present or look back to the past. Even if that past is understood as a constructed "overlapping consensus,"[2] and not just the simple recollection of norms, the process of reconstruction through the overlapping consensus is still directed to the past. The deconstruction of the traditional conception of time also provides us with an account of critique that can successfully answer the argument of Stanley Fish, who asserts that critique, in any strong sense, is impossible. For Fish, we are inevitably caught in the logic of recursivity, which enforces the apparent adequation between the legal system and justice. It is this logic of recursivity that makes the following of the pregiven legal roles or norms, "Doing What Comes Naturally."[3] Judges and lawyers would, as a result, be caught in a mechanism of repetition from which they could not escape. Judgment, then, could not be separated from calculation. Memory would *just* be rote, a replication in consciousness of an objective reality. Deconstruction challenges the possibility that the lawyer or the judge can be identified with the mere instrument for replication of the system. The judge and the lawyer "act" when they remember precedent.

The newest brand of legal positivism is offered by Niklas Luhmann and goes by the name autopoiesis. But if the name is new, the ultimate project of legal positivism, which is to solve the problem of *validity* of legal propositions through an appeal to the *mechanism* of validation internally generated by an existing legal system, remains the same. In order to achieve a satisfactory solution to the post-modern problem of *Grundlosigkeit*—the loss of grounding of legal rules in foundationalist principles—the positivist, in any of his guises, must postulate a self-maintaining, even if evolving, *cognitive system* in which there is what Luhmann calls normative closure. At the very heart of the conception of law as autopoiesis is this idea of the self-maintenance of a normatively, if not cognitively, closed system.[4]

This conception of self-maintenance, and its corresponding notion of recursivity, implies an understanding of time. In terms of its definition within the framework of law understood as an autopoietic system, recursivity means that the normativity of law can only be established by reference to the legal norms already in place as they are *authorized* and, *therefore justified* by the system. The legal system, in other words, grounds the validity of its own propositions by turning back on itself. Without recursivity there would be no operative, normative closure and, therefore, no system present to itself that could be considered self-maintaining.

Luhmann explores the iterative use of temporal modalities (past presents, future presents, etc.) as they are relevant to his social theory and more specifically to his conception of law as autopoiesis. For Luhmann, following the tradition of Western metaphysics, any theory of modal forms must privilege the present. It is this privileging of the present that lies at the very heart of Luhmann's conception of social evolution as the only way to make sense of change in a legal system which nevertheless remains normatively closed. Validity is found only by circling within the system. Luhmann's well known anti-utopianism is inseparable from his view of time.

LAW AS NORMATIVE AUTOPOIESIS

But let me turn now to a brief discussion of what autopoiesis means within the context of Luhmann's systems theory of law. I will not attempt to discuss autopoiesis in all its subtlety but only as it incorporates a conception of time as it is relevant to the very possibility of the establishment of validity within law. The central thesis of autopoiesis as it has been succinctly summarized by Luhmann is that legal validity is always circular. Legal propositions or norms can only claim validity within a self-generating system of communication which both defines relations with the outside environment and provides itself with its own mechanism of justification. Autopoiesis postulates law as an autonomous system that achieves full normative closure through epistemological constructivism. To quote Luhmann:

> Epistemological "constructivism" concludes from this that what the system, at the level of its operations, regards as reality is a construct of the system itself. Reality assumptions are structures of the system that uses them. This can be clarified once more using the concept of recursiveness. The system controls the environment, operationally inaccessible to it, by verifying the consistency of its own operations, using for this a binary scheme which can record agreement or nonagreement. Without this form of consistency control, no memory, could arise, and without memory there can be no reality.[5]

Practically speaking, then, recursiveness allows for the consistency control that enables the system to function as a system. The system, legal or otherwise, is a system only to the degree that it is operationally closed. As Luhmann himself explains:

[S]tructures of the system can be built up only by operations of the system. This too must take place in such a way as to be compatible with the system's autopoiesis; in the case of social systems, for instance, with communication. There is accordingly no input and no output of structures or operations of the system, and at this level, there are no exchange relationships with the environment. All structures are operationally self-specified structures of the system, which orients its operations to these structures. In this respect, too, the system is a recursively closed system.[6]

For Luhmann, then, law is a specialized system of information processing. Law constructs legal reality through the very recursiveness of its system of communication. But even so, the legal system is not autonomous in the sense that it is completely disengaged from the rest of society, the economy, the political arena, etc. Indeed, Luhmann argues that it is the very nature of the legal system to engage with events that are fed to it by the outside environment. As a result, there is always a material continuum between the law and its environment. The legal system is only autonomous in the sense that it is a self-reproducing mechanism for information processing.

The postulation of operational closure explains why systems theory is a form of epistemological constructivism in which reality comes to "be" only within the recursiveness of the system. But, of course, reality is only given in language. What words mean can only be deciphered from within the relevant system of communication, not through a more general system of definition. As Luhmann explains:

> The law need not and cannot concern itself with whether particular words like "woman" "cylinder capacity", "inhabitant", "thallium" are used with sufficent consistency inside and outside the law. To that extent, it is supported by the network of social reproduction of communication by communication. Should questions such as whether women, etc., really exist arise, they can be turned aside or referred to philosophy.[7]

The reality of law, for Luhmann, is a normative reality. Or, to put this another way so as to explain the distinction he makes between normative closure and cognitive openness: normative closure is based in the definitional recursiveness of the law. Normative closure creates the seeming adequation of law and justice. This formulation of law as logically recursive can, of course, be understood as a reformulation of the positivist hypothesis. The nomos of the law can only be found in law's thesis. But there is an important difference in Luhmann's conception of autopoiesis that separates him from the traditional legal positivist. In Luhmann's systems theory, the thesis is not an outside foundation, but the postulation of law itself as its own origin. For Luhmann, the thesis of law cannot be the will of the legislator. Rather the thesis is the already-in-place legal system with its recursive system of normative self-reproducing definitions.

Law is a normatively closed system in the sense that the opposition between *nomos* and *thesis* is practically overcome in the functioning of the legal system. But at the same time, law is not a cognitively closed system. This distinction is connected to Luhmann's position that while the legal system's normative autopoiesis is self-referential, it is not self-transparent. Luhmann denies that any complex system can achieve perfect self-reflexivity. This is why Luhmann distinguishes his own systems theory from all forms of neo-Kantianism. The biological metaphor of autopoiesis is supposed to capture this distinction between self-thematization or self-referentiality, and self-transparency. A biological system can be self-referential without necessarily knowing itself to be such.[8] Because law is not self-transparent and, therefore, not able to verify all of its operations, the legal system remains cognitively open. However, it is cognitively open only in a very special sense. For example, the legal system can take account of the notion that electricity can be stolen. But even as it *recognizes* this idea, it can do so only within the normative autopoiesis that recursively defines what it means for something to be stolen. Moreover, the normative definition of theft can only be what the legal system says it is. Recursivity also replaces the assumption of an *a priori* which could serve as an outside ground for justice by which to justify legal principles within a legal system. Without recursivity there would be no self-reproducing system that could come full circle to claim itself as its own origin.

THE ITERATIVE USE OF THE MODALITIES OF TIME
WITHIN SYSTEMS THEORY

Luhmann's basic hypothesis is that time, as well as its conceptualization, is changed through the mechanisms of social evolution. Time, as Luhmann defines it, is "the social interpretation of reality with respect to the difference between past and future."[9] Modern societies can be distinguished from traditional societies because of what he calls the temporalization of being. According to Luhmann, temporalization of being discredits any theory of natural forms, which would always turn us toward the past as the fundamental pivot of a society's time frame. Temporalization of being means that the past can no longer be grounded in an initial event or origin. This loss of origin shifts the very ground of time in modern societies and is reflected in the iterative use of temporal modalities within social theory. For Luhmann, the chief features of social evolution, at least in terms of how it has changed the concept of time, is to be found in what he calls the non-temporal extension of time.

Luhmann associates his conception of the non-temporal extension of time with his basic notion of a social system as a mechanism for processing information through communication with the "outside" environment:

> This nontemporal extension of time by communication creates temporal horizons for selective behavior—a past that can never be reproduced because it is too complex and a future that cannot begin.[10]

The nontemporal extension of time in turn implies time's reflexivity. As Luhmann rightfully explains, a theory of time that is distinguishable from chronology must make use of the iteration of temporal modalities. Even though Luhmann insists that the reflexivity of time in modern society turns around our orientation to the future, the future can only be understood from within the present. The future and, indeed, the past only "are" as horizons of the present. To quote Luhmann:

> [T]he *relevance* of time (in fact, I would maintain, "relevance" as such) depends upon a capacity to interrelate the past and the future in a present. All temporal structures relate to some sort of present.[11]

The present interrelates time and reality and represents a set of constraints on the temporal integration of the future and the past. Meaning can only arise if there is this shared "present." This set of constraints establishes the recursivity of the system. Social communication demands that there be a "present" that is "there" for the temporal actors. The nonextension of time—by which Luhmann indicates the evolution of society as the continued development of the present—implies the recursivity of the systems pattern, or what Luhmann calls self-thematization.

This process of self-thematization is what makes a system self-constituting in and through the present. The actors in the system can interact only because there is a shared present.

> The concept of the present contains rules for using the idea of simultaneity, which itself underlies the possibility of communication in social life.[12]

The system depends on temporal integration because without such integration it would not maintain its identity. The very distinction between the system and its environment means that there is an inevitable temporalization of the system. The system, in other words, is not there all at once in an eternal present. It is always coming to be. Recursivity is a mode of temporal integration of the past and the future as both these conceptual horizons have come to present themselves within the frame of modern society.

> As has recently been made clear, underlying this schema is the idea that *the differentiation of system and environment produces temporality* because it excludes an immediate and point-for-point correlation between events in the system and events in its environment. Everything cannot happen at once. Preserving the system requires time.[13]

In modern society the present now contains possibilities and, in this sense, the present future has conditional possibilities. Luhmann distinguishes between societies and social systems on the basis of whether or not they are expanding or curtailing the possibilities of the present future. But even so, the non-extension of time means that the present remains the basis for the iteration of all temporal modalities even if the present view includes the future present and the present future.

According to Luhmann, once we see the future as the storehouse of possibilities of the present—both as the future present and the present future—we can no longer conceive of time as containing a turning point where it veers back to mythical past or where the order of the present is to be apocalyptically transformed as a truly different future. For Luhmann, there is no telos in history which leads us to the ideal through the progressive realization of the potential that inheres in the origin and which ultimately has the power to make itself real. Luhmann believes himself to be enriching the iterative use of temporal modalities so as to develop a unique, modern conception of time.

For modern society, it is especially important that we be able to distinguish between our future presents and our present future. We can even speak, if necessary, about the future of future presents, the future of past presents (*modo futuri exacti*), and so on. This iterative use of modal forms has always been a problem for the theory of modalities. For example: why not speak of the "future of futures" like the "heaven of heavens" (*coelum coeli*)? Only phenomenological analysis can justify the selection of meaningful combinations of modal forms. What it shows, in fact, is that all iteration of temporal forms must have its basis in a present.[14]

For Luhmann, rooting the iteration of all temporal modalities in the present has implications for the way we think about historical time and systems history.

Historical time is constituted as the continuity and irreversibility of this movement of past/present/future as a whole. This unity of historical time lies in the fact that the past and future horizons of each present intersect with other (past or future) presents and their temporal horizons. This guarantees each present a sufficient continuity with other presents—not only temporally, but materially and socially as well.[15]

It is because the future and past move around the present that Luhmann can speak of his theory of time as reflexive. The horizons of the past and the future are reflexively integrated and thematized into a system through the non-temporal extension of time. This integration must take place through the present precisely because the notion of a past origin, which would constitute the true meaning of the present, is undermined.

It must now be recognized that the future (and this means past futures as well as our present future) may be quite different from the past. Time can no longer be depicted as approaching a turning point where it veers back into the past or where the order of this world (or time itself) is apocalyptically transformed.[16]

Once we accept Luhmann's proposition that the future is reflexively integrated into the present, we can understand exactly what he means when he insists that the future cannot begin.[17] For Luhmann the future is both the *present future*, as the conditional possibilities inherent in any complex modern social system, and the *future present*, expressed as the utopian projections of social critics. These projections of the utopian future, however, are only expressible as the negations of the present and, therefore, are contained in the very systems history they purport to reject. They serve as images to give body to the aspirations of the future present.

A future that cannot begin inheres in the reflexive view of time Luhmann associates with complex modern societies based on advanced technology. An open-ended future ironically involves the loss of the future as the promise of a truly "new beginning." The present of the systems theory is not a simple present, because it is relativized through the horizons of the past and the future, still constitutes reality. The future, in the sense of what would be truly different, an "apocalyptically" transformed world, cannot begin because the future "is" only as a horizon of the present.

This view of the time of social systems and of world history has specific implications for legal interpretation, the conception of justice, and the possibility of social criticism. For Luhmann, if there is no *telos* of history, the pull of the regulative ideal cannot be introduced into social theory or systems history. This is what Luhmann means when he says that history has been neutralized. History no longer has normative implications. As a result, there can be no use for utopian or redemptive visions within legal interpretation or within social theory generally. Luhmann uses legal positivism as one of the examples of what the neutralization of history entails.[18] The past can no longer provide us with an origin that can serve as the basis for normative justification for the present or for the projection of a truly different future as the truth of the past. In Luhmann's conception of the legal system's autopoiesis, justice can only be what the legal system defines it to be. The idea of justice as a projected horizon is completely rejected. The horizon, of course—Habermas' ideal speech situation or Kant's Kingdom of ends, for example—is only an ethical horizon to the degree that the projected ideal is beyond the logic of recursivity. The "ought to be," in other words, cannot be captured by the present. Kantianism, in all its forms, maintains a transcendental divide between the is and the ought. But in Luhmann, any norm, legal or otherwise, only means something to the degree that such a norm expresses the present understanding. The legal system can develop, but only as the legal system. For Luhmann the victory of legal positivism inheres in the very mode of the temporalization of modern society.

THE DECONSTRUCTIVE CHALLENGE TO LUHMANN'S
CONCEPTION OF TIME

Deconstruction challenges the idea that a theory of modal forms must have its basis in the present. As we will see, this challenge is crucial for the development of an anti-positivist conception of legal interpretation in which the divide between justice and law is always maintained.

But first I will turn to the deconstruction of the traditional conception of time which privileges the present. In order to do so, we must turn with Derrida around *différance*. Heidegger forcefully pointed to the privileging of the present in traditional conceptions of time in Western metaphysics. Derrida clearly recognizes the explosive power of Heidegger's attempt to follow through on the implications of *Dasein's*[19] finitude and its potential to undermine the traditional conception of time. But it is not this aspect of Heidegger's analysis that is crucial for the deconstruction of Luhmann's theory of temporal modalities.[20] Therefore, I will focus instead on the significance for legal theory of the Derridean *différance*. Because *différance* is not a traditional philosophical concept, it is difficult to define it directly. Indeed, Derrida himself circles around the play of *différance* as it operates within several different theoretical parameters.

Différance can be understood as the "truth" that being is only represented in time; therefore, there can be no all encompassing ontology which claims to tell us the truth of all that is. *Différance*, to use Derrida's word, *temporizes*. It breaks up the so-called claim to fullness of any given reality, social or otherwise, because reality only "presents" itself in intervals.

> An interval must separate the present from what is not in order for the present to be itself, but this interval that constitutes it as present must, by the same token, divide the present in and of itself, thereby also dividing, along with the present, everything that is thought on the basis of the present, that is, in our metaphysical language, every being, and singularly substance or the subject.[21]

The intervals through which reality is "presented" also make possible the presentation of reality out of what would otherwise be sheer density, "or the night in which all cows are black." In order for reality to "present" itself, it must already be spaced, which implies temporization and time. "The present," in other words, is what is already past and, therefore, "presented." But this condition is only reachable as the "effects" of temporization; one of which is that time is itself a diachronic force. Time, understood in this way, cannot function as both an integration and a unit of the past and future through the present, as in Luhmann. Any reality is always already divided against itself. Thus, the disruption of temporizing turns us toward the past, even if only in a very specific sense, because this past can just as well be conceived as the trace of the future.

> It is because of *différance* that the movement of signification is possible only if each so-called "present" element, each element appearing on the scene of presence, is related to something other than itself, thereby keeping within itself the mark of the past element, and already letting itself be vitiated by the mark of its relation to the future element, this trace being related no less to what is called the future than to what is called the past, and constituting what is called the present by means of this very relation to what it is not: what it absolutely is not, not even as past or a future as a modified present.[22]

The statement that the trace is related "no less to what is called the future than to what is called the past" may seem strange indeed. Yet it is precisely this insistence on the constitutive power of the "not yet" of the never has been that separates the Derridean understanding of temporization from Luhmann's conception of time and sets Derrida against Luhmann's assertion that the future cannot begin.

For Derrida, the future has already begun—although it is, of course, inappropriate to use the word beginning here since temporization belies an absolute beginning—as the trace of the unreachable origin. Derrida would agree with Luhmann, then, that there is no way back to the origin. As we approach the origin it recedes. For Derrida, the receding of the origin is inevitable because we have always already begun once there is a reality that has been presented. The origin only "is" as this recession of the never has been of an absolute beginning; this is why it can also be related to the future of the not yet. The past is not the past of chronology, which can be traced back through a linear succession of moments. Nor is it one of the horizons that extends back from the present, what Luhmann would call the present past. Rather, the past is the primordial constitution of temporality, which in turn is the condition of presentation. The present, as a result, itself becomes a sign, pointing beyond itself. Thus, it can no longer be the basis for meaning as Luhmann would have it.

Derrida would also agree with Luhmann that the recognition that we can never grasp the origin has implications for the way we think about the future. The central difference is that for Derrida it is the present that is postponed, because the present "moment" must refer to the trace of the not yet of the never has been that cannot be conceived as simply a modification of the now. In order to be what it is, the now or the present must refer back to an anterior/posterior that is the basis for presentation. As we have seen, this "movement" of temporalization is already "there" in presentation. As a result, the "present" is always belated. It cannot arrive except as a constitutive power of the not yet of the never has been, which can be evoked as either the "not yet" past or future. The future in this specific sense of the "not yet" cannot be reduced to the present future or future present. It remains the "not yet." To use Luhmann's language, the future as the "not yet" cannot be lost. But as that power it has always already begun. This is why *différance* implies a diachronic view of time. Time disrupts the very pretense of full presence at the very moment that it makes presentation possible. Time, in this primordial sense, is the limitation of the ontology of presence.

We can now put very simply what the diachronic view of time means for the critique of Luhmann's systems theory. Luhmann claims that his epistemological construct view is "past-ontology." And, of course, it is in the sense that Luhmann gives to post-ontology. For Luhmann, ontology claims privileged access to an "eternal reality" outside of the autopoietic system. Since the very idea of recursiveness belies the possibility of directly reaching the outside of the system, if we accept autopoiesis, ontology is impossible. Sociology replaces philosophy. We no longer attempt to know Being, only social systems. This displacement of philosophy is crucial to Luhmann's conception of "post-ontology."

But in another, more profound sense, the very idea of recursiveness implies exactly what Derrida means by the ontology of the full presence. Recursiveness implies a view of time that necessarily privileges the present. The whole point of Luhmann's theory of autopoiesis is to show us how a social system makes itself real through operative closure in the present. Through autopoietic closure, the system becomes the only reality. As such, it fills the universe; it becomes a kingdom which reigns over possibility and excludes the dream of a truly different future. Derrida challenges this idea that the system can reign in the beyond of the not yet through the demonstration of the significance of the play of *différance*.

> It is the domination of beings that *différance* everywhere comes to solicit, in the sense that *sollicitare*, in old Latin, means to shake as a whole, to make tremble in entirety. Therefore, it is the determination of Being as presence or as beingness that is interrogated by the thought of *différance*. Such a question could not emerge and be understood unless the difference between Being and beings were somewhere to be broached. First consequence: *différance* is not. It is not a present being, however excellent, unique, principal or trascendent. It governs nothing, reigns over nothing and nowhere exercises any authority. It is not announced by any capital letter. Not only is there no kingdom of *différance*, but *différance* instigates the subversion of every kingdom. Which makes it obviously threatening and infallibly dreaded by everything within us that desires a kingdom, the past or future presence of a kingdom.[23]

Recursiveness establishes the kingdom or the system as ontology, the "truly" real; *différance*, on the other hand, explodes from within its very claim to rule over the future by reducing the future to a horizon of the present. There is a sense, of course, in which Derrida would agree with Luhmann that the future cannot begin, because the very idea of the not yet is both anterior and *posterior* and, therefore, not merely "future" in the traditional meaning of the word. But, as we have seen, the very posterity of the future as the not yet of the never has been means that it has already begun as a consitutive force that disrupts the presence of the present. The future "is" as *redemption* from enclosure in the present.

Within a legal system, the future as the promise of justice "is" as the possible deconstruction of law or right. The destabilization of "the Kingdom" is also the destabilization of the functional or practical identity of *nomos* and *thesis* within a given legal system. As we have seen, in Luhmann, the logic of recursivity functions so as to postulate itself as its own origin, therefore urging *nomos* and *thesis* into accord. It is this endless process of turning in on itself that replaces the myth of origin. But it is precisely the legal system, turning in on itself, postulating itself as its origin, that deconstruction exposes as an impossibility. The legal machine is itself violence, as the erasure of the violent founding of the state. Think, for example, of the significance for legal interpretation of the replacement of the founding of the United States in revolution with the myth of the origin of the Constitution in the heads of the Founding Fathers. This replacement is what deconstruction shows to be the mythical foundation of authority.

Derrida agrees with Luhmann—and we will return to the significance of this agreement in his discussion of Rousseau—that there is no "real" normative origin from which all the values and norms of the legal system can be returned so they can be adequately assessed. But, unlike Luhmann, Derrida does argue that this origin cannot be displaced by the logic of recursivity:

> Since the origin of authority, the foundation or ground, the position of the law can't by definition rest on anything but themselves, they are themselves a violence without ground. Which is not to say that they are themselves unjust, in the sense of "illegal." They are neither legal nor illegal in their founding moment. They exceed the opposition between founded and unfounded, or between any foundationalism or anti-foundationalism. Even if the success of performatives that found law or right (for example, and this is more than an example, of a state as guarantor of a right) presupposes earlier conditions and conventions (for example in the national or international arena), the same "mystical" limit will reappear at the supposed origin of said conditions, roles or conventions, and at the origin of their dominant interpretation.[24]

Instead, the logic of recursivity is itself another myth that erases the founding violence from which the state and the legal system are constituted. Or, put somewhat differently, Luhmann's own insight can be deconstructed to show the fallacy of his own conclusions. As a result, the exposure of the violent act of constitution and the mystical foundations for authority is also the opening to the deconstruction of law and, correspondingly to the law of recursivity which would identify law and justice through the replication of the legal machine.

Law, as a construct, is always deconstructible. The endless deconstruction of law destabilizes the machine and exposes the cracks in the system. As a result of this destabilization, the displacement of the origin can never be completed through the functioning of the legal system, or through the postulation of a Master Rule of Recognition which supposedly replaces the founding moment of violence with a norm of foundation. This destabilization is itself done in the name of legal transformation and reform and, ultimately, in the name of justice. To quote Derrida:

The structure I am describing here is a structure in which law (*droit*) is essentially deconstructible, whether because it is founded, constructed on interpretable or transformable textual strata (and that is the history of law (*droit*), its possible and necessary transformation, sometimes its amelioration), or because its ultimate foundation is by definition unfounded. The fact that law is deconstructible is not bad news. We may even see in this a stroke of luck for politics, for all historical progress. But the paradox that I'd like to submit for discussion is the following: it is the deconstructible structure of law (*droit*), or if you prefer of justice as *droit*, that also insures the possibility of deconstruction. Justice in itself, if such a thing exists, outside or beyond law, is not deconstructible. No more than deconstruction itself, if such a thing exists. *Deconstruction is justice.*[25]

Why *is* deconstruction justice? There are several levels on which this question must be answered. Deconstruction, as we have seen, undermines the legal machine that claims to find authority in its own functioning. The tyranny of the "real," and with it the appeal to a present "reality" as the basis of the law, denies possibilities of legal reform that have yet to be articulated. The attempt to positively establish the nature of justice is rejected as incomplete because descriptive justification, the appeal to what is, still stands in for prescriptive justice. If we say this is what justice is through descriptive justification, (no matter how sophisticated the argument, if a victim's claim can still not be adequately translated, her claim goes unnoticed) to identify any existent state of affairs as justice is to impose silence on the other who dares not speak in that system.

Luhmann's conception of a legal system's evolution, which allows for a limited role for reform, obviously reinstates notions of mimetic adequation to pre-given standards, standards which themselves inevitably reflect preexisting inequalities. "The recognition that justice, if it is defined immanently, reinstates a circular mode of justification that turns on what already is and, therefore, cannot be fully prescriptive but only descriptive is one dimension of deconstruction's insistence on the maintenance of the divide between the is and the ought, law and justice. This resistance is in and of itself ethical.

But if justice is not immanent to any legal system, how can we conceive of justice as transcendent without simply reverting to Kantian metaphysics in which the is and the ought are clearly divided into realms? In other words, how can deconstruction destabilize the traditional dichotomy between nature and freedom, so crucial to Kantian ethics, while at the same time insisting on justice as transcendent to any set of immanent norms in any legal system? As we have seen, this destabilization can itself only be conceived within the deconstruction of the traditional modality of time. The legal system is never simply present to itself so as to self-generate purely immanent norms. This destabilization of the relation between the immanent and the transcendent is done in the name of justice, but it is not itself justice. Justice "is" the limit of the immanent of the present. But for Derrida, this limit is not projected as a transcendental ideal. Rather, it is an unsurpassable aporia. Justice, in other words, operates, but it operates as aporia.

Derrida gives us three examples of the operational force of justice as aporia.[26] The first aporia is between "épokhe and rule." If law is just calculation, then it would not be self-legitimating, because the process of legitimation implies an appeal to a norm. The judge is called to judge, which means that she not only states what the law is, but she also confirms its value as what ought to be.

> In short, for a decision to be just and responsible, it must, in its proper moment if there is one, be both regulated and without regulation: it must conserve the law and also destroy it or suspend it enough to have to reinvent it in each case, rejustifying it, at least reinvent it in the reaffirmation and the new and free confirmation of its principle. Each case is other, each decision is different and requires an absolutely unique interpretation, which no existing, coded rule can or ought to absolutely guarantee. At least, if the rule guarantees it in no uncertain terms, so that the judge is a calculating machine—which happens—we will not say that he is just, free and responsible. But we also won't say it if he doesn't refer to any law, to any rule or if, because he doesn't take any rule for granted beyond his own interpretation, he suspends his decision, stops short before the undecidable or if he improvises and leaves aside all rules, all principles.[27]

But at the same time, the judge is called to judge according to law. That is part of the responsibility of a judge: he must judge what is right. This means he appeals to law, to rules and not only to his opinion. So the judge is caught in a paradox. He must appeal to law and yet judge it through confirmation or rejection. But this act of judgment, if it were simply a calculation of law, would not be a "true" judgment, nor a fresh one. As a result:

> It follows from this paradox that there is never a moment that
> we can say *in the present* that a decision *is* just (that. is, free
> and responsible), or that someone *is* a just man—even less, "*I
> am just.*"[28]

To be just is to be in the throes of this paradox.

The second aporia is the "undecidable," an aporia which is
close to the first, and to some degree reflects a transcendental
deduction of the conditions of a decision.[29] A legal decision is an
interpretation which "exists" in the first aporia. If a decision is
merely calculation, it is not a decision.

> There is apparently no moment in which a decision can be
> called presently and fully just: either it has not yet been made
> according to a rule, and nothing allows us to call it just, or it
> has already followed a rule—whether received, confirmed, con-
> served, or reinvented—which in its turn is not absolutely
> guaranteed by anything; and, moreover, if it were guaranteed,
> the decision would be reduced to calculation and we wouldn't
> call it just. That is why the ordeal of the undecidable that I just
> said must be gone through by any decision worthy of the name
> is never past or passed, it is not a surmounted or sublated
> (aufgehoben) moment in the decision.[30]

The third aporia[31] is, perhaps, most significant for the purposes of our discussion here, because it most clearly distinguishes the Kantian divide between the noumenal and the
phenomenal from the Derridean conception of justice as the limit
of the immanent as aporia. The third aporia is created by the
very urgency of justice. As we have seen, every case calls for a
decision and a "fresh" judgment. The judge is called to decide
now. In Habermas or Lyotard, two modern interpreters of Kant,
justice ultimately "is" only as the projection of the ideal. The
content of the ideal differs in Habermas and Lyotard, but not the
Kantian mode of argumentation. But we are not in Habermas'
ideal speech situation now, nor are we in Lyotard's paganism.
And yet, we must judge. As a result, Derrida states:

> One of the reasons I'm keeping such a distance from all these
> horizons—from the Kantian regulative idea or from the
> messianic advent, for example, or at least from their con-
> ventional interpretation—is that they are, precisely, horizons.
> As its Greek name suggests, a horizon is both the opening and
> the limit that defines an infinite progress or a period of
> waiting.[32]

Justice does not wait. We judge in our present. But the ideal cannot guide us precisely because it is the ideal and thus not present. For Habermas, truth and rightness in the ideal speech situation demand the projection of a regulative ideal to guide us. As a regulative ideal, it is not realizable. Yet, we do not have the ideal speech situation and, indeed, as an ideal we cannot have it.

There is another concern. In spite of ourselves, the ideal will not be other to the real, therefore ideal; it will only be a rationalized protection of our current norms. Justice demands the recognition of the possible contamination of the ideal itself.

> Paradoxically, it is because of this overflowing of the performative, because of this always excessive haste of interpretation getting ahead of itself, because of this structural urgency and precipitation of justice that the latter has no horizon of expectation (regulative or messianic). But for this very reason, it *may* have an *avenir, a "to-come," which I rigorously distinguish from the future that can always reproduce the present.* Justice remains, is yet, to come, *à venir,* it has an, it is à-venir, the very dimension of events irreducibly to come. It will always have it, this à-venir, and always has. Perhaps it is for this reason that justice, insofar as it is not only a juridical or political concept, opens up for *l'avenir* the transformation, the recasting or refounding of law and politics. "Perhaps," one must always say perhaps for justice.[33]

Justice as the perhaps that must be said, also separates Derrida from Luhmann, for whom there is no perhaps, no possibility, only the evolution of an established system of communication in the present. The legal system as the present norm silences the perhaps. The machine may or may not operate. But, as a machine, in Derrida's sense, it demands only calculation of those who operate it. For Derrida, unlike Luhmann, and as we will see, for Fish, judgment begins where calculation ends. Ultimately, the deconstruction of the traditional modality of time, which privileges the present, and with it the destabilization of the traditional dichotomies, is connected to a reconceptualization which moves within Kantianism to find a beyond to its own metaphysical presuppositions.

Here we see the affinity of Derrida's conceptualization of the aporias of justice with Emmanuel Levinas' "Jewish humanism," in which justice provides the sanctity for the Other. Justice does not begin with the "I" that strives to establish *his* rights and protect *his* due share of the pie. The right of the Other is infinite, meaning that it can never be reduced to a proportional share of an already established system of ideality, legal or otherwise. Justice understood as distributive justice always implies an already-established system of ideality in which the distribution takes place. For Levinas, distributive justice is never a question of justice, but only of right. It is the Other as other to the present that echoes in the call to justice. The echo breaks up the "present," because the Other is there before the conception of a system of ideality and remains after.

For Derrida, the future is distinguished from the present that merely reproduces itself. Justice as a limit or as the call of the Other that cannot be silenced is the opening of the beyond that makes "true" transformation to the new possible. Without this appeal to the beyond, transformation would not be transformation, but only evolution, and in that sense, a continuation. The very concept of continuation as evolution of the system implies the privileging of the present.

THE IMPLICATION FOR LEGAL INTERPRETATION

The distinction between transformation and evolution is crucial in order to distinguish Derrida from a writer such as Stanley Fish, who is also identified as post-modern. I focus on Fish because he has developed his own conception of legal interpretation. In the view of deconstruction I have offered here, "post-modern philosophy" is certainly not just positivism in a new guise. Justice is radically separated from law. Yet, someone like Stanley Fish,[34] who has adopted many of what he sees as deconstructive insights, has argued that the identification of law with justice is inevitable.

For Fish, what deconstruction or post-modern philosophy more generally has shown us is that all reality, including the self, is socially constructed. This in turn means for Fish that "we" are what our reality makes us. We could not be otherwise. This position, of course, is almost identical to Luhmann's "epistemological constructivism." The result of this position as Fish sees it, is that social criticism and radical transformation is impossible. In order to have social criticism in legal interpretation, and a standpoint by which to know that real transformation had happened, we would have to appeal to a transcendental viewpoint. Since we have no transcendental or outside viewpoint, it follows that there can be no social criticism and no critical consciousness. Change can take place only as slow evolution, but not through transformation. The system "is" differently, but there is no true difference from the system. There is only evolution, not transformation. Here again, we see how close Fish is to Luhmann, because his argument implicitly relies on the logic of recursivity.

For Fish, in other words, law is always evolving, but at the same time, and in spite of his remarks to the contrary, law is not deconstructible. As Derrida reminds us, the deconstructibility of law is possible through the paradox that it is only the non-deconstructibility of justice that makes deconstruction possible.

> 1. The deconstructibility of law (droit) (for example) or of legitimacy makes deconstruction possible. 2. The undeconstructibility of justice also makes deconstruction possible, indeed is inseparable from it. 3. The result: deconstruction takes place in the interval that separates the undeconstructibility of justice from the deconstructibility of *droit* (authority, legitimacy, and so on).[35]

Because for Fish there is no divide between justice and law, the deconstruction of law is not possible. In this sense, Fish is not a deconstructionist, but a positivist.

The significance of Fish's positivism for legal interpretation is as follows: We have seen in the discussion of the aporias of justice that judgment as judgment demands the suspension of rule following, otherwise, application of the law would not be judgment, but only calculation. Fish, unlike Derrida, does not indicate the aporias of justice. Instead he argues that what "is" is a system of rules from which no one can extract himself or herself. The suspension of rule following that Derrida rightfully argues is necessary for judgment is exactly what Fish insists cannot exist. As a result, "Doing What Comes Naturally," does not include judging. The problem, of course, is that a judge who does not judge cannot claim to do justice. And yet, the claim of legitimacy of law cannot be separated in its articulation from justice. This claim is part of running the very machine Fish calls law. Fish cannot avoid the confrontation with justice as easily as he thinks.

Fortunately, as we have seen, there is also an effective challenge to legal positivism through the deconstruction of the traditional conception of time, which helps us solve the dilemma inherent in Fish's own work. There is no system present to itself which can fill the universe, and ourselves as containers for that universe, and by so doing "foreclose" the future or reduce it to the continuation of the present.

> This *same time* never is, will never have been and will never be
> *present*....There is only the promise and memory, memory as
> promise, without any gathering possible in the form of the
> present. This disjunction is the law, the text of law and the law
> of the text.[36]

Deconstruction calls us to that promise and leaves us with that
hope. The utopianism, if it can be called that, is in the reminder
"that what took place humanly has never been able to remain
closed up in its site."[37] But as we have seen, this reminder at
least within the legal system, also opens up the space for,
indeed, demands utopian imagination. As suggested in the last
section, this reminder is crucial for distinguishing between
evolution and transformation. The impossible, Justice, is what
makes the possible possible.

Given this, we must now rethink the significance of Derrida's
deconstruction of Rousseau's political theory and its implications
for legal interpretation. Many claim Derrida's deconstruction of
Rousseau theoretically undermines the very possibility of
political and ethical thought by showing that it must rely on an
origin that does not exist. However, once we put Derrida's
deconstruction within the understanding of time and temporization I have presented here, we can see why this is not the case.
For Derrida, the Rousseauean community postulates an originary instant of coming together without a trace of what has gone
before. This originary instant is the festival based on an
unmediated unity in the face to face relations of the participants.
As Derrida points up, Rousseau's vision privileges the living
voice. Speech is the vehicle of co-equals who are literally present
to one another as they determine their fate, as if they could start
again from the absolute beginning, the origin.

There is also a more profound point which has been completely missed and one which shows the significance of temporization for legal interpretation. Derrida shows us how the
inevitable failure to find the origin as the full presence that
Rousseau so desperately seeks opens up the space for the
conditional mood. Derrida wants us to see that what masks
itself as simple discovery is in fact discovery through a projection
of the ought to be. Rousseau argues from the logic of discovery,
as if we could just discover the origin in which oppositions of
nature and spirit, man and woman, etc. did not exist so as to
rend the soul apart. Rousseau seeks reconciliation in the Past
as if it were "there." But the power of his message actually lies in

its eschatological anticipation, in Derrida's sense of the "not yet." If there is no simple origin that we can find our way back to in the future, then we cannot escape the conditional mood of political and ethical vision. We project forward the truth of the past of the never has been as the "ought to be." As Derrida reminds us again and again, when we remember the past to find the ethical truth of the origin, we are, in truth, remembering the future. But we do so within the rhetoric of memory, because the future only is as the anterior/posterior.

> Memory is the name of what is no longer only a mental "capacity" oriented toward one of the three modes of the present, the past present, which could be dissociated from the present present and the future present. Memory projects itself toward the future, and it constitutes the presence of the present. The "rhetoric of temporality" *is* the rhetoric of memory.[38]

But this rhetoric is also a tension toward the future as the ought to be since memory can never exactly institute what was.

> The memory we are considering here is not essentially oriented toward the past, toward a past present deemed to have really and previously existed. Memory stays with traces, in order to "preserve" them, but traces of a past that has never been present, traces which themselves never occupy the form of presence and always remain, as it were, to come—come from the future, from the *to come*. Resurrection, which is always the formal element of "truth," a recurrent difference between a present and its presence, does not resuscitate a past which had been present; it engages the futures.[39]

In this sense, legal interpretation must be both discovery and invention because there can be no simple origin of legal meaning, whether we call it intent of the founders of the Constitution or some other name. We cannot escape the conditional mood of legal interpretation. In this sense, interpretation is always an act; moreover, an act from which we cannot escape responsibility.

THE EXAMPLE OF *ROE V. WADE*[40] AND ITS PROGENY: THE ACT OF REMEMBRANCE OF JUDGING

We can now turn to how this understanding of memory as inevitably involved in the remembrance of the future should shift our conception of the judge's role in "perpetuating" precedent. Let us take as an example, the line of decisions following *Roe*. In these cases, the Supreme Court examined state and municipal laws restricting a woman's right to choose whether to terminate her pregnancy. In *Roe*, the Supreme Court was presented with whether or not the constitutional right to privacy recognized in previous decisions such as *Griswold v Connecticut*[41] should apply to abortion. *Roe*, as Catharine MacKinnon has *described* the decision, "guaranteed the right to choose abortion, subject to some countervailing considerations, by conceiving it as a private choice, included in the constitutional right to privacy."[42] MacKinnon, among others has challenged the normative bases of grounding the decision in the right to privacy. My focus, however, is not on the normative basis for the decision, but on the mistaken "phenomenology" of judging that has now been used to justify the undermining of the principles on which *Roe* was based. The argument, supposedly legal, not moral, goes something like this: there is no origin in the Constitution itself for the right of privacy, let alone for the right of privacy to be "applied" to abortion.

We will now turn to how the judges, when they enunciated the decision in *Roe*, were unfaithful to their designated role as judges. The charge is that they did not simply re-collect precedent and then enunciate its reading as if this could be done without involving an evaluation. Instead they made up the law to fit the "new" situation, the demand of Women for reproductive rights.[43] It is not just that the judges had competing constitutional views which could be understood to "fit" the example of abortion and they chose the wrong one—although I think it is evident that had such norms available for their imaginative "re-collection."[44] There is no firmly rooted constitutional precedent for the judge to re-collect that could justify *Roe*. If the only correct act for the judge who enunciating a legal decision is the re-collection of past decisions that are understood to be based on the intent of the fathers, or on some other notion of the foundational origin of constitutional meaning, there can be no justification for *Roe* that is consistent with this view of judging.[45] I have argued, elsewhere[46] and in the course of this essay that this understanding of the relationship of law and judging completely misunderstands the role of interpretation in legal decisions because such interpretations always involve the justification, not merely the perpetuation, of the norms "embodied" in past decisions. Even if judging was understood primarily to involve memory in the sense of re-collection of precedent, memory itself can never just capture the past.

Derrida's analysis of the limit to memory as well as the responsibility to it, is thus crucially important to an adequate understanding of what judicial memory involves. This more adequate understanding of the phenomenology of memory in judging can be used in turn to critique any justification for the reversal of *Roe* as the correction of an irresponsible act of judging.

We can use the progeny of *Roe* to show that the deconstruction of the traditional conception of the modalities of time has implications for the way we think about the role of the judge. The judge can never be reduced to the instrument of the system who simply re-collects precedent. Her subjective role is not merely the passive one of re-collecting what is there in the origin. She also cannot just do what comes naturally, that is, follow the rules as if such a following were a form of automatic writing. She is responsible for her memory and the future which she promotes in the act of remembrance itself.

I am using responsibility in the sense that we are accountable for our own actions and our judgments. We are responsible precisely because we cannot be reduced to automatons who cannot choose to do other than what comes naturally. Responsibility has often been thought to turn on a positive account of a transcendental or autonomous subject. Only a subject that can rise above circumstances, so the argument goes, can be held accountable, because only an autonomous subject can achieve meaningful freedom.to choose. If we cannot do otherwise, responsibility becomes a misnomer. But such a view, which completely identifies the subject with the "machine" or system, depends on the myth of the full presence and the privileging of the present which has been deconstructed. Similarly the machine or system is not just a self-replicating presence. The machine is *only presented* through its enforcers. The very functioning of the machine demands its enforcers. It is our irreducibility and the irreducibility of the machine to a self-contained context, that makes our responsibility inescapable. This is not, admittedly a *positive* account of the subject. But deconstruction reinforces an account of the irreducibility of the subject to a context which is necessary for the strong sense of responsibility that Derrida emphasizes.

We have to think again about the responsibility to memory that is demanded by deconstruction and the very deconstructibility of law.

> The sense of a responsibility without limits, and so necessarily excessive, incalculable, before memory; and so the task of recalling the history, the origin and subsequent direction, thus the limits, of concepts of justice, the law and law [*droit*], of values, norms, prescriptions that have been imposed and sedimented there, from then on remaining more or less readable or presupposed. As to the legacy we have received under the name of justice, and in more than one language, the task of a historical and interpretive memory is at the heart of deconstruction, not only as philologico-etymological task or the historian's task but as responsibility in face of a heritage that is at the same,time the heritage of an imperative or of a sheaf of injunctions.[47]

In this unique sense, genealogy becomes a part of judicial integrity itself.[48] The tradition is called to remember its own exclusions and prejudices. We are called upon to remember the history in which women did not have the right to an abortion. We have to remember what the general conditions of women were during those times in history in which abortion was disallowed. Genealogy is not invoked for the sake of de-bunking. Genealogy, in the sense that I use it, is crucial to the integrity to justice that demands that we also examine the existing limits of actualized concepts of justice, particularly as these exist in, and perpetuate, the patriarchal order of society. Integrity to justice, the attempt to be just with justice, demands no less than this responsibility, to expose the limits of what has been established as law, as well as in other circumstances, its confirmation or reinstatement.

> This responsibility toward memory is a responsibility before the very concept of responsibility that regulates the justice and appropriateness (*justesse*) of our behavior, of our theoretical, practical, ethicopolitical decisions. This concept of responsibility is inseparable from a whole network of connected concepts (property, intentionality, will, conscience, consciousness, self-consciousness, subject, self, person, community, decision , and so forth) and any deconstruction of this network of concepts in their given or dominant state may seem like a move toward irresponsibility at the very moment that, on the contrary, deconstruction calls for an increase in responsibility.[49]

In *Roe*, justice Blackmun confessed that the question of when life begins was not one the Justices could answer.[50] Blackmun, however, was able to *decide* whether and when a fetus becomes a *legal* person. In a profound sense, Blackmun responsibly operated within the first aporia of justice. He imaginatively recollected a legal norm from within our heritage that would allow us to make crucial distinctions about the status of the fetus for the purposes of law. He had to make a fresh judgment in the new conditions created by women's demand for the right to abortion. In this sense, he applied the norm of privacy developed in *Griswold* to a new situation. This "application" clearly was also a judgment about what right women should have to privacy and why abortion was part of that right. In terms of the second aporia, he was called to make a decision in response to the woman's movement's call to justice, and he did. Once we read Blackmun's judgment within the aporias of justice, we can see his decision as the kind of activism that is *inevitable* in judgment and decision, but an activism exercised in accordance with responsibility and the call to justice. As we will see, Rehnquist is no less an activist, just less responsible, and deaf to the call of justice for women. Blackmun constructed the trimester framework[51] based upon the State's shifting interests in the respective lives of the woman and fetus. In dissent, Justice Rehnquist found himself "in fundamental disagreement" with almost every segment of the *Roe* framework.[52]

Sixteen years later, in *Webster v. Reproductive Health Services*,[53] Justice Rehnquist failed to re-collect precedential history. First, he maintained that *stare decisis* is a constitutional principle applicable only where used to re-collect "good" law. Then, by identifying *Roe* as "unsound in principle and unworkable in practice,"[54] he substituted his own standards in lieu of those which already existed, while maintaining that differences in fact justified not revisiting *Roe*.[55] We can now see just how deconstruction, with its emphasis on responsibility to history, differs from the position that would argue that all judges do is make things up as they go along. Rehnquist was responsible for considering the history in which women were not allowed to have abortions and what that meant for the exercise of their bodily integrity. But, equally important, he was called by the demand of justice for women to consider the reasons for the compromise in *Roe*. The *Webster* decision certainly shows why the deconstructibility of law promotes anxiety. As women, our rights can always be undermined. But we cannot protect against the deconstructibility of law by denying its possibility. Our only protection is in the call to responsibility, which is precisely why the recognition that law is always deconstructible increases rather than decreases responsibility.

For Rehnquist, the fact that the *Roe* framework was difficult to apply statutorily led him to question whether it had any constitutional basis. To quote Rehnquist:

> In the first place, the rigid *Roe* framework is hardly consistent with the notion of a Constitution cast in general terms, as ours is, and usually speaking in general principles, as ours does. The key elements of the *Roe* framework-trimesters and viability are not found in the text of the Constitution or in any place else one would expect to find a constitutional principle. Since the bounds of the inquiry are essentially indeterminate, the result has been a web of legal rules that have become increasingly intricate, resembling a code of regulations rather than a body of constitutional doctrine.[56]

Therefore, although Rehnquist acknowledged that "[s]tare decisis is a cornerstone of our legal system,"[57] he nevertheless felt that the indeterminacy of the *Roe* framework was sufficient justification to ignore it as precedent.

Perhaps the most striking aspect of Rehnquist's decision was its undermining of the principle which justified the erection, and I use that word deliberately, of the *Roe* framework.[58] This is most clearly shown in Rehnquist's interpretation of the preamble of the contested law restricting abortion.[59] The preamble stated:

> "findings" by the [Missouri] state legislature that "[t]he *life* of each human being *begins at conception*," and that "unborn children have protectable interests in life, health, and well-being." The Act further requires that all Missouri laws be interpreted to provide unborn children with the same rights enjoyed by *other persons*, subject to the Federal Constitution and [Supreme Court] precedents.[60]

As Rehnquist explained, "[t]he preamble can be read simply to express...a value judgment favoring childbirth over abortion."[61] Of course, that value judgment, cast as a finding of fact, undermines the fundamental basis upon which the *Roe* Court limited the states' interference with a woman's right to choose whether to have an abortion. The preamble establishes that life begins at conception and that a "fetus is a "person"[62] with "protectable interests in life, health, and wellbeing."[63] Therefore, the case for a woman's right choose whether to terminate her pregnancy "collapses, for the fetus's right to life would then be guaranteed specifically by the [Fourteenth] Amendment."[64] By allowing the Missouri statute to stand, the *Webster* plurality authorized the supersession of the woman's privacy right. Rehnquist interpreted the preamble of the statute in deliberate disregard of the genealogical considerations demanded by integrity. These considerations are demanded by the call of the Other for justice.

Likewise, in *Akron v. Akron Center for Reproductive Health*,[65] Justice O'Connor, in dissent (joined by Justices White and Rehnquist), characterized

> [t]he *Roe* framework...[as] clearly on a collision course with its self. As the medical risks of various abortion procedures decrease, the point at which the State may regulate for reasons of maternal health is moved further forward to actual child-birth. As medical science becomes better able to provide for the separate existence of the fetus, the point of viability is moved further back toward conception.[66]

This, she felt, would render the principle of the trimester approach worthless. The compelling state interest at the point of viability in the potential life of the fetus would clash with the woman's right to decide whether to terminate the pregnancy. This looming confrontation would create in fact what Justice O'Connor already believed true. O'Connor appealed to what was already understood as the state's interest in protecting the fetus, to undermine the woman's call for justice.

> The choice of viability as the point at which the state interest in potential life becomes compelling is no less arbitrary than choosing any point before viability or any point afterward. Accordingly, I believe that the State's interest in protecting potential human life exists throughout the pregnancy.[67]

O'Connor, then, engaged in an irresponsible act of judging not by imaginatively re-collecting her projection of the future, but by failing her responsibility to remember the actual conditions women would again face if the *Roe* framework was dismantled. Those conditions had been graphically described. They needed to be addressed. Instead, O'Connor appealed to the state's interest in the law, rather than to justice for women. Viability, as essential to the *Roe* framework, was clearly a compromise. As we have seen, in my interpretation, the compromise should be understood within Blackmun's attempt to operate within the aporias of justice. The call of women was for justice. What they got, indeed the only "thing" they could get from the legal system, was law. But the law, the new application of the norm of privacy, was an act of responsibility to memory in that it recognized the actual conditions in which women had been denied the right to abortion. Of course, the fetus can itself be recognized as Other, with infinite right. But whether or not this recognition is to be embodied in law must directly confront the woman as Other, who called for her right and for justice.

We can now return to why the deconstruction of the traditional conception of the modalities of time has implications for the way we think about the role of the judge. We have seen that when we remember the past we do so through the "ought to be" implicit in the not yet of the never has been. But we can also see the difference between this conception of the future of justice and the projection of a horizon. In the first place, it should be obvious that such horizons, as traditionally defined within our heritage, have projected rational persons as interchangeable, yet it is unclear whether an ideal premised on interchangeability can really help us justify abortion. Here we see a specific example in which the projected ideal, premised on interchangeability itself, may be contaminated by history, in this case patriarchal ignorance of the specificity of femininity. Secondly, as the slogan from the 1970s asserted, "women want abortion now." Thus we return to the third aporia of justice: Justice does not wait.

We do not remember through the logic of recursivity, although Justice O'Connor implicitly relied on such a logic when she established state interest. If we undermine the "ought to be," we can only do so through a direct appeal to a counter normative justification, in this case an appeal that would discuss whose life counts more, woman or fetus. Changing technology, which is what O'Connor pointed to, is not the issue. An "is" cannot simply undermine an "ought." Interpretation is not the calculation that "fits" pieces into a puzzle. The question of fit can never be legitimately used to enunciate an articulated norm. If the norm is wrong, it must be condemned through evaluation. I have suggested that a part of this evaluation must be a recognition of the conditions of woman and the conditions in which the right of abortion had been denied. Both aspects of this evaluative process are demanded by the exercise of responsibility to memory. The question is not whether *Roe* fits into our constitutional scheme, because every new decision raises the question of whether our constitutional system is just. Again, we are returned to the first aporia of justice. *Roe* was an attempt at fresh judgment based on this responsibility to memory. Privacy may not have been the "best norm." I would translate the call of justice into the right of bodily integrity. But the attempt was still made to heed the call to Justice. In the recent decisions, we find the failure to heed the call; it is hidden by the rhetoric of fit. And yet, even Rehnquist recognized that only good law is to be followed. Unless one can show that there is a past present or a present past that merely evolves, the reliance on the logic of recursivity including the rhetoric of fit, is an impossibility. It is precisely the contribution of deconstruction to show us that such a present past does not exist. By doing so it shows us why we cannot avoid appealing to the "ought to be" when we interpret precedent. Integrity demands that we face the call to Justice and the endless transformative demands on the legal system which justice demands of us. We are left with a simple command and an infinite responsibility. Be just with Justice.

NOTES

1. *See* Derrida, *Force of Law: The "Mystical Foundation of Authority"* 29 (forthcoming in 11 Cardozo L. Rev., Summer 1990). I am deliberately echoing Derrida's reference to Stanley Fish's expression "fresh judgment" in his article *Force*. S. Fish, *Doing What Comes Naturally* (1989).

2. *See generally* Rawls, *The Domain of the Political and Overlapping Consensus*, 64 N.Y.U. L. Rev. 233 (1989).

3. *See generally* S. Fish, *supra* note 1.

4. For a discussion of the conflict within autopoiesis between the autonomy of a normatively closed system and the dynamism of a cognitively open system, see Jacobson, *Autopoetic Law: The New Science of Niklas Luhmann*, 87 Mich. L. Rev. 1647 (1989).

5. N. Luhmann, *Closure and Openness: On Reality in the World of Law* in Autopoietic Law: A New Approach to Law and Society 337 (G. Reubner ed. 1987).

6. *Id.*

7. *Id.* at 340.

8. As Luhmann himself explains:
First of all with a comparable theoretical approach, it [the concept of autopoietic closure] replaced Kantian premises. This has chiefly affected epistemological questions. Autopoietic systems need not be transparent to themselves. They find nothing in themselves that could be regarded as an undeniable fact of consciousness and applied as an epistemological *a priori*. The assumption of an *a priori* is replaced by recursivity itself...It may be that continuing application of the operations available to the system to the results of precisely those operations

produces stable states (which means states that repeat themselves in further operations, so-called "eigenstates"), or it may not, and depending on the type of operation, many, or few, or only one of these self-referentially stable states may exist. How far the system itself possesses reflexive capacity to observe its own states and finds its own "identity" in them is another question.
Id. at 336.

9. N. Luhmann, The Differentiation of Society 274 (1982) (emphasis omitted).

10. *Id.* at 283.

11. *Id.* at 276 (emphasis in original) (endnote omitted).

12. *Id.* at 308.

13. *Id.* at 292 (citations omitted).

14. *Id.* at 278 (citations and endnotes omitted).

15. *Id.* at 307 (citation omitted).

16. *Id.* at 272.

17. *See generally id.* at 271–88.

18. *See id.* at 318.

19. The concept of *Dasein* is one which is familiar to those who engage with German philosophy and especially with Heidegger. Generally, it is "[t]his entity which each of us is himself and which includes inquiring as one of the possibilities of its Being." M. Heidegger, Being and Time 27 (J. Macquarrie & E. Robinson trans. 1962) (footnote omitted). More specifically:

in everyday usage it [*Dasein*] tends to be used more narrowly to stand for the kind of being that belongs to *persons*. Heidegger follows the everyday usage in this respect, but goes somewhat further in that he often uses it to stand for any *person* who has such Being, and who is thus an "entity" himself.

Id. at 27 n. 1 (emphasis in original).

20. *See generally id.*

21. J. Derrida, *Différance*, in Margins of Philosophy 13 (A. Bass trans. 1982).

22. *Id.* at 13 (emphasis in original).

23. *Id.* at 21–22.

24. Derrida, *supra* note 1, at 17.

25. *Id.* (italics in original, emphasis added).

26. *See id.* at 28–37.

27. *Id.* at 29.

28. *Id.* at 29–30.

29. *See generally id.* at 30–33.

30. *Id.* at 31.

31. *See generally id.* at 33–37.

32. *Id.* at 33.

33. *Id.* at 35 (emphasis added).

34. *See generally* Fish, *Anti-Professionalism,* 7 Cardozo L. Rev. 679 (1986).

35. Derrida, *supra* note 1, at 18.

36. J. Derrida, *Acts,* in Memories for Paul de Man 145 (C. Lindsay, J. Culler & E. Cadava trans. 1986).

37. E. Levinas, Otherwise Than Being 184 (A. Linges trans. 1981).

38. J. Derrida, *The Art of Mémoires,* in Memories for Paul de Man, *supra* note 36, at 56–57 (emphasis in original).

39. *Id.* at 58 (emphasis in original).

40. 410 U.S. 113 (1973).

41. 381 U.S. 479 (1965).

42. C. MacKinnon, Feminism Unmodified 93 (1987). Two separate state interests have been identified. The first is preserving and protecting the health of the pregnant woman. The second is protecting the potentiality of human life. "Each grows in substantiality as the woman approaches term, and at a point during pregnancy, each becomes "compelling." *Roe,* 410 U.S. at 162–63. The Court considered these interests sufficiently compelling to authorize the state to override a woman's privacy interest.

43. For background on the history of, and demand for, reproductive freedom, see generally, L. Gordon, Woman's Body, Woman's Right: A Social History of Birth Control in America (1977); R. Petchesky, Abortion and Woman's Choice: The State, Sexuality, and Reproductive Freedom (1985).

44. For a more completed discussion of the concept "collective imagination", see Cornell, *Institutionalization of Meaning, Recollective Imagination and the Potential for Transformative Legal Interpretation*, 136 U. Pa. L. Rev. 1135 (1988).

45. "The fundamental aspiration of judicial decision-making [is]...the application of neutral principles "sufficiently absolute to give them roots throughout the community and continuity over significant periods of time...." City of Akron v. Akron Center for Reproductive Health, 462 U.S. 416, 458 (O'Connor, J., dissenting) (quoting A. Cox, The Role of the Supreme Court in American Government 114 (1976)).

46. *See generally* Cornell, *supra* note 44.

47. Derrida, *supra* note 1, at 24.

48. I am using "integrity" here in the sense given it by Ronald Dworkin in Law's Empire (1989).

49. Derrida, *supra* note 1, at 25.

50. As Blackmun himself explained: "We need not resolve the difficult question of when life beings. When those trained in the respective disciplines of medicine, philosophy, and theology are unable to arrive at any consensus, the judiciary, at this point in the development of man's knowledge, is not in a position to speculate as the the answer." *Roe*, 410 U.S. at 159,

51. The trimester framework was set out as follows:
(a) For the stage prior to approximately the end of the first trimester, the abortion decision and its effectuation must be left to the medical judgement of the pregnant woman's attending physician.
(b) For the stage subsequent to approximately the end of the first trimester, the State, in promoting its interest in the health of the mother, may, if it chooses, regulate abortion procedure in ways that are reasonably related to maternal health.
(c) For the stage subsequent to viability, the State in promoting its interest in the potentiality of human life may, if it chooses, regulate, and even proscribe, abortion except where it is necessary, in appropriate medical judgment, for the preservation of the life or health of the mother.
Id. at 164–165.

52. *Id.* at 171 (Rehnquist, J., dissenting).

53. 109 S. Ct. 3040 (1989).

54. *Id.* at 3056 (quoting Garcia v. San Antonio Metro. Transit Auth., 469 U.S. 528 (1985)).

55. *See id.* at 3057–58.

56. *Id.* at 3056–57.

57. *Id.* at 3056.

58. *See supra* notes 50–52 and accompanying test.

59. Mo. Rev. Stat. §§ 1.205.1(1)-(2), 1.205.2 (1986).

60. *Webster*, 109 S. Ct. at 3049.

61. *Id.* at 5027. In his dissenting opinion, Justice Blackmun voiced an eloquent appeal for justice for women: "I fear for the future. I fear for the liberty and equality of the millions of women who have lived and come of age in the 16 years since *Roe* was decided. I fear for the integrity of, and public esteem for, this Court. I dissent." *Id.* at 3067 (Blackmun, J., dissenting).

62. Roe v. Wade, 410 U.S. 113, 156 (1973).

63. Mo. Rev. Stat. § 1.205.1(1)-(2).

64. *Roe*, 410 U.S. at 156–57.

65. 462 U.S. 416 (1983).

66. *Id.* at 458.

67. *Id.* at 461.

Dossier III

THE POLITICAL

8

EUGENE D. GENOVESE_____

Critical Legal Studies as Radical Politics and World View

> I am a democrat because I believe in the Fall of Man. I think most people are democrats for the opposite reason. A great deal of democratic enthusiasm descends from the ideas of people like Rousseau, who believed in democracy because they thought mankind so wise and good that everyone deserved a share in the government....The real reason for democracy is just the reverse. Mankind is so fallen that no man can be trusted with unchecked power over his fellows. Aristotle said that some people were only fit to be slaves. I do not contradict him. But I reject slavery because I see no men fit to be masters.
>
> C. S. Lewis,
Present Concerns

As an act of simple justice to Professor Mark Kelman and his *A Guide to Critical Legal Studies*, I must begin with a caveat. Every author has the right to expect a reviewer to criticize the book he has written, not the one he might have written. I have tried to meet that obligation but probably failed. Accordingly Professor Kelman has a right to get sore. Still, the Critical Legal Studies movement entails a good deal more than quarrels over strictly legal questions, however discretely important. It proudly proclaims itself the cutting-edge of a new radical politics and a new social theory. He who would guide us through CLS but obscures that larger program is asking for trouble.

Guide consists of nine chapters that might have been grouped in three parts. As a bonus, Kelman offers fifty-eight pages of annotated notes that provide an invaluable bibliography of CLS writings. The first three chapters discuss rules and standards, the subjectivity of value, and intentionality and determinism. Together, they constitute a synthesis of CLS's familiar, controversial, slashing attacks on the premises and practices of the legal system. The synthesis contains some fresh contributions by Kelman, but its primary value lies in its systematic recapitulation of the arguments the Critics have been scattering throughout a variety of law journals.

The middle three chapters contain a powerful attack on the law-and-economics school, which Kelman views as the principal embodiment of the liberal ideology and program that CLS has set out to combat, and a noticeably less powerful attack on the legal-process school. Kelman adds fresh contributions, some of them excellent, to debates that will be familiar to those who follow the law journals.

The three remaining chapters discuss the contributions of CLS to legal history, its critique of the rule of law, and its effort to construct a theory of legitimation. Here we might expect the constructive side of CLS to emerge with full clarity. It does not, and Kelman only strengthens the gnawing feeling that there is not much there to emerge. But then, were there much, Kelman might have opened his book with a "Here We Stand." Instead, he assures us throughout that the Critics' destructive work should be understood as Prolegomena to its work of construction. If so, we are left with *Hamlet* without the Dane. This failure reflects no lack of talent on the part of an admirably talented author; it reflects the lack of the promised constructive work in CLS itself. That lack proves illuminating, for it exposes the inadequacies of the utopianism that has plagued the Left, including the Marxist Left, from its beginnings and that once again threatens to ruin its efforts.

Kelman does shed some light on the implicit theoretical and political program, but, primarily, he seems determined to repel mean-spirited and ignorant attacks by demonstrating that CLS should be regarded as a respectable tendency within the legal profession and the law schools. He has performed well. As John Stick observes, "One of the interesting results of Kelman's intellectual style is that much of the current notoriety surrounding CLS is made to look quite silly."[1] Those words might be translated to mean that Kelman has performed too well and accomplished the astonishing feat of making CLS appear dull.

Guide is poorly written. Normally, civility would call for silence or at most a passing rebuke, but in this case the style of the book captures its content. Sentences, paragraphs, pages need to be reread, sometimes more than once, to be understood even by Kelman's fellow lawyers.[2] Clauses within clauses abound for no apparent reason. Guide could easily provide fodder for the *New Yorker's* illustrations of the undecipherability of academic prose. Kelman invites ridicule for a performance that reeks of mandarinism. After all, an exponent of radical egalitarianism might be expected to display a strong preference for "the plain style" and to reach out for the widest possible readership. The problem is not that Kelman cannot write well, for we have good reason to know that he can. His article on "Trashing," for example, is clear and, at its peak moments, elegant and witty.[3] The contrast suggests that *Guide*, for all its preaching against mandarinism, has a mandarin purpose, and that, for all its assault on the muddleheadedness of the despised liberals, it is trapped by the muddleheadedness of its own point of view.

Kelman's Introduction invites a nonlawyer to proceed no further. With disarming frankness he tells us what *Guide* is not about, notably the political and institutional history of the CLS movement. In other words, Kelman mercifully spares us a recitation of the nasty quarrels that have been disgracing our law schools and flooding Academia with gossip. For that we should be grateful. Less mercifully, he spares us an explication and critique of all except the minimum of the CLS world view. For that we should not be grateful.

There is a limit beyond which any viewpoint becomes dull when it remains on the attack, content to assail other intellectual positions. *Guide* launches an attack on the theoretical basis of the liberal legal system and its dichotomies of rules and standards, the objectivity and subjectivity of values, and the recourse to assumptions of intentionality and determinism. But it suffers from the easy assumption that the contradictions themselves, rather than their specific forms, should be attributed to liberalism instead of being seen as inherent in human nature and therefore inherent in any society we might construct. Time after time, a reader wants to cry out: "Doubtless, it is all a mess. But what, exactly, do you propose to put in place of the legal system you are attacking?"

Kelman scorns to suggest something to put in its place. By exposing the contradictions and inconsistencies in the liberal legal system, he seems to think he has done his job. But if, as

Calvin Massey, among other opponents, points out, contradictions and inconsistencies arise from the predicament of man in society, then any legal system—any social system—may be expected to suffer accordingly. Thus Massey scores a point when he notes that Kelman's often cogent critique of the privileging of rules over standards does not begin to demonstrate that rules should be dispensed with, but, as Massey says, it is no accident that Kelman winds up with the embarrassing rhetorical flourish, "Rules are the opiate of the masses."[4]

Similarly, Mark Hager, in a friendly review finds "puzzling" Kelman's discussion of the contradictions of liberalism. "I cannot see," he writes, "what could be thought specifically '*liberal*' about the contradictions identified—rules/standards, value objectivity/subjectivity, free choice/determinism. They can more plausibly be viewed as *existential* or *structural* than as specifically *liberal*." And he adds, "A given legal order is characterized not by the existence of contradictions, but rather by the nuances of how the contradictions are, if you will, 'mediated.'"[5] In fact, Kelman and the Critics do not deny that unreconcilable contradictions exist in human nature. Rather, they charge liberal society and the legal order with obscuring them. So far, so good. But they then assume that by opening up the society and legal system to participatory democracy and by exposing the contradictions to full view, we could somehow reduce the consequences to a bare minimum and usher in a much healthier social order. That far, not so good. And nowhere convincingly demonstrated.

The present social order and legal system may well be much worse than a practical alternative, as Kelman, the Critics, and many others believe, but that notion is precisely what needs to be elaborated and defended. Kelman does not do so. How could he, since he admits that CLS embraces an array of political tendencies and lacks a positive program? Instead he offers an exhortation to risk a plunge into the unknown. That exhortation may fire the faithful but is likely to chill those who have counted the corpses piled up in such projects, especially during this century.

Thus, the alarmed protest of Harold Berman against the cavalier treatment of rules and standards cannot readily be turned aside by ever more cutting exposures of the philosophic pretensions, ambiguities, and inconsistencies in the rule of law. Berman properly scoffs at the notion that the replacement of the emphasis on rules by one on substance would end well, especially if carried as far as many of the Critics seem willing to go. "What is to prevent discretionary justice," he asks, "from being an instrument of repression and even a pretext for barbarism and brutality, as it became in Nazi Germany?" Nor does an appeal to the benign effects of a strong sense of community serve well, for as Berman observes, "Most communities of more than face-to-face size can hardly survive for long, much less interact with one another, without elaborate systems of rules, whether customary or enacted."[6]

The Critics do have a strategy for social change, but they never outline the content of the desired change itself. They invoke "participatory democracy" and "equality," as if those code words speak for themselves. On principle they refuse to identify the specific content since, in their view, the content must emerge from practice and thereby define itself. The strategy calls for a demand that counter-principles be given equal weight with principles (e.g., substance with rules) so as to force society and the legal system to realize their own professed ideals. Kelman stands with the redoubtable Roberto Mangabeira Unger in rejecting siren calls to revolutionary violence and the transformation of society in a single stroke. Unger insists that radicals undertake the patient work necessary for the steady transformation of existing institutions. His program therefore respects existing democratic and constitutional procedures.[7]

But how far does this respect extend? During the 1960s the New Left experimented with a strategy of raising demands that roughly conformed to prevalent ideals and of escalating those demands immediately upon having them granted. Thus, in effect, no institution could continue to meet the demands without destroying itself. The cynicism of the strategy doomed it from the start, for it quickly became obvious that a large and largely hidden agenda lay behind seemingly innocent proposals. Unger displays no such cynicism and palpable bad faith. He lays his cards on the table in seven books that work out the theory of a transformation to an egalitarian society. Rejecting both socialism and capitalism, as those terms are commonly understood, he outlines a new economic and social order that would transcend the familiar concepts of state and private property.

Were the Critics to make his vision and program their own, they could no longer be fairly charged with negativism, much less nihilism. But, if Kelman guides us aright, as I believe he does, they make a virtue of the ideological disarray in their ranks, treat Unger's work as one interesting possibility, and settle for a transformative strategy without committing themselves to a definite outcome. They thereby fall into the same trap as the New Leftists of the 1960s did, and they lay themselves open to the charge of deliberately hiding their true objectives. Those who file that charge make the doubtful assumption that the Critics could agree on true objectives.

The Critics' strategy threatens unforeseen and ominous consequences. If their quest for participatory democracy and equality constitutes a will-o'-the-wisp, then their work of destruction, instead of clearing away rubbish in the fight for a better society, would probably lead to new and worse forms of domination. Without a commitment to Unger's program for restructuring property relations, or some coherent alternative to it, the CLS's attack on the legal system can only work destructively in the idle hope that increased popular empowerment must end with desirable results. We have been there before.

Cultural radicalism underlies Kelman's kind of political radicalism and is reflected in his writing style, which invites objections, large and small. Here let us settle for a small one with large implications. I make no apology to the ladies for usually writing "men" instead of "persons" and always writing "his" instead of "his/her" or God knows what, for I cannot fathom how a commitment to justice and equity for women requires a trashing of the great English language. Kelman, who enjoys deconstruction, does not agree. Throughout his book he concedes this ground to the radical feminist ideologues he drolly assumes to speak for progressive women. We are treated to an orgy of "persons" and, for good measure, to "she" and "her," as well as "he" and "his," when the antecedent is not gender-specific. And in almost every case, Kelman treats us to "she" and "her" when the gender-unspecific antecedent is a good guy (a Critic, a victim of oppression, a defenseless child, a noble soul), and to "he" and "his" when the antecedent is a bad guy (a law-and-economics professor, an egotist, a murderer, a sadist).

I regret to learn that they still play cops and robbers at Stanford Law School, where Kelman teaches, but since I have greater respect for institutional autonomy than he seems to, I shall mind my own business. In any case, Kelman is by no means alone among the Critics in playing this childish game.

What have we come to when men who aspire to speak seriously of serious things degrade themselves by cowering before threatened accusations of sexism? For myself, I can only offer a para-phrase of the retort given by Mike Quill to some slob who red-baited him: I would rather be called a sexist by a damned fool than a damned fool by a sexist.[8]

The Critics may well be cowering, as I fear, but they are also doing something a good deal worse. Apparently, they have embraced androgyny and, with it, much else, including the reduction of social standards to a matter of "sexual preference" on the basis of some high principle I cannot wait to hear explicated and defended.[9] They are entitled to their point of view, but their tactics speak volumes. Rather than compel a national debate over issues of capital importance, they invite us into an imperceptible reordering of social, political, and moral standards by a series of irreversible steps taken in response to "small" demands allegedly designed to remove residual bigotry. The tactics conform to a strategy, the strategy to a world view—the very world view Kelman labors mightily to obfuscate.

The problem arises from the Critics' method, which identifies a counter-principle for every principle. Up to a point the exercise proves fruitful. But the Critics insist that the legal system embraces a liberal bias that privileges the principle in such a way as to make it seem natural and to make the counter-principle seem either deviant or merely a stratagem to accommodate exceptions. It may do just that, but the case made against it raises hackles. Surely, as the Critics charge, the procedure creates a powerful tendency toward the legitimation of the principle and throws the burden of proof on those who would like to reverse matters and privilege the counter-principle. But that is what any legal system ought to do, if only because it is difficult to imagine social order on any other basis.

The Critics reply that we need to unmask the arbitrariness beneath the pretense of objectivity in deciding upon the principle to be privileged. Very well. But, that we could hope to avoid such arbitrariness in the absence of transcendent and revealed truth remains to be demonstrated. The Critics want us to accept the recognition of inherent contradictions and to present principle and counter-principle on equal terms. In that way we may discipline ourselves through constant practice to revolutionize the legal system and indeed our lives in a continuous way. We may discipline ourselves, that is, to live in a state of permanent revolution as a method for constantly widening the possibilities for self-expression and the realization of the creative potentialities in our personalities. We have their word for it: Such a world would exhibit a social order superior to the one we now have. I see no reason to believe it and know of no historical evidence to encourage me to. To the contrary, I can only see the prospect of what Louisa Susanna McCord of antebellum South Carolina, a social critic of parts who opposed the utopianism of her day, referred to as "a wrangling dog kennel."[10]

The Critics demonstrate that liberal society and its legal system do not sustain their own professed democratic and egalitarian premises in practice. They everywhere find not democratic and egalitarian practice but oppression and hierarchy, and wherever they find hierarchy, by which they seem to mean any structure of authority, they conclude, to their own satisfaction, that they have found oppression. On these and related matters we confront the book not written, for much of the difficulty arises from the lack of a theoretical and political consensus in the CLS movement itself. Kelman punts: He tells us that the movement is a house of many mansions and should be understood as a coalition of radicals of different kinds. Thus he reduces his discussion of the CLS world view to its negative common denominator. To Kelman's credit, he does not spare other Critics, including Unger, criticism, and he thereby makes worthwhile contributions to the clarification of secondary issues. But he succeeds primarily in revealing, if inadvertently, that the Critics are not rallying to the standard of Unger, their most intellectually powerful social critic, however much they accord him a guru status he probably does not aspire to.

Unger does have a positive vision, does struggle to transform negative criticism into constructive theory, does advance the outlines of a political program. To review Kelman's book in the customary professional manner would mean to bypass Unger. To focus upon the corpus of Unger's work would be to do Kelman dirty. To include a truncated review of Unger's work would mean to treat a powerful social theorist superficially. Not to risk the inclusion would mean to discuss CLS without attention to everything in it worthy of general consideration. Now it is my turn to get sore.

I shall do my best but must insist that Unger's rich, complex, and carefully nuanced work deserves to be studied and evaluated on its own terms and with due respect for its subtleties.

But a special problem arises from those subtleties, and from the subtleties of Kelman and the best of the Critics. They display an extraordinary talent for anticipating criticism: Unger is a perfect genius at it. Much may be learned from the qualifications and refinements they constantly introduce, and any brief critique of their views risks some unfairness and distortion. But in the end, their rhetoric overwhelms their dialectics. For no matter how many qualifications they introduce into their discussions of democracy, equality, and much else, their intentions and ideological stance come, shining through.

Let us begin with the never-defined term "hierarchy," which the Critics assail in a manner that passes into a broadside attack on authority per se. In Kelman's book, as in all CLS writing, authority appears as illegitimate, oppressive, exploitative. Even Unger, who wisely warns against the delegitimization of all authority, hardly begins to make a convincing case for a legitimate authority.[11]

Consider the CLS insistence that men should be free to move from one situation to another as the best guarantee against majoritarian tyranny and oppression.[12] That admirable goal ought to mean, for example, that if faculty members or students experience negatively the policies and arrangements of a university, they ought to be able to move to one more congenial. But if the experienced oppression stems from the imposition of a democratic consensus, then the reigning attitudes may be expected to reappear in the substituted university and produce a similar result. The only assurance against such institutional flattening would lie in the university's ability to project and defend autonomous goals and procedure's and to assert dissident values. If all were compelled to adhere to standards established in society as a whole whether established democratically or not, the freedom to move would become a sham. And the Critics' appeal to a plethora of communities and institutions within society only brings us back to the same problem.

Specifically, since the Catholic Church, appealing to the revealed word of God, regards homosexuality as a sin, it could not tolerate homosexuality on its campuses without prostituting itself. More generally, if a Catholic university could not discriminate in the hiring of its faculty and could not infuse its curriculum, not merely its theology courses, with its own version of Christian ethics, it would cease to be Catholic in any respect other than in its claims on government subsidies. (Please do not tell me that Catholic universities do just that. I repeat: They could not do so without prostituting themselves and ceasing to be Catholic. I am painfully aware that a good deal of prostitution is taking place.) A Catholic university must be allowed to discriminate and to stand on its prejudices. But to allow it to do so, society must acknowledge the legitimacy of some claims of discrimination and prejudice. It does not follow that any institution should be allowed to discriminate at will. Collective historical experience has prior claims. The United States has paid a terrible price for racism, and nothing should prevent its placing racial discrimination beyond the pale. But it does follow that such strictures should be held to the barest minimum.

And it also follows that a democracy imposed upon, say, a Catholic university would threaten institutional autonomy and distinctiveness, especially if the university were prevented from prejudicing the hiring of faculty to guarantee a critical mass of Catholics. At that, anyone who had received confirmation in the church could claim to be a Catholic and yet be ready, as so many are these days, to treat the standards of the Church with contempt. How long would it take for such a faculty, acting democratically, to destroy the very Catholicity of the university? To put it another way, only a strong dose of institutional authority and hierarchy could preserve such distinctiveness, which even the Critics claim to regard as essential to the preservation of democracy and freedom in the larger society.

A question: Are the critics prepared to impose their egalitarian and anti-hierarchical notions on the episcopal churches? If so, what become of religious freedom? And never mind that they could reasonably crow that, even in the Catholic Church, the laity is doing it for them. Sanity may yet return to the laity, or the laity may be put down by a Pope who, whatever his faults, gives no sign of being a fool or a marshmallow.

Unger, sensitive to the inevitable complaint that his egalitarianism could undermine social order, argues that only an expanding experience of equality could reveal what equality really is.[13] The same might be said for a lot of things sensible people would rather not try. To demonstrate that inequality causes pain and comes at a high personal cost is hardly enough to tempt those who are not desperate.

The CLS strategy of self-revolutionizing legal reform proceeds on undefended assumptions. The liberals and free-market right-wingers have no right to complain since they generally proceed on similar assumptions. I regret the clumsy reference to "free-market right-wingers," but whatever these Chicago school chaps may be, conservatives they are not. The traditionalists, who are conservatives, have every right to complain, but since, with the partial exception of Unger, neither the Critics nor their leading opponents bother much with them, their viewpoint is rarely heard in today's polemics. The assumptions at issue concern democracy and equality, which presumably embrace proper values and constitute worthy goals. One of the finest achievements of CLS criticism has been its ruthless exposure of the contradictions and failures of what in the old days, the Left called "bourgeois democracy" and "the parliamentary swindle." Most notably, Unger offers a marvellous critique of the social deadlock that arises from the cycles of parliamentary shifting between defenders of the status quo and reformers.[14] As Kelman shows, virtually all of the Critics, in one way or another, share Unger's view on this matter. Invariably, the proposed solution emerges as more and more "participatory" democracy. We get hardly a word in defense of the concepts of democracy and equality themselves. Thus the largely implicit attacks on republicanism demonstrate its contradictions, weaknesses, and failures in a way that merely assumes the existence of a constructive alternative.

Republicanism implies a measure of democratic control, for it acknowledges an ultimate appeal to the people, whom it recognizes as the ultimate source of political authority. In this sense, even most modern traditionalists subscribe to Churchill's celebrated *bon mot* that democracy is the worst form of government except for all the others. But the kind of democracy implied here necessarily succumbs to charges of building in hierarchy—the Critics' *bête noire*. The transformation of the CLS critique from a destructive assault on what might arguably appear as the best we could get into a constructive program for social change would require a defense of direct or "participatory" democracy—require, among other things, a demonstration that it could work in a technologically complex modern society or indeed in any civilized society at all. Instead, we are asked to assume that which must be demonstrated, presumably on the grounds that if the liberals and free-market rightwingers also speak as egalitarians and democrats, we have no problem.

This romance with "participatory democracy" leave little room for the protection of minorities or for dissident individuals for that matter, except perhaps for those who chatter in the name of ever more democracy. The American Left, or most of it, today joins the Center and Right in cheering wildly over the "democratization" of Eastern Europe. To read the left-wing press is to learn that, shucks, that is what the Left had in mind all along but was just too busy to mention. Like the Center and even much of the Right, it may soon have to swallow hard, as the Rumanians, Hungarians, Albanians, Serbs, Croats, Azerbaijanis, Armenians, and other shiny new democrats democratically resume their age-old pastime of slaughtering each other—a pastime the nasty Reds undemocratically kept them from indulging in for nearly half a century. Still, in one respect we may see a democratic consensus across tribal lines: They may yet democratically agree to settle accounts with their Jews. And what we may expect from the democratic wonders of a democratically reunited Germany I, for one, would rather not think about, although I know I have to.

The assumption that democracy is intrinsically wonderful—that the more of it we have the better off we are—exposes the deeper and more difficult problem of equality. All the leading contributors to the current debates stand on the principle that "all men are created equal"—a principle announced as self-evident though nowhere seriously defended; a principle the flagrant cant of which could hardly be more apparent. The traditionalist critique of equality thereby goes unanswered. The tactic serves the Critics well and allows them to embarrass their principal opponents, for, on one issue after another at law and in society generally, the Critics effectively show that the legal system perpetuates inequality in some form.

Unger makes a telling point, which echoes in Duncan Kennedy's essay on Blackstone, lurks just beneath the surface of Kelman's book, and says much too much: "Even reliance on merit becomes suspect when its dependence on the distribution of genetic endowments is taken into account, for people may begin to doubt whether a man's social place should be determined by a fact of which he is not the author."15 Indeed, "men may begin to doubt." But could any statement of the politics of envy be clearer? And if we place in doubt not merely all authority based on social convention but all authority based on natural endowment, on what grounds could we respect any authority at all? Unger, throughout his work, defends religious thought and sensibility as necessary for the construction of the new metaphysics we require. Kelman, Kennedy, and the Critics in general show little taste for religious thought and sensibility, and they thereby undermine their theoretical project since they have nothing to substitute. Whatever their personal views, they may well sense a trap. For on religious premises, intelligence and talent must surely rank as a special gift of God and therefore, as a firm basis for legitimate authority. And no such gift would be relevant unless developed and disciplined by the individual effort that the Critics tell us constitutes no authorship.

Unger, Kelman and other sensible Critics—we may leave aside the dummies and cranks—know that without some measure of authority civilized life would be impossible. Unger specifically warns that liberal thought and practice are undermining all authority, with appalling consequences for society. We need, he argues, "to make [individual] autonomy compatible with authority."[16] But an occasional admonition is as far as even he goes. If there is a concept of legitimate authority anywhere in Unger's books or in Kelman's *Guide* or anywhere else in CLS writing, I have somehow missed it. The Critics have left themselves wide open to the charge that they seek to enforce not equality of opportunity, which they recognize as an impossibility and a fraud, but an equality of condition that makes no sense in a world of economic scarcity and that would require what they themselves confess to be a violation of nature. Skeptics may be excused for wondering about the kind of society that would arise on a principle so transparently cynical. The problem does not lie primarily in CLS negativism per se, as many of their opponents charge and as Kelman himself focuses on.[17] For, in response, Kelman makes out a reasonable case for the constructive uses of negative criticism. Rather, it lies in the particular kind of negativism, which the Critics themselves insist upon as a political program. They wish to tear down liberal society and its legal system in the hope that whatever replaces them, if guided by an egalitarian ethos and sensitive to the demands of participatory democracy, would probably be better. As opponents of determinism, they offer no guarantees, but they do try to make a case for an overwhelming probability the basis for which remains elusive.

A long and depressing history tells a different story, which is full of murderous attempts to realize the beauties of egalitarianism and a world without hierarchy. In the wake of such attempts, particular forms of inequality and hierarchy have repeatedly given way to new forms. The exchange has often proven salutary, but the human cost has surely run high enough to make us wary. A case for social revolution and the acceptance of fearful blood-letting could, nonetheless, be made. Whatever the miseries of the French and Russian revolutions, our world would arguably be worse off had they not occurred, and slavery in the United States might not have been abolished without a ghastly war. But such a case would not readily offer aid and court to CLS utopianism. Indeed, as Unger has bravely insisted throughout his work, such revolutions, however defensible, have proven the worst possible way to solve the problems of particular historical injustices.

Kelman and the Critics justifiably fear that any grammar of assent must lead to a politics of resignation, to a hardening of the heart to human suffering, to apologetics for the status quo. Such fear from adherents of radical indeterminacy inspires some mirth, but we should not be too quick to laugh. Those outcomes may not be foreordained, but they remain strong possibilities. The Critics' discomfiture is also ours. In a world that rejects the revealed truth of religion and that has not yet discovered the new metaphysics Unger calls for, where do we turn for the wisdom that can steer society between Scylla and Charybdis?

The closest Kelman comes to a reply occurs in his essay on "Trashing," and it is unworthy of him. He attacks Robert Ellickson for a "purely theoretical refutation" of the critique of hierarchy and adds that Ellickson "falls back on the most laughable 'history' imaginable: Hierarchy must be fine because 'hierarchy is ubiquitous within all organizations of any size.' Unless one is ready to dismiss *a priori*, the very *possibility* of power and illegitimate domination, universality is hardly proof of necessity."[18] It is striking that Kelman reads a defense of authority as necessarily a defense of illegitimate authority, but that too we may let pass. True, ubiquity is not proof of necessity, but it creates a powerful case for proceeding as if it were. Surely, it places the burden of proof on those who would sustain the contrary. And to what do the Critics appeal beyond "purely theoretical refutation"? They do not themselves invoke a laughable history, for they invoke no history at all in support of their contention that civilized life would be possible without some form of hierarchy. All they say is that there is a first time for everything. Like hell there is.

Kelman does seem troubled by this point. After referring proudly to the CLS's work as "utopian," Kelman writes: "I see too little reason to believe either that history has a significantly predetermined teleological path, particularly a progressively bettering one, or that we could discern such a path if it did exist, to believe that the precise nature of our better tomorrows can be understood by looking more carefully at the hands we've already been dealt."[19] It is too bad that those fine words have been enlisted in an unworthy defense of playing politics *va banque* and, in effect, for absolving oneself in advance for the consequences of doing so. For no anti-utopian could say it better. Is it possible that Kelman does not recognize how far those words go toward undermining his own political position?

On this matter Philip Johnson rams the Critics' words back in their craw. Unger, he observes, admits that a solution to the conflict between community and personal autonomy would require a new metaphysics. Johnson comments: "Whatever may have been the author's intentions, the political implications of these messages seem conservative to me. If we not only do not know how to get there from here but also don't know where 'there' is, doesn't it follow that we should stay here until more information comes along?"[20] Other, more mean-spirited opponents have accused the Critics of totalitarianism, and some have even called for purging them from the law schools. They conflate the sin with the sinner and the possible outcome with the intent. In doing so, these liberals are remarkable. They never stop flaunting their anti-Stalinism, but what are they doing if not invoking Comrade Stalin's glorious dictum that the "objective" outcome reveals the intent? The possible, indeed probable, outcome nonetheless cannot be swept aside. In criticizing the CLS for its personal liberationism, I may seem to have advanced an argument that cannot coexist with the charge that the program of the CLS contains totalitarian dangers. In fact, it coexists easily. The history of utopianism demonstrates, in case after case, that movements dedicated to the creation of a social equality designed to liberate the individual to realize a presumably benevolent inner will have ended, usually quickly, in the opposite.[21] A dubious psychology condemns it in the first instance. If people are good and "altruistic"—more accurately, if the goodness and "altruism" in them are capable of extraordinary expansion through political struggle—and if the regime, whatever its specific characteristics, presents a communitarian agenda that liberates them to become truly human, then they should respond on cue. Unhappily, they rarely if ever do. From which it follows that these particular people, no matter how numerous, must not be quite human to begin with and should expect to be dealt with accordingly.

Kelman and the Critics cannot easily turn aside the charge that they seek to impose upon others their own notion of what everyone else's inner will needs in order to achieve fulfillment. Their open acceptance of the need for what they call "paternalism" in human affairs does not in itself make the case against them, but the specific kind of argument they are compelled to make does.[22] And that kind of argument betrays the radical individualism that lies at the core of their supposed communitarianism. For, in rejecting the traditionalist (organicist) premise that society remains prior to the individual and has superior claims, they must scramble to postulate for all humanity a complex of mutual love, faith, and sympathy that needs to be released from the repressions of hierarchical controls. Their whole doctrine of solidarity rests upon this presumed goodness, in contradistinction to the doctrine of the organicists, which postulates the prior claims of community and has no need for a descent into high comedy. In passing, let us note that Kelman and the Critics talk much about rights but rarely if ever about the duties that must accompany rights, at least if we are to proceed on sensible communitarian principles.[23] Kelman does mention duties, but, somehow, they always turn out to be the duties imposed on those who should be made to surrender privileges.

Unger goes to the extraordinary lengths of proposing that a good (democratic, egalitarian) society ought to allow people to opt out. That is, every man ought to be guaranteed the "right" to a decent standard of living even if he refuses to work and to share the ordinary social burdens.[24] Unger apparently assumes that few would choose to do so or at least too few to disrupt society. I doubt that I am alone in assuming the reverse and in refusing to take the gamble. And Unger must assume that those who do the work, having had their altruistic sentiments expanded by the joys of participatory democracy, would cheerfully tolerate those who lived off them. He must also assume that socially useful work itself need not be viewed as essential to character formation and need not be viewed by society as a duty and a matter of honor. Nothing in *Passion* or Unger's other books supports such assumptions, unless we count as something a long list of hopeful assertions.

Kelman, for his part, falls silent on such questions, much as he falls silent on the implications of his radical egalitarianism for such urgent questions as the fate of the steadily widening class of sociopaths our society is producing. The Critics' rejection of a doctrine of the prior rights and exigencies of the community, reinforced by their rejection of hierarchy, lies at the root of the totalitarian tendencies they certainly do not want to see realized, as well at the root of Kelman's intellectual evasions. For if the interdependency of men and the need for "paternalism" are to be accepted without a capitulation to totalitarianism, then hierarchy, legitimate authority, and a healthy dose of repression cannot be avoided.

Kelman and the Critics abhor dependency relations and people who give orders. Their defense of "paternalism" would seem to imply the one and countenance the other, but they make no effort to square the circle. Their argument, as Kelman presents it, comes close to an assertion that dependency is not really dependency when it realizes the dependent's inner will. In contrast, the southern slaveholders, who had daily experience with paternalism, never claimed that they were realizing their slaves' inner wills, only that they were protecting their slaves' rights, as defined by capacity. They were deceiving themselves, ma non troppo, in comparison with the Critics. Having no wish to engage in satire, I only suggest that the Critics make a greater effort to clarify their ideas. Unger in fact is more careful, but not careful enough. He hints that, after all, the problem is to reduce arbitrariness and oppression to a bare minimum by making all leaders accountable to the greatest possible degree.[25] Nazis aside, who would argue? Even law-and-economics professors might be able to live with that formulation since it smuggles in an acceptance of some kind of legitimate authority and leaves all the knotty theoretical issues and organizational specifics up for grabs.

The problem of institutional autonomy recurs since the Critics want to politicize everything and virtually eliminate the private sphere. Once again, they are good on the attack, demonstrating the ways in which ostensible respect for privacy permits not only oppression but atrocities no civilized society should tolerate. But their solution treats the right to privacy lightly. To democratize everything means to politicize everything, and since everything that happens in social life has some political implications, the case for the total politicization of the family and everything else is supposed to be invincible. In fact a dose of common sense would take care of the general problem. Much of family life may be put beyond the purview of the state without giving a blank check to wife-beaters and child abusers. The privacy of the family has long been respected while limited. But that arrangement requires the recognition of a legitimate authority in both state and family and an acceptance of such dreaded hierarchy as that of parents over children.

We neither have nor should expect to have a formula that could satisfactorily divide the public from the private sphere. Here too, historical experience offers the safest guide, but the interpretation of historical experience will always be ideologically charged. Indeed, as the Critics would be the first to insist, the very distinction between the spheres makes an ideological statement. But it remains difficult to imagine any degree of individual freedom worthy of the name without a wide swath for privacy and the institutional autonomy upon which freedom and privacy often depend. The problem concerns the bias brought to bear on the large and unavoidable gray area between the claims of privacy and the necessity for intervention to curb atrocities. On that question, the burden of the Critics' argument points toward the privileging of the claims of the state. I should suggest that even those of us who place community cohesion above individual right would do well to resist that siren call, lest we undermine the measure of individual freedom that ought to be compatible with social safety.

Today we are all democrats, if only for want of an alternative, but the Critics espouse a democracy that is radically egalitarian and "participatory." Hence the demand to politicize everything. The realization of the vision of the good society that Unger projects and that peeps through Kelman's blasts at hierarchy would require every man's constant participation in politics, for it must depend upon the direct politicization of all intermediary institutions and arrangements between the individual and the state: businesses, unions, churches, schools, the family. If Oscar Wilde could recoil from socialism because it would take too many evenings, what would he think of this project? Unger makes his customary brave effort to avoid his colleagues' facile utopianism and to meet the issue. Sensitive, as most Critics are not, to the nightmares in which all dreams of the revolutionary creation of "New Men" and "New Women" have ended, he outlines a process of the expansion of participation in the step-by-step ordering of institutions and rejects all calls to play *va banque* with society as a whole. When, therefore, he says that we must experience equality in order to know what it is, he is not speaking frivolously.

In Unger's view each new measure of participation in decision-making deepens individual consciousness and releases untapped energies. Doubtless it does—up to a point—and who would object to a reasonable testing of limits? But his project is open-ended, and, notwithstanding warnings against adventurism and excessive demands on people in time and place it rests on a faith in a quasi-egalitarian outcome that only a willingness to live in a state of permanent revolution could sustain. At first glance the vision has a genuine nobility, but a nobility that demands immeasurably more of people than we have reason to believe they could sustain threatens to collapse into its opposite.

Since a defense against the tyranny of the majority can no longer practicably rest on the consensual morality of Christian revelation, it must rest on a man-made alternative. Thus Unger calls for a new metaphysics—a project he surely knows is easier to call for than to effect. Meanwhile, our only guide would appear to be historical experience as read, however arbitrarily, by those prepared to invoke the Christian dogma of the moral equality of man. Moral equality, however, does not imply physical, intellectual, or civil equality and cannot logically be invoked to support CLS assumptions. And I fear that history compels us to stand-gagging, if we must—with Burke in regarding government as company of the living, the dead, and the unborn. The permanent revolution implicit in the CLS project could not flourish on such ground, and the project itself offers no other ground to stand on.

The Critics' project of human liberation—for that is what it amounts to—stands or falls on its assessment of human nature. One looks in vain in Kelman's *Guide* for such an assessment, although there are hints, Unger, as is his wont, does confront the issue and does contribute valuable insights on the ways in which what is assumed to be bedrock reveals itself a historical product. But he does not refute the fundamental insight of Christian theology, albeit an insight abandoned by the mainline Protestant churches more than a century ago, and of such secular doctrines as Freudian psychoanalysis before they too succumbed to liberal bastardization. I refer to the doctrine, however secularized, of original sin and the depravity of man.

Let us leave the theology to the theologians on the pretext that it need not concern such enlightened secularists as ourselves. Translating it into other terms, we may appeal to the historical record of human experience, which science has not yet effectively contradicted, to postulate warring tendencies in everyone: the drive for self-expression and the unavoidable dependency on others. This contradiction cannot be reduced to a question of freedom versus social order, autonomy versus authority, the individual versus the collective. It will not do to note that man's freedom is itself a product of social life and then to cry out with Duncan Kennedy, "But at the same time it forms and protects us, the universe of others...threatens us with annihilation....Numberless conformities, large and small abandonments of self to others are the price of what freedom we experience in society."[26] These remarks appear dialectically sound, if somewhat ambiguous, out rhetorically they reduce their own dialectical truth to nonsense. For "the price we pay" necessarily defines the freedom itself. Only by identifying freedom with personal desire could Kennedy threaten us with "annihilation." Kennedy here apes the moral stance of the liberals he sometimes caricatures—the kind of people who, when confronted by the dilemmas of life, offer up the only prayer they know: "May God have mercy on us."

From start to finish, in Kelman's *Guide* and without, the Critics proclaim their war against individualism, and from start to finish they wallow in the individualism they purportedly war against. Kelman, like Unger, Kennedy, and others, begins with the conflicted concerns of the individual and ends with his liberation or, more accurately, with a commitment to push for a presumably maximum liberation against all odds. They extol the community (society, group) and insist that the individual expand his personality with due respect for the personalities of others, but they reject, virtually out of hand, the alternate concept of the prior rights and imperatives of the community. In this respect they follow proudly in the tradition of the great bourgeois theorists from Hobbes to Locke and Blackstone and Burke, and beyond.

Those great theorists argued that man has a God-given natural liberty and, with it, rights. Yet they also argued that man willingly sacrifices much of his natural liberty in order to secure some of it. Why? Because natural liberty entails murderous—"mischievous" was Blackstone's preferred word— impulses, which, if released, would unleash anarchy and destroy liberty itself. Now, how could the God-given gift of natural liberty entail murder, mayhem, and mischief? Was God drunk? What could liberty conceivably mean other than a liberty that would be secured, healthy, and constructive? The answer does not emerge from the Critics' secularization of the problem, any more than it emerged from the secularization offered by Hobbes. Thus Albert Taylor Bledsoe, taunting Blackstone and the liberals of the nineteenth century in which he lived, denied the existence of any liberty other than that which arises from society's repression of our negative impulses. Society, he argued, made liberty possible, and therefore liberty has no meaning apart from society's constraints.[27] Accept this view and the Critics' theoretical edifice crumbles.

The Critics implicitly answer that the organicist vision rests on a myth—that the prior claims of society cannot be grounded empirically or in an undisputed metaphysics. That answer proves no answer at all. Kelman seems to think that, because his politically strongest opponents, the free-market rightwingers and the liberals, also dismiss the organicist argument, he need pay it no mind. The organicist notion does in fact rest on a myth, but so do the alternatives. Kelman might reflect on his own work of deconstruction, which proves inherently incapable of demonstrating that we could do without one or another such myth. In the absence of a superior social science and an adequate metaphysics, we are compelled to choose among contending myth for the work of deconstruction and the revelations of negative dialectics do no more than remind us that life is hard. Choose we must, and good sense dictates that we choose the myth that conforms most closely to historical experience.

Freedom, however defined, has arisen historically within and as a product of society, which remains prior to the individual not merely chronologically but—*pace* all CLS warriors against false necessities—as a matter of undiminished historical necessity. Its claims, therefore, are also prior. A "free" society may, accordingly, be viewed as one that expands individual freedom to the utmost consistent with an imposed sense of social order, and that places the burden of proof on those who would limit the individual's claims against society and the state. It proceeds on the assumption that, were men left wholly free to express themselves, they would eat each other alive.

The Critics seem to think that the massive historical evidence easily arrayed in support of such an assumption is beside the point—that historical contingencies could be overcome by revolutionary praxis. Maybe. But it requires a dangerous mindset to toss out the whole record of human experience in favor of a riverboat gamble on the patently utopian imagination of men who admit the antisocial nature of our deepest desires but who hope that it could be neutralized by love, faith, and sympathy.

In a perceptive critique of the communist regimes, Unger defines their central contradiction as the juxtaposition of hierarchical political and economic structures and their professed goal of an egalitarian society that liberates the individual to maximize autonomy and self-expression.[28] He is right, but he never does question the professed goal, much less note that Marx himself arbitrarily imposed it on a power interpretation of history with which it had no logical connection. We need not close our eyes to the grievous faults of the particular form and content of the communists' hierarchy to see that heir failure should be attributed primarily to the impossibility of sustaining adherence to an unrealizable ideal.

Kelman could not easily have obscured or trivialized these issues had he taken the measure of the attack on individualism mounted by the traditionalist or organicist Right. The free-market rightwingers and most liberals may be able to reject organicist theory out of hand since they unabashedly take individualist ground, but those who, like the Critics, advocate a communitarianism dare not. Communitarian theory, whether in conservative organicist or Marxist and socialist versions, has always accepted or accommodated to principles of leadership that the Critics call hierarchical. The one thing the Critics cannot get away with is the pretense that communitarianism per se implies nonhierarchical relations. To the contrary, their problem is to demonstrate that a practicable communitarianism could be reconciled with a repudiation of hierarchy at all.

The organicists pose a double challenge, the one political, the other theoretical. While Kelman directs his fire against the free-market rightwingers, and Duncan Kennedy directs his against the left-liberals, Unger has his eye on new political alliances.[29] His proposals for constructive social change might well attract people from across the ideological spectrum, and it is a measure of his political seriousness that he wants few doors closed. Unfortunately, despite some feints, he seems unwilling to open the door to the organicists, with whom he may well share more than he would like to—certainly, much more than other Critics would want to hear about.

Kelman does not match Unger's effort to meet the arguments of the organicists. In *Law and Society* Unger dismissed organicist theory by observing that it could not account for social conflict.[30] But it does account for it, after a fashion. It should be enough to recall Roland Mousnier's remarks in his illuminating history of early-modem peasant uprisings. The "cause" of social conflict, he wrote, lies in original sin and man's inability to live in accordance with the laws of God.[31]

Unger returns to the organicists in his recent books, but he does so uneasily, as if he suspects that he is still not doing them justice.[32] Part of the problem may arise from his being riveted on certain European and Latin American schools of thought, particularly those associated with Catholicism. He nowhere discusses the primary American variant, that of the southern conservative tradition from Thomas Roderick Dew, John C. Calhoun, and Bledsoe down to Allen Tate and the Agrarians, Richard Weaver, and such contemporary figures as M. E. Bradford and Thomas Fleming.[33] Hence he avoids a confrontation with a distinctly republican body of thought that, especially since Tate, has claimed for itself the "modernist" ground Unger wants the Left to occupy. Instead, Unger offers a discussion of "moderate organicists" whose views are presented with a noticeable lack of clarity. Who these moderates might be and what they stand for remain obscure.

To add to our frustration, Unger bravely alludes to the intellectually serious streak of corporatism in early fascist thought and hints that it might have something to offer.[34] It does, but who would be crazy enough to pursue the matter in the virtuous climate of "diversity" that now prevails in our universities? A hint, in any case. is all we get. But by ignoring the southern conservatives, who have grounded their own version of individualism in a community with prior claims, and by sidestepping the fascists, Unger, in effect, strikes his colors. No wonder, then, that Kelman and his colleagues proceed as if the challenges need not be noticed.

American traditionalists, as they prefer to be called, appeal to Christian theology to ground their view of human nature, however secular the form it may take in the writing of a particular individual. Unger ought to welcome the challenge since he makes his own strong and arresting appeals to religious thought. We may doubt that many if any of his colleagues among the Critics take him seriously in this respect, but if they do not, they cannot easily build on his thought. This is a big subject in itself, which will have to be left for another day. Let it suffice for the moment that Unger's repeated invocations of religion refer to God "if He exists" and, more to the point, refer to the all-loving and forgiving God of liberal and especially Universalist theology. The organicists, including the occasional atheists among them, have a different God in mind: the God of wrath, who proclaimed Himself "a jealous God." Do not get mad at me. Unger, not I, introduced the questions, even if Kelman has seen fit to ignore them. All I say is that if we are to take up the theological aspects of the relevant issues, then let us meet the responsibility to evaluate the long and illuminating record of theological debate.

It is true that, on balance, the organicists tend to flatten social conflicts in their defense of historically evolved community life, but that tendency may flow less from the exigencies of their world view than from the exigencies of their embattled political opposition to capitalism, liberalism, and socialism. The problem with their version of communitarianism arises from their acceptance of a consensus elucidated by elites whose social and institutional power rested on social foundations that were shattered in the 1860s. Southern conservatives therefore speak of their tradition as "at bay." Indeed it is, for the valued consensus prevailed as hegemonic doctrine only in the Old South under the social relations of slavery. These conservatives want no part of the legacy of slavery, but they have yet to figure out how to defend and develop a world view the roots of which have been severed.

At the moment they find themselves in the absurd position of defending "traditional values" in a Reaganite coalition that trumpets capitalism and the free market, which have always been anathema to them and which have proven to be history's most powerful solvent of traditional values. A refusal to confront the rich thought of these tradtionalists has nonetheless cost the Left dearly, especially since their though has important things in common with the petty-bourgeois thought Unger deeply admires. The cost of that refusal may be expected to mount as the Left struggles to come to terms with a corporatist future. Unger has to prefer his radical-democratic, petty-bourgeois heroes to these conservatives, not because they had a better critique of bourgeois property and better proposals for replacing it—they did not—but because they stood for equality and against hierarchy. Regrettably, on that issue the southern conservatives have had much the better case.[35]

Meanwhile, Kelman has largely succeeded in doing the limited job he set out to do. He has written a book that ought to put every socially conscious lawyer, judge and law professor and student on his mettle. Kelman, on his chosen terrain, shows himself to be an intellectually acute and worthy representative of the best in CLS by exposing the contradictions between the professed principles of the law and actual practice and its attendant injustices. Kelman and the Critics may fairly be accused of a negativism that conflates the corrigible at law with the consequences of human frailty, but better that error than the easy assumption that all blatant contradictions and injustice may be accepted as the way things are and must be. It has often been observed that men have an infinite capacity to bear with equanimity the misfortunes of others. The Critics, like the legal realists, are determined not to convict themselves on that score.

Whatever the frustrations aroused by Kelman's book, it provides powerful ammunition for those lawyers who seek to compel liberal society to live up to the finest of its own professed goals and who seek to combat gross injustice and the genuinely illegitimate structures of authority. Implicitly at least, it also provides ammunition for those who recognize the corporatist tendency of the model world and who understand that a critical view of its dynamics is essential for any effort to defeat its sinister features. Kelman's performance nevertheless invites the words of simultaneous praise and rebuke uttered by John Stick in his generally respectful review: "Critics of the CLS like Paul Carrington should wake up and realize that the Crits are just lawyers. Kelman is an excellent lawyer who has written a fine book—but one that addresses the concerns of lawyers, not political theorists or activists."[36] I am afraid so, for Kelman takes much of the "bite" (a favorite word of his) out of CLS and drowns the larger and more interesting questions it flirts with. Kelman seems intent upon turning Unger's demand for a "total criticism" of social theory into the safer channel of a critique of legal practice. To the admittedly unpracticed eye of one without legal training, he has done himself proud. But in so doing, he has played Bernstein to Unger's Marx, González Prada to Duncan Kennedy's Bakunin. And at that I may be doing an injustice to Bernstein and González Prada.

The political question remains. However unsatisfactory CLS theory may be, some parts of its strategy retain merit. The collapse of socialism in Europe has compelled the Left in the West as well as the East to reconsider social relations and the forms of property that undergird them—a reconsideration begun by Unger more than a decade ago. Much of the interesting work of the CLS on contract law contributes to a transformation of absolute or bourgeois property into social property of a kind radically different from that heretofore experimented with in the Soviet Union and the other socialist countries. Thus there arises a vision that recognizes the claims of capital to property in factories while also recognizing the claims of labor to that same property. In this sense all economic property becomes social and necessarily requires legal structures to mediate and arbitrate the conflicting claims that must arise from diverse titles to ownership and control.[37]

The possibilities for a restructuring of the economy call attention to the responsibilities of the national state. The Critics support a strong state capable of riding herd on a largely decentralized political and economic system. The state must intervene to guarantee economic growth and adherence to democratic practices throughout society.[38] At the same time the state itself must emerge from below as a product of the democratic practices in the institutions that mediate between it and the individual. A thousand objections suggest themselves, but it may suffice to ask how the state could impose its authority on those to whom it is wholly accountable, not in the sense of classical republican accountability, but directly, not to say absolutely? Unger assures us that this wonder could be performed without recourse to hierarchy. His extensive discussions, while ingenious, provide little to convince those who do not share his faith in radical democracy and his willingness to put aside historical experience for speculation. And Unger knows that he is speculating. More than once he warns that the society to which he aspires may well prove unattainable.[39]

A long shadow fills between Unger's stimulating explorations of the property question and state power and the politically incoherent stand of CLS as a movement. Potentially, the legal practice of the Critics could contribute to those who speak of "market socialism" but whose thought points toward a left-wing version of the corporate state. And some form of corporate state is precisely what we are likely to get, indeed are getting in both East and West. No such state is likely to be able to accommodate itself to the utopianism of the crusade against authority, leadership, and social stratification.[40]

The Critics could justify their negativity only by laying out a minimal social vision that gives people a sense of where they are being led. The internal disorder in the CLS movement may be excused politically: All political movements that aspire to be broad coalitions must project alternate visions, albeit within principled limits. But to make a virtue of political incoherence while trying to destroy an existing social order means to risk a capitulation to demagogy and deceit. Unger has a vision. The Critics may wish to dissociate themselves from it, but then they have a responsibility to present an alternative that could represent them as a movement. To proceed as Kelman does means to play a dangerous game that simultaneously threatens to betray those who rally to the CLS standard and to display a breathtakingly elitist contempt for the uninitiated.

The most discouraging feature of the story of CLS so far emerges from its inadvertent revelation of the condition of the American Left as a whole. For it shows the extent to which the flower of the left-wing intelligentsia perceives the need for a political agenda attuned to the realities of a corporate state for which it has little stomach, and the extent to which it is unwilling to shed its utopian egalitarianism and destructive view of authority. The ability of a largely deranged Left to contribute to, much less lead, a political movement appropriate to the corporatism it woos and fears remains, to say the least, doubtful.

NOTES

1. John Stick, *Charting the Development of Critical Legal Studies*, 88 COLUMBIA LAW REVIEW 409 (1988).

2. Kelman's style has drawn especially heavy fire in a generally harsh review by Richard L. Barnes, *Searching for Answers without Questions*, 24 SOUTH DAKOTA LAW REVIEW 220–225 (1989).

3. M. G. Kelman, *Trashing*, 36 STANFORD LAW REVIEW 293–348 (1984).

4. Calvin R. Massey, *Law's Inferno*, 39 HASTINGS LAW JOURNAL 1274 (1988); Kelman, GUIDE at 63.

5. Mark Hager, *Against Liberal Ideology*, 37 AMERICAN UNIVERSITY LAW REVIEW at 1057–1058 (1988). Emphasis here and throughout in the original. *See also* Philip E. Johnson, *Do You Sincerely Want to Be Radical?*, 36 STANFORD LAW REVIEW 257 (1984).

6. HAROLD J. BERMAN, LAW AND REVOLUTION: THE FORMATION OF THE WESTERN LEGAL TRADITION at 40–41; *see also id.* at 590–591, n. 88 (1983).

7. Unger's books deserve careful study by those interested in social theory and historical interpretation and are essential for an evaluation of CLS: ROBERTO MANGABEIRA UNGER, KNOWLEDGE AND POLITICS (1975); LAW IN MODERN SOCIETY: TOWARD A CRITICISM OF SOCIAL THEORY (1976); THE CRITICAL STUDIES MOVEMENT (1986); PASSION: AN ESSAY ON PERSONALITY (1984); SOCIAL THEORY: ITS SITUATION AND ITS TASK. A CRITICAL INTRODUCTION TO POLITICS, A WORK IN CONSTRUCTIVE SOCIAL THEORY (1987); FALSE NECESSITY: ANTI-NECESSITARIAN SOCIAL THEORY IN THE SERVICE OF RADICAL DEMOCRACY. PART I OF POLITICS, A WORK IN CONSTRUCTIVE SOCIAL THEORY (1987); PLASTICITY INTO POWER: COMPARATIVE-HISTORICAL STUDIES ON THE INSTITUTIONAL CONDITIONS OF ECONOMIC AND MILITARY SUCCESS. VARIATIONS ON THEMES OF POLITICS, A WORK IN CONSTRUCTIVE SOCIAL THEORY (1987). Throughout he rejects all-or-nothing politics and calls for a strategy of piecemeal institutional transformation.

8. Quill, who led the Transport Workers Union in New York City before and after World War II, was famous for his marvellous Irish brogue and militant left-wing politics, at least until he broke with the Communists shortly before the war. The oft-quoted words attributed to him were: "I'd rather be called a Red by a rat than a rat by a Red any day."

9. Kelman might be surprised to learn that many staunch feminists associated with the Left do not share the position of the radicals on these and other questions and, in fact, find them imprisoned by individualist ideology. *See, e.g.*, ELIZABETH FOX-GENOVESE, FEMINISM WITHOUT ILLUSIONS: A CRITIQUE OF INDIVIDUALISM (1991) and its references to the works of others.

10. Louisa Susanna McCord, *Woman and Her Needs*, 13 DEBOW'S REVIEW 275 (1852). Alas, Mrs. McCord was defending slavery and the subordination of women. I regret the uses to which she put her learning and good sense, but learning and good sense she had.

11. Unger's warnings may be found throughout the books. In a similar vein he warns that the decline of the rule of law could endanger freedom and unleash a new tribalism. *See* LAW IN MODERN SOCIETY at 237–239.

12. *SEE E.G.*, UNGER, KNOWLEDGE AND POLITICS at 279–280; LAW IN MODERN SOCIETY at 239.

13. UNGER, LAW IN MODERN SOCIETY at 240.

14. UNGER, CRITICAL LEGAL STUDIES MOVEMENT at 28–32; FALSE NECESSITY, ch. 2.

15. UNGER, LAW IN MODERN SOCIETY at 172. Duncan Kennedy similarly frets over "hierarchical structures of power, welfare, and access to enlightenment that are illegitimate, whether based on birth into a particular social class or on the accident of genetic endowment." *See* Kennedy, *The Structure of Blackstone's Commentaries*, 28 BUFFALO LAW REVIEW 212 (1979). Unger was troubled by the implications and returns to the subject in FALSE NECESSITY, where he makes excellent points on the nature and danger of envy and admits that some inequality may be unavoidable. He allays his doubts by again invoking love, faith, and sympathy. FALSE NECESSITY at 169–173, 212–217, 220–221, 270–271.

16. UNGER, LAW IN MODERN SOCIETY at 237.

17. Kelman, *Trashing* at 296–297.

18. *Id.* at 306, n. 37.

19. *Id.* at 336, 343.

20. Johnson, *supra* note 5 at 283.

21. Kelman might well deny that CLS invokes the doctrine of inner will—*see, e.g.,* GUIDE at 137—but I see no other way to read him and the Critics generally.

22. KELMAN, GUIDE at 137–141 and *passim.* Kelman shows the CLS to be uneasy about paternalism, and he makes some useful distinctions. But he also shows that, by any other name, a strong dose of paternalism lies implicit in CLS thought.

23. It is noteworthy that the index to GUIDE refers to three places and six pages under "rights discourse," but has no entries for "duties," "obligations," or "responsibilities." Whoever made the Index performed in a manner faithful to the spirit of the text.

24. Unger, False Necessity at 526. Unger does write "if the wealth of society permits," and a variety of sermons could be preached on that text. Again, the rhetoric and its implicit view of human nature overpower all dialectical qualifications.

25. This too is a running theme in Unger's work. *See, e.g.,* FALSE NECESSITY at 432–436. Kelman remains unclear but could easily be read to make similar concessions.

26. Kennedy, *supra* note 15 at 212.

27. ALBERT TAYLOR BLEDSOE, AN ESSAY ON LIBERTY AND SLAVERY, ch. 1 (1856).

28. UNGER, LAW IN MODERN SOCIETY at 233.

29. *See esp.* Unger's opening remarks to SOCIAL THEORY.

30. Unger discusses organicist theory and a number of points in LAW IN MODERN SOCIETY and KNOWLEDGE AND POLITICS and, as usual, has many valuable things to say about the history as well as the theory. In KNOWLEDGE AND POLITICS at 82–83, he concedes that it has been a staple of modern Western thought. But he nonetheless ends dismissively, arguing, *e.g., id.* at 250, that it has largely sought to reestablish older orders of estates and roles. Clearly, it is the organicists' commitment to hierarchical authority that he cannot swallow.

31. ROLAND MOUSNIER, PEASANT UPRISINGS IN SEVENTEENTH-CENTURY FRANCE, RUSSIA, AND CHINA at 306 (1970).

32. *See, e.g.,* UNGER, FALSE NECESSITY at 384–389.

33. The work of Richard M. Weaver offers the best introduction to traditional southern thought. *See esp.* THE SOUTHERN TRADITION AT BAY: A HISTORY OF POSTBELLUM THOUGHT (1968); IDEAS HAVE CONSEQUENCES (1948); and VISIONS OF ORDER (1964).

34. UNGER, FALSE NECESSITY at 386.

35. The celebration of petty-bourgeois radicalism constitutes a principal theme of FALSE NECESSITY. UNGER, *supra* note 7 at 29–31, chides the radicals for clinging to the ideal of a world of small property-holders—an ideal shared by the southern traditionalists.

36. Stick, *supra* note 1 at 432.

37. *See, e.g.,* UNGER, FALSE NECESSITY, at 491–502.

38. This view of the state, explicit throughout Unger's work, under-girds Kelman's GUIDE, which, however, contains no explicit statement.

39. *See* UNGER, KNOWLEDGE AND POLITICS at 231. Statements to this effect appear throughout his books. Kelman issues similar caveats. *See* ch. 9 of GUIDE and especially note the tone of the last few pages.

40. *See esp.* the regular contributions of Louis Ferleger and Jay R. Mandle to SOCIALIST REVIEW.

9

PETER GOODRICH _____

Sleeping with the Enemy:
An Essay on the Politics of Critical Legal Studies
in America

> The task of extremist writing is to put through the call for a
> justice of the future. Henceforth. Justice can no longer permit
> itself to be merely backward looking or bound in servility to
> sclerotic models and their modifications (their "future"). A
> justice of the future would have to show the will to rupture.
>
> Avital Ronell[1]

There seems little doubt within the contemporary American legal
academy that critical legal studies represented the emergence of
a left intelligensia in law.[2] While there are indeed few other
intellectual criteria by which to demarcate either a critical movement or position within legal theory, there remains the basic
common denominator of a commitment to a radical political
position both within and without the legal institution.[3] Critical
legal studies is the 'leftist' inheritor of legal realism, it is a
'political location', 'subversive', 'deviationist' and on occasion
even 'nihilistic', the extremist political position of a critical
movement which ironically no longer believes in critique.[4] The
movement or network thus both defines itself in terms of an
oppositional practice and is in its turn criticised by its detractors
for its commitment to fundamental change if not abolition of the
extant rule of law.[5]

This article is dedicated ironically to the proposition that
critical legal studies in America has failed in its radicalism: it has
neither gone to the roots of the tradition, in the sense of philosophical radicalism, nor pursued any consistent commitment to

299

fundamental change, in the sense of political radicalism. It is in many respects unsurprising to observe that the left in law shares the 'disintegrative' fate of its European counterparts,[6] that in conditions of political seclusion and existential isolation it treads the same path as Western Marxism, towards philosophical idealism focused upon questions of method applied, if at all, to the field of aesthetics in a vein of speculative pessimism.[7] At the level of specifically American culture, the movement expresses an instance of the failure or evasion of philosophy in America; while at a political level it confirms the absorption of the left and of the literate dialogue of the public sphere into the institution, the mass University and the 'ruminations' of higher education.[8] It offers little more than a politics of pragmatism, disjunctive theories of practice and the analysis of a reality whose object is defined by the citation of other critical legal texts.[9]

In common with the European left and with the broader critical tradition located in a rapidly changing public sphere, critical legal studies is faced by numerous contradictions of institutional circumstance and existential compromise—an unhappy consciousness which has become the condition and privilege of postmodern intellectual culture.[10] At its best critical legal studies is a species of neo-scholasticism, and like its scholastic forebears it faces the geopolitical or translational risks of reviving or receiving an alien, imported or borrowed discipline and its accompanying tradition.[11] Far more frequently it appears closer to the dogma of patronage, the fashionable pedagogy of an institutional elite or high clergy, concerned not so much with a culture of the left as with the preservation and reproduction of its own institutional place and status.[12] In both aspects, it will be argued, the political survival of critical legal studies depends upon the development of an institutional radicalism which both recognises the specific character and limitations of the scholarly field and in turn commits itself to the intellectual values which constitute the place, the institution and the social force of scholarship.

SHOOTING ON LOCATION

It is the function of scholarship both to remember and to reproduce, to repeat and to transmit. The role of the scholar—who has historically incorporated the cleric, the scribe and the priest—is thus an admixture of curator, lector, tutor and visionary. At the centre of the intellectual project was the institutional recollection and passing on of tradition, of the bonds of identity and community that are signalled by the very term religion, *re-ligare*, to bind again.[13] On the margins of scholarship there are historically the poets, the artists and those other heretics or critics "whose discourse wavers";[14] while on the periphery within the institution there are those who seek to devote their professional careers entirely to research and to writing. Here too, however, the reverie of the transcendent, the romanticism of vision or the narcotic aura of textuality can scarcely hide the positive pedagogic mission or frequently the celebrity status of marginal or 'critical' intellectuals. They too seek to convert, to expose to, pontificate and to persuade. Even the modest clerical message of doubt, of irony, of transcendental uncertainty or epistemic indeterminacy is programmatic and performative, it seeks to bind its audience, to move its constituency or identify and cohere its community. Nihilists have often been the most successful orators, the most charismatic of religious figures, the most purposive of clerics.[15] Nor should the homonymy of spirit and spirit, of phantasm and alcohol be entirely ignored.

Whatever the self-perception of critical legal studies in America, whether marginal or central to the academy, its most striking attribute from a sociological perspective is its media status and international profile. In superficially descriptive terms, critical legal studies had all the glamour of schism within the Vatican, dissent amongst the synod or Teresa amongst the Spanish nuns. It also had the high visibility of foreign fashion, of the importation of European trends, new vocabularies and a commitment to political culture which for once extended far beyond the cloisters of the legal academy. To the extent that the movement represented an intellectual departure from the earlier theory of legal realism, it did so not least by virtue of its neo-scholasticism, its return to the philosophical tradition and its importation of European social theory.[16] While copious reference to the translated works of continental philosophy are no guarantee of any substantial theoretical genealogy,[17] they do have the elite function of identifying a community and of legitimating an esoteric marginality in relation to traditional doctrinal scholarship. In terms of the sociology of intellectuals, however, there is an undoubted irony in the opposition between the critics claim to an outsider status, to a leftist marginality and the elite hubris or kudos of continental theory. Critical legal studies as

an imported phenomenon, as a politics of intellectual credentials, also finds itself bound to the patronage of the Ivy League
law schools and the media decor that those schools attract. The
defining criterion of high intellectual culture in mediatic terms is
simply the "ability to gain access to the means of mass
communication,"[18] and that, more than anything else defines the
power of the elite institutions.

One interpretation of this phenomenon would be to argue
that the postmodern path to intellectual success, to star status
and political preferment does not lie in the traditional route
through the academic institution. Critical legal studies may in
this sense represent the first moment of an intellectual 'mediology' within the legal academy.[19] It would be in one sense a
method of bypassing the established institutional route to
preferment, while in a more substantial sense it would reflect the
changed political and technical context of intellectual work.
Empirical studies of European intellectual culture indicate that
the social space of intellectual success and of international
recognition does not stem from institutional academic conformity
but rather from marginal disciplines and from the polemical
work of the institutional outsider, the researcher or writer who
defines their social identity in terms of writing rather than in
terms of academic commitment or institutional service.[20] While
the American media may still reserve the full focus of publicity
for intellectuals associated with the highest status schools, the
role and transhumant career of the media intellectual is an
established fact of an electronic culture of "paratexts', graphic
simulations and liquid crystal transmission.[21]

The media intellectual is frequently presented as a figure of
inauthenticity and of an active immorality. The move from text
to paratext, from the linearity of script to the nodal constellation
of video text, is viewed ethically as a move from a world of
reference to a world of simulation, from substance to fantasy,
from signs that signal something to signs that signal nothing
beyond themselves: "a degree xerox of culture."[22] The irony to be
observed in the present context is not that of the essentially
puritanical or properly protestant rejection of images and of the
intellectual imaginary but rather the mediological proposition
that there is a massive overproduction of texts and, in more
technological contexts, of signs. While this argument has been
levelled generally at the self-referential culture of the contemporary university and at the academicisation or co-optation of

the left, it has been encountered also in relation to criticisms of the style and jargon of critical legal studies.[23] The new legal intellectuals, it is argued, write for themselves in an esoteric and exclusory rhetoric which circulates internally within the academy and signifies nothing much more than the fact of having been published. Such publication confers a certain symbolic credit within the institution but it has no wider significance beyond that of creating a class of nouveau riche intellectuals whose publications represent a constant aspiration towards upward mobility.[24]

Without here entering debate as to the politics of rhetoric or the institutional consequences of legal academic style, there is a further significance to the critical aspirations of the more visible or prominent of the movement scholars, the patrons, merchants and middlemen of the new legal art. This is simply to observe that the reproductive function of scholarship, its institution of an order of succession, is predicated upon production. In medio-logical terms, the positivity of critical legal studies must be viewed in terms of its literary produce, in terms of its material output and the institutional consequences of its graphematic substance, its writing. Here the politics of critical legal studies becomes more opaque. The claim to being a 'political location,' 'subversive,' 'oppositional' or simply leftist does not appear to necessarily carry to the alternately febrile and flippant produce of its harbingers. Aside from an early and now dated Marxist sociology of law which has been largely abandoned and which was itself imported,[25] the defining feature of the critics was arguably that of a naive and somewhat bowdlerised translation of continental social theory into an American legal idiom.[26] One consequence of such a characteristic of the literature was the limited audience which such a product or positivity was likely to have in the legal academy itself. Its success was its failure, its external visibility was its strongest form of internal secession, its text was its context. More interestingly and ironically, however, a literature bent upon importation and translation across languages, continents and jurisdictions has only an indirect relation to the immediate politics of the institution or practice of law. Such may yet, however, be the critics greatest strength: not only does the repressed return,[27] but those that are either literally or figuratively expelled can use the rupture of institutional place as the most striking of emblems of injustice and as the strongest of ethical grounds for the call to change. This is certainly one aspect of the critical movement's biography but it is not yet a defining feature of its politics.

In a bureaucratic age, the scholar is by profession a teacher. What is striking about the literature of critique is its almost complete absence of relation to teaching practice and so to the immediate politics of the institution which it otherwise supports and publicises. It could be termed 'critique without copula' in the sense that it offers an order of succession of academics, a transmission of a self-referential and so exclusory form of symbolic capital which refers only by way of the most distant signals to the lifeworld of the legal pedagogue. If critical legal studies purportedly offers a local politics[28] it is not at all clear what or where the locale is; if it offers a 'relational politics' it is equally hard to discern with what or to whom the relationship is made.[29] It would seem to be divided at best between heterotopias of literature and difference on the one hand and the moralism of the outsider seeking domicile on the other. While both projects may well have an ethical value, such a value or ethics is not yet connected to the life or practice of the academic institution. The most striking facet of American critical legal studies is its failure to penetrate, subvert or deviate from the established norms of legal educational practice. With only occasional exceptions[30]— and these exceptions do not involve substantially changing the syllabus or the classificatory grid of educational practice—the casebook and the Socratic method reign supreme. In an observational or empirical sense, critical legal studies has nothing to do with legal education, it has nothing to do with the teaching practice of legal scholars, it has only the most marginal of relations to the academic disicipline of law, if that discipline is defined in doctrinal or pedagogic terms. It rather obeys a mediological law: "for the media, the objective world—the thing there is something to speak of—is what other media are saying. Be it hell or heaven, from now on we are going to have to live in this haunted hall where mirrors reflect mirrors and shadows chase shadows."[31]

The radicalism of American critical legal studies does not appear to extend to the lives of its practitioners. It does not threaten the institutional safety, tenured security, economic comfort or frequently elite status of the critics. Were its product not so frequently intellectually tawdry, it would be tempting to regard the movement as a form of designer chic within the legal academy, an imported fashion, the latest in pre-packaging 'from the shelf to you' without need for alteration. At one level it can simply and cynically be argued that legal academics in America were long ago bought out by the size of their professional salaries, that they suffer "an enlightened false consciousness," a thoroughgoing cynicism or modern form of "unhappy consciousness."[32] Such unhappy consciousness is a species of pseudo-critique in which critical stances are subordinated to professional roles, the immediate politics of the institution to totalising theories of the particular, conflicts of value in the workplace to the exigencies of privatised therapies which order happiness or at least good relations.

Let us be more specific as to the features of the counter-revolution. The American law professor is too well paid to be politically committed, too status conscious to be intellectually engaged and too insular—too bound to the parochial and mono-lingual culture of the Law Review—to be scholarly. These are the progeny of mass legal culture, of the stupefaction which passes for legal education and at best produces a blend of intellectual naivety and doomed political enthusiasm. Its history appears from the outside to have been one of therapeutic self-confirmation hiding behind a legitimatory romanticism which views political radicalism as a species of patronage: critique is in pragmatic terms no more and no less than the essentially liberal yet nonetheless imperialistic desire to embrace and to include any stranger, any other, any nomad, any political infant or any woman who can plausibly represent an outside within the academy. These, however, are the tokens of radicalism, the coinage of hubris, whereby an inauthentic and uneasy bureaucratic elite salvages its conscience by buying in representatives of repressed, marginalised or disadvantaged groups. More than that, however, the American translation of European social theory, of the 'new philosophies' and the 'new politics' seems predicated upon the belief that by supporting the marginal, the foreign, the peripheral or the outsider the intellectual within the institution becomes, presumably by projection, marginal or foreign—and so *ipso facto* politically radical himself. As if the greatest injustice known to the world were the indignity of being fired from Yale, refused tenure at Harvard or barred from promotion at Stanford or Pennsylvania. As if a political biography which ends at the law school in Georgetown, Washington or in Madison, Wisconsin or Cardozo, New York or Hampshire College, Amherst or the New School, San Francisco or Amsterdam, Mars or Kansas somehow spelled out the injustice of the American polity, of the marginal, the unloved or the ignored, in its entirety. In these terms the time of critique has surely run out, for critique is a matter of distance, of prospect and perspective, whereas the network or the group is altogether too close for comfort or at least too close for criticism.

It seems almost appropriate that Mark Tushnet, in a most unpolitical 'political history' of critical legal studies should propose a rather anodyne yet peculiarly telling emblem, or more properly icon, for the movement: it is a place, a location, a heading, an umbrella.[33] This place or location is in the law school and it is interesting to contemplate further and from a variety of perspectives why an umbrella might be useful in the law school. First, and most interestingly, from the perspective of the social moralist Stevenson we learn that "...it is the habitual carriage of the umbrella that is the stamp of Respectability. The umbrella has become the acknowledged index of social position."[34] It is tempting to prolong and emphasise the metaphor of moral place that the umbrella offers: it is the icon of bound space as well as of transient refuge or mobile structure. Yet it is also, as Stevenson does not fail to recognise, a portable icon and constitutes a mystical space.[35] From the perspective of those that do not believe, it is potentially duplicitous or mendacious.[36] In Stevenson's moralistic terms the duplicity of the network, movement or place lies in a critique or critical stance which seeks little more than institutional respectability or a place within the hierarchy for the radical and the marginal, but also— it might be suggested—for the naive and the incompetent; the tired, the masculine, the white and the obscure.

The same point could be made by reference to the symbolism of the umbrella. It is in Freudian terms a phallic symbol, the pleated gingham or silk hides, veils or secrets away "an organ which is at once aggressive and apotropaic, threatening and/or threatened".[37] There is a certain modesty to the symbol but there is also an ideology or a paranoia which pitches artefact against nature, culture against tempest, style against expression. Nietzsche forgets his umbrella,[38] which is possibly to say that in a life devoted to the proximity of thought to nature, of mind to body, it was impossible to hide from either fate or thunder, destiny or storm, by the artifice of the umbrella. Nor did Nietzsche hide his writing behind the artifice or conventions of genre or of style: for the philosopher as aesthete, the style *was* the thought, a life lived as art: "like a woman or like writing, it passes itself off for what it passes itself off for".[39] Writing does not need to shelter, it is rather the institution and the law which imposes a standardised rhetoric, a writing for essays, trials, tests and examinations, a writing for bureaucracy, a prose for conformity and for defeat.[40]

Nor, finally, should one fear to be wet. The umbrella suggests a place that is dry, a liberal location which keeps nature and fluid at bay. As Drucilla Cornell has observed, 'wetness' is associated with femininity, with bodily fluids, and occasionally with uncleanness.[41] Fluid—pluvial, aquaeous, oceanic, vaporous or internal—is the allegory of femininity, for fluid dissolves and escapes, it is inconsistent, disequilibriated and changing, "fluid has to remain that secret remainder".[42] Could the umbrella keep these aquarian phenomena away? Is it appropriate to be "stiff" and dry, to erect barriers against nature and against the writing or thought of the body? Again there is a potential duplicity or at least an irony, the umbrella is not an utopian instrument, it is at most heterotopic and as such should be used only occasionally and terroristically. It need simply be reiterated that in psychoanalytic terms this particular symbolism of critique is tied to aspirations of acceptance, to the desire to be accepted, to the desire for proximity or to be close and incorporated. Nor does the emblem of the umbrella exhaust itself in the metaphor of community. As a reference to the carapace of style, it can be argued further that it is precisely in relation to writing that law is most directly and disturbingly threatened. It is precisely in challenging the normativity of genre or the rhetoric of writing that critical legal studies can find a space that awaits its appropriate politicisation.[43] Writing differently or writing otherwise are far more threatening to the academic institution and indeed to bureaucracy generally than many more overtly radical strategies or politically subversive messages.[44]

NO PARTICULAR PLACE TO GO

The politics of form is necessarily accompanied by substantive effects. Indeed it is arguable that the two cannot be differentiated but rather are dialectically bound.[45] In that respect critical legal studies continues the ancient war of texts.[46] It goes further than the Romanists, the glossators, the commentators or the common lawyers—the Anglican legists—by recognising that the gloss is also an intervention rather than a simple or neutral repetition, precis, concordance, paraphrase or rephrasing. It obscurely recognises that what is at stake in the text, namely the constitution of legal subjectivity, is a matter of textual politics as well as of a linguistic inhabitation of the text.[47] Moreso, for a politics located in the academy it should not be hard to recognise that the text is the normative territory of legal life and the discourse of law the constitution of the sociality—the civility—of legal subjects, 'the children of the text.'[48] Here then there can be no question but that discourse and text are themselves a politics, or in more formal terms that the ontology—the being—of law and so too of legal subjectivity is located in the material circulation, access to, storage of and transmission by texts.[49] While—in a strictly schematic sense—the ensuing analysis moves from form to substance, from place to purpose and from style to intellectual circumstance, it is not intended to imply anything more than a descriptive account of philosophical and political oppositions identified with critical legal studies. If the umbrella is an unfortunate emblem for a putatively radical movement, it may be more effective to seek an intellectual identity or political space in the conflictual trajectory of the academic literature produced by and descriptive of the movement, network or place of critique.

The discourse of identity is most usually the product of denial, the unitary identity of legal subjects in particular being the positive consequence of the negation of the fragmentary *personae* and fractured experiences of institutional biography and collective belonging. Our group or individual identity is a product of the claims we make to difference, we are by virtue of what we claim we are not.[50] In this respect an intellectual and political cartography of American critical legal studies could well begin with the attribution of nihilism to the critical stance: this designation is both an exemplar of negation and an instance of ethical mis-translation.[51] It is further the most obvious space of political conflict within the legal academy: in a reprise of certain of the denunciations of the legal realists, those that were deemed neither to believe in the enterprise of law nor to express adherence to the values of established doctrine, were to be labelled nihilists and irrationalists and were explicitly and implicitly invited to leave the legal academy.[52]

Nihilism or Nowhere Left to Go

The antirrhetic,[53] polemical as opposed to philosophical, character of the aspersion of nihilism deserves momentary emphasis.

In its negative connotation it would appear to mean—if such is not too strong a term—a combination of existential hopelessness, doctrinal libertinism, political anarchism, philosophical amoralism, irrationalism, immodesty and faithlessness. In its positive connotation, it would appear rather as a varied and eclectic advocacy of what is inelegantly termed anti-foundationalism, a combination of philosophical pragmatism and political romanticism. Neither field of connotations accords with any recognised historical or philosophical sense of nihilism, a term deriving from *nihilum*, signifying nothing or nil, of no value or without value, but taken philosophically by Nietzsche to mean negation, the will to annihiliation of fixed and sedentary values.[54] Nihilism was not the coincident or generic expression of *ressentiment* or passivity but rather an active political and historical force engaged with preparing a post-theistic secular world for recognising that being was without foundation, and that the absence of foundation was constitutive of the human condition.[55] Being, in Heidegger's terms, was not foundation but rather the site of disappearance, of the *mise en abyme* of thought.[56]

In political terms the European philosophical tradition which develops from Nietzsche has tended to argue for an 'accomplished' or positive perception of nihilism. The nihilist recognises the death of the highest values—of a particular Judaeo-Christian order of corporeal and spiritual repression—as a point of ethical and political opportunity, as the meeting of history and destiny as the inauguration of a novel "mobility of the symbolic"[57] as the beginning of a secular social world which can only ever begin, only ever aspire to becoming. The pertinent point is that however the concept of nihilism is interpreted there is little sense in which critical legal studies could be designated intelligently as nihilistic in either a positive or a negative connotation. It has neither the philosophical acumen to know what nihilism designates nor the political will to rupture, reappropriate or translate a being without foundation into an historical constellation of legal or counter-legal values.[58] Critical legal studies refers at most to a hermeneutic nihilism, a specific loss of faith first in the constitutional text and subsequently in the determinacy of all legal meanings. While the seemingly interminable lucubrations of the critics and others on the method and theory of interpretation may come close to a species of textual nil or nothingness, to the circulation of texts that have become "empty speech" or "gray on gray,"[59] the specific problem of the legal consequences of semantic indeterminacy are hardly the same thing as a fully fledged philosophical nihilism to which critical legal studies neither approaches nor in all probability aspires.[60] More than that, the assertion of an absolute indeterminacy could only express the alienation, estrangement or distance of critical legal studies from institutional legal acts, sentences and enforcement: judgment, after all, occurs within a terrain of inscriptions of pain upon the body.[61] As Lacan once remarked, the real may be elusive yet "when we bang our heads against a stone wall, we are struggling with the real" and in that context it might be added, the real leaves us dazed, either delirious or unconscious.[62]

The question surrounding critical legal studies is not that of any direct, conscious or substantial adherence to nihilistic philosophical positions. The most that can be said is that the strategy of self-identification pursued by the movement—presumably so as to indicate the points between which movement or (e)motion occurred—is predicated upon a species of negation or denial: the critics cluster around a series of portenteous negations: they do not believe in objectivity, (semantic) determinacy or neutrality as attributes of legal judgment.[63] The identificatory thesis is most usually developed around the concept of indeterminacy, the proposition that in all rule application there is a variable element of variation or uncertainty, choice or discretion. The interesting question to be posed, however, is not that of the degree of variation nor of the extent of uncertainty—these are antique and unexceptionable jurisprudential themes—but rather the form of denial of certainty itself. The claim of the indeterminacy thesis is that of negation of determinacy. It can initially be argued that this negation simply retains the determinacy thesis in an attenuated form: "the subject-matter of a repressed image or thought can make its way into consciousness on condition that it is *denied*. Negation is a way of taking account of what is repressed....The result is a kind of intellectual acceptance of what is repressed, though in all essentials the repression persists."[64] More interestingly, however, it is possible to endeavour to pursue the image of indeterminacy and to ask what is at stake in an apparently vague or essentially uncontroversial realist claim. How does the recollection of the function of judgment—of discrimination, taste or political choice—lead so suddenly to aspersions of nihilism, to allegations both of a life and of a law deprived of meaning? No more than a partial answer can be offered.

The etymological root of determinacy is *terminus*, connoting both boundary and conclusion or end. The question becomes what is it that ends in the law? What is it that ends with the law? With this law? A question of the intellectual history of jurisprudence and of doctrine that takes the analyst deep into the unconscious structures of law. First, however, the notion of boundary and of going beyond the pale: it is not the by and large conscious semantic indeterminacy of law that immediately threatens the citadel, it is the mixing of genres, the conflation, non-recognition or transgression of boundaries, texts and territories that engenders a terror of criticism. What happens when the law is treated as literature or worse when literature plays the law and fiction becomes the figure of the truth?[65] At one level the response may be that the literature of legal criticism is of little aesthetic interest, that it is beyond the pale of good or discriminating taste.[66] Perhaps it ceases to be literature.[67] Such a response, however, misses the point. The degree to which the proponents of the indeterminacy thesis seek determinacy or ineffectively mourn its loss is symptomatic of a greater stake than that of simple jurisdiction. At an analytic level the question of the boundary marked by law is that of the separation and opposition of pleasure and pain, life and death, *eros* and *thanatos*.[68]

The indeterminacy thesis exposes the mystical foundation of law.[69] It suggests a level or depth of uncertainty that affects not simply legal judgment but equally the prejudices or prejudgments of law. It asks the question of tradition and of the traditionality of law: if this is common law, to whom is it common? It was not, after all, common to the peasant who stood before the law, who died before the law, for whom the law was ever a secret. But even this is not the stake. The stake is death itself and the lie which suggests that through law, through the law as an order of succession, death may in some measure be evaded. Death is the zone of indeterminacy, of an absolute and never ending indeterminacy. It is in Blanchot's terms "the utterly indeterminate, the indeterminate moment and not only the zone of the unending and the indeterminate".[70] It is the residual christian sensibility of doctrine, of established modern jurisprudence, which is appalled by indeterminacy, by the prospect of eventually becoming an indeterminate element in a zone of unending indifference. And yet that is our fate, such is human destiny: historical being is necessarily being towards death.[71] The question posed by the indeterminacy thesis is the question of closure. What is it that law excludes? What is it that law represses? What is it of which the law will not speak?

One answer, offered by recent strands of critical legal studies—if, as is I believe possible, feminist jurisprudence and critical race theory can be aligned with the movement—is autobiographical. The literature and politicisation of autobiographical accounts of law is in philosophical terms an attempt to respect the facticity, the historicality and finitude of being.[72] In recognising the exigency of being towards death, the literature of legal autobiography engages with a legality of the contingent, an historical and social as well as literary law, a linguistically and politically constructed governance or rule of law. In terms of intellectual history, the return to the 'voice' of law (*viva vox iuris* or *lex loquens*), to a bodily writing or bio-graphy (*bios-graphien*), is a return to (though also projection of) an earlier discourse of law, that of the fates or *fata*, the daughters of necessity who would predict or foretell—like the oracles at Delphi—the structure if not always the events of human existence. Here the law is directly called into question. The issue is that of the legitimacy of the legal construction of the institution: if the institution is our fate then the law is the medium and manner of our resistance to, accommodation of or love for it.[73] It is in this sense of law as a response to fate, as an aspect of the discourse of the fates, that critical legal concern with indeterminacy—with the issues of openness and closure—can be politicised in terms of hedonism or nihilism, *eros* or *thanatos*, nascence or nemesis. To which it should be added that only the most fervently puritanical, complacently ignorant or deeply pessimistic can propose that hedonism is either apolitical or amoral.[74] Hedonism is nothing less than the political expression of *amor fati*, of fate as character,[75] or at a collective level of an active and dramatic historical and ethical gnosticism. In a more aphoristic and more potent vein, it may simply be observed that the critique of law is the philosophy of its history.

Translation or Nothing Left to Hold on to

The question of law as a question of fate or fortune, of destiny as the external force which historical being defines itself against, leads to a further consideration and a second identificatory feature of critical legal studies. It was Gadamer who perhaps most clearly posed the question of death as being at the hermeneutic basis of tradition.[76] For Gadamer all institutional speech is a matter of translation, transmission, across the temporal, geographic and linguistic boundaries that separate generations, cultures, communities and institutions.[77] Translation was the always desired and constantly impossible goal of all speech, though its archetype was writing and the textual corpus of tradition. Tradition was ever the stranger whom the present must come to know; tradition was *nomos* as language and as law. The problem of translation is in that sense also the question of justice: "that which is here named Babel: the law imposed by the name of God which simultaneously both prescribes and prohibits translation in both showing and hiding the limit."[78] It is impossible to translate, and yet justice requires translation as the only available means of accounting, of taking account of, the native, the slave, the foreigner, the stranger, the aegyptian, the nomad, the woman, the other that comes before the law.

As is well known, to translate connotes both to carry over or across, to move from one place to another, *trans-latum*, and more remotely to give up, hand over, transmit or betray, from *tradere*, which lies also at the root of tradition. In a direct sense, to translate is to figure, simulate or trope, to move or transfer a meaning from one place to another, where in classical rhetorical terms it does not naturally or properly belong.[79] It is to simulate, to act 'as if' the borrowed word or phrase belonged, or were no longer alien or strange. The translation posts, it sends on, it sends something borrowed, perhaps at a certain rate of interest or loan. Its relation to its source is one of transference, conscious or unconscious, it cannot let go, it betrays by remaining bound to an origin, a sovereign, a law.[80] The geopolitical metaphor of translation, of transfer and transference, of the tradition that traduces, is of considerable—though arguably unwitting—significance to critical legal studies. It may be addressed either geographically or temporally in terms of those purloined letters, those languages, posted from Europe to America and returned unopened or in inverted form. The question in geopolitical terms must be simply stated as 'what is America?' What is America to the critique of law? An unanswerable question perhaps, for America is a place one passes through.[81] The United States are after all most obviously a series of relations, of imaginary boundaries and imaginary communities. Their relation to Europe must be as various and several as their relation to themselves. How, in legal terms, could American critical legal studies be bound by an acceptance posted in Europe?

As a preliminary observation, might it not be the case that the pre-history of critical legal studies drew much, if not all, of its radicalism from the translation of European sources? The more iconoclastic realists turned to Freud, Nietzsche and to Marx.[82] It may be, of course, that these figures are simply those that are recognisable to Europeans, that the real radicals were Peirce, Dewey, James, Morris or even Rorty—"he created a space in American philosophy in which former New Leftists could go continental"[83]—as sources of legal realist critique and its critical progeny.[84] Yet it seems unlikely in the context of their future, for critical legal studies developed from a European left associated with Lukacs, Heller, Althusser, Foucault, Adorno and Habermas, but also and more improbably from the work of Levi-Strauss, Ferdinand de Saussure, Jacques Lacan, Julia Kristeva, Jacques Derrida and most recently (in law) Niklas Luhmann. And their attraction was also their otherness, that they were continental, their language foreign, their ideas opaque. It is necessary to ask whether this importation represents an exotic escape from politics? A co-opted deferral of engagement? Lapsed commitment or a politics of apostasy of the outside, of transgression, of fear? Is it simply a question of the subordination of jurisprudence to broader cultural trends within the academy? Is it rather that American jurisprudence is neither autonomous as a discipline nor free of the legal profession as a practice? That it was never intended as a form of scholarship but rather as a form of technical-practical service?

The dominance of European theory, of the phenomena of importation, translation and visitation, is marked by several ironies.[85] While American critical legal studies returns to Europe as a peculiarly American phenomenon concerned with a peculiarly American jurisdiction, its history is nonetheless that of displaced continental theory, its philosophy one of a thorough-going eclecticism and its method a combination of precis, paraphrase and circumlocution. On one level this could be deemed a wholly postmodern phenomenon, a politics of the marginal and the fragmentary in which the student edited Law Review revels in new possibilities: Derrida applied to law and economics, Levi-Strauss to torts cases, Lacan to contractual gap-filling, Luhmann to the constitution.[86] It is a one way street and arguably a transcendental politics repeating old errors in new forms.[87] Yet this is no greater a sin of over-consumption than any other aspect of the American commodity market, it is indeed relatively liberal, pluralistic and free of the xenophobia whereby the English (legal) academy steadfastly resists the incursions of foreign or otherwise 'unsound' theories. At the same time, however, there is a sense of ironic disorientation that accompanies much of this work. The translation of continental theory is market led and subjects critical scholarship to a breathless journalism which follows the immediate fashions one after another like papparazzi. One name gives way to another while cultural memory dissolves into the immediacy of the limelight: we can all be critical scholars for a quarter of an hour.

The root of the problem in all probability lies somewhere in the sub-cultural character and conventions of legal scholarship. The Law Review is a steadfastly monolingual institution: what has not been translated does not yet exist. Such an editorial norm is symptomatic of two separate problems. One is the obvious limitation of scholarship to those works which it is commercially viable to translate, while more legally relevant yet more specialist work in, for example, 'Critique du Droit,'[88] philosophy of law or the cultural history of European law remains in the obscurity of its native tongues. The monolingual limitation of citation and reference in the Law Review points to a further problem: to what public sphere does the critique of law speak? The restriction of scholarship to the vernacular would have a justification if its political design were to foster a specific public discourse or dialogue as to legal change. Such is far from the case. The stylistic criterion has nothing to do with the vast glut of over-lengthy Law Review articles being read by any but professional academics. The critics speak to and write for the critics within the relative privacy of the law school. Their circle of acquaintance can be reconstructed in large measure from the frequency of citation of other American critical authors.[89] Put differently, if the theory translated, summarised, examined and explained in the Law Review article belongs initially to a European dialogue and corresponding public sphere, its legal significance is likely to be attached in some measure to that jurisdiction and its institutions. Not only is available theory constrained by the economics of publishing but the potential practice or advocacy of legal change aligned to such theories is limited to continental jurisdictions which are procedurally and substantively different to American law. The irony is deepened once it is realised that it is most often legally harmless texts that are translated: if critical lawyers were to act on the political implications of the theoretical works which are most often cited, they would end up designing different housing, filming according to new theories of cinematography, reforming the practice of literary criticism, developing designer jeans, scribble-writing or body-building. The relation between translated cultural and literary criticism and an American public sphere of legal reform or of radical legal change is complex, diffuse and to date remote. In one respect this is a reflection of the decline of the public sphere as a site of intellectual or scholarly dialogue. In another sense it may yet reflect a politics by other means. In either case, it is necessary to ask "what can intellectual life be, if it is subject to the phenomena of fashion?"[90] Is the everyday world of fashion the only access to politics, to the public sphere, that remains within the institution? Is it the only escape available from a dogmatic theology of law? Is it rather a sign of the loss of intellectual authenticity, of a market led scholarly journalism in which the dedicated academic follower of fashion is subjected to repeating traditions to which they do not belong, translating ideas which they do not understand and more generally instituting an idolatry or romanticism of great theorists, great names and great men.

Abstractionist Theory: New Left or Old Rite

The preceding remarks may appear unduly negative: the political and cultural pluralism from time to time engendered by American pragmatism has in its way been a virtue. Nor is the left in Europe in any very competent or ethical position to criticise or chastise its American counterpart. The easy *ad hominem* arguments that have pursued the political compromise of Nietzsche, Heidegger or Paul de Man have seldom been predicated upon any reasoned political position nor has the critique of postmodernity generally been impeded by any very closely defined conception of the object—period, space or position—subjected to criticism. Like most intellectual novelties, critical legal studies provokes fear and dogma in equal measure. It is in that respect at least postmodern and on occasion post-scholarly as well. Its plural or diffuse identity—a feature it also shares with legal realism[91]—is not necessarily a commitment either to simple confusion or to a politics of parody perplexity, pessimism or passivity. The deconstruction of identity, the denial of a unitary form or cause which is reflected amongst other things in theoretical eclecticism, is simply a denial of identity as foundation or ground of being: "deconstruction...establishes as political the very terms through which identity is articulated".[92]

The identity of the legal critic or critical movement is dialectically tied to or parasitic upon that of the legal or juridical field itself.[93] While the movement of the critics may be contrasted to the stasis of the establishment or of doctrinal scholarship, the two cannot be separated in either political or conceptual terms. If it is the closure of legal doctrine that criticism seeks to subvert, it may well be that it proffers for law a wider cultural and political significance but that significance, that politics and culture are nonetheless bound to or derivative from a practice of law.[94] The political goal of exposing legal doctrine to cultural analysis, the history of legal practice to theoretical reconstruction, is threatening because it challenges the boundaries of the discipline and particularly the seclusion—the innocence—of its practice. At the risk of repetition, or at least of returning to the starting point of this article, a third feature of critical legal studies is the distance between its theory and the discipline of law as a practice. More particularly, the abstractionism of the theory disengages critical legal analysis from the politics of what is primarily or at least in the first instance an educational practice, a politics of the discipline of law in an academic age.

It is perhaps the ironic fate of the postmodern intellectual to be tied to a specific institution and its practice. It is certainly as yet unclear what the consequences or limitations of that position are likely to be. In the meantime, critique still refers to scholarship and to a species of enlightenment although it may well be an ambiguous and contradictory enlightenment, a double agency or *double entendre*, illumination designed to preclude illumination and to subvert the institution.[95] In the meantime it remains a question of the extent, direction and audience or public sphere of the critique of dogmatic reason, of the relationship between the inside and the outside of the institution and of conceiving of discourse "as a violence that we do to things."[96] In particular critique must address the question of tradition that underpins so much of the confusion or despair associated with the question of identity: "our inheritance, because of the manner of its textual survival and the spasmodic mode of its reconstruction, is a conspicuously muddled one."[97] The inheritance or specific tradition of western left intellectual culture is further both disorientated by events and confused by long term stasis if not outright failure. Our inheritance, however, is two thirds of our identity, genealogy our first character or fate. In this sobering yet salutary sense it needs to be reiterated that the demarcation of the disciplines, the disciplinary canon, the subject, the treatise, casebook or textbook, is the object language of law and the site of critical legal practice.

One example will suffice. The preface to the much commented and much used Dawson, Harvey and Henderson, *Contracts*,[98] makes the striking assertion that it is not the function of the textbook to merely convey a technical knowledge. Neither is it the purpose of the course in contracts—which the book, needless to say, represents—to simply inculcate the analytic skills of the intellectual discipline of Contracts. The work is dedicated to a higher end, one which acknowledges that "there is a language and a culture to be passed on."[99] There, in an explicit and direct yet nonetheless overlooked form, is the stake of critique. The question at issue is that of how one would pass on, disseminate or diffuse another language and a different culture, or simply other texts, other portraits, other promises. The first stage of critique must be to reconstruct the history of that discipline, that language and culture of contracts, to ask what or who was contracted over the long time span of historical and institutional structures, over the *longue durée* of contractual language.[100] There are in these historical terms at least three discernible stages in the development of critique in the specific context of a sub-discipline such as contract. Somewhat idiosyncratically they will here be labelled laconically in terms of grammatology, judgment and representation.[101]

Considerable work has been done in the history of Anglo-American contract law. A.W.B. Simpson, whose philosophical position would be better described as that of hedonist and cynic rather than as self-conscious critic, amongst other things has traced the history of assumpsit as the pre-history of contract and has related the development of the doctrine of mistake to an early version of the futures market,[102] as well as indicating the civilian basis and borrowings of English contract doctrine.[103] James Gordley has provided a meticulous account of the medieval glossatorial conceptualisation of contracts and traces the mailbox rule to the *Digest*.[104] P.S. Atiyah has written an extensive and largely critical history of the concept of freedom of contract, while the approach of the major American treatise writers and of Dawson, Harvey and Henderson in particular is structured by extensive historical extracts and by the archaisms of American contracts law.[105] It is perhaps for this reason that many of the more interesting works in critical legal studies have engaged with aspects of contract law and with the problems of teaching it.[106] To suggest something more than a simple history or politics of contract law may in this context seem perverse. On the other hand, instrumental histories of the effects of contract doctrine or internal histories of the structure of contractractual relations provide only a very partial opening of the discipline.

The philosophy of contractual history is initially and at its best a grammatological endeavour.[107] The legal concept of contract develops through the materiality of the signs of contract: the *symbolon* was classically a thing divided, then a creed or literal inscription or enunciation of faith, an ecclesiastical and social pact, and latterly an instrument, tract, deed or obligation, a confession of will.[108] Contract, tract or treatise, is both literally and figuratively a species of writing, of memory and inscription but also of law. Arthur Jacobson develops this theme in an argument that translates the Judaeo-Christian tradition, and specifically the decalogue, into a theory of writing law. The commandments or laws are written three times in a narrative that centres around the destruction of a false image, an idol: "the struggle over writing in Names—between Elohim and Yahweh, between Yahweh and Moses—rescues it from idolatry. The struggle supplies the necessary collaborations. To write is to rewrite. To rewrite is to erase. To erase is to rescue writing from idolatry."[109] Writing in this tradition is not simply, immediately or only the speech of or 'in the name of' the father.[110] It is a complex negotiation, at base an agreement not only to respect the text or to follow the law according to the later maxim of *pacta sunt servanda*, but also it is a contract as to words and as to language itself. In short, the complex combination of writing and erasure, speech, record and interpretation, that make up the law—its instruments, its deeds, its faiths—impose a duty of interpretation on the ground that law can always change, that a theistic conception of creation cannot treat either world or law as closed: "to consider rules complete, from Moses' perspective, is to treat them as engravings. To apply rules to cases as if they are already formed bows to rules as idols. Creation is not complete, even if we want to treat it so."[111]

It is not simply a question of the history of contracts being a semiotic endeavour. The history of contracts is a history of a particular tradition of sociality, of a symbolic structure, a particular discipline, a particular culture and its graphic instruments, its inscriptions, its writing: "But was it not the Judaeo-Christian, rather than the Graeco-Roman, tradition which inserted the question of law in the innermost recess of the question of Being? Only history can get at what this means for us."[112] At the level of the history of judgment, contracts mean specific assignations of subjectivity, particular constructions of language and of silence, the implication and interpretation of pricing (*inter-pretium*)[113] of certain actions, behaviours and words. At the risk of stating the obvious, the contract is a sign and is subject or party, as Dawson remarked, to a social language or tradition of contracts. Hence the covenant, charter, compact or contract would traditionally begin by invoking the deity (*dei gratia*) and the crown (*fidei defensor*) to indicate both good faith (*bona fide*) and also the universal community of the text (*omnibus christi fidelibus ad quos praesentes literae pervenerint*).[114] The contract is the insignia, effigy or emblem of admission to that community, it is the recognition that the condition of possibility of interpreting the contract in law is the socio-linguistic contract which guarantees our initial access to the law. The contract is not my language but our language, not my law but rather my part—my act, my deed, my confession—before the law. Hence the gender and the sociality of contracts: according to a classical principle of *imitatio imperii* each subordinate sovereignty—each child of the text—imitates the sovereign constitution and so too each minor contract imitates a sovereign social compact. Such is the order of succession, of contraction, "the charter or contract for the following, which quite stupidly one has to believe: Socrates comes *before* Plato, there is between them—and in general—an order of generations, an irreversible sequence of inheritance. Socrates is before, not in front of, but before Plato, therefore behind him, and the charter binds us to this order: this is how to orient one's thought, this is the left and this is the right, march."[115] The condition of judgment which critical legal studies has begun to reconstruct is itself a judgment and not a foundation, it is a contract, a social pact, a tradition. It represents us to ourselves, it is our continuity, our identity, our law. It is also our word, our sign, our text.

Finally, how should these ties, these solemn prejudices or articles of faith be transcribed in postmodern conditions? At the very least a critical legal analysis of the history of contract doctrine can build upon deviationist internal analyses. The great failing of deconstruction in America has not been that it was playful, obscure or endlessly interpretative but rather that it uncritically translated and arguably absorbed deconstruction into an existing network of disciplinary practices and their rhetorical forms. When it comes to the demarcation of disciplines, it is the function of critical thought to cross boundaries and to mix genres both in a reflexive political sense and in a stylistic and rhetorical sense of an alternative practice of writing destined to address a future that is not yet formed, neither bound to our existing contract nor subject to the schemata that spell out the conceptual proprieties of its tradition. To 'contract' is to do things with texts, to circulate, send and reinvest texts with a reflexive political significance: in an immediate and vital sense, they *are* the locality, the terrain and the community of critical legal thought. In addressing the texts of law, the critic engages with the desire to comprehend the material history, the circulation, interpretation and passing on of the text. Critical thought would also understand the conceptual conditions of possibility of the text and its interpretation. In rethinking the latter issue, the paramount aim is to influence and to change the political community that determines, according to a pre-defined series of hierarchies and oppositions, both the continuance and the fate of contractual language, its speech and its silence.

The contract, in the words of one recent account, "is a sexual-social pact, but the story of the sexual contract has been repressed...the missing half of the story tells how a specifically modern form of patriarchy is established."[116] The narrative of contract begins not simply with Hobbes' materialist absolutism grounding law in the violence of monarchy, but similarly with Robert Filmer's *Patriarcha* and with the adoption of a Roman conception of sovereign will and jurisdiction, of the father as legislator, as *Pater patriae*, King and patriarch.[117] The question of who contracts becomes more complex when the legal conception of subject and will is traced to the power—to the name—of the father. Yet even here the boundaries are not discrete or singular. The sexual repression is predicated also upon a specific conception of genealogy as legitimacy and upon succession as passing from father to son. At issue here is not simply a linguistic coincidence, that legitimacy is a familial expression, but a further contract which founds the tradition as history, language and narrative structure upon these figures of domestic descent: upon what we call power "a word derived from Roman law where it originally designated the domestic power of the father."[118] Our contract, according to Roman law at least, is to obey our parents and our country.[119]

PAST AS PROLOGUE

The brief excursus above on the possibility of critique in contract law can serve to illustrate three pre-conditions to the politicisation of critical legal studies. The first consideration is that of the use of history in reconstructing the intellectual development of the doctrinal tradition. Critical legal studies, particularly as a development from some Anglo-American version of historical materialism, has always paid a certain passing due to the power of history.[120] The reconstruction of American law, however, cannot credibly base itself upon the short term historical journalism of American institutions. Sensitivity to history should face critical legal studies with a series of geo-political questions as to the destiny and transmission of culturally specific forms of law and of their critique. It would be a history of tradition, of the long time span, of representation, repetition and reproduction. Second, the perspective of the *longue durée* forces critique to focus upon the systems of classification, the conceptual grids or schemata, whereby doctrine divides, categorises and represents the subject-matter, the disciplines of law. The re-writing of the disciplines, the reformation of what the legal academy does, is a question of a return to the epistemic structures, the forms of knowledge that pass as law. It is for this reason the more radical strands of critical legal studies have chosen to ignore the piecemeal pragmatism of post-realist legal reform and to develop instead novel forms of writing law.[121] Included in the concept of novel doctrinal rhetorics, in biography, the novella, body writing, grammatology or philosophical deconstruction as proper epistolary forms for critical legal scholarship, is a profound change in the object of critical thought in law.

In one respect the issue returns to the question of identity but in this instance it is the identity of the intellectual in law that is called into question. It is a matter of the role of a radical scholarship, but it is also a question of the self-definition, the insecurity and the fate of personal investment in or commitment to challenging the established institution and its pedagogy of law. It is a question also of the complicity of the critic in repressive institutional practices, a complicity that extends into a hierarchical programme, an elitist curriculum, an intellectually complacent if not overtly anti-intellectual syllabus and a largely passive relation to the inheritance, transmission and reproduction of the legal tradition. In this respect it will be argued in conclusion that the politics of legal critique are the politics of a particular profession, a questioning of the law of law but also a questioning of our place within and responsibility for the tradition. The marks of politics in the discourse of critique are neither familiar nor obvious: they do not relate directly to a specific content or programme but rather to an ethics, they do not belong directly to a given tradition but rather to a necessarily ambiguous and potentially subversive place or space in the legal academy, they do not share the organisational framework or umbrella of previous or pluvious movements but rather stand for a critique of organisational or managerial forms of rationality.[122] The politics of reason is not simply a local politics, it is oppositional, fragmentary and frequently obscure. It remains in many respects a politics of style and is in consequence resistant to normative forms of analysis.

The dice are loaded against a politically radical critical legal studies. In sociological terms intellectual radicalism has been the product of institutional insecurity or of externality to the institution.[123] Whatever else the critics may argue, law is the least threatened and one of the best paid of academic disciplines. At most the bulk of critical legal scholars could lay claim to the comfort but insignificance of less privileged law schools. Even here, however, critical scholars have tended to move on, their career trajectories taking them to more privileged schools: the American legal academy can hardly be accused collectively of refusal or inability to 'buy out' or co-opt the radicals where such seemed the easiest course. Secondly, the history of the Western Left hardly encourages optimism as to the future of a revolutionary or politically radical institutional tradition. Anderson summarises several histories of Western oppositional movements in arguing that "no matter how otherwise heteroclite, they share one fundamental emblem: a common and latent pessimism. All the major departures or developments of substance within this tradition are distinguished from the classical heritage of historical materialism by the darkness of their implications or conclusions."[124] This seemingly prescient 'pervasive melancholy' is frequently interpreted as leading from politics to aesthetics—to the "hyperinflation of aesthetic discourses"[125]—and from activism to passivity if not *ressentiment*.[126]   Worse still, the tradition is neither indigenous nor comprehensible to the native intellect.   It is taken at best to augur poetry rather than politics, careerism rather than critique, fashion rather than passion.

The question remains, however, as to why a politics of writing, a stylistic radicalism, a purely discursive opposition or subversion should engender such hostility, such grandiloquent rejection from the legal academy.   The answer must be linked in some way to the institutional threat that these critics represent. In an important sense the politics of writing brings radicalism home to the academy and challenges, at the very least, the languages of law or in one recent coinage, the 'law of texts in the texts of law.'[127]   In marked contrast to the disillusion and disfavour with which the traditional left has dismissed 'continental theory' and post-marxist politics as pretentious, opaque and even dishonest, it is quite possible that the politics of writing will popularise critique both within and without the legal academy.   At an immediate level concern with grammatology, with modes of discourse and with the traditions and mechanisms of transmission makes this particular radicalism well placed to gain access to the new media that now dominate cultural life.   As a form of hedonism of writing the body, it is also possible that critical legal studies could not simply oppose but also seduce in the sense of taking the politics of law into the sphere of enjoyment, into the media of representation and reproduction.[128]   The question of justice, of the possibility of ethical judgment, is both a question of style or form of representation but equally a politics of inscription, of the link between writing and erasure from the text, between communication and excommunication, freedom and guilt, innocence and bodily sacrifice.[129]

In more directly or at least classically political terms, it can be relatively uncontentiously observed that the politics of the institution, of the academy, revolve around the constitution and policing of sites of enunciation.   The institution qualifies, regulates and ordains through patterns of discourse.   It establishes rights of speech, jurisdictions, through linguistic examinations, through essays, dissertations, moots, bolts, writing programmes and other verbal performances.   It assesses, grades, classifies, marks, assigns, defines, simulates and litigates through the institution of protocols or rhetorics of writing.[130]   While it might be argued that threatening the procedures of normalisation within the law school is a far cry from the politics of any genuinely politicised public sphere, it can equally be argued not only that the institution is the last remaining habitus of radicals but that the media of transmission, of teaching and of repro- duction, are the site of a new politics, that the educational institution is a fundamental element in the future of radicalism. Whether such a conclusion should be greeted with optimism or pessimism remains an open question. Critical legal studies both represents and transgresses the politics of law: in being an important dimension of a wider legal politics it evidences both the potential and the limitations of that politics, it shows us what politics there is and it shows that such a politics is not yet that significant or radical a cultural force. In so doing it indicates that there is much intellectual space yet to be filled, it indicates that while critical legal studies is a radical force in the legal institution it is not yet radical enough.

NOTES

1. Avital Ronell, *Crack Wars: Literature, Addiction, Mania* (1992) Lincoln: University of Nebraska Press, at p 21.

2. The expression is taken from D. Kennedy, 'Critical labour Theory: A Comment' (1981) 4 *Industrial Relations LJ* 503, 506. It is reiterated in D. Kennedy, 'Cost Reduction Theory as Legitimation' (1981) 90 *Yale Law Journal* 1275 and confirmed in a. Hutchinson and P. Monahan, 'Law, Politics and Critical Legal Scholars: The Unfolding Drama of American Legal Thought' (1984) 36 *Stanford Law Review* 199. See further A. Hunt, 'The Theory of Critical Legal Studies' (1986) 6 *Oxford Journal of Legal Studies* 1; M. Tushnet, 'Critical Legal Studies: A Political History' (1991) 100 *Yale Law Journal* 1515; Schlegal, 'Notes Toward an Intimate, Opinionated, and Affectionate History of the Conference on Critical Legal Studies' (1984) 36 *Stanford Law Review* 391; D. Kairys (ed.), *The Politics of Law* (1990, 2nd ed.) New York: Pantheon Books.

3. Peter Gabel introduced the session at which this paper was delivered in terms of critical legal studies being "the most radical show in town." While there are several radical connotations to the carnivalesque, to festivals, circuses and travelling shows, the metaphor also suggests a transience and abnormality restricted to theatre or to the stage. The recourse of critical legal studies to metaphors drawn from theatre, drama, cinema, rock music and indeed jazz as well as a more general strain of popular culture, has been remarked upon frequently and will not be engaged with here. See J. P. Oetken, 'Form and Substance in Critical Legal Studies' (1991) 100 *Yale Law Journal*

2209 at 2214–16; A. Chase, 'Toward a Legal Theory of Popular Culture' (1986) *Wisconsin Law Review* 527; or G. Frankenberg, 'Down by Law: Irony Seriousness, and Reason' in C. Joerges and D. Trubek (eds.), *Critical Legal Thought: An American-German Debate* (1989) Baden-Baden: Nomos Verlag, 315. Alternately the most stylistically frightening and bemusing example of such style probably remains A. Hutchinson, *Dwelling on the Threshold: Critical Essays on Modern Legal Thought* (1988) Toronto: Carswell.

4. The aspersion or attribution of nihilism seldom achieves this level of philosophical coherence, but such a theme is implicit in J. Singer, 'The Player and the Cards: NihiDsm and Legal Theory' (1984) 94 *Yale Law Journal* 1; P. Gabel and D. Kennedy, 'Roll Over Beethoven' (1984) 36 *Stanford Law Review* 1; G. Peller, 'The Metaphysics of American Law' (1985) 73 *California Law Review* 1151. See, for a discussion of this point in relation to the French left, the excellent V. Descombes, *Modern French Philosophy* (1979) Cambridge: Cambridge University Press, pp 110–131; also P. Dews, *Logics of Disintegration* (1987) London: Verso, at p xvi: "the fundamental issue here, of course, is the sense in which a philosophical position which assumes the foundations of the classical forms of critique to be necessarily and oppressively identitarian can itself continue to perform a critical function".

5. P. Carrington, 'Of Law and the River' (1984) 34 *Journal of Legal Education* 222; O. Fiss, 'The Death of Law?' (1984) 69 *Cornell Law Review* 1; O. Fiss, 'The Law Regained' (1989) 74 *Cornell Law Review* 245; C. Fried, 'Jurisprudential Responses to Legal Realism' (1988) 73 *Cornell Law Review* 331; N. Duxbury, 'Some Radicalism about Realism? Thurman Arnold and the Politics of Modern Jurisprudence' (1990) 10 *Oxford Journal of Legal Studies* 11.

6. The notion of disintegrative reason comes from T. Adomo, *Negative Dialectics* (1973) London: Routledge; see also Peter Dews, *Logics of Disintegration* (1987) London: Verso. Further development of this theme can pursued through N. Geras, *Prophets of Extremity* (1990); E. Laclau, *New Reflections upon the Revolution of our Times* (1991) London: Verso.

7. P. Anderson, *Considerations on Western Marxism* (1976) London: New Left Books, at p 93, concluding a magisterial account of the Western left aphoristically: "Method as impotence, art as consolation, pessimism as quiescence: it is not difficult to perceive elements of all these in the complexion of Western Marxism". See further, P. Anderson, *In the Tracks of Historical Materialism* (1983) London: Verso.

8 The most striking version of this argument is to be found in R. Jacoby *The Last Intellectuals*, (1987) New York: Noonday Press; see also

J. Wiener, *Professors, Politics and Pop* (1991) London: Verso, especially pp 339-47 ('Footnote or Perish'); Cornel West, *The American Evasion of Philosophy* (1989) Madison: University of Wisconsin Press. See also P. Buhle, *Marxism in the United States* (1990) London: Verso; R. Debray, *Critique oi Political Reason* (1983) London: Verso. C.f. A. Bloom, *The Closing of the American Mind: How Higher Education has failed Democracy and Impoverished the Souls of Today's Students* (1987) New York: Viking Books; also A. MacIntyre, 'Reconceiving the University as an Institution and the Lecture as a Genre', in MacIntyre, *Three Rival Versions of Moral Inquiry* (1990) London: Duckworth.

9. This is the modest programmatic conclusion arrived at, for example, in A. Hunt, 'The Big Fear: Law Confronts Postmodernism' (1990) 35 *McGill Law Journal* 507 533. See also, R. Coombes, 'Toward a Theory of Practice in Critical Legal Studies' (1989) *Law and Social Inquiry* 69; A. Hutchinson, *Dwelling on the Threshold: Critical Essays on Modern Legal Thought*, op cit.; J. Boyle, 'The Politics of Reason: Critical Legal Theory and Local Social Thought' (1985) 133 *University of Pennsylvania Law Review* 685.

10. For a political analysis of this Hegelian term, see J. P Sartre, '"The Concrete Universal', in J. P. Sartre, *Between Existentialism and Marxism* (1974) London: New Left Books. The theme is philosophically central to the unjustly overlooked J.P. Sartre, *Critique of Dialectical Reason: Theory of Practical Ensembles* (1976) London: New Left Books. On the conditions of postmodern intellectual life, the 'locus classicus modernus' is J. F. Lyotard, *The Postmodern Condition* (1984) Minneapolis: University of Minnesota Press; together with H. Foster (ed), *Postmodern Culture* (1986) London: Pluto Press.

11. For an historical account of critique in law, see P Goodrich, 'Critical Legal Studies in England: Prospective Histories' (1992) 12 *Oxford Journal of Legal Studies* 195; also P Goodrich, 'A Short History of Failure: Law and Criticism 1580–1620', in idem, *Languages of Law: From Logics of Memory to Nomadic Masks* (1990) London: Weidenfeld and Nicolson.

12. For an implicit recognition of this point, see D. Kennedy, 'Psycho-Social CLS: A Comment on the Cardozo Symposium' (1985) 6 *Cardozo Law Review* 1013. J. Schlegel, 'American Legal Theory and American Legal Education', in C. Joerges and D. Trubek (eds.), *Critical Legal Theory* op cit.

13. For an extensive discussion of this etymology and function, see R. Debray, *Critique of Political Reason* (1983) London: Verso, at pp 184–217. In one etymology the word 'law' can also be traced to *ligare* as well as to *legere* (to read) and *legein* (to speak). For a brief discussion, see G. Rose, *The Dialectic of Nihilism* (1984) Oxford: Blackwell; P. Stein,

Regulae Iuris (1966) Edinburgh: Edinburgh University Press; and more extensively, E. Benveniste, *Le Vocabulaire des Institutions Indo-Europeenes* (1969) Paris: Minuit.

14. P. Legendre, *Paroles Poetiques Echapees du Texte* (1982) Paris: Seuil, at p 12.

15. Thus the myth of Hegesias, according to which Hegesias preached the valuelessness of life so successfully that his audiences would regularly commit suicide, leading Ptolemy to ban him from Egypt. See G. Puttenham, *The Arte of English Poesie* (1589) London: Field, at p 118. The various heretical traditions of gnosticism and nihilism have seldom refrained from building communities or organising groups. See, for examples in a religious context, N. Cohn, *The Pursuit of the Millenium* (1970) London: Paladin and M. Gauchet, *Le Desenchantement du Monde: Une Histoire Politique de la Religion* (1985) Paris: Gallimard; see also R. Debray, *Cours de Mediologie Generale* (1991) Paris: Gallimard; R. Debray, *Le Scribe* (1980) Paris: Grasset; J. Derrida, 'Scribble (writing-power)' (1979) 58 *Yale French Studies* 116.

16. See particularly J. Boyle, 'The Politics of Reason: Critical Legal Theory and Social Theory' (1985) 133 *University of Pennsylvania Law Review* 1135; D. Cornell, 'Institutionalisation of Meaning, Recollection, Imagination and the Potential for Transformative Legal Interpretation' (1987) 135 *University of Pennsylvania Law Review* 1135; and more recently, D. Cornell, *The Philosophy of the Limit*, (1992) New York: Routledge. Generally, see D. Carlson, D. Cornell and M. Rosenfeld (eds.), *Hegel and Legal Theory* (1991) New York: Routledge; idem (eds.), *Deconstruction and the Possibility of Justice* (1992) New York: Routledge.

17. This point is made extensively in relation to English critical legal studies in W. T. Murphy, 'The. Habermas Effect: Critical Theory and Academic Law', in (1990) 42 *Current Legal Problems* 135.

18. R. Debray, *Teachers, Writers, Celebrities: The Intellectuals of Modern France* (1981) London: Verso, at p 32 (translating R. Debray, *Pouvoir Intellectuel en France* (1979) Editions Ramsay).

19. For the development of mediology, see R. Debray, *Teachers, Writers, Celebrities*; and Debray *Cours de Mediologie*, op cit. where mediology is defined as the study of "the mediations by means of which an idea becomes a material force, mediations of which the 'media' are simply a particular belated and overgrown prolongation". (14) Mediology traces the political genealogy of the contemporary intellectual from the cleric and the scribe but also has the more substantial and technical role of studying the materiality of thought, "the technically determined material ensemble of supports, rapports and means of transmission which assures thought [la pensee] its social existence in each epoch." (17) This comes close to a grammatology as spelled out in

J. Derrida, *Positions* (1986) Chicago: University of Chicago Press. and in J. Derrida, *Of Grammatology* (1976) Baltimore: Johns Hopkins University Press. In somewhat more conventional historical terms, see D. Kelley, *The Beginning of Ideology* (1981) Cambridge: Cambridge University Press.

20. This is one of the principal findings of P. Bordieu, *Homo Academicus* (1988) Cambridge: Polity Press, ch 3. It is also a central theme of R. Debray, *Teachers, Writers, Celebrities*, op cit. On the legal 'field', see P. Bordieu, 'The Force of Law: Toward a Sociology of the Juridical Field' (1987) 38 *Hastings Law Journal* 814.

21. On paratexts in law, see M. Ethan Katsh, *The Electronic Media and the Transformation of Law*; R. Collins and D. Skover, 'Paratexts' (1992) 44 *Stanford Law Review* 509; and for a more general critique, in addition to works cited, see A. Ronell, *The Telephone Book: Technology, Schizophrenia, Electric Speech* (1989) Lincoln: University of Nebraska Press; J. Baudrillard, *La Transparence du Mal* (1990) Paris: Galilee; J. Derrida, *The Post Card: From Socrates to Freud and Beyond* (1987) Chicago: Chicago University Press. As regards the secondary literature, see M. Poster, *The Mode of Information: Poststructuralism and Social Context* (1990) Oxford: Polity Press; G. Ulmer, *Teletheory: Grammatology in the Age of Video* (1989) New York: Routledge.

22. J. Baudrillard, *La Transparence du Mal*, op cit at 82. For a comparable argument made from a more properly sociological perspective, see J. Conselot, *L'Invention du Social: Essai sur le declin des passions Politiques* (1984) Paris: Fayard; and in a literary critical context see E. Said, *The World, the Text and the Critic* (1984) London: Faber and Faber; E. Said, 'Opponents, Audiences, Constituencies and Community, in H. Foster (ed.), *Postmodern Culture* (1985) Bay Press. More broadly, see the historical analysis of intellectuals—though primarily literary critics—in F. Lentricchia, *After the New Criticism* (1980) Chicago: Chicago University Press; T. Eagleton, *Literary Theory* (1983) Minneapolis: Minnesota University Press; T. Todorov, *Literature and Its Theorists* (1987) Ithaca: Cornell University Press. See also, B. Robbins (ed.), *Intellectuals: Aesthetics, Politics and Academics* (1990) Minneapolis: University of Minnesota Press; J. Kristeva, *Desire in Language* (1987) New York: Columbia University Press; F. Jameson, *The Political Unconscious* (1981) London: Methuen; M. Foucault, *Power/Knowledge* (1980) New York: Pantheon Books.

23. For criticism of obscurity, pretention and fraudulence, See P. Carrington, 'Of Law and the River', op cit, pp 222–223: C. Fried, 'Jurisprudential Responses' op cit.; O. Fiss, 'The Death of Law?', op cit.

24. E. Said, in H. Foster, *Postmodern Culture*, op cit.; J. Baudrillard, *La Transparence du Mal: Essai sur les phenomenes extremes* (1990) Paris: Galilee.

25. D. Jacoby, *The Last Intellectuals*, op cit at p 167: "As in many American industries, imports dominate the Marxist academy—for roughly the same reasons as with cars. Although the final product is sometimes assembled in the United States, foreign Marxism seems snappier better, designed; it accelerates more easily. It is more finished and polished". See. for an example, M. Jay, *Marxism and Totality* (1984) Berkley and Los Angeles: University of California Press; and D. Lehman, *Signs of the Times*, op cit at 22–24.

26. For a recent and by and large sophisticated example of this project, see M. Kramer, *Legal Theory, Political Theory and Deconstruction: Against Rhadamanthus* (1991) Bloomington: Indiana University Press, at pp 2-3: "For those not familiar with the more arcane pathways of recent French philosophy, the preceding paragraphs may be somewhat obscure. It is the aim of this introductory chapter, and indeed of this whole book to start to gain wider currency for the insights of French scholars among jurisprudes and political theorists in the Anglo-American tradition." The work, in common with the bulk of American critical legal theory, is one of importation, translation and appropriation. For some interesting observations on this theme from a feminist perspective, see S. Gibson, 'Continental Drift: The Question of Context in Feminist Jurisprudence' (1990) 1 Law and Critique 173. C.f. A. Jardine, *Gynesis: Configurations of Woman and Modernity* (1985) Cornell University Press, ch 1.

27. On the return of the repressed in law, see A. Sarat and T. Kearns (eds.), *The Fate of Law* (1991) Ann Arbor: University of Michigan Press, at p 12: "perhaps it is the ironic fate of law to be reconstructed or revitalised by those very ideas, for example, compassion, engagement, even politics, that law has for so long tried to exclude." See also P. Goodrich, 'Fate as Seduction: The Other Scene of Legal Judgment' in A. Norrie and J. Macahery (eds.), *Closure or Critique* (1993) Edinburgh: Edinburgh University Press.

28. J. Boyle, 'Politics of Reason', op cit; M. Tushnet, 'Some Current Controversies in Critical Legal Studies', in C. Joerges and D. Trubek, *Critical Legal Theory*, op cit. Also Sarat and Kearns, 'A Journey through Forgetting: Toward a Jurisprudence of Violence', in Sarat and Kearns, *The Fate of Law*, op cit, especially pp 253–65. For a comparative view, see R. de Lange and K. Raes (eds.), *Critical Legal Studies in Europe* (1991) Special Issue, 10 *Recht en Kritiek*.

29. The theory of a relational account of law is best expressed in A. Hunt, 'The Critique of Law' in A. Hunt and P. Fitzpatrick (eds.), *Critical Legal Studies* (1987) Oxford: Blackwell.

30. See particularly the essays collected in D. Kairys (ed.), *The Politics of Law*, op cit.

31. R. Debray, *Teachers, Writers, Celebrities*, op cit at p 118.

32. For development of these and related themes, see P Sloterdijk, *Critique of Cynical Reason* (1987) Minneapolis: University of Minnesota Press, ch 1 and 2. See further, G. Hegel, *Phenomenology of Spirit*; J.P. Sartre, *What is Literature?* (1984 ed.) London: Methuen.

33. Tushnet, 'Critical Legal Studies', op cit, particularly at 1515-1519. On the 'umbrella' movement of critical legal studies, see also P. Rush, 'Killing them Softly with his Words' (1990) 1 *Law and Critique* 21, at 23.

34. R. L. Stevenson 'The Philosophy of Umbrellas' in idem, *Lay Morals* (1911 ed.) London: Chatto and Windus, at 151. He argues further "that...are almost inclined to consider all who possess really well-conditioned umbrellas as worthy of the Franchise...they carry a sufficient stake in the commonweal below their arm". (153)

35. A. Schmemman, *L'Eucharistie* (1985) Paris; Y Brilioth, *Eucharistic Faith* (1930) London: Dent.

36. Having argued that "umbrellas, like faces, acquire a certain sympathy with the individual who carries them; indeed they are far more capable of betraying his trust...", Stevenson, concludes, that "a mendacious umbrella is a sign of great moral degredation" (ibid. at p. 154).

37. Derrida, *Spurs: Nietzsche's Styles* (1979) Chicago: Chicago University Press, at p 129. For extensive further analysis, see D. Noguez, *Semiologie du Parapluie* (1990) Paris: Editions de la Difference, pp 11–29, developing a neo-logistic science of 'parahyetology'. He remarks at one point—of the symbolism of the umbrella—"the phallus is...at one and the same time desire and repression, the blind continuity of a plenitude and the yawning sight of the void."

38. "I have forgotten my umbrella". Fragment classified no. 12,175 in the French edition of *Joyful Wisdom*, p 147 and discussed at length in J. Derrida, *Spurs*, op cit pp 123–140.

39. Derrida, *Spurs*, opcit at p 127. On art, language and life, see particularly Nietzsche, *The Will to Power*, on writing, and particularly the writing of the body, see H. Cixous, *Coming to Writing* (1991) Cambridge: Harvard Universtiy Press; L. Irigaray, *Marine Lover: Of Friedrich Nietzsche* (1991) New York: Columbia University Press; J. Derrida, *The Post Card*, op cit. S. Sellers, *Women and Writing* (1991) London: Macmillan. For a fascinating historical relation of the sins of flesh and language, see C. Casagrande and S. Vecchio, *Les Peches de la Langue* (1991) Paris: Editions de la Cerf.

40. Reference is particularly to the informatic prose of technological massification. For critiques of information, see J. Baudrillard, *La Transparence du Mal*, op cit; P Legendre, *Paroles Poetiques Echapees du Texte*, op cit.

41. See D. Cornell, *Beyond Accommodation* (1991) New York: Routledge ch 1; also D Cornell, 'What Takes Place in the Dark' (forthcoming).

42. L. Irigaray, *Speculum of the Other Woman* (1985) Ithaca: Cornell University Press, at p 237 See further, L. Irigaray, *This Sex which is not One* (1985) Ithaca: Cornell University Press. ('The mechanics of fluids').

43. Again the principal proponent of this thesis in J. Derrida, *The Post Card*, op cit, and again in J. Derrida, *Dissemination* (1981) Chicago: Chicago University Press. See also the remarkable discussion of writing and law in A. Jacobson, 'The Idolatry of Rules: Writing Law According to Moses' (1990) 11 *Cardozo Law Review* 1079; and for further discussion, P. Goodrich, 'Contractions' in *Languages of Law: From Logics of Memory to Nomadic Masks* (1990) London: Weidenfeld and Nicolson; C. Douzinas and R. Warrington, 'Posting the Law: Social Contracts and the Postal Rule's Grammatology' (1991) 4 *International Journal for the Semiotics of Law* 115.

44. This point is made at length in M. Foucault, *Power/Knowledge* (1982) New York: Pantheon Books; M. Foucault, *Language, Memory, Counter-Practice* (1977) Ithaca: Cornell University Press. See also, J. Derrida, 'Response', in C. McCabe (ed.), *The Linguistics of Writing* (1989) Manchester: Manchester University Press. The theme is also present in R. Unger, *The Critical, Legal Studies Movement* (1986) Cambridge: Harvard University Press.

45. For an interesting example of this thesis put into practice, see P Schlag, 'Cannibal Moves: An Essay on the Metamorphoses of the Legal Distinction' (1988) 40 *Stanford Law Review* 929. For another example, see P. Rush, 'Killing them Softly', op cit.

46. For a history of the 'war of texts', see P. Legendre, *Le Desir Politique de Dieu: Etude sur les montages de l'Etat et du Droit* (1988) Paris: Fayard. More broadly, see P. Legendre, *Jouir du Pouvoir: Traite sur la Bureaucratie Patriote* (1976) Paris: Editions de Minuit; P. Legendre, 'The Lost Temporality of Law' (1990) 1 *Law and Critique* 3.

47. In American critical legal terms, this thesis returns to K. Klare, 'Law-Making as Praxis' (1979) 40 *Telos* 123. For further discussion, see A. Hunt, 'The Theory of Critical Legal Studies', op cit at pp 37–43; and A. Hunt, 'The Big Fear: Law Confronts Postmodernism' (1990) 35 *McGill Law Journal* 507. For further discussion in a European context see P. Goodrich *Languages of Law*, op cit ch 8.

48. On which, see P. Legendre, Les Enfants du Texte (1992) Paris: Fayard. In the American context, see the excellent P. Schlag, 'Le Hors de Texte, C"Est Moi: The Politics of Form and the Domestication of Deconstruction' (1990) 11 Cardozo Law Review 1631.

49. For an historical analysis of this point, see P. Goodrich, 'Literacy and the Languages of the Early Common Law' (1987) 14 Journal of Law and Society 422. More broadly, see M. Foucault, 'The Discourse on Language', in M. Foucault, The Archaeology of Knowlege (1972) New York: Pantheon Books; J. Kristeva, Revolution in Poetic Language (1984) New York: Columbia University Press; P. Goodrich, Legal Disourse (1990) New York: St Martins Press.

50. Freud, 'Negation' in Freud. 6eneral Psychological Theory (1963) New York: Macmillan; H. Bhabha (ed.). Nation and Narration (1990) London: Routledge; B. Anderson, Imagined Communities (1983) London: Verso; P. Goodrich, 'Poor Illiterate Reason" (1992) 1 Social and Legal Studies 7.

51. I have analysed and criticised this debate previously, in P. Goodrich, Reading the Law (1986) Oxford: Blackwell. at ch 7. On the philosophical genealogy of the concept of nihilism, of which American critical legal studies seems so easily ignorant, see F. Nietzsche, The Will to Power (1991) Edinburgh: Foulis; M. Heidegger, Nietzsche: Nihilism (1982) New York: Harper and Row; 6. Vattimo, The End of Modernity (1990) Oxford: Polity.

52. P. Carrington, 'Of Law and the River' (1984) 34 *Journal of Legal Edication* 222, responding to the closing remarks of R. Unger, 'The Critical Legal Studies Movement' (1983) 96 *Harvard Law Review* 563, 675; P. Carrington, 'Butterfly Effects: The Possibilities of Law Teaching in a Democracy' (1992) 41 *Duke Law Journal* 741; O. Fiss, 'The Death of Law?" (1986) 72 *Cornell Law Review* 1; O. Fiss, 'Objectivity and Interpretation' (1982) 34 *Stanford Law Review* 739. For the more general debate as to nihilism in legal studies, see Singer, 'The Player and the Cards', op cit. Stick, 'Can Nihilism be Pragmatic?' (1986) 100 *Harvard Law Review* 332; and the literature reviewed in D. Chow, 'Trashing Nihilism' (1990) 65 *Tulane Law Review* 221. On irrationalism and nihilism, see G. Lukacs, *The Destruction of Reason* (1980) London: Lawrence and Wishart; P. Dews, *The Logics of Disintegration* (1987) London: Verso; N. Geras, *Prophets of Extremity* (1989) London: Verso; E. Laclau and C. Mouffe, *Hegemony and Socialist Strategy* (1986) London: Verso; T. Docherty, *After Theory* (1991) London: Routledge.

53. 'The antirrhetic is the rhetorical form of discourses of denunciation, archetypically discourses against iconoclasts. For an extended historical account of the antirrhetic, see P Goodrich, 'Antirrhesis: The Polemical Structure of Common Law Thought' in A.

Sarat and T. Kearns, *Law and Rhetoric* (1993) Ann Arbor: University of Michigan Press. In a strictly rhetorical sense the critical legal studies movement could be designated nihilistic insofar as the iconodules would of rhetorical or antirrhetical necessity paint an anti-portrait of the iconoclast as sacrilegious, irrational and against nature.

54. See G. Deleuze, *Nietzsche and Philosophy* (1983) London: Athlone Press, for an interesting account of this sense of nihilism in Nietzsche.

55. R. Camus, *The Nihilists*, (1969) Harmondsworth: Penguin; G. Vattimo, *The End of Modernity*, op cit ch 1.

56. See M. Heidegger, *What is Metaphysics?* (1976) New York: Harper and Row. Also, P. Virilio, *The Aesthetics of Disappearance* (1991) New York: Semiotexte; J. Baudrillard, *Simulations* (1983) New York: Semiotexte; J. Derrida, *Writing and Difference* (1978) New York: Routledge; J. Derrida, *The Truth in Painting* (1987) Chicago: University of Chicago Press.

57. G. Vattimo, *The End of Modernity*, op cit at p 28.

58. This argument is made most strongly by J. P Sartre, *Critique of Dialectical Reason*, op cit.

59. The concept of "empty speech" (*parole vide*) is taken from J. Lacan, *Ecrits: A Selection* (1980) London: Tavistock, at pp 40–56; the "gray on gray" comes from D. Jacoby *The Last, Intellectuals*, op cit at p 236. For an emotive version of this argument applied to the legal academy, see J. Boyd-White, *Justice as Translation* (1990) Chicago: Chicago University Press, especially ch 1. In a different tone, there is also S. Fish, 'Dennis Martinez and the Uses of Theory', reprinted in S. Fish, *Doing What Comes Naturally* (1990) Oxford: Oxford University Press.

60. For a critical appraisal of the indeterminacy debate, see C. Yablon, 'The Indeterminacy of the Law: Critical Legal Studies and the problem of Legal Explanation' (1985) 6 *Cardozo Law Review*; D. Cornell, The Philosophy of the Limit, op cit, pp 91–95

61. An observation made most forecefully in the history of imprisonment, see M. Foucault, *Discipline and Punish* (1978) Harmondsworth: Pelican; M. Ignatieff, *A Just Measure of Pain* (1980) London. In an American context, see R. Coover, 'Violence and the Word' (1986) 95 *Yale Law Journal* 1600. See also the powerful analysis in C. Douzinas and A. Warrington, 'A Well-Founded Fear of Justice' (1991) 2 *Law and Critique* 115.

62. Cited in S. Turkle, *Psychoanalytic Politics*, op cit at p 243. See further, C. Clement, *Lives and Legends of Jacques Lacan* (1985) Princeton: Princeton University Press.

63. Chow, 'Trashing Nihilism', op cit at p 224–25, summarising J. Singer, 'The Player and the Cards: Nihilism and Legal Theory' (1984j 94 *Yale Law Journal* 1. See also G. Peller, 'The Metaphysics of American Law' (1985) 73 *California Law Review* 1151; also G. Peller, 'Reason and the Mob: The Politics of Representation' (1987) 2 *Tikkun* 28.

64. Freud, 'Negation', in *General Psychological Theory*, op cit at p 214. For discussion, see Kristeva, *Revolution in Poetic Language*, op cit; M. Borch-Jacobsen, *Lacan: The Absolute Master* (1990) Stanford: Stanford University Press; G. Deleuze, *Difference and Repetition* (1968) Paris: Presses Universitaires de France.

65. The question is asked most forcefully in J. Derrida, 'Prejuges: Devant la Loi' in J. Derrida et al., *La Faculte de Juger* (1985) Paris: Editions de Minuit, at p 134: "Literature has perhaps come to occupy, in these specific historical conditions which are not only linguistic, a space which remains open to a certain subversive legality *(juridicite)*...it makes the law, it comes into view in the place where the law makes itself...in the elusive instant where it plays the law, literature passes literature. It finds itself on both sides of the line which separates law from the outside of law..." More broadly on the medieval maxim *fictio figura veritatis*, see E. Kantorowicz, *The King's Two Bodies* (1956) Princeton: Princeton University Press; P. Legendre, *L'Empire de la Verite* (1983) Paris: Fayard; and Lacan, *Ecrits*, op cit pp 74–75, 305–306.

66. As, for example, remarked of Singer by A. Hunt, 'The Big Fear', op cit at p 528: "Singer's edifying legal theory of opposition to cruelty, misery, hierarchy and loneliness is just too mushy and indeterminant for my tastes".

67. As could be remarked, in a different context, of the final chapter of C. Douzinas. R. Warrington and S. McVeigh, *Postmodern Jurisprudence: Texts of the Law in the Law of Texts* (1991) London: Routledge.

68. Deleuze, *Difference et Repetition*, op cit; Freud, *Beyond the Pleasure Principle* (1961) London: Hogarth Press.

69. On the mystical foundations of law, see Nietzsche, *Birth of Tragedy* (1905) Edinburgh: Foulis, at p 174; "the state itself knows no more powerful unwritten law than the mythical foundation which vouches for its connection with religion and its growth from mythical ideas"; also Derrida, 'Force of Law: The Mystical Foundation of Authority' (1990) 11 *Cardozo Law Review* 919.

70. M. Blanchot, *The Space of Literature* (1982) Lincoln: University of Nebraska Press, at 99.

71. M. Heidegger, *Being and Time* (1962) Oxford: Blackwell; A. Lingis, *Deathbound Subjectivity* (1989) Bloominton: Indiana University Press; P. Goodrich, 'Fate as Seduction: The Other Scene of Legal Judgment', in J. McCahery and A. Norrie (ed.s), *Closure and Critique* (1992) Edinburgh: Edinburgh University Press. Generally, Cicero, De Fato (1942 ed.) London: Heinmann; Boethius, *The Consolation of Philosophy* (1987 ed.) London: Elliot Stock.

72. R. Delgado; P. Williams, *The Alchemy of Race and Rights* (1991) Cambridge, Mass.: Harvard University Press; D. Kennedy, 'Spring Break'; D. Bell.

73. For a particularly powerful expression of this thesis, see A. Papageorgiou-Legendre, *Filiation: Fondement genealogique de la psychanalyse* (1990) Paris: Fayard. See also R. Debray, *Critique of Political Reason*, op cit; and on *amor fati*, see Nietzsche, *Daybreak* (1881/1982 ed.) Cambridge: Cambridge University Press, at p 258: "my formula for greatness in a human being is amor fati: that one wants nothing to be different, not forward, not backward, not in all eternity. Not merely bear what is necessary, still less conceal it—all idealism is mendaciousness in the face of what is necessary—but *love* it".

74. S. Zizek, *For they Know not What they Do: Enjoyment as a Political Factor* (1991) London: Verso. The literature on hedonism is of varied quality, but it is possible to recommend particularly P. Sloterdijk, *Critique of Cynical Reason*, op cit (arguing for a philosophy of disinhibition or classical cynicism); Nietzsche, *Ecce Homo* (1911 ed.) Edinburgh: Foulis; Marcuse, 'On Hedonism' in Marcuse, *Negations* (1976) London: Allen Lane; Feyerabend, *Against Method* (1975) London: New Left Books.

75. W. Benjamin, 'Fate as Character' in *One Way Street* (1979) London: New Left Books, at 124, at 125: "the system of signs of character is generally confined to the body".

76. H-G. Gadamer, *Truth and Method* (1979) London: Sheed and Ward. For further accounts of legal hermeneutics, see *Southern California Law Review*; *Texas Law Review*; and in a European context, P. Goodrich, *Reading the Law*, op cit, at ch 5; C. Douzinas, R. Warrington, S. McVeigh, *Postmodern Jurisprudence*, op cit, ch 2. See also, D. Michelfelder and R. Palmer (eds.), *Dialogue and Deconstruction* (1989) New York: New York University Press.

77. Gadamer, *Truth and Method*, op cit pp.

78. J. Derrida, 'Des Tours de Babel' in *Psyche* (1987) Paris: Galilee, p 234. The literature on the impossible philosophy of translation is extensive but mention should at least be made to W. Benjamin, 'The Task of the Translator' in *Illuminations* (1969) New York: Shocken; G.

Steiner, *After Babel* (1975) Oxford: Oxford University Press; P. de Man, *Resistance to Theory* (1986) Minneapolis: University of Minnesota Press; J. Derrida, *The Ear of the Other: Octobiography, Transference, Translation* (1988) Lincoln: Nebraska University Press. A. Benjamin, *Translation and the Nature of Philosophy* (1989) London: Routledge. On the stranger, see J. Kristeva, *The Stranger* (1991) New York: Columbia University Press.

79. Thus Quintilian, *Institutio Oratorio* (1966 ed.) Cambridge, Mass.: Harvard University Press, Book IX. 1: 4–5: (defining trope) "the transference (*translata*) of words and phrases from the place which is strictly theirs to another where they do not properly belong."

80. See particularly J. Derrida, *The Post Card*, op cit 339–47, 384–90. Arguing, inter alia, that transference is the mechanism whereby the analyst reduces or overcomes the patient's 'resistances' (334).

81. See the brief remarks on America in J. Derrida, *Memoires for Paul de Man* (1986) New York: Columbia University Press, pp 12–20. Additionally, see J. Baudrillard, *America* (1989) London: Verso; and in a more sociological vein, J. Baudrillard, *In the Shadow of the Silent Majorities...Or the End of the Social* (1983) New York: Semiotexte. The tradition of French letters home from America goes back to Alexis de Tocqueville and is continued quite strikingly by Sartre and Foucault. In terms of self-description I would recommend Venturi et al., *Learning from Las Vegas* (1977) Boston: MIT Press; F. Jameson, *Postmodernism or the Cultural Logic of Late Capitalism* (1990) Durham, N.C.: Duke University Press; M. Davis, *City of Quartz: Excavating the Future in Los Angeles* (1990) London: Verso.

82. For an interesting analysis of the "house radicalism" of realism, see J. Brigham and C. Harrington, 'Realism and its Consequences: An inquiry into Contemporary Sociological Research' (1989) 17 *International Journal of the Sociology of Law* 41. See also Livingstone, 'Round and Round the Bramble Bush: From Legal Realism to Critical Legal Studies' (1982) 95 *Harvard Law Review* 1670; Frankenberg, 'Down by Law' op cit at 338 ff; D. Kennedy, 'A Rotation in Contemporary Legal Scholarship' in C. Joerges and D. Trubek (eds.), *Critical Legal Thought*, op cit p 353; and G. Binder, 'On Critical Legal Studies as Guerrilla Warfare' (1987) 76 *Georgia Law Journal* 13. C.f. N. Duxbury, 'Some Radicalism about Realism? Thurman Arnold and the Politics of Modern Jurisprudence' (1990) 10 *Oxford Journal of Legal Studies* 11.

83. N. Fraser, *Unruly Practices* (1989) Minneapolis: University of Minnesota Press, p 5.

84. See T. Grey 'Holmes and Legal Pragmatism' (1989) 41 *Stanford Law Review* 787; R. Summers, *Instrumentalism and American Legal*

Theory (1982) Ithaca: Cornell University Press; F. Kellogg, 'Legal Scholarship in the Temple of Doom: Pragmatism's Response to Critical Legal Studies' (1990) 65 *Tulane Law Reveiw* 15; and as an implicit theme see R. Kevelson, *Law as a System of Signs* (1988) New York: Plenum Press. Richard Rorty is the last in the line of an indigenous American pragmatism, yet his work and certainly his fame are largely products of his continental connections. C.f. P. Goodrich, 'Law and Modernity' (1986) 49 *Modern Law Review* 545.

85. The debate as to the relationship between European philosophy and American theory can be followed in its various phases in J. Wierner, *Professors, Politics, and Pop*, op. cit; Lehman, *Signs of the Times* (1991) London: Deutsch; C. West, *The American Evasion of Philosophy*, op cit; A. Bloom, *The Closing of the American Mind* (1987) New York: Viking Books; D. Jacoby, *The Last Intellectuals*, op cit; and A. MacIntyre, *Three Rival Versions of Moral Inquiry* (1990) London: Duckworth.

86. D. Carlson, 'On the Margins of Micro-Economics: Price Theory as Logocentrism' in D. Carison, D. Cornell and M. Rosenfeld (eds.), *Deconstruction and the Possibility of Justice*, op cit ch 8; D. Kennedy, 'A Semiotics of Legal Argument' in R. Kevelson (ed.), *Law and Semiotics III* (1990) New York: Peter Lang; J. Balkin, 'Ideological Drift' in R. Kevelson (ed.), *Action and Agency* (1991) New York: Peter Lang; J. Boyle, 'The Anatomy of a Torts Class' (1985) 34 *American University Law Review* 1003; on Lacan and contracts, see D. Caudill, 'Lacan and Legal Langauge: Meanings in the Gaps/Gaps in the Meanings' (1992) 3 *Law and Critique*; and on Luhmann, see the symposium in volume 13 *Cardozo Law Review* (1992); also G. Teubner (ed), *Autopoietic Law* (1987) Florence: European University Press.

87. An argument forcefully made in N. Fraser, 'The French Derrideans: Politicising Deconstruction or Deconstructing the Political', reprinted in N. Fraser, *Unruly Practices*, op cit, pp 69–93; and see also the analysis of the psychoanalytic left in S. Turkle, *Psychoanalytic Politics: Freud's French Revolution* (1979) London: Deutsch; and also in E. Roudinesco, *Jacques Lacan and Co.* (1990) Chicago: University of Chicago Press. See further J. Jenson, 'Representations of Difference: The Varieties of French Feminism (1990) 180 *New Left Review* 127. See also G. Rose, *Dialectic of Nihilism: Post-Structuralism and Law* (1984) Oxford: Basil Blackwell. For further discussion, specifically related to law, see W.T. Murphy, 'Memorising Politics of Ancient History' (1987) 50 *Modern Law Review* 384.

88. The title of an untranslated series of critical legal work in France, published by an established Parisian publishing House, Francois Maspero. The early volumes in the series, particularly M. Miaille, *Une Introduction Critique au Droit* (1976) Paris: Maspero, are discussed in I. Stewart, 'Critical Legal Studies in France' (1981) 9

International Journal oi the Sociology of Law 225, but the work has otherwise met with silence. I. Stewart, 'Pour One Science Critique du Droit' (1985) 23 *Annales de Vaucresson* 201; I. Stewart, 'Law and Closure' (1987) 50 *Modern Law Review* 908, provide some interesting and important comparative analyses of critique in law. See also W. Paul, *Marxistiche Rechtstheorie als Kritik des Rechts* (1974) Frankfurt; and the German essays in C. Joerges and D. Trubek (eds.), *Critical Legal Thought*, op cit. In relation to French critical legal thought see also F. Ost and M. Van de Kerchove, *Jalons pour une Theorie Critique do Droit* (1987) Brussels: Presses Universitaires de Bruxelles; also the earlier work, J. Lenoble and F. Ost, *Droit, Mythe et Raison* (1980) Brussels: Presses Universitaire de Bruxelles. It is also something of a scandal that F. Ewald, *L'Etat Providence* (1987) Paris: Grasset; and none of the work of Pierre Legendre have yet been translated. See for recent reviews of the latter, Y. Hachamovitch, 'One Law on the Other' (1990) 3 *International Journal of the Sociology of Law*; P. Goodrich, 'Law's Emotional Body: Image and Aesthetic in the Work of Pierre Legendre', in *Languages of Law*, op cit ch 7; A. Pottage, 'Crime and Culture: The Relevance of the Psychoanalytical' (1992) 55 *Modern Law Review* 421.

89. I owe this melancholic observation to Professor Arthur Jacobson who has developed an elaborate and entertaining theory of the 'citation condominium', a self-circulating group of cross-references, a network of mutual citations inhabiting a largely hermetic or self-enclosed sphere of its own, an autopoietic system of (eternally) recurrent names.

90. Debray, *Teachers, Writers, Celebrities*, op cit at p 8.

91. See, most obviously, K. Llewellyn, 'Some Realism about Realism—Responding to Dean Pound' (1931) 44 *Harvard Law Review* 1222; and the discussion in W. Twining, *Karl Llewellyn and the Realist Movement* (1985) London: Weidenfeld and Nicolson.

92. J. Butler, *Gender Trouble: Feminism and the Subversion of Identity* (1990) New York: Routledge.

93. For an analysis of the legal field, see P Bordieu, 'The Force of Law' op cit; and more. generally, *Knowledge and Social Control* (1976) Milton Keynes: Open University Press.

94. On which point, see particularly D. Kelley, *The Human Measure: Social Thought in the Western Legal Tradition* (1990) Cambridge, Mass.: Harvard University Press.

95. P. Sloterdijhk, *Critique of Cynical Reason*, op cit, ch 4; Debray, *Critique of Political Reason*, op cit ch 7.

96. Foucault, 'The Order of Discourse' in the *Archaeology of Knowledge* (1972) New York: Pantheon Books.

97. W.T. Murphy, 'Memorising Politics of Ancient History' op cit at p 405, and remarking earlier there are some things on which it is so hard to make up one's minds (393). See further, *Writing and Difference* (1978) New York: Routledge; P Legendre, *L'Inestimable Objet de la Transmission* (1985) Paris: Fayard.

98. J.P. Dawson, Harvey and Henderson, *Contracts: Cases and Materials* (1985 ed) Foundation Press.

99. Ibid at p xxiii.

100. The term derives from the work of Fernand Braudel. See F. Braudel, *On History* (1980) Cambridge, Mass.: Harvard University Press; and for an example, F. Braudel, *The Mediterranean and the Mediterranean World* (1972) New York: Viking. See further W.T. Murphy, 'The Oldest Social Science? The Epistemic Structures of Common Law Thought', op cit; D Kelley, 'Gaius Noster: Substructures of Western Social Thought' (1979) 84 *American History Review* 619.

101. I here respond in part to comments of N. Duxbury, 'Postmodernism and its Discontents' (1991) 11 *Oxford Journal of Jurisprudence.* More generally on the theoretical context of critical legal histories, see R. Gordon, 'Critical Legal Histories' (1984) 36 *Staniord Law Review* 57; A. Hunt, 'The Theory of Critical Legal Studies', op cit pp 37–43; P. Hirst and P. Jones, 'The Critical Resources of Established Jurisprudence' (1987) 14 *Journal of Law and Society* 21; N. Rose, 'Beyond the Public/Private Division: Law, Power and the Family' (1987) 14 *Journal of Law and Society* 61; P. Goodrich, 'Ars Bablativa: Ramism, Rhetoric and the Genealogy of English Jurisprudence' in G. Leyh (ed.), *Legal Hermeneutics: History, Theory and Practice* (1992) Berkley and Los Angeles: University of California Press; G. Rubin and D. Sugarman (eds.), *Law, Economy and Society* (1984) Abingdon: Professional Books; J. Minson, *Genealogies of Morals* (1985) London: Macmillan.

102. A.W.B. Simpson, *A History of the Law Contract* (1978) Oxford: Oxford University Press; idem, 'Contracts for Cotton to Arrive' (1987) 8 *Cardozo Law Review.*

103. Simpson, 'Innovation in Nineteenth Century Contract Law' (1977) 91 *Law Ouarterly Review* 247.

104. J. Gordley *Philosophical Origins of Modern Contract Doctrine* (1991) Oxford: Oxford University Press, citing Bartolus and the Digest.

105. P.S. Atiyah, *The Rise and Fall of the Freedom of Contract* (1976) Oxford: Oxford University Press; Corbin, *Treatise on Contracts.*

106. Unger, 'Critical Legal Studies Movement', op cit; C. Dalton, 'An Essay in the Deconstruction of Contract Doctrine' (1985) 94 Yale Law Journal 997; M.J. Frug, 'A Feminist Analysis of Contracts Casebooks'

(1984) 35 American University Law Review; M.J. Frug, 'Impossibility in Contract, Doctrine' (1992) 140 University of Pennsylvania Law Review; P. Gabel and J. Feinman, in Kairys (ed.), The Politics of Law, op cit; M. Rosenfeld, 'Contract and Justice: The Relation between Classical Contract Law and Social Contract Theory' (1985) 70 Iowa Law Review 769; M. Rosenfeld, 'Hegel and the Dialectic of Contract' (1989) 10 Cardozo Law Review 1199; H. Collins, Law oi Contract (1984) London: Weidenfeld and Nicolson; P. Goodrich, 'Contractions' in A. Carty (ed.) Post-Modern Law (1990) Edinburgh: Edinburgh University Press; C. Pateman, The Sexual Contract (1985) Oxford: Polity Press; B.S. Jackson, Law, Fact and Narrative Coherence (1989) Merseyside: Deborah Charles; R. Abel, 'Torts' in D. Kairys (ed.) The Politics of Law, op cit; A. Hutchinson, Dwelling on the Threshold, op cit at ch 6 and 10. It is interesting also to note in this context that E.B. Pashukanis, Law and Marxism (1978) London: Ink Links, developed a marxist theory of law specifically predicated upon the historical linking of modern law to contractual relations. See further, R. Fine, Democracy and the Rule oi Law (1984) London: Pluto Press; R. Cotterrell and B. Bercusson (eds.), 'Law Democracy and Social Justice' (1988) 15.1 *Journal of Law and Society.*

107. On, or of, grammatology, see J. Derrida, *Of Grammatology* (1976) Baltimore, MD: Johns Hopkins University Press, where grammatology is depicted as the study of systems of inscription: "if writing signifies inscription and especially the durable institution of the sign...writing in general covers the entire field of linguistic signs" (44) Grammatology proposes an interrogation into the significance of the fact that law is written. More than that, "the science of writing should...look for its object at the roots of scientificity. The history of writing should turn back toward the origin of historicity. A science of the possibility of science? A science of science which would no longer have the form of *logic* but that of *grammatics?* A history of the possibility of history...?" (27–28) See also J. Derrida, *Positions* (1981) Chicago: Chicago University Press. For an analysis of grammatology in terms of the history of legal writing, see P. Goodrich, 'Rhetoric, Grammatology and the Hidden Injuries of Law' (1989) 18 *Economy and Society* 167. See also P. Goodrich, 'Specula Laws: Image, Aesthetic and Common Law' (1991) 2 *Law and Critique* 233.

108. On which, see particularly William West, *Symbolaeography: The Art or Description or Image of Instruments, or the Paterne of Presidents or the Notarie or Scrivener* (1590/1603 ed.) London: Society of Stationers; also T. Phayr, *A New Boke of Presidentes, in Manner of a Register* (1544) London: E. Whytchurche. On the use of icons and objects as signs of donation, contract and law, see M.T. Clanchy, *From Memory to Written Record* (1979) London: Arnold; J. Goody, *Writing and the Organisation of Society* (1987) Cambridge: Cambridge University Press.

109. Jacobson, 'The Idolatry of Rules', op cit at 1095.

110. As in Plato, on which see J. Derrida, *Dissemination* (1981) Chicago: Chicago University Press. See further, J. Lacan, *Four Fundamental Concepts of Psychoanalysis* (1978) London: Pelican; J. Lacan, *Seminaire V: L'Ethique de Psychanalyse* (1985) Paris; P. Legendre, *Le Crime de Caporal Lortie: Traite sur le Pere* (1988) Paris: Fayard; D. Cornell, *Beyond Accommodation* op cit, especially pp 41 ff.

111. Jacobson, 'Idolatry of Rules' op cit at p 1132.

112. Murphy, 'Memorising Politics of Ancient History', op cit at p 387. See further, P. Legendre, 'Les Maitres de la Loi: Etude sur la fonction dogmatique en regime industriel', in Legendre, *Ecrits Juridiques du Moyen Age occidental* (1988) London: Variorum; W.T. Murphy, 'The Oldest Social Science? The Epistemic Properties of the Common Law Tradition' (1991) 54 *Modern Law Review* 182. C.f. G. Rose, *Dialectic of Nihilism*, op cit pp 77–84.

113. On which fascinating etymology, see E. Benveniste, *Le Vocabulaire des Institutions Indo-Europeenes*, op cit. vol I.

114. In West, *Symbolaeography*, op cit, passim.

115. J. Derrida, *The Post Card*, op cit, p 20.

116. C. Pateman, *The Sexual Contract*, op cit at p 1.

117. R. Filmer, *Patriarcha or the Natural Power of Kings* (1680) London: W. Davis, at p 20.

118. See particularly P. Legendre, *L'Inestimable Objet de la Transmission*, op cit, at p 35.

119. *Digest* 1.1.2.

120. Thus, for example, D. Kennedy, 'The Structure of Blackstone's Commentaries' (1979) 28 *Buffalo Law Review* 205. J. Boyle, 'On Hobbes'; C. Gordon.

121. The list is not a long one, but for dramatic—and perhaps dramatistic—examples, see particularly A. Hutchinson, *Dwelling on the Threshold*, op cit, (particularly 'Indiana Dworkin and Law's Empire'); P. Williams, *The Alchemy of Race and Rights* (1991) Cambridge, Mass.: Harvard University Press; D. Cornell, *Beyond Accommodation*, op cit; P. Schlag, 'Normative and Nowhere to Go' (1991) 43 *Stanford Law Review*, and for a remarkable European example, C. Douzinas, R. Warrington, S. McVeigh, *Postmodern Jurisprudence*. op cit Part III.

122. This point has been made in many different ways. M. Foucault, 'Intellectuals and Power' in Foucault, *Language, Counter-*

Memory, Practice, op cit, and M. Foucault, *Power/Knowledge* (1980) New York: Pantheon Books, probably provides one of the more important analyses of new kind of politics. See also J. Derrida, *Du Droit a la Philosophie* (1991) Paris: Galilee, Part III. Specifically in relation to the legal tradition, see J. Derrida, 'Force of Law' op cit; P. Schlag, 'Le Hors de Texte C'Est Moi', op cit; D. Cornell, *The Philosophy of the Limit*, op cit, pp 170–183; G. Bruns, 'Law and Language' in G. Leyh (ed.), *Legal Hermeneutics: History, Theory and Practice*, op cit., pp 23–40.

123. P. Bordieu, *Homo Academicus* op cit at pp 125–127, associates political radicalism with marginal disciplines or with institutionally threatened individuals. R. Debray, *Teachers, Writers, Celebrities*, op cit, similarly associates the new high intelligensia with a structurally co-opted clericism, and see also R. Debray, *Modeste Contribution aux discours et ceremonies officiels du dixieme anniversaire* (1978) Paris: Maspero, taking a position close to that of the classic P. Nizan, *Les Chiens de Garde* (1932) Paris. In an American context, see D. Jacoby, *The Last Intellectuals*, op cit, at p 186 and 190: (discussing the movement of the new left intelligensia into the universities) "In the United states, however, a dissenting or Marxist culture has never been firmly established; it is diffuse, fragile and frequently lost...the influx of left scholars has not changed the picture; reluctantly or enthusiastically they gain respectability at the cost of identity". For discussion of law and intellectual radicalism, see P Goodrich, *Legal Discourse*, op cit, at pp 205–212; P. Fitzpatrick, 'The Abstracts and Brief Chronicles of the Times: Supplementing Jurisprudence' in P. Fitzpatrick (ed), *Dangerous Supplements* (1991) Durham, NC: Duke University Press; C. Smart, *Feminism and the Power of Law* (1989) London: Routledge, ch 1.

124. P. Anderson, *Considerations on Western Marxism*, op cit, at p 88; and the later analysis in P. Anderson, 'Modernity and Revolution' (1984) 144 *New Left Review* 96.

125. J. Baudrillard, *La Transparence du Mal*, op cit at pp 19–21.

126. D. Jacoby, *The Last Intellectuals*, op cit, especially pp 180–190; P. Dews, *Logics of Disintegration*, op cit at pp xiv–xvii. C.f. F. Jameson, *Late Marxism* (1990) London: Verso, pp 227–250.

127. See P. Goodrich, *Languages of Law*, op cit; and Douzinas, Warrington, McVeigh, *Postmodern Jurisprudence*, op. cit. ch 2.

128. On the politics of seduction, see particularly J. Baudrillard, *Seduction* (1990) London: Macmillan; also S. Zizek, *For they Know not What they Do*, op cit. C.f. A Callinicos, *Against Postmodernism: A Marxist Critique* (1989) London: Polity Press; also T. Eagleton, *The Ideology of the Aesthetic* (1990) Oxford: Blackwell. More generally, J. Kristeva, *Revolution in Poetic Language* (1984) New York: Columbia University Press; R. Braidotti, *Patterns of Dissonance* (1990) Oxford:

Polity Press; H. Cixous, *Coming to Writing* (1991) Cambridge, Mass.: Harvard University Press.

129. For a preliminary analysis of this issue, see P. Goodrich, 'Eating Law: Commons, Common Land, Common Law' (1991) 12 *Journal of Legal History* 246.

130. In this respect D. Kennedy, *Legal Education as Training for Hierarchy* (1982) Cambridge: Afar, is perceptive and informative. See additionally, C. McCabe (ed.), *The Linguistics of Writing* (1991) Manchester: Manchester University Press; P. Goodrich, 'Psychoanalysis in Legal Education', in Kevelson, R (ed.), *Law and Semiotics I*, (1988) New York, Plenum Press.

10

TERESA L. EBERT _____

Writing in the Political: Resistance (Post)Modernism

(POST)MODERNISM AND THE CRISIS OF (TRANSFORMATIVE) POLITICS

This text stems from a concern over the present situation in which the (post)modern is increasingly seen as the end of transformative politics.[1] Different critics attribute this eclipse of the political to a variety of factors, from Jean Baudrillard's "disaffected masses,"[2] Jean-François Lyotard's "incredulity toward meta-narratives,"[3] to the overwhelming commodification and fragmentation of reality in advanced capitalism, making the (post)modern what Fredric Jameson calls the "logic of late capitalism".[4] As I argued at the 1990 conference on *Rewriting the (Post)Modern: (Post)Colonialism/Feminism/Late Capitalism*, at which an earlier version of this text was presented, what is urgently necessary is a sustained retheorization of the crisis of the political in (post)modernity. Instead of simply asserting the common view of the political as "outside" of and opposed to the (post)modern, what is needed on the contrary is not only a critique of the current situation but also a (re)writing of the political back into the (post)modern.

I would like to address my remarks here to the political consequences of the more "philosophical" side of this crisis where politics—as the basis for a transformative practice—has largely been displaced by the advent of politics as rhetoric: politics as an issue of signification. The deconstruction of grand narratives, of totality, the referent, experience and truth as unfounded and self-divided has in effect erased not only the question of economics but also the struggle of the subject in history toward a society free from exploitation. The consequences of this shift in the concept of the political in (post)modern discourses are profound for how we understand our world and effect social change. In terms of what knowledge—what "truth"—do we act? What is the basis for an emancipatory practice? In fact, the (post)modern critique of the founding concepts of Western thought, particularly those inherited from the Enlightenment, has even called into question emancipation itself as a political agenda. In its place we find the post-structuralist notion of politics as merely the disruption of the ready-made meanings of culture—a notion that is becoming so dominant, it is now common to call our age "post-political."[5]

The urgent issue at stake in turning (post)modern politics from a "post-politics" into a "transformative politics," to my mind, is the issue of *difference*: how to conceive of difference politically rather than rhetorically or textually, as well as how to rethink "collectivity" in/after "difference." To do so, we first need to distinguish between what I call "ludic (post)modernism" and "resistance (post)modernism." Ludic (post)modernism finds its articulation in the disappearance of the transcendental signified, as in such writers as Jacques Derrida, Lyotard and Baudrillard, for whom reality is a theatre of "simulation" marked by the free play of images, disembodied signifiers and the heterogeneity of difference. According to this metanarrative (which denounces metanarratives and denies being a metanarrative), (post)modernism does not know historical boundaries—or rather "history" itself becomes a free-floating trace of textuality—thus (post)modernity, for ludic (post)modernists, is the name of a recurring crisis in the metanarratives of culture, whether in the Renaissance or in the present.[6] (Post)modernism, for these thinkers, is the mark of a subversive practice that displaces those grand narratives—such as "exploitation" and "emancipation"—that provide the larger frames of intelligibility for culture and legitimate specific constructions of reality.

Ludic (post)modernism is best conceptualized as a crisis of the mode of signification, a crisis in which texts constituted by difference can no longer provide reliable knowledge of the real because meaning itself is self-divided and undecidable: the access of the signifier to the signified is delayed and deferred, divided by a *difference within*. Ludic (post)modernism emphasizes this traffic of differ*a*nce as dividing and dispersing all cultural practices—including "politics." Thus politics and its foundations, for ludic (post)modernists, are traversed by differance, making them self-divided, dispersed and unreliable. This movement of differance deprives politics of its groundedness in such categories of seeming identity, "presence" and plenitude as race, class, gender and state. Moreover, differance dismantles the notion of politics itself as being an "outside" to representation —as a clear, unmediated "referent" for action. Politics, for ludic (post)modernists, is instead a textual practice (e.g., parody, pastiche, fragmentation...) that obscures prevailing meanings: it disrupts the oppressive totality of what Lyotard calls "cultural policy" through "play," "gaming," experimentation in writing and transgressive readings that subvert the "rules" of grand narratives and prevent the easy circulation of meaning in culture.[7] Thus radical politics for ludic (post)modernists problematizes signifying practices and established meanings, demonstrating that in every entity there is a surplus of meaning—an "excess"—a difference that prevents any given category from being a reliable ground for reality in general and politics in particular. Such a subversive politics of signification is seen as a liberating gesture, deconstructing the totalities—the grand narratives—organizing reality. Ludic (post)modernism substitutes a politics of differences within entities for the politics of differences between identities such as race, class and gender.

Ludic (post)modernism—whether in poststructuralism or in the pastiche of "styles" in Michael Graves' architecture;[8] Terry Gilliams' film, *Brazil*; Madonna's videos or Donald Barthelme's fiction[9]—is in effect a cognitivism and an immanent critique that reduces politics to rhetoric and history to textuality and in the end cannot provide the basis for a transformative social practice. However, I would argue that we should not easily dismiss it, because it does effectively denaturalize and destabilize the dominant regime of knowledge and the naturalization of the status quo in the common sense. And in problematizing politics it prevents a simple, positivistic practice and calls into question a politics based on essentializing *differences between* seemingly self-contained and stable identities. But this seems to be all it does: ludic (post)modernism removes the ground from under both the revolutionary and the reactionary and in the name of difference effectively conceals radical difference. It does not transform practices; it merely prevents their continuation. Ludic politics is, in the last instance, a Socratic, dialogic, discursive apparatus. It helps to clarify the issues from the perspective of representation, but in doing so, it turns politics into ethics. The issue then for radical politics is how to rewrite the (post)modern *difference within*—differance—not as a ludic difference but as a historical, *political difference*, a materialized, resisting differance.

I would like to propose *resistance (post)modernism* as the activation of this political difference. Resistance (post)-modernism contests the ludic notion of difference as textuality, as a formal, rhetorical space in which representation narrates its own trajectory of signification and argues, instead, that difference is social and historical. Resistance (post)modernism does not simply reject textuality or rhetoric, nor does it return to a pre-determined reference, but rather contends that textuality and difference—the relation of signifier and signified—are themselves the sites of social conflict and struggle. They are not panhistorical spaces of eternal ahistorical slippage and excess. In short, significations acquire meaning not from their formal system—as Ferdinand de Saussure's *Course in General Linguistics* proposes—but from their place in the social struggle over "meanings": the "sign" itself is an arena of social conflict, to paraphrase V. N. Volosinov-Bakhtin in his *Marxism and the Philosophy of Language*.[10]

But what specifically does it mean to say the sign is the arena of social struggle? First, we need to retheorize the sign not as the correspondence between a single signifier and signified (as in humanist linguistics) nor as a free-floating chain of signifiers (as in poststructuralist semantics). Instead, we can rewrite the sign as an ideological process formed out of a signifier standing in relation to a matrix of historically possible or suspended signifieds. The signifier becomes temporarily connected to a specific signified through social struggle in which the prevailing ideology and social contradictions put forth a particular signified. Such a relation is insecure, continually contested and changeable. Signifieds are challenged, struggled-over and displaced by opposing ideologies asserting other signifieds in relation to a particular signifier in order to support their own signifying practices and regime of representation and thus to propose their own "real" for culture. The signified which gets picked-up and inscribed in the relation of signification is the one that contributes to the legitimation of the prevailing ideology—obviously, the prevailing ideology is not always the dominant one; in a specific local site of struggle, the prevailing ideology can temporarily be the opposing ideology. Also, keep in mind, that since the relation between signifier and signified is continually struggled-over, the assertion of an oppositional meaning or signified can be readily displaced and appropriated by the dominant ideology. Examples of the social struggles over signifiers and their signifieds include those over the terms "negro," "black" and "African-American," or those over the signifieds assigned to fetuses—whether these should include the full legal rights and meanings of persons.

Radical political action for a resistance (post)modernism then is not merely a subversion of signification but a *critique* and *intervention* in social struggle in order to provide equal access to social resources and to transform the dominant power relations which limit this access according to class privilege, race and gender. Resistance (post)modernism acknowledges that these restrictions are naturalized in the dominant systems of representation, and as such it addresses the way social struggle is enacted in signification and the ways signification is used for oppression.

I would like to suggest that the main conflict over politics in (post)modernity is thus the contestation between two radically different notions of politics:

(1) Politics as open access to the free play of signification (through parody, irony and experimentation) in order to dissemble the dominant cultural policy (the totality) that tries to restrict and stabilize meaning; and

(2) Politics as the practice aimed at "equal" access for all to social resources and an end to the exploitative exercise of power.

One of the main points of contention between these two notions of the political, I would argue, is the issue of "totality." To transform people's access to social resources and to end exploitation requires a notion of totality in order to critique the systematicity and global relations of oppression. But the first mode of politics—"ludic politics"—does not merely disrupt specific totalities, it discredits any inquiry into the concept of totality as an instance of totalitarianism, and thereby occludes any critique of power as a *system* of unequal relations involving the powerful and powerless. Ludic politics relies on an immanent notion of power, and instead of systems of power such as capitalism or patriarchy, it proposes localities (like prisons or clinics) in which power is not merely repressive but positively enabling since it produces its own "resistance."[11] Power in ludic politics is aleatory and asystematic. Thus for many (post)-modernists, the main agenda of ludic politics follows Lyotard's battle cry to "wage a war on totality."[12] And this ludic "non-totalization," according to Derrida, can be "determined...from the standpoint of the concept of *play*. If totalization no longer has any meaning, it is...because the nature of the field—that is, language and a finite language—excludes totalization. This field is in effect that of *play*."[13] In short, ludic (post)modernists reject totality as a political concept in favor of a pluralistic difference in which concrete specificity seems all-inclusive and capable of countering the exclusions of the repressive hierarchical regimes of grand narratives. But pluralism itself involves a very insidious exclusion as far as any politics of change is concerned: it excludes and occludes global or structural relations of power as "ideological" and "totalizing." It excludes, in effect, the systematicity of regimes of exploitation on the flimsiest of all grounds. In Jameson's words: "at least a few of the most strident of the anti-totality positions are based on that silliest of all puns, the confusion of 'totality' with 'totalitarianism.'"[14]

In contrast to the detotalizing, Foucauldian micropolitics of ludic (post)modernism, the second form of politics—a transformative politics—reasserts the necessity of totality. But not totality seen as an organic, homogeneous, unified whole, as a Hegelian expressive unity. Rather, we need to reunderstand totality as both a system of relations and an *overdetermined structure of difference*. For difference, as I argue resistance (post)modernism rewrites it, is always *difference in relation*, that is, *difference within a system of power and the social struggle it engenders*. A system is thus always self-divided, different from itself and multiple: it is traversed by *differences within*, by differance. Or to be more precise, a system (a social totality) is divided by historical contradictions and social conflicts. But in much (post)modern thought, ludic difference—a dislocated, free-floating difference—displaces and substitutes for social contradictions. However, when we rewrite difference as *difference-in-relation*, we show how differences are never free-floating or isolated differences within such formal ensembles as language. Rather differences coalesce into social contradictions, into the "other" inscribed within the system. Moreover, most existing systems of differences are organized into patterns of domination and subordination; they involve power relations, oppression and exploitation and thus social conflict. Since such patterns are never fixed and stable, but are always themselves divided by difference—divided, that is, by their "other(s)"—they are split by contradictions and thus open to change. This concern with the economy of relations of difference within historically specific totalities is the key issue of transformative politics—and its main difference from ludic politics—for transformative politics sees its task as intervening in the power relations organizing difference in order to end the oppression and exploitation grounded on them. If totalities are structures of differences, and thus multiple, unstable, and changeable arenas of contradictions and social struggle, then they are open to contestation and transformation.

But such transformations are themselves contingent on analyzing the ways in which the operations of power and the organization of differences in a specific system are *over-determined* by other systems of difference. Systems of differences are also situated in a social formation—which is itself a structure of differences made up of other systems of differences, including the social, economic, political, legal, cultural and ideological. Thus systems of differences are determinate, but they also act on each other and their relations and differences in *overdetermined ways.*

RESISTANCE (POST)MODERNISM AND FEMINISM

What are the consequences of this rewriting of difference for understanding historically specific totalities such as patriarchy? Also, what is the contribution that resistance (post)modernism can make to social movements such as feminism? Despite the diversity and conflict within feminism over (post)modern discourses, feminists, by-and-large, share ludic politics' rejection of totality and immersion in the concrete, the local and specific— whether that specificity is defined as women's experience or as a tropic excess. One need only compare such different feminists as Elaine Showalter, Jane Gallop, and Denise Riley to see that all their writings have the same *effect* in their focus on the local and specific avoidance of the issue of systematicity.[15] Moreover, feminists are increasingly embracing ludic micropolitics with its aleatory, diffuse, nonsystematic notion of power as evident in Donna Haraway's text, "A Manifesto for Cyborgs," which has become the exemplar of ludic (post)modern feminism. In short, feminists tend to regard (post)modernism as synonymous with ludic discourses and practices and fail to see that (post)-modernism is itself divided by a radical difference.

As a result such different feminists as Haraway, on the one hand, and Linda Nicholson and Nancy Fraser, on the other, are articulating a politically very counter-productive form of (post)-modern feminism in their celebration of a local pluralism and their "war" on other feminists as totalizing. For instance, Nicholson and Fraser, in their widely disseminated essay, "Social Criticism Without Philosophy," reproduce Lyotard's confusion of totality with universal metanarratives and use it to discredit a number of feminist theories as "quasi-metanarratives." They advocate instead a "concrete," "localized, issue-oriented" inquiry into difference: one that "would dispense with the idea of a subject of history."[16] Similarly Haraway attempts, in "A Manifesto for Cyborgs," to rewrite a socialist, materialist feminism as an "argument for pleasure in the confusion of boundaries"; as a local network of differences among women, and as a rejection of any notion of system and totality because it is an "erasure of polyvocal, unassimilable...difference."

In feminism the war on totality, as both these essays demonstrate, has meant especially a war on those feminist theorists who have attempted to articulate the systematicity of patriarchal oppression and gender exploitation. The core of Haraway's "Manifesto," for example, is an attack on Catharine MacKinnon's radical feminism as "a caricature of the appropriating, incorporating, totalizing tendencies of western theories of identity grounding action."[18] In fact, MacKinnon has become the most prominent "straw-woman" for attacks on feminist totalizing—so much so that *The Nation's* reviewer called her both "Lenin" and "Hitler."[19] Such attacks on committed feminists like MacKinnon, who has long been on the frontlines of critique and intervention in the systematic exploitation of women's sexuality and labor, should be a serious warning to us to rethink the political consequences of feminist involvement in ludic (post)modernism.[20] The local pluralism of ludic (post)modernism and much recent feminism is far from being a new, nonrepressive inclusivity: as I have already emphasized, it excludes and occludes the critiques of global or structural relations of power by calling them "totalizing." In contrast, resistance (post)modernism, as I am articulating it here, enables feminists to retheorize totality and to insist on the critique of systematicity for any transformative politics.

The concept of totality is basic to feminism—perhaps even more than the notion of identity which is the focus of so much current debate. The specific, historical totality of patriarchy, I would argue, is the fundamental category of a transformative feminist politics. It is, as the socialist-feminist Maria Mies argues, the necessary "struggle concept" for feminism because it conveys both "the totality of oppressive and exploitative relations which affect women...as well as their systematic character."[21] Yet, the interrogation of patriarchy as a system has largely been abandoned by much recent feminism under the pressure of the critique of grand narratives and totalities by ludic (post)-modernism. These feminisms—from poststructuralists and psychoanalytic critics to social theorists and gynocritics—attempt a critique of the *effects* of patriarchy without adequately addressing the operation of patriarchy as a *system*, an ongoing regime of exploitation.[22] In short, they commonly dismiss patriarchy as an essentialized, universal and transhistorical concept and, instead, reduce it to merely a specific, local "context," or simply a descriptive marker, such as "male dominated," "Masculinist," "androcentric," "phallocentric" and "phallogocentric," all of which are metonymically substituted for patriarchy as the systematic exercises of gender exploitation. Patriarchy, in short, has become suppressed (the *unsaid*) in recent feminist theory. Moreover, for many feminists and (post)-modern critics alike, the decline of traditional forms of patriarchy is read as the advent of a "post-patriarchy."

However, when we rewrite patriarchy in terms of a conjunc-tion of resistance (post)modernism and feminism—what I call a *(post)modern materialist feminism*—we can understand patri-archy as an *economy of differences* and not as a unified, homo-genous "totalitarian totality" nor as a fragmented, dispersed, free-floating power. Patriarchy organizes all differences according to a hierarchy of gender divisions which it represents as natural and inevitable. But such an organization of dif-ferences is not fixed and stable but traversed by contradictions and continually contested and struggled-over by the other: that is, by differences excluded, suppressed and exploited. *Patriarchy is thus a totality in process*, a self-divided, multiple arena of social struggle. The differences and contradictions within patriarchy congeal at specific historical moments, providing sites of oppositions and producing scenes of alternative subjectivities and significations in which individuals can take-up their place as resisting agents. Feminism is thus generated out of the confluence of differences and contradictions within patriarchy itself. Thus the site from which I speak as a feminist rewriting feminism rewriting patriarchy is an unstable, fluctuating place within the convergence of some of those contradictions, struggles and differences within patriarchy.

Although patriarchy is multiple, fragmented and divided, it is able to represent itself as a seeming unity that is coherent, inviolable and always the same, in other words, continuous; but this is an ideological effect—which is not to say that this highly differentiated and contradictory structure is not hegemonic. Obviously it is hegemonic, and patriarchy as such has been extraordinarily effective in reproducing its hegemony and projecting its illusory unity throughout recorded history so that it *seems* transhistorical and synonymous with human nature and society. But this seeming historical "continuity" is not so much the continuity of the same as it is, rather, a historical series of *different* reconfigurations (reforms) of the patriarchal, gendered ordering of difference in conjunction with other systems of difference. In other words, different reconfigurations of an ongoing structure of oppression. More specifically, patriarchy reproduces itself differently in relation to diverse modes of production—for example, the variations between feudal patriarchy and capitalist patriarchy.

Patriarchy is a global relation of oppression based on a hierarchical organization of gendered differences in which men as a group are privileged and women as a group are exploited. At the same time, patriarchy is "different from itself" and "different in history"; in other words, the specific articulation of oppression is diverse and varied. Patriarchy, then, is continuous on the level of the structure or organization of oppression and dis-continuous (different from itself) on the level of the enunciation of particular, local practices of oppression. In short, patriarchy is a differentiated, contradictory structure that produces *identical effects* differently. For instance, the specific configuration of the economy of differences in (post)modern, late capitalist patriarchy in the United States is quite distinct from the configuration of differences in contemporary fundamentalist Iran, and both of these vary from those found in feudal Europe. Yet for all their *differences-in-relation* to each other, they share the same dominant organization of differences according to the binary opposition of male/female. They produce the same *effects*: the oppression and exclusion of woman as other. Women in (post)modern patriarchal America, Islamic fundamentalist Iran and feudal Europe share the same collective identity that results from—is an effect of—their shared position (their "post") within the global patriarchal structure of oppression. But women occupy the "same" position within patriarchy differently. Thus their "identity" is not identical; they are not the "same" as each other although they are all subjects of the same structures of oppression. Nor are they the "same" in their difference from men: within the economy of power relations they are all situated in the same asymmetrical position, but they are subjugated in that position differently.

Moreover the position of women is not necessarily synonymous with their biological sex and cultural subjectivity as women. Benazir Bhutto, for instance, was, until recently, Prime Minister of Pakistan, a fundamentalist Islamic country, but this did not in any way alter the position of women within that patriarchal system of oppression. She was in that position in spite of the fact that she is biologically and culturally female— perhaps even *because of* this fact. She was in the position of Prime Minister as the patriarchal agent and heir of a specific familial and class domination of power, which she has represented and enforced. She was unable to oppose and alter the specific hegemony of patriarchal power—in other words, to govern from the position of woman, from the position of opposition to women's exploitation—to do so would have jeopardized her position as Prime Minister and her power as patriarchal agent. Bhutto's situation was made especially clear in her interview with Tom Jarriel on a segment of ABC's *20/20*, entitled "Veil of Darkness,"[23] when she admitted that she could not overturn the "Zina Laws." This legal regime, also known as the "Hudood Ordinance," is an especially oppressive set of fundamentalist Islamic laws enacted by the previous Prime Minister Zia, according to which a woman can be publicly flogged and jailed for up to ten years (although many remain in jail indefinitely) on charges of adultery made without any evidence or cause for suspicion, simply on the word of a neighbor. Even more alarming, a woman who reports being raped can be prosecuted for adultery on her own evidence while the rapist goes free.[24] Hundreds of women remained in jail under "Bhutto's reign," with her knowledge, and in spite of concerted protests by Pakistani women's organizations, because she can only govern from the overdetermined position (the "post") of patriarchal agency.

Thus for all her power, Bhutto has occupied the "same" position differently within the patriarchal structure of oppression than has a young Pakistani village girl who, during Bhutto's reign, refused to marry the middle-aged widower who "asked" for her hand and was gang-raped by the village men for violating patriarchal "Law." On the specific level of the enunciation of oppression, women are produced differently as women in each system and in relation to the differences in the other systems. For the specific position of each woman is "overdetermined" in that she is produced differently in conjunction with the other systems acting on her in terms of class, race, nationality, ethnicity, age and so on. Benazir Bhutto, for instance, has been produced by the "overdetermined" conjunction of colonialism and Westernization—she was educated at Radcliffe and Oxford—along with the wealth, power and political position of her extended family and class, whereas the position of the young Pakistani village girl has been "overdetermined" by the specific articulation of poverty, rural isolation, lack of education and rigidly intact, traditional forms of patriarchy. The two women are thus situated very differently in the "same" position in patriarchal structures of oppression—they share a collective identity as women, as the Other. Should either woman step outside the parameters of variation and limited resistance allotted them by the specific articulations of patriarchy—again these parameters vary for women in different conjunctures—and should they fundamentally oppose the structures of patriarchal oppression, Prime Minister and village girl alike will be harshly penalized—*but in different ways.*

Obviously an effective political critique and a (post)modern materialist feminist intervention needs to investigate specific, local enunciations of patriarchal oppression. But it cannot rest there, as many ludic (post)modern and feminist critiques do; instead it must also relate the specific position and differences of women back to the global relations of patriarchal oppression and critique the systematic operation of these relations. As my example of the Pakistani Prime Minister and the village girl demonstrated, for all the immense diversity among women on the level of the local manifestations of patriarchy, we must also analyze their relation to the dominating structures of oppression, no matter how differently they occupy that "same" position, in order to understand the dimensions of patriarchal oppression which extend from the seemingly powerful Prime Minister down to the obviously powerless village girl.

Thus an emancipatory politics that seeks to intervene in and transform patriarchal structures of oppression which organize and "overdetermine" every woman (and in a different way, every man) can only be formulated, I propose, through the critique of the global relations of difference, through an intervention in the structures of oppression: both at the macropolitical level of their structural organization of domination and at the micropolitical level of different and contradictory manifestations of oppression. Ludic (post)modernism and much recent feminist theory, whether *l'ecriture feminine* or the current advocacy of pluralism, all tend to confine their analysis to the micropolitics of oppression and the local level of differences and thereby inhibit any effective intervention in the structures of totalities like patriarchy. I believe resistance (post)modernism and (post)modern materialist feminism, with their dialectical critiques of both the macro-structures of difference-in-relation and the specific enunciations of these micro-differences, will develop a transformative theory and practice that can contribute to the end of patriarchal exploitation.

NOTES

1. For a fuller elaboration of the arguments presented here, in relation to "ludic" and "resistance" (post)modern feminism, see my essay, "Ludic Feminism, the Body, Performance, and Labor: Bringing *Materialism* Back into Feminist Cultural Studies," *Cultural Critique*, no. 23 (Winter 1992-93): 5–50, and my book, *Ludic Feminism and After* (forthcoming). Also of interest is Peter McClaren's deployment of the concepts of "ludic" and "resistance" (post)modernism articulated here for a multicultural critical pedagogy. See his text, "Multiculturalism and the Postmodern Critique: Towards a Pedagogy of Resistance and Transformation," *Cultural Studies*, special issue on The Politics of Pedagogy/The Pedagogy of Culture(s) guest edited by Henry A. Giroux and Peter McLaren, vol. 7:1 (1993): 118–46. [The conference, *Rewriting the (Post)Modern: (Post)Colonialism/Feminism/Late Capitalism*, was organized by Teresa Ebert and held at the University of Utah on March 30–31, 1990. —Ed.]

2. See Jean Baudrillard, *In the Shadow of the Silent Majorities...or, the End of the Social*, trans. Paul Foss et al., New York: Semiotext(e) (1983); *Simulations*, trans. Paul Foss et al., New York: Semiotext(e) (1983); *For a Critique of the Political Economy of the Sign*, trans. Charles Levin, St. Louis: Telos (1981); and *The Mirror of Production*, trans. Mark Poster, St. Louis: Telos (1975). See also Charles Levin, "Baudrillard, Critical Theory and Psychoanalysis," *Canadian Journal of Political and Social Theory*, vol. 8:1–2 (Winter/Spring 1984) : 35–52.

358 *Ebert*

3. See Jean-Francois Lyotard, *The Postmodern Condition: A Report on Knowledge*, trans. Geoff Bennington and Brian Massumi, Minneapolis: University of Minnesota Press (1984 xxiv).

4. See Fredric Jameson, "Postmodernism, or The Cultural Logic of Late Capitalism," *New Left Review*, no. 146 (1984): 53–92; see also Anders Stephanson, "Regarding Postmodernism—A Conversation with Fredric Jameson," in *Universal Abandon?: The Politics of Postmodernism*, ed., Andrew Ross, Minneapolis: University of Minnesota Press (1988): 3–30.

5. See Ernesto Laclau and Chantal Mouffe, *Hegemony and Socialist Strategy*, London: Verso (1985).

6. See, e.g., Jonathan Goldberg, *Voice Terminal Echo: Postmodernism and English Renaissance Texts*, New York: Methuen (1986); Herman Rappaport, *Milton and the Postmodern*, Lincoln: University of Nebraska Press (1983).

7. See Lyotard, *The Postmodern Condition* at 6–17, 73–79.

8. See Charles Jencks, *The Language of Post-Modern Architecture*, 4th rev. ed., New York: Rizzoli International Publications (1984); Fredric Jameson, "Architecture and the Critique of Ideology," in *The Ideologies of Theory: Essays 1971–1986*, Minneapolis: University of Minnesota Press (1988): 35–60.

9. See Teresa Ebert, "Postmodern Politics, Patriarchy and Donald Barthelme," *The Review of Contemporary Fiction* (Summer 1991).

10. Compare Ferdinand de Saussure, *Course in General Linguistics*, trans. Wade Baskin, New York: McGraw-Hill (1966), and V.N. Volosinov-Bakhtin, *Marxism and the Philosophy of Language*, New York: Seminar Press (1973) at 23.

11. See Michel Foucault, *The History of Sexuality, Volume I: An Introduction*, trans. Robert Hurley, New York: Vintage (1980) at 92–102.

12. See Lyotard, *The Postmodern Condition* at 82.

13. See Jacques Derrida, "Structure, Sign, and Play in the Discourse of the Human Sciences," in *Writing and Difference*, trans. Alan Bass, Chicago: University of Chicago Press (1978) at 289.

14. See Fredric Jameson, "*History and Class Consciousness* as an 'Unfinished' Project'," *Rethinking Marxism*, vol. 1:1 (1988) at 60.

15. See Elaine Showalter, "Feminist Criticism in the Wilderness" and "Towards a Feminist Poetics," in *The New Feminist Criticism*, ed., E. Showalter, New York: Pantheon (1985): 243–70, 125–43. See Jane Gallop, *Thinking Through the Body*, New York: Columbia University

Press (1988); and *The Daughter's Seduction: Feminism and Psycho-analysis*, Ithaca: Cornell University Press (1982). See Denise Riley, *"Am I That Name?" Feminism and the Category of "Women" in History*, Minneapolis: University of Minnesota Press (1988).

16. See Linda Nicholson and Nancy Fraser, "Social Criticism Without Philosophy: An Encounter Between Feminism and Post-modernism," in *Feminism/Postmodernism*, ed., Linda Nicholson, New York: Routledge (1990) at 31–34. See T. Ebert, "Postmodernism's Infinite Variety," *The Women's Review of Books*, vol. 8:4 (Jan. 1991): 24–25, and responses in vol. 8:6 (Mar. 1991): 4–5.

17. See Donna Haraway, "A Manifesto for Cyborgs: Science, Technology, and Socialist Feminism in the 1980's," in *Feminism/Postmodernism* at 191, 201.

18. See Haraway, "A Manifesto for Cyborgs," 200.

19. See Maureen Mullarkey, "Hard Cop, Soft Cop," *The Nation* (30 May 1987): 720–26.

20. Another telling example of the ludic feminist delegitimation and exclusion of MacKinnon and interventionist feminism in the name of (post)modernism is a recent experience of mine. One of my essays on resistance (post)modern feminism was rejected by two editors of a special issue on feminism and (post)modernism for two main reasons: first, my critique of ludic (post)modernism; and second—significantly— my use of MacKinnon's statistics on rape in developing a materialist (post)modern critique of Jane Gallop's ludic feminist celebration of the Marcuis de Sade because, as the editors said, MacKinnon's statistics "are after all embedded in a hiqhly polemical argument many of whose essentializing premises don't seem at all compatible with yours!" The issue here for resistance (post)modern feminism is to question and critique this blanket rejection of radical, interventionist feminist theories, such as those of MacKinnon, as "essentializing" and "totalizing" and to recognize the way such exclusion participates in the reactionary ludic (post)modern attack on systematic critiques of gender exploitation and oppression.

21. See Marie Mies, *Patriarchy and Accumulation on a World Scale: Women in the International Division of Labour*, London and Atlantic Highlands: Zed Books (1986) at 37.

22. See, e.g., Luce Irigaray, *Speculum of the Other Woman*, trans. Gillian Gill, Ithaca: Cornell University Press (1985); Alice Jardine, *Gynesis: Configurations of Woman and Modernity*, Ithaca: Cornell University Press (1985): Gayatri Chakravorty Spivak, *In Other Worlds: Essays in Cultural Politics*, New York: Methuen (1987); Constance Penley, *The Future of an Illusion: Film, Feminism, Psychoanalysis*,

Minneapolis: University of Minnesota Press (1989); and Joan Scott, *Gender and the Politics of History*, New York: Columbia University Press (1989).

23. Tom Jarriel's "Veil of Darkness" aired in the United States on ABC's *20/20* on September 29, 1989.

24. See Khawar Mumtaz and Farida Shaheed, *Women of Pakistan: Two Steps Forward, One Step Back?*, London and Atlantic Highlands: Zed Books (1987).

A SELECTIVE BIBLIOGRAPHY IN LEGAL STUDIES AS CULTURAL STUDIES

JERRY LEONARD _____

This bibliography has been constructed to enable further reading/research on the lines of the general project of legal studies as cultural studies. I wish to point out that this is a decidedly selective and thus an incomplete list: like the theory and the construction of this volume as a whole, this bibliography is partisan. For the most part I have included here all of the works cited in the tests of Drucilla Cornell, Costas Douzinas and Ronnie Warrington, Teresa Ebert, Nancy Fraser, Eugene Genovese, Gayatri Spivak, and my own introduction and contribution. I have not listed such things as newspaper articles; while the inclusion of such "daily" texts in contemporary studies of law/culture is quite important, in my view it is ultimately the broader theory, analysis and critical registration of such tests which are most significant for the progressive development of critical theory. While this is so, I should point out as well that I have not listed the many tests by Freud which are cited throughout David Caudill's work; with the ever-increasing attention to psychoanalytic theory (crystallised, for instance, by the emergence of Slavoj Zizek) in the aftermath of the de Man cover-up, one can be fairly certain that an archive such as that of Freud will neither be forgotten nor rendered very difficult to access. This bibliography, then, is broadly aimed at *producing a space of access to the theoretical connections between (post)modern legal and/as cultural studies*, and thus will provide readers with an organized means of continuing and extending their critical interrogations.

Regarding the contributions of Marie Ashe, David Caudill, and Peter Goodrich, while I have tried to include a number of key citations from their works (notes), I have not by any means included all of the works that they have cited or referenced.

Their extensive documentation, like most texts which in one form or another manage to survive the amazingly elaborate institution of law reviews, makes them quite bibliographical already; a re-listing of the entirety of their "sources" or "authorities" would in my view have been fairly redundant and unproductive. Even more to the point, due to the rather confusing rules of citation among law reviews—rules of intricacy which themselves reflect the shrouded, Kafkaesque institutional isolationism of the entire juridical apparatus in the contemporary world—the inordinate labor required in tracking down the complete bibliographical information (e.g., full names of authors, book publishers, etc.) for each and every work cited seemed as ludicrous to me as the notes themselves in most instances. Of course, there is enough basic information provided in the notes for interested readers to pursue further studies as they wish.

As I argued in the introduction, the main question is not the (canonical) one of *what* is read, nor primarily the technical, mechanical, processual question of *how* to read, but rather *why* any and all readings/texts operate in the ways that they do under and within the institutional and historical conditions of their production and dissemination. In short, why "knowledge" is produced in the (post)modern moment. Contrary to the implicitly pluralist "moderacy" of the dominant and most pervasive modes of "critical" cultural/legal studies, I believe it is necessary to insistently argue that "reading" is not simply a matter of the confluence, the easy co-existence, for instance, of the "aesthetic" *and* the "political," but rather is a primarily or fundamentally *political* mode of cultural activity, wherein the questions of the boundaries of "the political" and the "theoretical" themselves become openly contested and subject to historical critiques, thereby opening new spaces of intervention and transformation toward collective social justice. In a historical moment, like the present, where the notion of "post-theory" acquires everyday currency throughout the First World academies, it is necessary to re-argue the case for radical critical theory in this way. The scope and consequences of this argument—basically an urgent defense of theory in the current situation—is such, I believe, that it impacts even the seemingly trivial practices like constructing a bibliography: this is because in such a "list" one is dealing once more with the problematics of inclusivity, the repetition of the *same* (names, signs, concepts...) and the emergence or resurgence of *others*. In short, a "bibliography," ordinarily at the end of "books," can itself be re-understood as mediating and registering "the ensemble of social relations."

I would like to specifically indicate a few (collectively oriented) sources which I believe would be particularly helpful to readers who may be approaching one or both of the axes of critical legal/cultural studies for the first time. While now dated by about ten years, the work by Duncan Kennedy and Karl Klare, "A Bibliography of Critical Legal Studies," is quite helpful and worth mentioning by itself as a wholly separate bibliography. In the domain of critical cultural studies, readers may wish to write for a current catalog of publications from the Maisonneuve Press Institute for Advanced Cultural Studies, Director Robert Merrill, P.O. Box 2980, Washington, D.C. 20013-2980. An extraordinarily broad range of historical materialist writings, from the introductory to more advanced levels, are available through Bookmarks. In the United States and Canada, current catalogs may be requested through Bookmarks, P.O. Box 16085, Chicago, Illinois 60616; and abroad through Bookmarks, 265 Seven Sisters Road, Finsbury Park, London N4 2DE, England. Finally, I have also included here a number of works (mostly anthologies) which for various reasons are not referenced in the texts of the present volume, but which I believe represent significant contributions to the general development of legal studies as cultural studies. I have marked these texts and some others with an asterisk (*) so as to further locate the present work in relation to the wider terrain of discourses in contemporary theory.

At the conclusion of a very short text called "Our Revolution," written in 1923, Lenin puts forth a decisive critique of what he calls the "faint-hearted pedantry" of intellectuals and critics who, in the effect of their practices, demonstrate a refusal to take seriously the centrality of dialectics in committed historical struggles to end social injustice through the openly confrontational and differential processes of oppositionality. "Where, in what books," asks Lenin, "have you read that such variations of the customary historical sequence of events ["deviations" and "breaks" from entrenched bourgeois protocols of order] are impermissible or impossible?" To this he responds, drawing upon Napoleon: *On s'engage et puis...on voit*—First engage in a serious battle and then see what happens. In this collection I have proposed the general concept of legal studies as cultural studies not as a dogmatic given but on the contrary as a developing and open site of struggle: a dialectical *ensemble of*

364 *Legal Studies as Cultural Studies*

social relations registered at the level of differential intelligibilities under (post)modern capitalist patriarchy. When Lenin stages the question, "Where, in what books..." he is—as I have done here— contesting the complacency and the seemingly de-classed or undivided unity of the "book"—of historically contested "signs"; and at the same time, Lenin's critique writes in an "other" way forward, a radically other historical possibility. *Legal Studies as Cultural Studies* begins and ends precisely in the dialectics of this "other" way forward.

As I remarked at the outset, this bibliography is "partisan"— selective and incomplete—and I will surely have left out a number of significant writings. The point, however, is *not* merely to reproduce such a commonsensical notion of the bibliography as the formally inclusive inventory of "the latest things"—theory commodified in (post)modern consumerism. Rather, what is necessary is to reconceptualize the "edge" of (post)modern critique in ways which are imbued and driven with a conscious- ness of the necessity to end the global ravages and injustices of exploitation. The "edge" is a highly variegated vanguard revolu- tionary movement whose constant task is to theorize its "newness" in terms of its practical capability of destroying and superseding the "old" historical contradictions between the controlling minority of racist patriarchal capitalism on the one hand and the diversely constituted laboring masses on the other. In these terms, the bibliography—like the anthology form in general—should not be trivialized into a moment of "celebration" (merely a new canonical registry, a reformist project) but rather, as I suggested earlier, needs to be seen as *a laying bare of a struggle in the process of uneven development.* The reader is in this way relocated in the active space of the critical advocate, and the enduring project of social transformation becomes the axis of radical judgment. To conclude by paraphrasing Lenin, what is essential then is to first *get in the struggle* and then see what happens.

ADORNO, Theodor. 1973. *Negative Dialectics.* London: Routledge.

*AGARWAL, Bina, ed. 1988. *Structures of Patriarchy: The State, Community and Household in Modernising Asia.* London: Zed Books.

ALTHUSSER, Louis. 1971. *Lenin and Philosophy and Other Essays.* Trans. Ben Brewster. New York: Monthly Review Press.

AMARIGLIO, Jack. 1988. "The Body, Economic Discourse, and Power: An Economist's Introduction to Foucault." *History of Political Economy* 20.4.

AMIN, Samir. 1976. *Unequal Development.* Trans. Brian Pearce. New York: Monthly Review Press.

ANDERSON, Perry. 1984. "Modernity and Revolution." *New Left Review* 144.

___ 1983. *In the Tracks of Historical Materialism.* London: Verso.

___ 1976. *Considerations of Western Marxism.* London: New Left Books.

___ 1974. *Lineages of the Absolutist State.* London: Verso.

* ARATO, Andrew and Eike Gebhardt, eds. 1993. *The Essential Frankfurt School Reader.* New York: Continuum.

ASHE, Marie. 1989. "Zig-Zag Stitching and the Seamless Web." *Nova Law Review* 13.

___ 1990. "Inventing Choreographies: Deconstruction and Feminism." *Columbia Law Review* 90.

___ 1991. "Abortion of Narrative: A Reading of the Judgment of Solomon." *Yale Journal of Law and Feminism* 4.

___ 1992. "The 'Bad Mother' in Law and Literature: A Problem of Representation." *Hastings Law Journal* 43.

___ "'Bad Mothers,' 'Good Lawyers,' and 'Legal Ethics.'" *Georgetown Law Journal* (forthcoming).

AUSTIN, Granville. 1972. *The Indian Constitution: Cornerstone of a Nation.* Bombay: Oxford University Press.

BARNES, Richard L. 1989. "Searching For Answers Without Questions." *South Dakota Law Review* 24.

BALKIN, Jack. 1987. "Deconstructive Practice and Legal Theory." *Yale Law Journal* 96.

BAUDRILLARD, Jean. 1990. *Seduction.* London: MacMillan.

___ 1983. *Simulations.* Trans. Paul Foss. New York: Semiotext(e).

___ 1983. *In the Shadow of the Silent Majorities...or, The End of the Social.* Trans. Paul Foss. New York: Semiotext(e).

___ 1981. *For a Critique of the Political Economy of the Sign.* Trans. Charles Levin. St. Louis: Telos.

___ 1975. *The Mirror of Production.* Trans. Mark Poster. St. Louis: Telos.

* BENHABIB, Seyla and Drucilla Cornell, eds. 1987. *Feminism as Critique: On the Politics of Gender.* Minneapolis: University of Minnesota press.

BENVENUTO, Bice and R. Kennedy. 1986. *The Works of Jacques Lacan: An Introduction.* London: Free Association.

* BHABHA, Homi K, ed. 1990. *Nation and Narration.* London: Routledge.

BIENENFELD, Franz Rudolf. 1965. "Prolegomena to a Psychoanalysis of Law and Justice." *California Law Review* 53.

BINDER, G. 1987. "On Critical Legal Studies as Guerilla Warfare." *Georgia Law Journal* 76.

BLACKBURN, Robin. 1988. *The Overthrow of Colonial Slavery. 1776–1848.* London: Verso.

BLANCHOT, Maurice. 1986. "The Absence of the Book." In *Deconstruction in Context: Literature and Philosophy.* Ed. Mark C. Taylor. Chicago: University of Chicago Press.

___ 1982. *The Space of Literature.* Lincoln: University of Nebraska Press.

BLAUSTEIN, Bert P. and Gisbert H. Flanz, eds. 1976. *Constitutions of the Countries of the World.* New York: Oceana.

BORDIEU, Pierre. 1988. *Homo Academicus.* Cambridge: Polity Press.

___ 1987. "The Force of Law: Toward a Sociology of the Juridical Field." *Hastings Law Journal* 38.

BORSCH-JACOBSEN, M. 1990. *Lacan: The Absolute Master.* Stanford: Stanford University Press.

BOYLE, James. 1985. "The Politics of Reason: Critical Legal Theory and Local Social Thought." *University of Pennsylvania Law Review* 133.

___ 1985. "The Anatomy of a Torts Class." *American University Law Review* 34.

BRANTLINGER, Patrick. 1990. *Crusoe's Footprints: Cultural Studies in Britain and America.* New York: Routledge.

BRIADOTTI, Rosi. 1990. *Patterns of Dissonance.* Oxford: Polity Press.

BRIGHT, Charles and Michael Gyer. 1987. "For a Unified History of the World in the Twentieth Century." *Radical History Review* 39.

BUHLE, Paul. 1990. Marxism in the United States. London: Verso.

BUTLER, Judith. 1990. *Gender Trouble: Feminism and the Subversion of Identity.* New York: Routledge.

* ___ and Joan W. Scott, eds. 1992. *Feminists Theorize the Political.* New York: Routledge.

CALLINICOS, Alex. 1989. *Against Postmodernism: A Marxist Critique.* London: Polity Press.

CARRINGTON, Paul. 1984. "Of Law and the River." *Journal of Legal Education* 34.

___ 1992. "Butterfly Effects: The Possibility of Law Teaching in a Democracy." *Duke Law Journal* 41.

CAUDILL, David. 1989. *Disclosing Tilt: Law, Belief and Criticism.* Amsterdam: Free University Press.

* ___ 1994. *Radical Philosophy of Law.* Ed. D. Caudill. New York: Humanities Press.

CHASE, Anthony. 1986. "Toward a Legal Theory of Popular Culture." *Wisconsin Law Review* 527.

CIXOUS, Helene. 1980. "The Laugh of the Medusa." In *New French Feminisms.* Ed. Elaine Marks. Amherst: University of Massachusetts Press.

___ 1991. *Coming to Writing.* Cambridge: Harvard University Press.

COLLINS, R. and D. Skover. 1992. "Paratexts." *Stanford Law Review* 44.

CONNOR, Steven. 1989. *Postmodernist Culture: An Introduction to Theories of the Contemporary.* Oxford and Cambridge: Basil Blackwell.

COOMBES, R. 1989. "Toward a Theory of Practice in Critical Legal Studies." *Law and Social Inquiry* 69.

COOVER, R. 1986. "Violence and the Word." *Yale Law Journal* 95.

CORNELL, Drucilla. 1987. "Institutionalisation of Meaning, Recollection, Imagination and the Potential for Transformative Legal Interpretation." *University of Pennsylvania Law Review* 135.

___ 1991. *Beyond Accomodation.* New York: Routledge.

___ 1992. *The Philosophy of the Limit.* New York: Routledge.

CRENSHAW, Kimberle. 1988. "Race, Reform, and Retrenchment: Transformation and Legitimation in Antidiscrimination Law." *Harvard Law Review* 101.

DALTON, Clare. 1985. "An Essay in the Deconstruction of Contract Doctrine." *Yale Law Journal* 94.

DELEUZE, Gilles and Felix Guattari. 1977. *Anti-Oedipus: Capitalism and Schizophrenia*. Trans. Robert Hurley et al. Minneapolis: University of Minnesota Press.

DERRIDA, Jacques. 1976. *Of Grammatology*. Trans. Gayatri Chakravorty Spivak. Baltimore: Johns Hopkins University Press.

___ 1979. *Writing and Difference*. Trans. Alan Bass. Chicago: University of Chicago Press.

___ 1979. "Scribble (writing-power)." *Yale French Studies* 58.

___ 1979. *Spurs: Nietzsche's Styles*. Chicago: University of Chicago Press.

___ 1981. *Dissemination*. Trans. Barbara Johnson. Chicago: Chicago University Press.

___ 1982. *Margins of Philosophy*. Trans. Alan Bass. Chicago: University of Chicago Press.

___ 1984. *Otobiographies*. Paris: Galilee.

___ 1986. *Positions*. Chicago: University of Chicago Press.

___ 1987. *The Post Card: From Socrates to Freud and Beyond*. Chicago: University of Chicago Press.

___ 1987. *The Truth in Painting*. Chicago: University of Chicago Press.

___ 1990. "Force of Law: The Mystical Foundation of Authority." *Cardozo Law Review* 11.

DEWS, Peter. 1987. *Logics of Disintegration*. London: Verso.

DOUZINAS, Costas and Ronnie Warrington. 1991. "Posting the Law: Social Contracts and the Postal Rule's Grammatology." *International Journal for the Semiotics of Law* 4.

DREYFUS, Hubert L. and Paul Rabinow. 1983. *Michel Foucault: Beyond Structuralism and Hermeneutics*. 2nd ed. Chicago: University of Chicago Press.

DUXBURY, Neil. 1990. "Some Radicalism About Realism? Thurman Arnold and the Politics of Modern Jurisprudence." *Oxford Journal of Legal Studies* 10.

___ 1991. "Postmodernism and Its Discontents." *Oxford Journal of Jurisprudence* 11.

EAGLETON, Terry. 1983. *Literary Theory: An Introduction.* Minneapolis: University of Minnesota Press.

EBERT, Teresa L. 1991. "Political Semiosis in/of American Cultural Studies." *The American Journal of Semiotics* 8.1/2.

___ 1991. "The 'Difference' of Postmodern Feminism." *College English* 53.8.

___ 1992. "Detecting the Phallus: Authority, Ideology, and the Production of Patriarchal Agents in Detective Fiction." *Rethinking Marxism* 5.3.

___ 1992/93. "Ludic Feminism, the Body, Performance, and Labor: Bringing *Materialism* Back into Feminist Cultural Studies." *Cultural Critique* 23 (Winter).

___ *Ludic Feminism and After.* Ann Arbor: University of Michigan Press (forthcoming).

___ *Patriarchal Narratives.* Ann Arbor: University of Michigan Press (forthcoming).

* ___ and Mas'ud Zavarzadeh, eds. *[Post]Modern Discourses on Ideology.* Gainesville: University Press of Florida (forthcoming).

EHRENZWEIG, Albert Armin. 1971. *Psychoanalytic Jurisprudence: On Ethics, Aesthetics, and Law.* Dobbs Ferry, New York: Oceana Publishers.

EISENSTEIN, Zillah. 1988. *The Female Body and the Law.* Berkeley: University of California Press.

FELMAN, Shoshana, ed. 1982. *Literature and Psychoanalysis: The Question of Reading—Otherwise.* Baltimore: Johns Hopkins University Press.

* FERGUSON, Russell et al., eds. 1990. *Out There: Marginalization and Contemporary Cultures.* Cambridge, Massachusetts: MIT Press.

* FINEMAN, Martha Albertson and Nancy Sweet Thomadsen, eds. 1991. *At the Boundaries of the Law: Feminism and Legal Theory.* New York: Routledge.

FISH, Stanley. 1986. "Anti-Professionalism." *Cardozo Law Review* 7.

___ 1990. *Doing What Comes Naturally.* Oxford: Oxford University Press.

FISS, Owen. 1982. "Objectivity and Interpretation." *Stanford Law Review* 34.

___ 1984. "The Death of Law?" *Cornell Law Review* 69.

___ 1989. "The Law Regained." *Cornell Law Review* 74.

* FITZPATRICK, Peter., ed. 1991. *Dangerous Supplements: Resistance and Renewal in Jurisprudence.* London: Pluto Press.

* FOSTER, Hal, ed. 1986. *Postmodern Culture.* London: Pluto Press.

FOUCAULT, Michel. 1970. *The Order of Things: An Archaeology of the Human Sciences.* New York: Vintage Books.

___ 1972. *The Archaeology of Knowledge.* New York: Pantheon.

___ 1972. "History, Discourse and Discontinuity." Trans. Anthony M. Nazzaro. *Salmagundi* 20 (Summer/Fall).

___ 1973. *Madness and Civilization: A History of Insanity in the Age of Reason.* Trans. Richard Howard. New York: Vintage Books.

___ 1975. *I, Pierre Riviere, Having Slaughtered My Mother, My Sister, and My Brother...: A Case of Parricide in the 19th Century.* Ed. M. Foucault. Trans. Frank Jellinek. Lincoln and London: University of Nebraska Press.

___ 1977. *Language, Counter-Memory, Practice: Selected Essays and Interviews.* Trans. Donald Bouchard and Sherry Simon. Ed. D. Bouchard. Ithaca: Cornell University Press.

___ 1978. *The History of Sexuality, Volume I: An Introduction.* Trans. Robert Hurley. New York: Vintage Books.

___ 1979. *Discipline and Punish: The Birth of the Prison.* Trans. Alan Sheridan. New York: Vintage Books.

___ 1980. *Power/Knowledge: Selected Interviews and Other Writings, 1972–1977.* Ed. Colin Gordon. New York: Pantheon.

___ 1984. *The Foucault Reader.* Ed. Paul Rabinow. New York: Random House.

FOX-GENOVESE. 1991. *Feminism Without Illusions: A Critique of Individualism.*

FRANK, Jerome. 1930. *Law and the Modern Mind.* New York: Tudor Publishing.

FRANKENBERG, G. 1989. "Down By Law: Irony, Seriousness, and Reason." In *Critical Legal Thought: An American-German Debate.* Eds. C. Joerges and D. Trubek. Baden-Baden: Nomos Verlag.

FRASER, Nancy. 1989. *Unruly Practices: Power, Discourse, and Gender in Contemporary Social Theory.* Minneapolis: University of Minnesota Press.

___ 1990. "Rethinking the Public Sphere: A Contribution to the Critique of Actually Existing Democracy." *Social Text* 25/26 (Fall).

___ 1992. *Revaluing French Feminism: Critical Essays on Difference, Agency, and Culture.* Bloomington: Indiana University Press.

* FRAZER, Elizabeth, Jennifer Hornsby and Sabina Lovibond, eds. 1992. *Ethics: A Feminist Reader.* Oxford: Blackwell.

FREEMAN, Alan. 1978. "Legitimizing Racial Discrimination Through Antidiscrimination Law: A Critical Review of Supreme Court Doctrine." *Minnesota Law Review* 62.

___ 1981. "Truth and Mystification in Legal Scholarship." *Yale Law Journal* 90.

___ and Betty Mensch. 1987. "Religion as Science/Science as Religion: Constitutional Law and the Fundamentalist Challenge." *Tikkun* 2 (Nov./Dec.).

FRIED, Charles. 1988. "Jurisprudential Responses to Legal Realism." *Cornell Law Review* 73.

FROMM, Erich. 1970. *The Crisis of Psychoanalysis: Essays on Freud, Marx and Social Psychology.* New York: Holt, Rinehart, Winston.

FROSH, Stephen. 1987. *The Politics of Psychoanalysis: An Introduction to Freudian and Post-Freudian Theory.* New Haven: Yale University Press.

FRUG, Mary Joe. 1992. *Postmodern Legal Feminism.* New York: Routledge.

GABEL, Peter. 1980. "A Critical Anatomy of the Legal Opinion." *ALSA Forum* 5.

___ 1984. "The Phenomenology of Rights-Consciousness and the Pact of the Withdrawn Selves." *Texas Law Review* 62.

___ 1989. "Dukakis's Defeat and the Transformative Possibilities of Legal Culture." *Tikkun* 4 (Mar. /Apr.).

___ 1989. "On Passionate Reason: Transcending Marxism and Deconstruction." *Tikkun* 4 (Nov. /Dec.).

___ and Duncan Kennedy. 1984. "Roll Over Beethoven." *Stanford Law Review* 36.

GABRIEL, Yiannis. 1983. *Freud and Society*. London: Routledge and Kegan Paul.

GALLOP, Jane. 1982. *The Daughter's Seduction: Feminism and Psychoanalysis*. Ithaca: Cornell University Press.

___ 1985. *Reading Lacan*. Ithaca, New York: Cornell University Press.

___ 1987. "Reading the Mother Tongue: Psychoanalytic Feminist Criticism." *Critical Inquiry* 13.

___ 1988. *Thinking Through the Body*. New York: Columbia University Press.

___ 1992. *Around 1981: Academic Feminist Literary Theory*. New York and London: Routledge.

* GATES, Henry Louis, Jr., ed. 1986. *"Race," Writing, and Difference*. Chicago: University of Chicago Press.

GAY, Peter. 1985. *Freud for Historians*. New York: Oxford University Press.

GEERTZ, Cliff ord. 1973. *The Interpretation of Cultures*. New York: Basic Books.

GIBSON, S. 1990. "Continental Drift: The Question of Context in Feminist Jurisprudence." *Law and Critique* 1.

GOLDBERG, Jonathan. 1986. *Voice Terminal Echo: Postmodernism and English Renaissance Texts*. New York: Methuen.

GOLDSTEIN, Joseph. 1968. "Psychoanalysis and Jurisprudence." *Yale Law Journal* 77.

GOODRICH, Peter. 1986. *Reading the Law*. Oxford: Blackwell.

___ 1986. "Law and Modernity." *Modern Law Review* 49.

___ 1987. "Literacy and the Languages of the Early Common Law." *Journal of Law and Society* 14.

___ 1987. "Psychoanalysis in Legal Education: Notes on the Violence of the Sign." In *Law and Semiotics*. Ed. Roberta Kevelson. New York: Plenum Press.

___ 1989. "Rhetoric, Grammatology and the Hidden Injuries of Law." *Economy and Society* 18.

___ 1990. *Languages of Law: From Logics of Memory to Nomadic Masks*. London: Weidenfeld and Nicolson.

___ 1990. *Legal Discourse*. New York: St. Martin's Press.

___ 1991. "Specula Laws: Image, Aesthetic and Common Law." *Law and Critique* 2.

___ 1991. "Eating Law: Commons, Common Land, Common Law." *Journal of Legal History* 12.

___ 1992. "Poor Illiterate Reason." *Social and Legal Studies* 1.

___ 1992. "Critical Legal Studies in England: Prospective Histories." *Oxford Journal of Legal Studies* 12.

___ 1993. "Fate as Seduction: The Other Scene of Legal Judgment." In *Closure or Critique*. Eds. A. Norrie and J. Macahery. Edinburgh University Press.

GORDON, Robert. 1982. "New Developments in Legal Theory." In *The Politics of Law: A Progressive Critique*. Ed. David Kairys. New York: Pantheon.

___ 1987. "Unfreezing Legal Reality: Critical Approaches to Law." *Florida State University Law Review* 15.

GRAFF, Gerald. 1992. "Teach the Conflicts." In *The Politics of Liberal Education*. Eds. Darryl J. Gless and Barbara Herrnstein Smith. Durham: Duke University Press.

* GREENBLATT, Stephen and Giles Dunn, eds. 1992. *Redrawing the Boundaries: The Transformation of English and American Literary Studies*. New York: Modern Language Association Publications.

* GRIGG-Spall, Ian and Paddy Ireland, eds. 1992. *The Critical Lawyers' Handbook*. London: Pluto Press.

* GROSSBERG, Lawrence, Cary Nelson and Paula Treichler, eds. 1992. *Cultural Studies*. New York: Routledge.

GRUNBAUM, Adolf. 1984. *The Foundations of Psychoanalysis: A Philosophical Critique*. Berkeley: University of California Press.

GUHA, Ranajit. 1981. *A Rule of Property for Bengal: An Essay on the Idea of Permanent Settlement*. 2nd ed. New Delhi: Orient Longman.

___ 1982. *Subaltern Studies I: Writings on South Asian History and Society*. Ed. R. Guha. Delhi: Oxford University Press.

GWYER, Maurice and A. Appadorai. 1957. *Speeches and Documents on the Indian Constitution*. New York: Oxford University Press.

HABERMAS, Jurgen. 1971. *Knowledge and Human Interests*. Trans. Jeremy Shapiro. Boston: Beacon Press.

HAGER, Mark. 1988. "Against Liberal Ideology." *American University Law Review* 37.

HALL, Calvin. 1954. *A Primer of Freudian Psychology.* New York: Octagon Books.

HARAWAY, Donna. 1990. "A Manifesto for Cyborgs: Science, Technology, and Socialist Feminism in the 1980's." *In Feminism/Postmodernism.* Ed. Linda Nicholson. New York: Routledge.

HARLAND, Richard. 1987. *Superstructuralism: The Philosophy or Structuralism and Post-Structuralism.* London: Methuen.

HELLER, Thomas. 1984. "Structuralism and Critique." *Stanford Law Review* 36.

HENNESSY, Rosemary. 1990. "Materialist Feminism and Foucault: The Politics of Appropriation." *Rethinking Marxism* 3.3/4 (Winter).

* HIRSCH, Marianne and Evelyn Fox Keller, eds. 1990. *Conflicts in Feminism.* New York: Routledge.

HORDEN, Peregrine, ed. 1985. *Freud and the Humanities.* London: Duckworth.

HORKHEIMER, Max and Theodor W. Adorno. 1972. *Dialectics of Enlightenment.* Trans. J. Cumming. New York: Herder and Herder.

HUNT, Alan. 1986. "The Theory of Critical Legal Studies." *Oxford Journal of Legal Studies* 6.

___ 1990. "The Big Fear: Law Confronts Postmodernism." *McGill Law Journal* 35.

___ and P. Fitzpatrick, eds. 1987. *Critical Legal Studies.* Oxford: Blackwell.

HUTCHINSON, Allan C. 1989. *Dwelling on the Threshold: Critical Essays on Modern Legal Thought.* Toronto: Carswell.

___ 1989. *Critical Legal Studies.* Ed. A. Hutchinson. Totowa, New Jersey: Rowman & Littlefield Publishers.

___ and P. Monohan. 1984. "Law, Politics and Critical Legal Scholars: The Unfolding Drama of American legal Thought." *Stanford Law Review* 36.

IRIGARAY, Luce. 1985. *Speculum of the Other Woman.* Trans. Gillian Gill. Ithaca, New York: Cornell University Press.

___ 1985. *This Sex Which is Not One.* Ithaca: Cornell University Press.

___ 1991. *Marine Lover: Of Friedrich Nietzsche.* New York: Columbia University Press.

JACOBY, Russell. 1987. *The Last Intellectuals.* New York: Noonday Press.

JACOBSON, A. 1990. "The Idolatry of Rules: Writing Law According to Moses." *Cardozo Law Review* 11.

JAMESON, Fredric. 1981. *The Political Unconscious: Narrative as a Socially Symbolic Act.* Ithaca: Cornell University Press.

___ 1984. "Postmodernism, or the Cultural Logic of Late Capitalism." *New Left Review* 146.

___ 1988. *The Ideologies of Theory: Essays 1971–1986.* Minneapolis: University of Minnesota Press.

___ 1988. "History and Class Consciousness as an 'Unfinished Project.'" *Rethinking Marxism* 1.1.

___ 1990. *Postmodernism, or the Cultural Logic of Late Capitalism.* Durham: Duke University Press.

* JANMOHAMED, Abdul R. and David Lloyd, eds. 1990. *The Nature and Context of Minority Discourse.* New York: Oxford University Press.

JARDINE, Alice. 1985. *Gynesis: Configurations of Woman and Modernity.* Ithaca: Cornell University Press.

JAY, Martin. 1973. *The Dialectical Imagination.* Boston: Little, Brown.

___ 1984. *Marxism and Totality: The Adventures of a Concept From Lukacs to Habermas.* Berkeley: University of California Press.

JENCKS, Charles. 1984. *The Language of Post-Modern Architecture.* 4th rev. ed. New York: Rizzoli International Publications.

JOHNSON, P. 1984. "Do You Sincerely Want to be a Radical?" *Stanford Law Review* 36.

* KAIRYS, David, ed. 1990. *The Politics of Law: A Progressive Critique.* 2nd ed. New York: Pantheon.

KAVANAGH, James H. 1990. "Ideology." In *Critical Terms for Literary Study.* Eds. Frank Lentricchia and Thomas MCLaughlin. Chicago: University of Chicago Press

KEITH, Arthur B. 1937. *A Constitutional History of India: 1600–1935.* 2nd ed. London: Methuen.

* KELLNER, Douglas, ed. 1989. *Postmodernism/Jameson/Critique.* Washington, D.C.: Maisonneuve Press.

KELLOGG, F. 1990. "Legal Scholarship in the Temple of Doom: Pragmatism's Response to Critical Legal Studies." *Tulane Law Review* 65.

KELMAN, Mark. 1984. "Trashing." *Stanford Law Review* 36.

___ 1987. *A Guide to Critical Legal Studies.* Cambridge: Harvard University Press.

KENNEDY, David. 1985/86. "Critical Theory, Structuralism and Contemporary Legal Scholarship." *New England Law Review* 21.

KENNEDY, Duncan. 1979. "The Structure of Blackstone's Commentaries." *Buffalo Law Review* 28.

___ 1981. "Critical Labour Theory: A Comment." *Industrial Relations Law Journal* 4.

___ 1981. "Cost Reduction Theory as Legitimation." *Yale Law Journal* 90.

___ 1982. *Legal Education as Training for Hierarchy: A Polemic Against the System.* Cambridge: Afar.

___ 1985. "Psycho-Social CLS: A Comment on the Cardozo Symposium." *Cardozo Law Review* 6.

*___ and Karl Klare. 1984. "A Bibliography of Critical Legal Studies." *Yale Law Journal* 94.

KEVELSON, Roberta. 1988. *Law as a System of Signs.* New York: Plenum Press.

___ 1990. *Action and Agency.* Ed. R. Kevelson. New York: Peter Lang.

KLARE, Karl. 1978. "Judicial Deradicalization of the Wagner Act and the Origins of Modern Legal Consciousness, 1937–1941." *Minnesota Law Review* 62.

___ 1979. "Law-Making as Praxis." *Telos* 40.

KRISTEVA, Julia. 1984. *Revolution in Poetic Language.* New York: Columbia University Press.

___ 1987. *Desire in Language.* New York: Columoia.

KURZWEIL, Edith. 1980. *The Age of Structuralism: Levi-Strauss to Foucault.* New York: Columbia University Press.

LACAN, Jacques. 1977. *Ecrits: A Selection.* Trans. Alan Sheridan. New York: Norton.

___ 1978. *Four Fundamental Concepts of Psycho-Analysis.* London: Pelican.

LACAPRA, Dominick. 1987. "History and Psychoanalysis." *Critical Inquiry* 13.

* ___ 1991. *The Bounds of Race: Perspectives on Hegemony and Resistance.* Ed. D. LaCapra. Ithaca: Cornell University Press.

LACLAU, Ernesto. 1987. "Psychoanalysis and Marxism." *Critical Inquiry* 13.

___ 1991. *New Reflections Upon the Revolution of our Times.* London: Verso.

___ and Chantal Mouffe. 1985. *Hegemony and Socialist Strategy.* London: Verso.

LAING, R.D. 1971. *The Politics of the Family and Other Essays.* New York: Vintage Books.

LAWRENCE, Charles. 1987. "The Id, the Ego, and Equal Protection: Reckoning with Unconscious Racism." *Stanford Law Review* 39.

___ 1983. "'Justice' or 'Just Us': Racism and the Role of Ideology." *Stanford Law Review* 35.

LEGENDRE, Pierre. 1990. "The Lost Temporality of Law." *Law and Critique* 1.

LENIN, V.I. 1975. *The Lenin Anthology.* Ed. Robert C. Tucker. New York: W.W. Norton & Co.

___ 1979. "Our Revolution." In *On Utopian and Scientific Socialism: Articles and Speeches.* Moscow: Progress Publishers.

* LENTRICCHIA, Frank and Thomas McLaughlin, eds. 1990. *Critical Terms for Literary Study.* Chicago: University of Chicago Press.

LERNER, Michael. 1986. "Surplus Powerlessness: The Psychodynamics of Everyday Life...and the Psychology of Individual and Social Tranformation." Oakland, California: Institute for Labor and Mental Health.

LEVIN, Charles. 1984. "Baudrillard, Critical Theory and Psychoanalysis." *Canadian Journal of Political and Social Theory* 8.1/2 (Winter/Spring).

* LEVINSON, Sanford and Steven Mailloux, eds. 1988. *Interpreting Law and Literature: A Hermeneutic Reader.* Evanston: Northwestern University Press.

* LEYH, G., ed. 1992. *Legal Hermeneutics: History, Theory and Practice.* Berkeley: University of California Press.

LLEWELLYN, Karl. 1931. "Some Realism About Realism—Responding to Dean Pound." *Harvard Law Review* 44.

LYOTARD, Jean-Francois. 1984. *The Postmodern Condition: A Report on Knowledge.* Trans. Geoffrey Bennington and Brian Massumi. Minneapolis: University of Minnesota Press.

MACKINNON, Catharine A. 1987. *Feminism Unmodified: Discourses on Life and Law.* Cambridge: Harvard University Press.

___ 1989. *Toward A Feminist Theory of the State.* Cambridge: Harvard University Press.

MANDEL, Ernest. 1978. *Late Capitalism.* Trans. Joris De Bres. London and New York: Verso.

MARCUSE, Herbert. 1955. *Eros and Civilization: A Philosophical Inquiry into Freud.* New York: Vintage Books.

MARX, Karl. 1970. *A Contribution to the Critique of Political Economy.* Trans. S.W. Ryazanskaya. Ed. Maurice Dobb. Moscow: Progress Publishers.

___ 1978. *The Marx-Engels Reader.* Ed. Robert C. Tucker. 2nd ed. New York: W.W. Norton & Co.

MASSEY, Calvin R. 1988. "Law's Inferno." *Hastings Law Journal* 39.

MCCLAREN, Peter. 1993. "Multiculturalism and the Postmodern Critique: Towards a Pedagogy of Resistance and Transformation." *Cultural Studies* 7.1.

MIES, Maria. 1986. *Patriarchy and Accumulation on a World Scale: Women in the International Division of Labour.* London and Atlantic Highlands: Zed Books.

MINAULT, Gail. 1982. *The Khilafat Movement: Religious Symbolism and Political Mobilization in India.* New York: Columbia University Press.

MITCHELL, Juliet. 1974. *Psychoanalysis and Feminism.* New York: Pantheon.

MOHANTY, Chandra Talpade, Ann Russo and Lourdes Torres, eds. 1991. *Third World Women and the Politics of Feminism.* Bloomington: Indiana University Press.

MOORE, Michael. 1984. *Law and Psychiatry: Rethinking the Relationship.* Cambridge: Cambridge University Press.

MORTON, Donald. 1987. "The Politics of the Margin: Theory, Pleasure, and the Postmodern *Conférance.*" *The American Journal of Semiotics* 5.1.

* ___ and Mas'ud Zavarzadeh, eds. 1991. *Theory/Pedagogy/Politics: Texts for Change.* Urbana: University of Illinois Press.

MUMTAZ, Khawar and Farida Shaheed. 1987. *Women of Pakistan: Two Steps Forward, One Step Back?* London and Atlantic Highlands: Zed Books.

MURPHY, W.T. 1990. "The Habermas Effect: Critical Theory and Academic Law." *Current Legal Problems* 42.

___ 1991. "The Oldest Social Science? The Epistemic Properties of the Common Law Tradition." *Modern Law Review* 54.

* NELSON, Cary and Lawrence Grossberg, eds. 1988. *Marxism and the Interpretation of Culture.* Urbana and Chicago: University of Illinois Press.

* NICHOLSON, Linda, ed. *Feminism/Postmodernism.* New York: Routledge.

NIELSON, Kai. 1989. "The Concept of Ideology: Some Marxist and Non-Marxist Conceptualizations." *Rethinking Marxism* 4.

NIETZSCHE, Friedrich. 1969. *On the Genealogy of Morals.* Trans. Walter Kaufmann and R.J. Hollingdale. New York: Vintage Books.

___ 1968. *The Will to Power.* Trans. Walter Kaufmann and R.J. Hollingdale. New York: Vintage Books.

NORRIS, Christopher. 1982. *Deconstruction: Theory and Practice.* London and New York: Methuen.

___ 1989. *Deconstruction and the Interests of Theory.* Norman and London: University of Oklahoma Press.

OETKEN, J.P. 1991. "Form and Substance in Critical Legal Studies." *Yale Law Journal* 100.

PASHUKANIS, E.B. 1978. *Law and Marxism.* London: Ink Links.

PELLER, Gary. 1987. "Reason and the Mob: The Politics of Representation." *Tikkun* 2.

___ 1985. "The Metaphysics of American Law." *California Law Review* 73.

PENLEY, Constance. 1989. *The Future of an Illusion: Film, Feminism, and Psychoanalysis.* Minneapolis: University of Minnesota Press.

PETCHESKY, Rosalind P. 1986. *Abortion and Woman's Choice: The State, Sexuality, and Reproductive Freedom.* London: Verso.

POSTER, Mark. 1990. *The Mode of Information: Poststructuralism and Social Context.* Oxford: Polity Press.

POTTAGE, A. 1992. "Crime and Culture: The Relevance of the Psychoanalytical." *Modern Law Review* 55.

PRASAD, Madhava. 1992. "The New (International) Party of Order? Coalition Politics in the (Literary) Academy." *diacritics* 22.1.

* PUNTER, David, ed. 1986. *Introduction to Contemporary Cultural Studies*. London: Longman.

RAGLAND-SULLIVAN, Ellie. 1987. *Jacques Lacan and the Philosophy of Psychoanalysis*. Urbana and Chicago: tiniversity of Illinois Press.

RAPPAPORT, Herman. 1983. *Milton and the Postmodern*. Lincoln: University of Nebraska Press.

RICOEUR, Paul. 1970. *Freud and Philosophy: An Essay on Interpretation*. Trans. Denis Savage. New Haven: Yale University Press.

___ 1978. *The Philosophy of Paul Ricoeur: An Anthology of His Work*. Eds. Charles Reagan and David Stewart. Boston: Beacon Press.

RILEY, Denise. 1988. *"Am I That Name?" Feminism and the Category of "Women" in History*. Minneapolis: University of Minnesota Press.

ROAZEN, Paul. 1968. *Freud: Political and Social Thought*. New York: Knopf.

* ROBBINS, Bruce, ed. 1990. *Intellectuals: Aesthetics, Politics and Academics*. Minneapolis: University of Minnesota Press.

ROBINSON, Paul. 1969. *The Freudian Left: Wilhelm Reich, Geza Roheim, Herbert Marcuse*. New York: Harper and Row.

RODINSON, Maxime. 1978. *Islam and Capitalism*. Trans. Brian Pearce. Austin: University of Texas Press.

RONELL, Avital. 1992. *Crack Wars: Literature, Addiction, Mania*. Lincoln: University of Nebraska Press.

___ 1989. *The Telephone Book: Technology, Schizophrenia, Electric Speech*. Lincoln: University of Nebraska Press.

ROSE, G. 1984. *The Dialectic of Nihilism*. Oxford: Blackwell.

ROSE, N. 1987. "Beyond the Public/Private Division: Law, Power and the Family." *Journal of Law and Society* 14.

* ROSS, Andrew, ed. 1988. *Universal Abandon? The Politics of Postmodernism*. Minneapolis: University of Minnesota Press.

RUSH, Peter. 1990. "Killing Them Softly With His Words." *Law and Critique* 1.

SAID, Edward W. 1991. *Covering Islam*. New York: Pantheon.

___ 1993. *Culture and Imperialism*. New York: Alfred A. Knopf.

* SARAT, A. and T. Kearns, eds. 1993. *Law and Rhetoric.* Ann Arbor: University of Michigan Press.

DE SAUSSURE, Ferdinand. 1966. *Course in General Linguistics.* Trans. Wade Baskin. New York: MCGraw-Hill.

SCALES, Ann. 1991. "Towards a Feminist Jurisprudence." *Indiana Law Journal* 56.

___ 1986. "The Emergence of Feminist Jurisprudence: An Essay." *Yale Law Journal* 95.

SCHLAG, Pierre. 1998. "Cannibal Moves: An Essay on the Metamorphoses of the Legal Distinction." *Stanford Law Review* 40.

___ 1990. "Le Hors de Texte, C' Est Moi: The Politics of Form and the Domestication of Deconstruction." *Cardozo Law Review* 11.

___ 1991. "Normative and Nowhere to Go." *Stanford Law Review* 43.

SCHOENFELD, Charles G. 1973. *Psychoanalysis and the Law.* Springfield, Illinois: Thomas Publications.

* SCOTT, Joan and Judith Butler, eds. 1992. *Feminists Theorize the Political.*

SHOWALTER, Elaine, ed. 1985. *The New Feminist Criticism.* New York: Pantheon.

SINGER, Joseph. 1984. "The Player and the Cards: Nihilism and Legal Theory." *Yale Law Journal* 94.

SKINNER, Quentin, ed. 1985. *The Return of Grand Theory in the Human Sciences.* Cambridge: Cambridge University Press.

SMART, Carol. 1989. *Feminism and the Power of Law.* London: Routledge.

SPIVAK, Gayatri Chakravorty. 1987. *In Other Worlds: Essays Cultural Politics.* New York: Methuen.

___ 1993. "Poststructuralism, Postcoloniality, Marginality, and Value." In *Literary Theory Today.* Eds. Peter Collier and Helen Geyer-Ryan. Cambridge: Polity Press.

___ 1994. *Imaginary Maps.* New York: Routledge.

STEWART, I. 1981. "Critical Legal Studies in France." *International Journal of the Sociology of Law* 9.

___ 1987. "Law and Closure." *Modern Law Review* 50.

STICK, John. 1988. "Charting the Development of Critical Legal Studies." *Columbia Law Review* 88.

THOMPSON, John. 1984. *Studies in the Theory of Ideology.* Cambridge: Polity Press.

TRUBEK, David. 1984. "Where the Action Is: Critical Legal Studies and Empiricism." *Stanford Law Review* 36.

TUSHNET, Mark. 1984. "Critical Legal Studies and Constitutional Law: An Essay in Deconstruction." *Stanford Law Review* 36.

___ 1984. "An Essay on Rights." *Texas Law Review* 62.

___ 1991. "Critical Legal Studies: A Political History." *Yale Law Journal* 100.

TWINING, W. 1985. *Karl Llewellyn and the Realist Movement.* London: Weidenfeld and Nicolson.

ULMER, Gregory. 1989. *Teletheory: Grammatology in the Age of Video.* New York: Routledge.

UNGER, Roberto Mangabeira. 1975. *Knowledge and Politics.* New York: Free Press.

___ 1976. *Law in Modern Society: Toward a Criticism of Social Theory.* New York: Free Press.

___ 1984. *Passion: An Essay on Personality.* New York: Free Press.

___ 1986. *The Critical Legal Studies Movement.* Cambridge: Harvard University Press.

VATTIMO, G. 1990. *The End of Modernity.* Oxford: Polity Press.

VIRILIO, Paul. 1991. *The Aesthetics of Disappearance.* New York: Semiotext(e).

VOLOSINOV, V.N. 1976. *Freudianism: A Marxist Critique.* Trans. I.R. Titunik. New York: Academic Press.

___ 1973. *Marxism and the Philosophy of Language.* New York: Seminar Press.

WAGENAAR, Willem Albert. 1988. *Identifying Ivan: A Case Study in Legal Psychology.* London: Harvester, Wheatsheaf.

WALLERSTEIN, Robert. 1990. "Psychoanalysis: The Common Ground." *International Journal of Psycho-Analysis* 71.

*WARHOL, Robyn R. and Diane Price Herndl, eds. 1991. *Feminisms: An Anthology of Literary Theory and Criticism.* New Brunswick, New Jersey: Rutgers University Press.

* WEISBERG, D. Kelly, ed. 1993. *Feminist Legal Theory: Foundations.* Philadelphia: Temple University Press.

WEST, Cornel. 1989. *The American Evasion of Philosophy.* Madison: University of Wisconsin Press.

WEST, Robin. 1986. "Law, Rights, and Other Totemic Illusions: Legal Liberalism and Freud's Theory of the Rule of Law." *University of Pennsylvania Law Review* 134.

___ 1988. "Jurisprudence and Gender." *University of Chicago Law Review* 55.

WHITE, James Boyd. 1990. *Justice as Translation.* Chicago: University of Chicago Press.

WIENER, J. 1991. *Professors, Politics and Pop.* London: Verso.

WILLIAMS, Bernard. 1981. *Moral Luck: Philosophical Papers, 1973–1980.* Cambridge: Cambridge University Press.

WILLIAMS, Patricia. 1991. *The Alchemy of Race and Rights: Diary of a Law Professor.* Cambridge: Harvard University Press.

WRIGHT, Elizabeth. 1987. *Psychoanalytic Criticism: Theory in Practice.* London: Methuen.

YABLON, C. 1985. "The Indeterminacy of the Law: Critical Legal Studies and the Problem of Legal Explanation." *Cardozo Law Review* 6.

ZAVARZADEH, Mas'ud. 1993. *Pun(k)deconstruction and the (Post)Modern Political Imaginary.* Washington, D.C.: Maisonneuve Press.

___ and Donald Morton. 1991. *Theory, (Post)Modernity, Opposition: An "Other" Introduction to Literary and Cultural Theory.* Washington, D.C.: Maisonneuve Press.

___ and Donald Morton. 1993. *Theory as Resistance: Politics and Culture After (Post)Structuralism.* New York: Guilford Publications.

ZIZEK, Slavoj. 1991. *For They Know What They Do: Enjoyment as a Political Factor.* London: Verso.

NOTES ON THE CONTRIBUTORS

MARIE ASHE, currently a member of the faculty of the Suffolk University School of Law in Boston, Massachusetts, has written extensively about legal regulation of female gender and female sexuality. Her work includes: "Zig-Zag Stitching and the Seamless Web" (13 *Nova Law Review* 1989); "Inventing Choreographies: Deconstruction and Feminism" (90 *Columbia Law Review* 1990); "Abortion of Narrative: A Reading of the Judgment of Solomon" (4 *Yale Journal of Law and Feminism* 1991); "The 'Bad Mother' in Law and Literature: A Problem of Representation" (43 *Hastings Law Journal* 1992); and "'Bad Mothers,' 'Good Lawyers,' and 'Legal Ethics'" (*Georgetown Law Journal* 1993).

DAVID S. CAUDILL, J.D., Ph.D., is Assistant Professor of Law at Washington & Lee University. He practiced law for seven years, in San Diego and Austin, before becoming a law professor. Professor Caudill is co-editor of *Radical Philosophy of Law* (1994), and author of *Disclosing Tilt: Law, Belief and Criticism* (1989) and numerous articles and essays on Lacanian psychoanalysis, land use planning, and law and religion.

DRUCILLA CORNELL is Professor at the Benjamin N. Cardozo School of Law. She is author of *Beyond Accommodation* and co-editor of *Deconstruction and the Possibility of Justice* and *Hegel and Legal Theory*.

COSTAS DOUZINAS is Rudolph Palumbo Lecturer in Law, Birkbeck College, University of London. His most recent publications, with Ronnie Warrington, include *Postmodern Jurisprudence* (1993) and *Justice Mis-Carried: Ethics and Aesthetics in Law* (1994).

TERESA L. EBERT teaches postmodern critical and cultural theory and feminism at the University at Albany, State University of New York. She develops a materialist postmodern feminist culture critique in her two forthcoming books, *Ludic Feminism and After* and *Patriarchal Narratives* and in such essays as "Ludic Feminism, the Body, Performance, and Labor: Bringing *Materialism* Back into Feminist Cultural Studies" (23 *Cultural Critique* 1992–93); "The 'Difference' of Postmodern Feminism" (53.8 *College English* 1991); "Detecting the Phallus: Authority, Ideology, and the Production of Patriarchal Agents in Detective Fiction" (5.3 *Rethinking Marxism* 1992); and "Political Semiosis in/of American Cultural Studies" (8.1/2 *The American Journal of Semiotics* 1992).

NANCY FRASER is Professor of Philosophy at Northwestern University, where she is also a Fellow of the Center for Urban Affairs and Policy Research and an affiliate of the Women's Studies Program. She is the author of *Unruly Practices: Power, Discourse, and Gender in Contemporary Social Theory* (1989) and the co-editor of *Revaluing French Feminism: Critical Essays on Difference, Agency, and Culture* (1992).

EUGENE D. GENOVESE is Distinguished Scholar-in-Residence at The University Center in Georgia. A specialist on the Old South, his most recent books are *The Slaveholders' Dilemma: Freedom and Progress in Southern Conservative Thought, 1820–1860* (1991) and *The Southern Tradition: The Achievement and Limitations of an American Conservatism* (in press).

PETER GOODRICH is Corporation of London Professor of Law and Chair of the Department of Law, Birkbeck College, University of London. He has taught law and legal theory at universities in Britain and the U.S. His most recent publications include *Languages of Law* (1990) and *Oedipus Lex* (1994).

JERRY LEONARD received his Juris Doctorate from the Syracuse University College of Law. Currently a doctoral candidate in the Department of English and Comparative Literature at the University of Wisconsin-Milwaukee, his dissertation concerns issues in Marxism and postcolonial cultural studies.

GAYATRI CHAKRAVORTY SPIVAK is Avalon Foundation Professor in the Humanities at Columbia University and teaches English and Cultural Politics. Before coming to Columbia, Professor Spivak taught at the University of Texas at Austin and Emory University and most recently was the Andrew W. Mellon Professor of English at the University of Pittsburgh. Among her publications are *Of Grammatology* (a translation with critical introduction of Jacques Derrida's *De La Grammatologie*), *In Other Worlds: Essays in Cultural Politics*, *The Post-Colonial Critic: Interviews, Strategies, Dialogues* (edited by Sarah Harasym), *Selected Subaltern Studies* (edited with Ranajit Guha), and most recently *Outside in the Teaching Machine* (1993) and *Imaginary Maps* (1994), a translation of three stories by Mahasweta Devi.

RONNIE WARRINGTON taught at the Universities of Middlesex and Lancaster. His recent publications (with Costas Douzinas) include *Postmodern Jurisprudence* (1993) and *Justice Mis-carried: Ethics and Aesthetics in Law* (1994).

INDEX